PENGUIN BOOK

BALLETOMANIA

Arnold Haskell was educated at Westminster and Trinity Hall, Cambridge, where he took an M.A. degree in Law. However, his 'emotional unreasoning passion' for ballet led him to give up a law career and embark upon a long and fruitful association with the dance.

He became the first ballet critic on an English newspaper (the *Daily Telegraph*). He toured Australia twice with the de Basil Ballet Russe, in 1937–8 and 1938–9. He became the first director of the Royal Ballet School in 1947, and was subsequently Governor of the Royal Ballet, the Royal Ballet School, and the Festival Ballet. He was a member of the jury at the International Ballet Contest at Varna on four occasions, three times as Vice-President and also on two occasions of the jury in Moscow.

Mr Haskell was awarded a C.B.E. in 1954, is a Chevalier de la Legion d'Honneur, and received an Honorary D.Litt (Bath) in 1974.

His many books on ballet include *Diaghileff*, *Dancing Round the World*, *Ballet: A Complete Guide to Appreciation*, *Waltzing Matilda*, *In His True Centre*, *The Russian Genius in Ballet* and *Ballet Russe*.

Arnold Haskell

BALLETOMANIA

An Updated Version of the Ballet Classic

PENGUIN BOOKS

Penguin Books Ltd, Harmondsworth, Middlesex, England
Penguin Books, 625 Madison Avenue, New York, New York 10022, U.S.A.
Penguin Books Australia Ltd, Ringwood, Victoria, Australia
Penguin Books Canada Ltd, 2801 John Street, Markham, Ontario, Canada L3R 1B4
Penguin Books (N.Z.) Ltd, 182–190 Wairau Road, Auckland 10, New Zealand

—

First published by Victor Gollancz 1934
Revised edition published by Weidenfeld and Nicolson 1977
Published with revisions in Penguin Books 1979

—

—

Made and printed in Great Britain by
Hazell Watson & Viney Ltd, Aylesbury, Bucks
Set in Linotype Juliana

Contents

PART II
BALLETOMANIA NOW

List of Plates

Preface

I AM delighted that this edition with some new material should appear under the Penguin imprint. My *Ballet: A Complete Guide to Appreciation* was the first Pelican Special to be commissioned by Allen Lane, over the port after an admirable dinner. It cost six old pennies, a fraction of the price of a theatre programme today! It made me friends all over the world.

Many critics wrote, with some reason, that in the last hardback edition which brought the book up to date the new material showed less enthusiasm than the original text. I have become more selective and, I hope, more discriminating. Moreover my horizon has widened outside the narrow sphere of one school of ballet. Some minor figures in the first edition have gained world fame; I have only to name de Valois, Markova and Ashton. There was no mention of Margot Fonteyn. In 1934 she had yet to emerge triumphantly, and so change the history of our ballet.

No, I have not lost my capacity for enthusiasm. Have I not enjoyed the supreme experience of watching Ulanova, too carried away to applaud, and been deeply moved by Chauviré whose French technique has been combined with a rare sensitivity? More recently Lynn Seymour has brought a new dimension to our ballet, a Brontë romanticism.

Babillée was a pioneer in re-establishing the male dancer, followed later by Vassiliev, Nureyev, Dowell and Baryshnikov. Roland Petit has thrilled and sometimes shocked deliberately, recreating the excitement of a Diaghilev première. I have gained some insight into the wealth of the Indian classical dance. No, I have not lost my capacity for enthusiasm, and having worked behind the scenes in ballet I have realized the difficulties as never before. I have watched dancing in schools and on stage in every continent thanks to the doors that *Balletomania* unlocked for me. I have been fortunate in being in the right place at the right time. I must stress that this is a personal and very subjective account.

I must thank Mary Clarke of the *Dancing Times* and Paul Sidey of Penguin Books for their help in selecting photographs, and not least my wife for her many helpful suggestions.

Bath 1978   ARNOLD HASKELL

Introduction

ON the occasion of my seventieth birthday my good friends Nadia Nerina and her husband, Charles Gordon, gave a dinner at the Ritz. They had invited dancers from all over the world, many other friends, and those closely connected with the arts (see Appendix). Eight countries were represented. The cast assembled could not have been gathered together by any impresario, even the mighty Hurok himself. I hastily counted eight Giselles. The party filled the beautiful Ritz dining room, but thanks to the skill with which it was arranged it remained an intimate affair. Nadia, wiser than most chairmen, had kept speeches to the minimum, limiting everyone to five minutes. All the speakers were ballerinas. I list them in alphabetical order: Alicia Alonso, Yvette Chauviré, Ninette de Valois, Alicia Markova, Galina Ulanova, and Nadia herself. I was deeply moved by the warmth of their references to what I had tried to do for ballet. I remembered that I had once written that in England, if you were lucky to live long enough, you became a 'grand old man', your errors overlooked; you entered a second childhood and were indulged. Seventy was a very comfortable age. As I looked round the room memories kept crowding in from every period in my life, all of them happy ones. I had been in the right place at the right time, able to see the Maryinsky ballerinas and the young Vaganova-trained dancers of the Soviet Union, to watch the growth of new schools in England, the United States, Cuba, and to see the revival of the ballet in France and the dance in India. I had travelled all over the world. The dance was a common language that made me feel at home everywhere, transcending political differences and bridging the generations. Phyllis Bedells, ten years my senior, was the doyenne; others had been pupils during my time at the Royal Ballet School. I thought of the many who were no longer there: Trefilova and Pavlova, who had started my enthusiasm and set a standard, and my old mentors Valerian Svetlov, Philip Richardson, and Prince Wolkonsky, all of whom had paid me the supreme compliment of taking me seriously when

I was a brash dilettante of great enthusiasm but little knowledge. Every one of the pile of telegrams awoke a fresh memory. In that short space I relived a lifetime as a drowning man is said to do – although the only liquid in which I might have been drowned was pink champagne.

All this came about through *Balletomania*. The title and subject matter I had thought of in my bath one morning and had rushed round to Victor Gollancz, who took it on trust, giving me a generous advance. It was the easiest book I ever wrote. Its instant success turned me away from a hard grind at medicine (I already had a law degree) and prevented me from becoming a perpetual student. In my innocence I took its success for granted. I know better now, forty books on.

Balletomania was written in a fever heat of enthusiasm. It was the very personal book of a young man. Over the years it went into thirty-five printings, made many converts, and turned a hobby into a vocation.

On re-reading it I felt that it had a certain value as an eyewitness account of an interesting transition period. In my original introduction I wrote that this would be the raw material for the historian of the future, and so it remains in the present edition – as will, I hope, the new section after a similar lapse of time.

When a book is over forty years old, it may smell either of mothballs or lavender, it may seem naïve or even prove unreadable. Ballet lovers have indulged me for so many years, the emotions that inspired the book were so genuine, and the material so new to a whole generation that I felt that it might be dusted and taken down from the shelves. I was further encouraged to see that first editions fetch an appreciable price in booksellers' catalogues and that the title is quoted in the appendix to the greater Oxford Dictionary. The fact that George Weidenfeld suggested at the dinner that I write another book under his imprint (I had written *Ballet Russe* for him in 1968) and approved the idea, clinched the matter.

I have decided to leave the original text unchanged, and not to appear wise after the events recorded. I have made certain excisions where the matter seemed irrelevant. I have written a postscript to certain chapters, either to indicate a changed point of view or to emphasize the extraordinary development of ballet that has taken place during my lifetime, a greater change than any in its long history.

Balletomania was the story of an obsession, one that has not diminished with the passing of time but rather has grown more selective, more critical, and, I hope, better informed. I concluded the book with the words, 'The End is the beginning of a new story. I will stay to learn.'

My basic outlook remains unchanged. It is still firmly linked to the classics. I have added a new section, 'Balletomania Now', relating the various experiences of performances and personalities that from time to time have rekindled my obsession, omitting my absorbing work with the Royal Ballet School and its remarkable founder Ninette de Valòis; I have written about this in two autobiographical works, and others have discussed it at length.

I have made less reference to the ballet scene in England today than it merits. It will be familiar to anyone who reads this book and certainly not through any lack of enthusiasm. Also, I have been, and am still, too close to it to write with spontaneity about the sudden impact of those experiences.

I hope that I do not appear didactic: such is not my intention. It is impossible to repeat in every case 'in my opinion'. I can only deal with my tastes and reactions – a method which, incidentally, is far more modest than telling the reader what he must think. I have tried whenever possible to give my reasons for feeling as I do, but however vivid in my memory are the bygone performances of which I write, and they are vivid, it is not always possible to reproduce them on paper. At times one is reduced to that useful postcard formula, 'I wish you had been with us.' For this reason many dancers to whom I owe a debt of gratitude are omitted. It may be an amusing pastime, one in which I sometimes indulge, to make a list of 'greats' and to assemble a dream cast of dancers, but it is a party game and should never be committed to print.

This will positively be my final appearance as a writer on ballet. This then is a record of over fifty years of exciting memories of performances that have moved me and still remain vivid as I write of them.

Once again I am deeply grateful to my friend and fellow writer Roma Fairley and her husband, Alan, for giving me the peace and the stimulus to write in their beautiful villa at Cap d'Ail, a stone's throw from Monte Carlo, where the original story started, and also to my wife, Vivienne, for her invaluable help.

Villa les Trois Ifs,
Cap d'Ail
1975–6

Introduction to the 1934 Edition

THIS is in no sense a history or a complete survey of contemporary ballet. Both the personal angle from which it is written and the recent rapid developments of this vigorous art make that an impossibility. It is written very definitely from a personal angle, the angle of a man madly, but let us hope not blindly, in love with a certain conception of ballet, and consequently uninterested in, and even hostile to, many other forms of the dance. That conception is, I believe, large enough to cover a very wide ground, and the love intense enough to be critical of everything that bears the name *ballet*, until it has proved itself by a whole series of performances. It is only then that a true perspective can be obtained; and when a work and a company are both so well known that carmine-coloured nails, objectionable at all times, can in *Les Sylphides*, by cutting off abruptly the fine line of the fingers and substituting bloody stumps, produce a feeling of profound irritation, then the right diagnosis is *balletomania*.

This is the story of an adventure in search of the experience that alone can give the very maximum of pleasure at a performance, an adventure that has led me into the classrooms of the world to dissect every movement, so that just as the concert-goer can follow with his score, I can solve the mysteries of movement with my mental score. It is cold-blooded perhaps, but when I applaud and shout I must know why, and if I know the reason first, then I am completely happy, without the fear that soon, after two or three performances, I shall be a little ashamed of my temporary intoxication.

Nothing is more difficult than to express dancing in words. The actual life of the dancer is so short. What can the seven-letter word *Pavlova* mean to those who never saw her, however many books in her praise are left behind? Yet how much it can convey to those of us who did, who can still see *The Dying Swan* on an empty stage, and relive its thrills, moment by moment, till that final unforgettable tremor, when the ruby brooch seemed to liquefy into an actual drop of blood from the heart of The Swan. A drama, a life's experience in two minutes, based on the classroom pas de bourrée and made up of a simple sequence of steps. No, analysis cannot be cold-blooded. It makes the achievement the nobler, Anna Pavlova still more supreme. Even the work of those dancers still with us dies as the curtain falls; the performance of each night remains unique.

I am fond of reading contemporary accounts of some great dancer of the past, of looking at drawings, old prints, and faded photographs. It was with a thrill that I spoke to an old lady who had taken lessons from Taglioni herself. She remembered it all so clearly : the apartment in Paris, the portrait dedicated by Rossini 'à la plus légère des Sylphides',* and the rather prim old lady 'with arms so unusually long that one wondered at her poetry'. She was fussily correct in her *tenue* and took the little girl severely to task one day : 'Il ne faut jamais dire "embêtant", ce n'est pas un mot qu'une jeune fille doit prononcer; dites "ennuyeux", mais jamais, jamais ce mot de domestique.'† That is sentimental, a memory of no real importance, but such sentimental links also serve to keep our art alive when the last farewell has been given. If we are to be cold-blooded, critical, analytical, we must leave space for gossip, too. Time can lend dignity to gossip.

Like the dancer himself, sometimes I shall be gossiping in the wings, sometimes busy on the stage. The actual criticism consists largely of those performances of the last few years that are still alive in repertoire and memory. Thus the reader will be able to re-live his own experiences as well as mine, point by point, and names will mean more than just a grouping of letters. There is a risk in this, too. The young dancers of today, the Toumanovas, Baronovas, Riabouchinskas, heroines of the latter part of my story, are developing rapidly. Already their charming, gawky rendering of a dance, which suddenly gives one a fresh vision of its meaning, is almost a thing of the past, replaced by a new-found perfection. But whatever their development and their ultimate goal, they have already coloured their whole period. The new 'Baby Ballet', patronized at first, is now assured of its place in history. Massine has guided them and made them dance, Derain, Miró, Masson, and others have dressed and decorated them, Auric has given them melody, and they have interpreted the music of the immortals.

* 'To the lightest of the Sylphides'.
† 'One must never say "boring", it's not a word a young lady should use; say "dull", but never, never that below-stairs expression.'

I have tried throughout to give those who are really moulding our art the chance to express themselves, away from the stage itself, as they have done to me in so many after-performance discussions. Sometimes I disagree with the conclusions expressed, sometimes they are difficult to reconcile with one another, but the remarks of a practical man give one a new stimulus that is worth pages of theory.

If this book contains any lesson or theme, or even has continuity, it is that ballet is so much more than just a pleasant evening's entertainment; like music or the drama, it has endless varieties of shades and subtleties not as yet fully understood outside dancing circles, and the dancer suffers both in pride and pocket from such a lack of understanding. When we consider that there are fewer truly great dancers than virtuosi of the piano or violin, that a Baronova is as amazing in her depth of expression as a Menuhin, and as brilliant and rare a phenomenon, and that there are far fewer choreographers than playwrights, composers, or painters, all first cousins, then we can realize that the dancer has still truly to be discovered, even by her most enthusiastic admirers. Ask anyone who has been applauding a great dancer or a good ballet his exact reasons, and the answer will most certainly be vague – something to do with beauty, grace, or lightness, a fraction of the truth. His instinct was correct, but he lacked the very necessary framework in which to fit the experience. My adventure has been the construction of such a framework for myself.

The more concrete historical theme is that Michael Fokine gave us the ballet we know and love, and that has had such a powerful effect on the whole artistic life of the century; for a time it was lost, bankrupt of ideas and hidden under a mass of literary and aesthetic conceptions, hostile to the dancer; recently Leonide Massine, after many experimental wanderings, has once again made of it a creative force with a future.

Finally, a word addressed to dancers in an attempt to preserve my future peace of mind. I believe that my many dear friends in ballet will take my criticism, at any rate of themselves, in good part, as they have done in the past, although each article or book has often meant an embarrassing reunion, until little points were straightened out. I have been entirely frank here. Too often in the past I have been tempted to become the propagandist at the expense of the critic, to see my subjects under the best possible light, to explain their virtues and not to dwell on their faults. At one time there were so few enthusiasts. For me this present book cancels everything I have ever written on the ballet; all of that past writing goes into one big bonfire, with perhaps a shadowy company dancing gleefully around it.

No, decidedly this will not be history, but it may well be the very raw material for history in the future.

New York – Paris – London
1933–4

PART I

Balletomania: The Story of an Obsession

*

This first part is dedicated to my dear friends Nadia Nerina and Charles Gordon in gratitude for a long and uninterrupted friendship and in souvenir of so many tastes in common. And to Alicia Markova who proved such an inspiration from the earliest days.

1. Balletomania

IT is my firm belief that human society is divided into three distinct castes: Russian dancers, dancers, and very ordinary people. This great truth must first have dawned upon me at about the age of six, for I have always been conscious of it. Whether it came direct from my mother, to whom ballet means much, or as a violent re-action from my father, to whom it means boredom, I cannot tell. Probably it requires both to make the complete fanatic. At any rate, now, after many years of close association with dancers, I still believe it firmly. Even a knowledge of their little intrigues and jealousies, which are fully as pronounced as in the case of writers or lawyers, if not quite so bitter as with the scientists, cannot make me recant. And I have suffered much from this failing. How well do I know the cold, awkward silence that follows a favourable answer to the challenging, almost threatening, 'And what did you think of X in *Le Lac des Cygnes*? – No, really?' Yet now I can understand and excuse it. When the dancer is jealous of her rival's performance, she is certainly even far more jealous of an abstrac-tion than an individual, a certain ballerina X, who represents an absolute standard of perfection, and it is in her rival that she can see some aspects of that ideal. She is also jealous of the opportunity to work and to develop. Later I will have much more to say about that jealousy, but already in mitigating it I have revealed myself. It is a symptom. Now I must make clear my reasons, not merely to others, but, what is more difficult still, to myself. What in fact is this dancer whom I worship? I know that in a country where so many take cricket in a similar spirit, study its finesses, respect its traditions, and make heroes of its exponents, sympathy at any rate will be with me from the very start. For the cricket-lover and the balletomane share many symptoms.

The dancer is perhaps the only true amateur in the theatre today, using that word in its finest sense. She lives definitely for her art, and not for what it can bring. Its rewards are painfully meagre; many years of overwork at a bare living wage, a very generous share of applause from a small public, a few press cuttings with her name misspelt, bouquets, photographs, with the end almost inevitably a school, and the grind all over again, this time vicariously. This is a chronicle of hard work. The dancer will never cut her rehearsals, but clamour for more, and when she is not herself dancing, she watches others, in acute discomfort, for she will make every movement inwardly and suffer with every fault. She has never finished learning. At the height of her triumph she must submit herself to the discipline, and often to the abuse, of her ballet-master. To him she is never '*Madame*', but always the small girl whose arabesque lacks perfection or whose elevation is weak. What a mental and physical training, this daily class. Frequently I refresh myself there and seek new vision. It is the very start of the whole story.

'One ... two ... Un ... deux ... Rass ... dva.'

No flattering costumes, even if the traditional revealing black dress is no longer enforced, no scenery, no music except that of a piano accompaniment. Every fault laid bare before the mirror and analysed, the sarcasms of the teacher, the amusement of the other pupils until their turn comes. I have yet to meet the truly conceited dancer – that is, the dancer who really believes in her own pathetic little attempts at bluff. There is always something new to be learned, something that X excels in and that she herself lacks. Her mother is there to blow the trumpet and beat the big drum; every mother's daughter is a genius (more of dancers' mothers, much more, later), but she herself really knows. Dancers are fêted, meet the most interesting people of their day, but they live in a world apart, a world of their own making – classroom, rehearsal, a hurried meal, shoes and tights to darn, and the stage. 'There is no time to be gay at all,' said a disillusioned girl to me, with visions of champagne and slippers. They think of dancing, dream of dancing. Their values are their own; they make and break reputations quite apart from popular estimation. And they respect the opinions of their little world above all else. They know that theirs is the responsibility, that they alone are the sole guardians of a great tradition. In practice nothing much is written down, it all lives in the memory. The spirit of the performance of *Giselle* we enjoy tonight has been handed down from person to person for over a hundred years, from country to country, yet only the smallest changes in detail must have crept in since its creation by Carlotta Grisi (1841), whom no dancer living today can ever have seen. Pavlova causes a revolution by discarding the ballet skirt in the second act for grave-clothes draperies that enhance her spiritual interpretation. Spessiv-tseva again reverts to tradition, but the spirit and substance remain unchanged. Massine at times forgets his own compositions, so great in number and diverse in feeling, but Woizikovski remembers them, and the ballet goes on. The art of the individual dancer may be ephemeral. Today we do not know how the great Taglioni danced – from the prints and lithographs we can only recognize the incorporeal effect she produced on her contemporaries – but her art is not dead. Some little girl in London, Paris, or Milan dances differently because Taglioni once existed. She will carry part of Taglioni with her onto the stage. Already Anna Pavlova, with so much of Taglioni in her, is only an exciting memory, but a memory that is creative, that has made and still is making dancers who will possess something of her poetry, even some of her technique, and especially the will to serve and to be artists. La Camargo, because of a pardonable pride in her shapely legs, has given us the conven-tional ballet skirt, which has altered the whole technique of danc-ing. Heinel of Stuttgart has left us with the pirouette. Today every ballet performance is a tribute to La Camargo and Heinel. Kchess-inska, Trefilova, Preobrajenska, and others of whom I will write, are daily giving something of themselves, so that ballet goes on living and growing, even if dancers themselves die.

The ballet dancer is the perfect example of the balance between the individual and the group. Her whole aim in life is to shine as a star, a *ballerina assoluta*, yet she subordinates herself to the whole, the ballet. Always she is under rigid, almost military discipline, a discipline that becomes so much a part of herself that, in extra-ordinary circumstances, a group of excitable, highly strung young girls can act with the courage and presence of mind of a ship's crew.

It happened in Bournemouth, before a packed house, on the last night of the Monte Carlo Ballet season.

It is the first ballet, *Le Lac des Cygnes*, with its dreamy romantic music, its comfortable old-fashioned scenery, so drab a background to the filmy white swans, princesses under a spell, and the audience is dazed with pleasure, perhaps under that selfsame spell. Danilova, with Eglevsky as her cavalier, is about to begin the great adagio, the most completely satisfying moment of all, when piercing shrieks are heard. The unusual in something so well known, so ordered and logical, is especially terrifying. After a pause, a white swan runs fluttering onto the stage, her dress and wings in flames, reaching high above her head. So long does this agonized fluttering seem to last that I can recognize Rostova, the beautiful leader of one flock of swans, and take in her whole dazed expression, as the dancers retreat from her in horror, clutching at their billowing tarlatans. But it is too late, already Tarakanova is well alight, isolated now, as the flock retreats still further. Then Grigoriev in mufti, an intruder on this scene of magic, rushes onto the stage, and seizes her in his arms, while Jan Hoyer embraces Rostova and the flames. The orchestra pauses for an instant, but Danilova nods violently. I can hear her say: 'Even if the theatre is on fire we *must* go on; play.' The beautiful adagio continues. Then a burned but reassuring hand is waved from the wings, the swans troop on again, Morosova stepping automatically into Rostova's place as leader. It has all been a question of a few bars of music, with nothing to show that the tragedies of poor Clara Webster and Emma Livry, burned alive on the stage, have nearly been reproduced before our eyes: an old-fashioned ballet for this old-fashioned tragedy of naked footlights and a dancer's tutu.

An old lady seated next to me is considerably amazed at my agitation and says: 'Well, I thought it was all a part of the show. You never do know in ballet. They *are* so clever nowadays,' and half the audience shares the same impression. They have not realized that Rostova, Tarakanova, the company, and perhaps they themselves owe their lives not only to the bravery and presence of mind of Grigoriev and Hoyer, who are badly burned, but to this whole conception of discipline on the stage. Not one of those girls realized that the entire theatre was not on fire, yet they backed into the wings and walked quietly into the street, as if it had all been a part of Petipa's choreography, and Danilova, defying the fresh wiles of the magician, added one more performance of this most difficult of roles to her brilliant record.

Then the last ballet, the complex *Choreartium*. Rostova appears, dances especially well, and the only sign of the incident is Hoyer lifting with a heavily bandaged hand. Behind the scenes there is far less excitement than I have known about the destination of a bouquet, so often a sore point. There are some kisses and hand-clasps, and a much repeated little joke that seems to give general satisfaction . . . 'This is *Lac des Cygnes*, but you gave a performance of *L'Oiseau de Feu*.' Danilova, too, is promptly dubbed 'The Captain', but that is all. It is Saturday night; dressing rooms are hurriedly cleared, and the company goes home. There is a very early start for Birmingham the next morning, supper to be eaten, packing to be done.

Afterwards Rostova told me how she had gone to the stage dressing room to touch up her make-up and looking in the glass had noticed a whole background of flames. Thinking that it was the theatre and not her own dress, she ran onto the stage to warn the others and was terrified as they drew away from her. I saw all that was left of the dress, which had been set on fire by a candle carelessly left alight, a small scrap of tarlatanless silk – yet she was untouched. Afterwards at the hotel just a simple : 'Has anyone got a French novel to lend me? I may not sleep very well tonight,' from a pale little girl of seventeen.

Rostova, after her adventure, danced in *Choreartium* because she was one of a group that needed her help, but she danced beautifully because she was an individual who wished to excel.

This is as much a digression here as it was at the performance that night, but it is all a part of the tradition, strong and unbreakable.

There are dynasties of dancers, and a true line of succession. In 1847 Marius Petipa of Marseilles, real founder of the Russian Ballet as we know it, goes to Russia and is received with all the warm Saint Petersburg hospitality to the visiting artist. He becomes a Russian, in spite of a stubborn Marseillais accent. Before his death in 1910 he composed fifty-four new ballets, mostly in five or six acts, and was entrusted with the formation of several generations of dancers. Christian Johannsen of Sweden also comes to Russia. He is a pupil of the Bournonvilles, who were themselves pupils of the Great Vestris : an unbroken line. Like all wise teachers, they too learn from their pupils, and the Russian school is born. To quote Nicolas Legat, whose own father was a visitor from Scandinavia : 'The Russian school is the French school that the French themselves have forgotten.'

Petipa composed fifty-four ballets. Today, when we see those that have survived – *Le Lac des Cygnes* and *Le Mariage d'Aurore* – Petipa, and all the dancers who have performed in them, live once again. The line goes on unbroken to our day. Fokine works with Petipa, Johannsen, and Legat, and then founds his modern ballet. Upon leaving Diaghilev, he teaches and produces in London, Paris,

New York, Milan, Scandinavia, South America, leaving everywhere not only his own influence but that which has gone before. Old *maestro* Cecchetti, a visitor from Italy and teacher of a thousand dancers the world over, receives his first lesson from Giovanni Lepri, pupil of Carlo Blasis, a founder of the art. All the dancing wisdom of the world meets in Theatre Street before being dispersed once again. One forgetful generation, and ballet would be dead for ever; but there is no risk of that. It can survive war and revolution.

Kchessinska, flying before the Bolsheviks, daily performs the exercises that might betray her; the first preoccupation on safe arrival in France is for a pair of ballet shoes. Nijinsky, a prisoner of war in Hungary, frets himself ill because he cannot dance, plans ballets, and devises an intricate system of notation, born of the stubborn knowledge that ballet must survive.

Diaghilev dies, Pavlova dies asking for her Swan dress, and there is a terrifying silence, but, in all the dancing schools, classes continue as if there were still something left for which to live. After a few false starts the broken threads are once more gathered together, and our art enjoys a glorious renaissance. The strength of this tradition, this will to survive, is tremendous. The exact lines it has followed are of immense interest to the historian. Here I have tried to convey something of the atmosphere of what is so essential to feel, if this story of great dancers and little girls struggling at the barre, of the painters and musicians who work for them, and with them as their medium, is to be understood and seen, not merely as a series of disconnected episodes and studies, which in form, as the experiences of one man, it may well be, but as a part of one vast structure. The consciousness of this, which grew in me only after many years, is present with the youngest dancer, her pride and part of her life. That is why, when people so often ask me, 'What are dancers really like off the stage?' I cannot reply with the obvious, 'Oh, just like other people.' The old legend of champagne in a dancer's slipper will die hard, but, if the dancer can be a bacchante, there is often much more of the nun in her outlook. Dancing has had its martyrs. But recently, a man has died for it. I will write the story of Simeonov, as it was told me by Michael Fokine.

' "If you knew how I loved the ballet" were the last words written to me by Nicolai Prokofievitch Simeonov, a few moments before he leapt into the turbulent waters of the Niagara Falls. Such words may seem strange to the layman in a suicide letter, but to me they are easy to understand, for I knew his ideals, his sincerity, his long-suffering. I knew how he loved the ballet, how he believed in its necessity. In each one of his letters to me he asks why ballet, one of the highest, purest, most beautiful achievements in art, must now pass through a long black period of neglect through a lack of comprehension.

'He was a member of the Russian Ballet in the stormiest period of its history, in the period of tumbling traditions and the struggle for new ideas. He was born in the classical school, participated in the creation of the new ballet, and went right through into the radical modernist experiments. The struggle between various tendencies in the art did not frighten him. He was deeply interested. It was a sign of vitality. What made him suffer was the gradual lack of appreciation of ballet in America, the countless new schools established without the smallest foundation in art or knowledge, and their "slander and persecution" of ballet in the press. "These people must surely hate ballet, for it calls for years of study," is how he explained it.

'Nicolai Simeonov worried – wrote to the newspapers ... wrote to me, till one day, 5 July 1932, I received this final tragic letter:

My dear Michael Michaelovitch – As you see from the enclosed, I am ending my life by suicide. I can no longer bear the slander and persecution of ballet. Maybe my jump into Niagara Falls will sufficiently disturb you and others, and give you the strength to puncture these inflated modernists ...

How I am longing for the Bolshoi Theatre, the Arts Theatre and the others ... there was enthusiasm, here is business.

A more detailed explanation of my death I have mailed to Valerian Svetlov. My heartiest regards to Madame Fokine.

Your N. Simeonov

P.S. I wanted to send you a kiss, but the dead are not interesting. Do you remember Monte Carlo, Paris? How excited we were, how enthusiastic. What a success. Here everything is asleep.

'The letter was supplemented by six pages; two were written on the 30th of September, 1931, and four on the 3rd of October. The September note starts like this: "I am fifty years old and in perfect health. I will have myself examined again, however, in the local hospital. Yet I must end my life by suicide."

'I received many letters from him between September 1931 and July 1932, but with no reference to his intentions to commit suicide. You will notice, from the very first thoughts of suicide he had himself examined, so that his death should not be attributed to ill health or insanity. Everything was carefully calculated. Again he writes: "When municipalities and colleges will be interested in the dance even in the same degree as they are at present in Music and the Drama, Ballet will come back into its own." In his final letter he sent me the programme of his last recital on June 26th, just a few days before his death. He had demonstrated the pupils of his school and had taught them thirty-one dances. What a degree of labour and of love he must have given in teaching them their roles, designing their costumes, and supervising their make-up. He was still full of power and energy.

'I have known Nicolai Simeonov since 1909, the beginning of the Diaghilev Ballet. I knew him as a man of self-respect and integrity, integrity in art and in business, who would protest against injustice however much damage it did to himself.

'I believe that his death for an ideal typifies and corresponds to his whole life.'

In a bygone age this death of a man for his ideal of beauty would have been understood and would have given rise to a legend, just as now a man's death for his ideal of speed is understood. Today the first is but an interesting study in morbid psychology, a few lines in the newspaper. Perhaps the balletomane will understand, assuredly the dancer. I like to think of Simeonov as having acted deliberately and in the full possession of his senses, of having believed in something strongly enough to be willing to die to rouse others in its defence. Mistaken or not, does it matter?

Dancers must remember the name of Nicolai Simeonov, who died by drowning on 5 July 1932.

2. My Debut as a Balletomane

'WHEN did your interest in dancing first begin?' I am asked that now almost daily. Unfortunately I cannot answer. My earliest memories are of the sparkling Genée at the Coliseum, of Nijinsky leaping out of a window, of Pavlova and Mordkin in the *Bacchanal*, Karsavina sadly awaking from her rose-haunted dream, and of the backcloth of *Thamar*, which has altered the whole vision of my generation and made it colour-conscious.

It seemed as natural for me in those days to know the names of every member of a corps de ballet as it was for my friends to reel off batting averages and the like. I decorated a screen with the portraits of dancers cut out of the illustrated papers, and I still have many of the photographs that hung on my dormitory walls, to the horror of one or two schoolmasters, who considered it a thoroughly unhealthy taste. By the age of ten I was completely obsessed.

Now no Russian has ever asked me that question, for the balletomane has always been a thoroughly Russian product and, from what I hear, is to this day, in spite of all the material hardships. With the biggest pull in government circles, it is necessary to arrange for seats several weeks in advance when Semenova, the great Maryinsky ballerina of today, is to dance, just as in the old days when the best seats were a coveted hereditary privilege. Ballet originated at a court, flourished under an emperor, but balletomania is the privilege of no one class, and is not the artificial exotic thing that some might think.

Perhaps the greatest of all cases of balletomania took place in the very midst of the terror itself. It is told by Tamara Karsavina. Her brother, Platon Karsavin, famous historian and philosopher, was thrown into prison with a group of the intelligentsia suspected of counter-revolutionary activities. One night he was fetched out of his cell for the customary inquiry, and the particular form of 'third degree' must have been something like this:

THE TCHEKIST: Your name?
THE PRISONER: Platon Karsavin.
THE TCHEKIST: Karsavin – any relation to Tamara Karsavina?

THE PRISONER: My sister.

THE TCHEKIST: Your sister! That is wonderful! Absolutely my favourite ballerina. I find her *Giselle* unsurpassed ...

THE PRISONER: ... and her *Lac des Cygnes*.

And so the discussion may have continued until dawn, all political differences forgotten, the prisoner's friends doubtless giving him up for lost. Perhaps he owed his life to that fact, for what balletomane could sentence La Karsavina's brother?

Then there was that prince of ballet enthusiasts, the Baron Dimitri Gunsbourg, who perished in the Revolution. It was he who made Diaghilev's first venture possible, when official help was withdrawn, proud and happy to devote his time and fortune to the art. His name must be especially honoured.

To go from the sublime to the ridiculous: Alexander Plestcheev, in his history of Russian ballet, tells of how a group of Saint Petersburg balletomanes bought a pair of La Taglioni's slippers for two hundred roubles, had them cooked, prepared with a special sauce, and ate them at a banquet. My Russian friends have told me endless stories of the forms that the obsession can assume; of a certain general (Russian stories are always told about generals) who was so far gone that he refused to eat out of any plate that was not decorated with some dancing figure. They feared that I might become the same – perhaps there was some risk – but I rapidly began to rationalize my obsession. Today my best definition of a balletomane is, that he is a person who is sad, very sad, on the first night of a season, just because he realizes that it is only for a season, and that a first night implies a last night, most exciting and melancholy of events.

My first actual contact with ballet came about through meeting a little girl at a children's party and later through seeing one of the greatest of all ballerinas dance in Diaghilev's unforgettable production of the Petipa-Tchaikovsky-Bakst *Sleeping Princess* at the Alhambra, ill-fated adventure that was ten years ahead of its time. The first gave me a human contact, a career to follow, to be interested in and to try to advance; the second, a deep lasting artistic experience that made me rationalize all that had gone before the vivid, confused mass of exciting impressions, and that gave me certain standards. Subsequently the great ballerina became my friend just as did the little girl. The extremes met – the beginnings of a career and the triumphant climax. Years later I was to sit with Vera

Trefilova and hear her enthusiasm about Alicia Markova in one of her own great roles.

I first heard of the little girl, Alicia Marks, through my mother, who often visited Astafieva's studio in the King's Road, Chelsea.

Seraphine Astafieva, a former pupil of the Imperial schools, and for a time a principal in the Diaghilev Ballet, the beautiful protagonist in *Cléopâtre* and *Prince Igor*, was the first Russian to open a school in London, and her classes were a revelation. By her link with the great tradition, her knowledge, enthusiasm, and vivid personality, she was beginning to do things with English dancers, and to break down the legend that they were only fit for the corps de ballet. I remember seeing a small girl called June there, who was spoken of as *the* coming English dancer, and there was also a boy, Patrick Kay, who seemed to have unusual talent. Astafieva was warm-hearted, quixotic, and incredibly untidy, her beautiful legs hidden by the most extraordinary woollen garment – 'It is not really dirty, just near-white' – her skirts hitched up around her waist with string or a safety pin, but she was always beautiful to watch and interesting to talk to. She had an inexhaustible storehouse of ballet legend and knowledge. She could and would help everyone save herself, and was, as a result, the constant prey of picturesque but unscrupulous persons. The more fantastic the hard-luck story, the more readily she believed in it, lending her sympathy and always her aid. Her studio was the meeting place for the most curious 'down-and-outs', as well as the most interesting people of the day, and she mixed them so well that her parties were a certain success. With a little less sympathy and more common sense in her make-up, she could have started almost unaided many of the subsequent English ballet movements. They all owe much to her and to the fine foundation she gave her pupils. I consider myself one of them. She guided my youthful enthusiasm and grounded me in the technical foundations of the dance. Since then I have met in nearly every company in the world someone who worked in the studio at that time. No less a person than Diaghilev, highly critical, especially where women were concerned, admired 'Sima's' great qualities and confided in her. He often talked of engaging her to take the classes, but feared the trouble that might be caused through having a temperamental teacher for temperamental pupils. To her English girls she gave something of her vitality; with the Russians there might have been explosions. For various reasons I have seen little of her since those days, but I have always retained my admiration and gratitude.

It appears that little Alicia Marks had made a highly dramatic entrée into the school. *Madame* had exploded into a voluble outburst in her particular mixture of English and Russian, and the pupils could talk of nothing else for days.

A pretty young woman with a very frail, timid little girl had come to the door during the morning class and asked to see Madame Astafieva.

'I am Astafieva. What you want, dahlink?'

Everyone was always 'darling' to her, including the coal-man one morning, to his great amazement and mine. There was a muttered explanation, a silence to gather up strength, and then the explosion.

'You mothers are all alike. You are a *doura*, yes, a *doura*; in English, eediot. You think because little girl can stand on toe and wobble she just like Pavlova – yes? You don't know how long it take to make Pavlova, what work, what tears, what art. You don't know what it mean. Good-bye.'

She promptly slammed the door in their faces. For the rest of the class she was too indignant to do anything but deliver a long tirade against all dancing mothers, the standard tirade I know by heart and have heard from every *maître de ballet* in turn. It appears that this particular mother had handed her a visiting card, with the daring words THE MINIATURE PAVLOVA printed on it, and was about to explain the merits of her little girl at considerable length.

A few days later Astafieva told me excitedly that she had a new pupil of quite exceptional promise – Alicia Marks, that selfsame child whom she had turned out and nearly terrified into a fit. Mother and daughter had discussed the matter on returning home, and had been so moved by the outburst and its obvious integrity of purpose that they had destroyed the offending cards, and had decided that Alicia must learn there and there alone. Incidentally, in justice to Mrs Marks, since that first day in the studio she has been a model 'dancing mother', as her speedy return proves, and has never again risked her daughter's career.

It was some time before I came to class again. In spite of Astafieva's commendation, I was strongly prejudiced against the 'wonder child'. Although not so long ago, those were still the days when children did not yet exist in ballet outside of charity functions, and when record numbers of fouettés were only for the very experienced, and then used sparingly. Today I would have gone out eagerly in search of new talent, for now I know that there are no longer any 'wonder children', only very young dancers, whose youth is an added quality. It was completely by accident, therefore, that I met Alicia at a Christmas party, where I had gone to play my great role of Santa Claus for a young cousin, a fellow pupil in the class, who has since fallen from grace by a passion for tap-dancing to the gramophone and other profanities. As usual, I gravitated toward the first person who was willing to discuss dancing, and the first person was this child, who was very shy, did not quite fit in, and was just as eager to talk dancing as I was. Immediately her whole outlook, her very great earnestness and her ambition, charmed me. The next day I went to see her dance, and the provoking words 'miniature Pavlova' no longer seemed quite so fantastic, and more than once I heard Astafieva herself make the comparison. Her legs were like arrows, she danced as if she meant it, and there was nothing of the conventional prettiness of the small child. She was then the complete ballerina in miniature. Although at that time English soloists in the ballet were quite exceptional, and Sokolova's English birth was still a mystery to the general public, I do not think that any of us who frequented the studio doubted for one moment that the boy, Pat, and little Alicia would make big names, and play their part in the main movement of ballet. Never for one moment did we identify them with panto-mime or cabaret, the chief destination of most of the pupils.

I saw a great deal of Alicia and her three mischievous sisters, mis-chievous doubtless by contrast, for the only naughty thing that she ever seems to have done was to wipe the floor with a facecloth, and she shuddered as it was told. Once she danced for me at a charity soirée at Cambridge, but my only positive recollections are of a smoky oil-stove in a draughty, hastily improvised dressing-room, and of the babble of a group of charitably minded spinsters who flocked around her making motherly sounds.

'Little girl, do you like dancing?'
'How it must hurt your poor little toes to stand on them.'
'You should have been in bed ages ago.'

*

My knowledge of dancing grew with Alicia's increasing technique. I watched her constantly in class, analysed her movements, learned with her.

Pat was the first to go, but his is another story. Diaghilev saw the little girl dance, watched her for his *Sleeping Princess*, and then gave up the idea, fortunately perhaps, on account of the difficulties in getting a labour permit. So she went on learning. Soon family reasons made it essential for her to earn a living. Any other dancing but ballet would have ruined her future. Astafieva reminded Diaghilev of the little girl. He had never had a child in the company before, and the regulations made it necessary for her to be accompanied by a governess. Would he take her and be saddled with all these difficulties? George Balanchine had just been engaged as *maître de ballet*, and a new version of Stravinsky's *Le Chant du Rossignol* was being planned, with décor by Matisse. Perhaps this frail child would do for the role of the nightingale? She was, I think, quietly confident, though she said little. She was still too young to be impressed by the names Stravinsky or Matisse, or to realize the importance of the work. The audition itself was undramatic, in front of Diaghilev, Nijinska, and Balanchine. Knowing him, as I now do, I can imagine his helpful sympathy, a sympathy that he showed later to the twelve-year-olds Toumanova and Baronova. Alicia was engaged; she would be taken on at the end of the Coliseum season to be rehearsed and 'made' at Monte Carlo, workshop of ballet for so many years. Here at last was a definite, thrilling contact with the thing I loved best. Now I, too, could make my debut as a true balletomane. There would be someone from home, someone whose problems mattered, in the very centre of activities. Doubtless then I realized the importance of the engagement far better than she did. I was fully as excited.

The next day she lunched with us in triumph. The immediate problem was to make Alicia Marks into a good Russian Ballet citizen, a process of naturalization I have since seen so many times. It may be hotly attacked, but it is not snobbery. She would dance just as well under the name Lizzie Smith, if we wish to be coldly logical, and yet I do not fully believe it.

The adoption of the Russian name is in a way symbolical, signifying the entrance into the fine tradition that is the living force in ballet, the motive of my first chapter. It is also a gracious compliment to those who made her and gave her the opportunity to shine. When England has a genuine ballet tradition of her own, the name Lizzie Smith may be in great demand.

After a heated discussion and references to Tolstoi and Dostoievski, we settled on the obvious *Markova*, and then watched this English girl gradually growing acclimatized, even to the extent of wrestling with her hair, which had then to be worn in a severe, well-defined manner. True, with no Diaghilev to protest, dancers are apt to bob it, and the true classical style is worn chiefly by autograph hunters and ballet-struck girls. I remember at that same luncheon two amazed questions of Alicia's:

'Why does everyone call Diaghilev, Sergy Pock?'

'Who is this man Basket they are always talking about?'

In spite of her hour-old name, she was not yet Russian enough to have heard of patronymics (Sergei *Pavlovitch*), or of the glory of Russia, Leon Bakst.

Her big ordeal was still to come, when Diaghilev presented his new protégée to the company. She was to dance for them at a party given by Astafieva at the studio. I was excited both on her account and mine. To think that at last I should meet Diaghilev and all the members of that glorious company ! I was still then more emotional in my approach than critical, though I had begun to formulate certain standards, but to this very day I am just as thrilled at meeting a dancer whose work I admire, and I have yet to be disillusioned, so perfectly is the character revealed in the movement. Perhaps in my own excitement I forgot that no more critical or frightening audience could have been chosen and that Alicia was not quite thirteen years old. They were not going to be impressed by any childish charm. The words 'dainty' and 'sweet' applied to dancing, which was a serious business, had no meaning for them. They too had danced at that age, though not in public, and some of them had daughters who knew the classical repertoire and could perform really well. I had just seen, at a children's party in the studio, Woizikovski's little girl, now a promising dancer, aged six, dressed in costume for the Bluebird pas de deux, going through all the movements of that dance, in the grand manner, in an unconscious parody of her elders. Many people, who have since become my friends, were there: Lubov Tchernicheva, the most beautiful member of the company; the severely classical Doubrovska, looking like a madonna, with a very great sense of humour; and the new dancers but lately from Russia: Tamara Gevergeva, one of the few fine talents that Diaghilev passed by, and who is certainly the richer for it as Tamara Geva of the Ziegfeld Follies; Alexandra Danilova, future ballerina of the company; and the piquante, angular Nikitina, a shooting star. There were doubtless many others, but my head was in a whirl, and these in particular held my attention. Dolin was watching anxiously. This studio was his home; he was host and somehow felt the responsibility. Once during the evening he drew me aside.

'I know you are interested. Well, you see that dark boy over there, romping in the corner. He is going to be a very great dancer, really great . . . His name? Serge Lifar.'

What a contrast to the children's party, although very much the same games were played, and there was noise, crackers, and paper caps. Late in the evening Markova danced. She had chosen the *Valse Caprice* and was made to improvise, as a still-sterner test. She danced with a new-found assurance and a personality that she was not to show again for many years. Her audience challenged her, and her whole future depended on the result. One could see there something of Pavlova's, and Pavlova herself had recognized it. That combination of strength, precision, and apparent fragility proved irresistible.

In an imagined story one would say that the audience was completely carried away, acclaimed her, and gave her an ovation. It was not so. They applauded a little, and I remember Tchernicheva voicing the general verdict: 'There is fine material there. She is young, has faults, and must first prove herself. She may become one of us in time.' It was not grudging, but a very real tribute, worth all the flattery and applause to which she had been used. Now she was truly one of a magnificent group, and Diaghilev was pleased, Dolin relieved, Astafieva radiant.

She left for Monte Carlo in a pea-soup fog, nearly missing the train; first taste of a life of continual, agitated hurry. The great adventure had begun in earnest.

The story of Markova in the Diaghilev Ballet is the story of a careful, slow preparation under expert hands, preparing for a big chance as prima ballerina that would surely have been hers had Diaghilev lived.

'Watch my little English girl,' he said in the very last interview he gave to the press. He genuinely loved 'his little English girl' and often told me, 'I will do big things for her when she really wakes up.'

Her first role of importance was the famous Act II *Le Lac des Cygnes* adagio, in a divertissement from that ballet. The costume, the smallest ever made in the studios, was afterwards presented to her by Diaghilev, accompanied by one of his very rare bouquets.

I went to Monte Carlo to follow that season carefully. Markova was technically almost flawless, and Cecchetti had given her a new strength. She had everything that she has now, save personality. Diaghilev never lived to see the mature artist, who has been the cornerstone of all our English endeavours. For him she danced Little Red Riding Hood in *Le Mariage d'Aurore* and much later the Blue-bird in the same ballet with Dolin, her school friend; the Child in *La Boutique Fantasque*, the Nightingale in *Le Chant du Rossignol*, her creation, the *pas de trois* in *Cimarosiana*, and *La Chatte*. Each time she showed a frigid perfection which never gave one the impression that some day she could give a really fine performance in *Giselle*. Her story, like that of all dancers, soon became one of ceaseless work, classes, rehearsals, trains, and 'digs'. When that happens there is little more that can be written that is not pure criticism. I heard from her, journeyed to the more accessible places, and was moved by her worries and difficulties. For the first time then I heard of those little jealousies and intrigues. They seemed dreadfully important, but I did not then know the game, the rapid change of friendships, the easy nervous tears, the reconciliations.

So the little English girl, eldest of four sisters, disappears from the story, to be replaced by the dancer.

Pat, my other 'school' friend, has already told his story in his book *Divertissement*, but there are many omissions that I can fill in. I have seen him dance more often than anyone, have followed him from the music hall to the Russian Ballet, and backwards and forwards again. His first ballet costume was confectioned by Asta-fieva from an old dress of my mother's, who would reward him with a box of chocolates for any difficult technical feat well accomplished.

Pat was the first to leave school for the real world of ballet. He was engaged for a small part in the vast production of *The Sleeping Princess*, an event that was to have its influence on the outlook of every dancer, even if the larger public did not at the time grasp its significance. He was to be found in the programme as Patrikeef; Dolin was not yet born. There the dancing of Spessivtseva affected him as deeply as Trefilova's did me. It gave him the ambition to dance with her one day. On his return to the studio we noticed a great difference in him. He worked all day and half the night too, throwing himself down on a couch, exhausted, to sleep. He was no more the 'star pupil', contented with himself, struggling for the best place in front of the mirror. In fact, he was now very far from self-content, for he knew what really great dancing meant, and he had a very definite ambition – to join the Russian Ballet as its *premier danseur*, perhaps to partner the divine Spessivtseva. Now he interested himself in music and prepared his mind as well as his body for the task. He was always studying forms of movement outside the syllabus of work. He would turn cartwheels or walk on his hands. With the aid of Astafieva he adapted these acrobatics to the strictly classical plastique, forcing the pointes. All this was an unconscious preparation for *Le Train Bleu*, led directly to its creation, and has made it up to the present day his alone. It gave rise to an entirely new type of dancing. But such apparent modernism was always classical in mechanism and feeling. Dolin has always been a classical dancer, even in his famous *Espagnol*. His excursions into the purely romantic *demi-caractère* of such a role as Harlequin in *Carnaval*, and *Le Spectre de la Rose*, although extremely well danced, seemed forced and have left me unmoved.

His true debut, and the birth of *Anton Dolin*, took place through one of those muddles, with brilliant results, that can only happen to Russians. One morning Astafieva suddenly found herself talked into putting on a large-scale programme, at the Albert Hall of all places, with just the talent available at her studio and a few days in which to arrange dances, improvise costumes, and see to the orchestration of the music. A pupil show, in fact, disguised under the high-sounding name of *The Anglo-Russian Ballet*.

As the programmes were being printed Pat suddenly conceived the idea of disguising himself under a Russian name. 'It will be an excellent joke. It is sure to mystify all my friends and annoy some of them intensely. What shall I be?' He reached for a volume of Chekhov. 'Anton, at any rate, is a good beginning.' The rest was not so easy. Most of the names were difficult to pronounce, and still more difficult to remember. Someone – it must have been

Astafieva, hit upon Dolin. 'It is simple and will look well in print. I can already hear the public calling out: "Dolin! Bravo, Dolin!"'

They did the very next night. I still have my programme, the first signed with the new name.

Much of the performance was amateurish, and looked still more so in the vast Albert Hall; also there was a hitch that nearly stopped the show at the last minute and made a Russian curtain even later than usual in rising. No one had remembered that there was an orchestra to be paid save the orchestra, who wisely insisted on immediate payment. After a delay and many Russian expletives when it seemed that all the hard work had gone for nothing, a generous friend of ours and of ballet, Nathan Golodetz, whose beautiful wife was an occasional pupil, came to the rescue. He may have played a big role that night by ensuring for Dolin his highly spectacular start. Now for the first time in history there was to be a truly English *premier danseur classique*. I must not insist on the word *English* without some qualification. It was one of the small contributory causes of Dolin's leaving the ballet. Well-meaning admirers, with a misplaced patriotism, started counting up the number of English dancers and got it into their heads that the Russian Ballet was being run by them, a fact that could not be expected to please Diaghilev, especially as there were only six – Sokolova, Savina, de Valois, Coxon, Markova, and Dolin – in a company of over forty, with a purely Russian choreography. Dolin himself has always insisted that as an artist he is a Russian who owes everything to Russian training and environment. Time enough to rejoice if, and when, like the Russians themselves *vis à vis* the Italians, we find a genuine and not an accidental individual supremacy.

After the performance we all went back to the studio to talk and wait for the papers, Dolin clutching his first wreath.

The press was enthusiastic and unanimous. J. T. Grein wrote in the *Daily Sketch*:

'A new dancer, Anton Dolin, carried us away in enthusiasm ... Dolin is as light as a feather, as graceful as a fawn, as wing-footed as Mercury. I for one believe that Dolin, wholly unaffected, immersed in his art, will ere long be proclaimed the rival and successor of Nijinsky, and, if he remains unspoilt, he may be the greater of the twain, for so far his great work is entirely free of pose.'

Not a little surprising, for the performance of a young boy at a pupil display. Astafieva sent the news to Diaghilev, and an audition was arranged in Paris. Dolin proceeded to Monte Carlo a year ahead of Alicia.

There were three sequels to this haphazard choice of a name. The first, by no means flattering, an advertisement in the Russian press stating that a certain family Dolin wished to disclaim all relationship with the dancer of that name; the second, a long, pathetic letter in Russian, which Diaghilev translated. 'I lost my son Anton [Dolin] in the early days of the Revolution. I am in despair. In spite of all my efforts I have failed to trace him. Now the news of your triumphs fills me with hope again. Can it be that you are he, and that God in His mercy will give you back to me once more?'

The third event occurred upon his first appearance in London, when the 'Irish dancer', Le Beau Gosse of *Le Train Bleu*, had become the rage. There was a very simple, obvious, and straightforward explanation to the name. Pure Irish, of course, and it did the boy credit : for Dolin read Dolan !

Dolin's great roles are now a part of ballet history, the subject of many accounts in nearly every language, but there are three outstanding performances I shall never forget which to some extent explain his temperament. The first was his own *Hymn to the Sun* at the Albert Hall; the next, *L'Oiseau Bleu* at the Coliseum, the last night of his first London season, which proved quite conclusively that he was no nine-days' wonder; the third, the last performance of *Le Train Bleu* the night he left the Ballet, danced in a violent temper, when, smarting under a sense of injustice, he wished to show Diaghilev and the company the full extent of their loss. It was the very first ballet, and so dramatic in effect that Jean Cocteau, realizing that it meant the end of his ballet, left the theatre. Each one of these performances was given under the stress of a strong emotion.

There is no more curious case in ballet than the career of this boy, who might so easily have become a successful public school athlete. Even when we pass over the extraordinary fact that Patrick Kay became so very completely Anton Dolin, he should have ruined his career time and time again through his flirtations with the commercial stage, with banality and bad taste. Few dancers can survive a season of music-hall appearances, certainly no young dancer. I have followed him carefully in the music hall, and it has hurt me, both for his sake and for the art that he represents, but he has always done the thing supremely well. 'If the audience want a little sensation, a little flattery too, then they'll get it' has been the attitude of this dancer, who on the ballet stage can be the embodiment of classical dignity, keeping his audience at a respectful distance. It has become a habit now, after seeing him in some trivial engagement, to talk of him as finished. People began to say so when he left the Ballet for the first time, but his colleagues never did. He has had an enormous share of the approbation of his fellow dancers, the appreciation that alone truly counts, and especially from the many ballerinas whose partner he has been. People may talk of the vanity of the male dancer – of course it is monstrous; it is a favourite topic of my own – but as a partner Dolin has always sought to put the ballerina in the limelight and to make of himself a fitting background. The audience can feel the obvious admiration that he has for his partner, and their pleasure grows with his.

'I can dance on my pointes quite naturally, as you will remember in *Les Fâcheux*. I have danced for my own amusement all the great ballerina parts; that is why, when I am partnering, I can feel and appreciate it so well. I get a real thrill in watching and trying to enhance the effect.'

Pat's ready appreciation of fine work reveals the artist. 'Quel magnifique collègue', said Lifar to me recently. It was Pat who first drew my attention to him and who told me with enthusiasm of a newcomer, then unknown – David Lichine.

It is this understanding and an extraordinary adaptability that have saved him from all the worst faults of the virtuoso, faults that are very near to him with his sense of showmanship and his ability to gain extra applause through an effective climax. He has done dreadful things, vapid, meaningless, flashy things; he knows it, and so far can always recover in time, and in the right surroundings. This adaptability has made him into the complete Russian dancer, as it has made only one other person, Lydia Sokolova, who can speak Russian, and curse in Russian too, like a muzhik, when occasion arises. Dolin assimilates with rapidity the atmosphere of an environment. One day he will greet me with :

'Seet down, Arnold, I weel be weeth you in just meenute.'

'Are you raving mad, Pat?'

'No, why?'

'That stage Russian.'

'Oh, I hadn't noticed it. I've just been speaking with Boris for the last hour.'

I have heard him speak Anglo-French, Anglo-Spanish at a corrida, and tolerable American. It is decidedly not a pose; his whole career proves that. It is the very thing that has made him a *premier danseur classique* or a cabaret artist as the occasion demands. His book *Divertissement* shows this, with its extraordinary enthusiasm at being included in a Royal Command music-hall performance, with acrobats and sea lions. In anyone else, especially a Russian, this would have meant a desertion of serious work, while with him it merely implied that he was a different person temporarily, doing a different job with wholehearted enthusiasm, and doing it well. Apathy is his only enemy.

Dolin may have done everything possible to damage his name with the casual ballet public, which may even bear him a slight grudge for not being born a Russian, but, when not lazy, he is a very great dancer and a considerable artist, who has influenced his whole period.

Now perhaps there is to be a new career, another essay in adaptability. After a performance in *Ballerina*, where I heard him speak his first lines on the stage, and was duly shocked, he said, 'Soon I may give up dancing altogether and try to become an actor. I don't want people to say about me: "You should have seen him when he was young" – it has made me suffer too much for others. I know quite well that the big name I made had something to do with my youth and freshness. As Le Beau Gosse in *Le Train Bleu* I created a new type of dancing. It was the one Diaghilev ballet that was never revived for anyone else. That is something to remember, and I don't wish people to forget it by leaving it too far behind.'

There is one memory he will never forget; Diaghilev made his last public appearance at a party in Pat's studio after the première of *Le Bal*, all differences between them forgotten.

These, then, were my fellow pupils.

3. *The Lessons of* The Sleeping Princess

PARALLEL with my emotional unreasoning passion for ballet, and my interest in my friends, came an experience that made me pause, take stock, and really 'discover' ballet, just as it had made Pat, on the other side of the footlights, feel less pleased with himself and revise his standards.

During the season of 1921, *The Sleeping Princess* was presented at the Alhambra, the most important event since the first coming of the Russians to Western Europe in 1909. Its failure altered the whole course of ballet, kept Diaghilev from London for some years, and made him bitter and disappointed.

'I was always years ahead of my time,' he said, 'but this time too many years.'

Yet this ultra-modern experiment, so much ahead of its time in Western Europe, was one of the great Petipa ballets, originally produced at the Maryinsky Theatre in 1890, with Carlotta Brianza, the Wicked Fairy of the 1929 revival, as the Princess Aurora, Paul Gerdt as the Prince Charming, and the beautiful Marie Petipa as the Lilac Fairy. It rapidly became an established success, and every great ballerina is associated with it, especially Mathilde Kchessinska, who took it from the Italians, and first proved the Russian worth. It is replete with magnificent dances; one fragment of it alone makes the brilliant *Le Mariage d'Aurore*; one dance even, *L'Oiseau Bleu* – the Bluebird pas de deux – the acid test of the male classical dancer, the success of any virtuoso programme today.

Diaghilev decided to put this on in lavish fashion, with new costumes and décor by Leon Bakst, to transfer Theatre Street to Leicester Square. Nor had he neglected his usual calculated precautions in preparing the public mind. There was the obvious danger that Tchaikovsky, the one great composer of 'ballet music', might not prove popular with his typical *dernier cri* audience. Tchaikovsky therefore must be sponsored by one of their idols, someone who was himself above suspicion and perfectly secure in position. A commendatory letter from Stravinsky, who had himself reorchestrated some of the music, appeared in the programme.

'... It is a great satisfaction to me as a musician to see produced a work of so direct a character at a time when so many people, who are neither simple, nor naïve, nor spontaneous, seek in their art simplicity, "poverty", and spontaneity.

'Tchaikovsky in his very nature possessed these gifts to the fullest extent. Tchaikovsky possessed the power of melody, centre of gravity in every symphony, opera, or ballet composed by him. It is absolutely indifferent to me that the quality of his melody was sometimes unequal. The fact is that he was a creator of *melody*, which is an extremely rare and precious gift. Among us, Glinka, too, possessed it, and not to the same degree, those others.

'And that is something that is not German. The Germans manufactured music with themes and *leitmotif*, which they substituted for melodies.

'Tchaikovsky's music, which does not appear specifically Russian to everybody, is often more profoundly Russian than music which has long since been awarded the facile label of Muscovite picturesqueness.

'... The convincing example of Tchaikovsky's great power is, beyond all doubt, the ballet of *The Sleeping Princess*.'

This interesting letter should have secured a success in certain circles, but Tchaikovsky was apparently still out in the dark. In this very theatre, twelve years later, *Les Présages* to Tchaikovsky's Fifth Symphony was a sensational success, repeated throughout the long season, which it had made possible, and Diaghilev himself, on his return, could fill his house with Tchaikovsky's *Mariage d'Aurore*, and *Le Lac des Cygnes* scarcely missed a performance.

Perhaps the greatest attraction of all lay in the quality of the dancers.

THE PRINCESS AURORA Vera Trefilova, Olga Spessivtseva,* Lubov Egorova, Lydia Lopokova (on alternate nights).

THE LILAC FAIRY ... Lydia Lopokova, Bronislava Nijinska.

THE OTHER FAIRIES: Felia Doubrovska, Lydia Sokolova, Bronislava Nijinska, Ludmila Schollar, Vera Nemchinova, Lubov Tchernicheva, and Carlotta Brianza.

THEIR PAGES: L. Woizikovski, N. Zverev, N. Kremnev, T. Slavinsky, A. Wilzak, E. Addison, S. Idzikovski.

THE PRINCE CHARMING ... Pierre Vladimirov.

*For a time the name was shortened to Spessiva to make it easier for a non-Russian public.

I do not say that we shall never see such an ensemble again; such rash statements contradict my whole attitude, and infuriate me in others, but this once I am very much tempted.

In this programme there are the names of two Russian prima ballerinas, Vera Trefilova and Olgo Spessivtseva. *Prima* and *ballerina* are much abused words today, when it is commonplace to read of Madame Smithova, former ballerina of the Imperial Theatres, to be deceived, and to enjoy the deception.

Actually, even in Russia, the home of ballet, the ballerina was a rarity. It was as definite and as official a rank as that of general, with the very important difference that generals abounded ('no wedding is complete without its general'), while there were only five ballerinas of the Maryinsky at any one time, five in an Empire!

In fact, the Russian life of the Russian Ballet is a very brief but brilliant period, within the experience of many. At first there is the fixed belief that only the Italians can dance, and the major roles are created for them. Legnani, the Italian, causes a sensation with her thirty-two fouettés; Kchessinska a still greater one, in which patriotic fervour is mixed, by being the first Russian to do the same thing. All this is recent history, but a few weeks ago I saw a ten-year-old, still a Russian, turn fifty faultless ones.

Of our times then there are but five ballerinas: Kchessinska, Preobrajenska, Trefilova, Pavlova, and Karsavina. Egorova was a courtesy ballerina on retirement, Spessivtseva in early Soviet days. I have known them all. Each one is an exceptional personality. Alas, I have never seen Kchessinska, the *ballerina assoluta*, dance, though the impression of her in class, demonstrating to her pupils, is quite unforgettable. Without hesitation I would say that her arm movements are the most expressive that I have ever seen. On that evidence alone – and the rest is hearsay – I must place her among the very few supreme artists of movement. Round that lightness, those supple, expressive arms and wrists, that beautifully poised head with its indescribable smile, I have built for myself a whole ballet. Previously Kchessinska meant to me the dancer who had first raised Russian ballet to Italian technical standards, the transition stage between Russia and Italy, as hard and as brilliant as the diamonds round her neck. People blindly praised the wrong thing. I have not seen the technique, I can imagine it, but I have seen the poetry that so many missed and cannot imagine. Again I

thought of Kchessinska as an important personage in history ...
'Lenin in occupation of Kchessinska's palace!' Now she is *the*
dancer, whom I have never seen dance, but only sketch in a movement lightly.

Each one of these five women had to be an impeccable virtuoso,
with an ear above the average and a faultless line. Each must combine the grace of France with the strength and precision of Italy,
and all must add something positive to the living tradition of the
dance. I would say that the age of such artists was over had not
Kchessinska herself indignantly contradicted me. In any case, the
new dancer must find her greatness in another direction; today the
whole machinery is different, and the balletomane, who demands
perfection and can recognize it, is at the moment scarce.

There is one point especially that each one of these dancers has in
common: she is *classical*. That word must be thoroughly understood because it is probably used more frequently than any other in
any conversation on dancing. It is necessary to know the classical
in the study of every branch of art. In the present case too it is frequently confused with so-called Greek dancing. I once defined
classical in a small monograph on the art of Vera Trefilova, the
very first results of this *Sleeping Princess*. I will repeat it, as it has
been accepted by those who have seen the greatest performances of
the type, and it is essentially a question of quality and not of
period. Such definitions and elaborations may appear dull, but they
are in reality tremendously exciting and of practical use in appreciation. *Ballet suffers from its tacit acceptance as something
beautiful.* No art has become more difficult to understand, just
because it is immediately pleasing and there is so little opportunity
to follow it to its sources. 'Classicism, very freely translated, means
pure dancing that is based on the five positions, that produces long
graceful lines, that is neither acrobatic, violent, nor lacking in dignity; the *classical* dancer, the dancer of perfect build and technique,
who has sought no short cuts to proficiency, and who can hold her
audience *by her movements alone, with no extraneous literary conception to divert them*; the *classical* ballet, ballet that is designed
first and last for the maximum exploitation of the dancer's gifts,
physical and artistic.'

The classical dancer has a very definite system, built up by years
of study, and it is only when that system has become second nature
that she is ready to be seen by the public. There is absolutely no

possibility of bluff in such work. I have seen one dancer, generally considered technically brilliant, dismally exposed in *Le Lac des Cygnes*. The opponent of classicism, and therefore of ballet itself, invariably raises the point that steps such as the pirouette, fouetté, pas de bourrée are monotonous and meaningless, and that the intelligent public requires something more. Of course, they are monotonous and meaningless when performed by a nonentity, but, apart from the sheer beauty of line that fine movement gives, the classical dance, to be true, must be full of character. These much-maligned steps, for which Simeonov died, are merely like the musical notes, limited in number, in themselves nothing. The effect depends upon how they are combined and executed. It is this *classicism* that is helping the dancer to express herself that leaves her so gloriously free, if only she is big enough. No mediocrity can exist in the true classical ballet without an exposure that the most untrained audience could feel. The classical ballet in theory is flawless, in practice usually full of those faults that Michael Fokine revealed and banished, but the classical dancer is truly flawless, both in theory and practice, and it was she he used to carry out his reforms.

By *classicism* so far I have meant *school*, but it can also mean temperament. Vera Trefilova has the true classical temperament, as well as the training. If Pavlova is the Poussin of the dance, Trefilova is the Ingres. It was that very reason that made her performance of *The Sleeping Princess* so full of meaning and opened up so many new avenues for exploration. It was just because Olga Spessivtseva, the other great 'discovery' of the season, danced the role with more evident warmth, and so placed something extra between the crystal purity of the part and myself, the something that made her *Giselle* a triumph, that it was Trefilova who moved me, and whom I shall always identify with the role. As each dancer had her partisans, and fierce argument persists to this day, the lesson was made all the clearer. It was impossible any more to see a ballet or a dancer with the same eyes, not so much because one compared them to her, but because her logical, classical conception of the dance, logical but not cold, or so cold that it burned, made things gradually clear.

At the time I was not conscious of this; all I realized was that I wanted to stand up on my chair and shout, which I most certainly did. No balletomane ever knew the meaning of restraint, and his infernal din is the dancer's main reward.

During this season my main interest was still centred on the dancer as an artist; ballet itself was unexplored. My many hours in the studio with Pat and Alicia had already given me a sound technical background. I believe that I understood Diaghilev's motives for this return to classicism. It was just to focus once again the attention on the dancer, so as to free ballet from the complications of décor, music, and literature, all with an aesthetic axe to grind, that were strangling it to such an extent that puppets might well have taken the place of human beings with no loss at all. In fact, Gorno's Italian Marionettes, one of my first outside lessons, provided a complete substitute for the post-1921 ballet in a parody that was revealing. *The Sleeping Princess* proved conclusively that only when choreography exploited to the full the artistic and physical capabilities of the dancer could it take its place among the other arts.

It is strictly logical to demand that a particular medium be put to its most effective use. Diaghilev had made the ballet the artistic force it was, apart from his own quite exceptional gifts, because of the Maryinsky in the background to provide the essential material, which had sent his own name and those of Bakst, Stravinsky, and others across the civilized world. It was now necessary to call a halt before ballet was too definitely committed to modern artistic activity, much of it ephemeral, and to return to the great Maryinsky principle, taking from it only what was best. Moreover, there was not much time to be lost, for the source of supply was being rapidly cut off. Such a pause would give him the time to realize what was definitely worthwhile in the contemporary movement and what new lines could be followed, for eventually new lines must be evolved if the art is to live. This whole nomadic existence, the feverish chase after new Parisian gods, was stimulating only up to a point, but saturation had been reached. Diaghilev carefully trained his audience for each new development, but now it had run away from him in its desire for novelty. It could be tickled only by unusual décor or music, a scandal, a name, or an idea, but the dancer, the start and the very *raison d'être* of the whole thing, was no longer understood.

This return to classicism was also in the main trend of the artistic development that had acclaimed Ingres as a great master again, not for the subject matter of his vast historic canvases, but for their line and composition. In ballet, it is the dancers who provide the line, the 'dessin' which is 'la probité de l'art', and the subject, the fairy tale or legend, could be accepted or ignored according to individual taste. Such ballet was not old-fashioned; in its essentials it was timeless. This throwing of the onus onto the dancer once more, giving her the main responsibility of boring or enchanting an audience, provided the possibility of producing dancers who were great personalities, great artists, and great performers. Vera Nemchinova, who was one of the few great dancers formed from within the company, and who saved it at a critical period, was purely the result of the opportunity to dance in such works. And just as the dancers themselves are best trained in the school of Petipa, so are the spectators. The dancer is fully revealed.

From that season I found certain standards of criticism from which I have never had to depart. They have added to my enjoyment a thousandfold, by giving me the thrill of watching developing talent with more system and certitude than when I assisted emotionally at the birth of Dolin and Markova, taking so much for granted that I could only verify later.

The very first consideration is physical beauty, face as well as body, the perfection of the instrument. There can be no question here of being charitably minded, just, decent people. Mary may be possessed of immense dramatic talent, have a fine musical ear, and a truly infinite capacity for hard work, but if she squints or her legs are unshapely then she is out of place in ballet. Yes, the squint counts. A Russian balletomane – I believe he was a general again – once said, 'Show me a girl's face, and I will tell you whether she can dance.' He may have expressed himself too positively. Had he put it, 'Show me her face, and I will tell you if she cannot dance,' I would have been with him every time. Twinkling legs alone are not enough. A fine head, well set on the shoulders, a smile that is a smile and not a grin, marks of the Russian ballerina, make one wish to look further and judge the dancer as a whole. So many Italian dancers have been ruined through concentrating exclusively on the legs. Beauty, fortunately, is a wide term that must be elastic enough to include the deep classical beauty of Karsavina or Toumanova, the ethereal quality of Pavlova, the radiant smile of Kchessinska, the wit and elegance of Preobrajenska, the romantic languor of Spessivsteva, the sparkle of Lopokova, the soul of Baronova.

Ballet dancing is the maximum exploitation of physical beauty in motion. In thinking of the various companies I have known well, I cannot remember one highly trained Russian dancer who was plain; I can think of a number who were exceedingly beautiful in a subtle, non-Hollywood way, for the classical system properly understood trains every portion of the body, from the tips of the toes to the chignon. It gives direction to every movement and gesture. It is organized beauty.

Another point that I would include here is natural grace. To many, grace and dancing are synonymous. This is by no means the case. The purely technical, non-artist dancer is usually clumsy. Faulty training can destroy natural grace, while the soundest training can only create the semblance of it.

Once we have satisfied ourselves about the instrument, bearing in mind the more obvious fact that Kreisler himself is helpless on a cigar box, the next consideration is technique.

Sound technique should be taken for granted. If it is stressed even favourably, there is usually something very much wrong with the performer. The words 'a technical dancer' are definitely insulting. Trefilova's technique is faultless. It would never occur to me to bring that up as a point in her favour. There are so many other interesting points to talk about. There is but one stage in the dancer's life when it is relevant, the first few years. It is a characteristic of the young dancer to say, 'My turns were perfect tonight,' just as it is characteristic of the non-subtle audience to applaud those turns especially loudly, as if they did not belong to the whole. There are obviously degrees of technique : Kchessinska may have had more than Karsavina, but the good technique is the one that is not noticed by the dancer or public, and that leaves her free to express the choreographer's intention and her own personality. Karsavina once told me that the dancer's personality developed with her technique, a fact that I have repeatedly verified. I do not believe in the performer who has immense personality and little technique. In the concert hall she would not be tolerated for a moment. People are always a little too indulgent of dancers.

Technique has developed enormously of late, a fact that must be borne in mind. Just as Kchessinska, when already famous, discovered the Italian secret of thirty-two fouettés, so have the smallest pupils today found the way to the almost endless fouetté, neatly, easily. It is now a definite part of the repertoire and cannot any more be condemned as an unworthy acrobatic feat. Modern choreography has used it with immense effect in such ballets as *Cotillon, Concurrence, Beau Danube,* and *Jeux d'Enfants,* just on account of the fact that Baronova and Toumanova can perform it with ease and grace, with no undue concentration, so that, with it, they can express something definite. This increase in technical resources gives the choreographer a richer vocabulary, without having to resort to distortion for his effects.

Technique means freedom for dancer and choreographer, while in so-called free dancing the performer is shackled by the difficulty of moving, the choreographer by the paucity of resources at his command.

So far we are on easy ground. Physical beauty and technique can be measured to a degree not only by the expert but by their effect on an audience, in spite of subtle differences of opinion. The great difficulty arises when it comes to a discussion of dramatic ability, temperament, and personality, all three of which are so closely bound up with the question of technique. The dancer who is beautiful and well trained, with nothing much else besides, can hold a certain type of audience through sheer pleasure in her line. There is an endless fascination in watching ballet that depends on line alone, and that is devoid of dramatic content.

A Russian physicist-artist has been undertaking some research on aesthetics, communicated in a paper to the French Académie des Sciences, that illustrates this vividly. He has based his whole theory on optics, the line of least resistance for the eyes, and has carried out a lengthy series of experiments, his subjects looking at pictures and dancing while the movements of their eyes are measured on sensitized paper attached to a drum. He has already demonstrated the truth of many artistic adages. He has found that two closely parallel lines in a composition are disturbing because the eye travels from one to the other rapidly and is wearied, while in the case of parallel lines far apart the eye travels comfortably down the path in the middle. The experiments that interested me specially, and that I followed with care, were those relating to pure dance technique. According to his experiments, the line of least resistance, his line of beauty, is a long, slow curve that the eye can follow at ease and caress. But if this stands alone, or is repeated indefinitely, it becomes monotonous, and some contrast is essential. According to this, the arabesque is the perfect pose, with its long, sloping line from fingertips to toes, with its inner strong contrasting angles formed by the legs and the arms. Whether this can be demonstrated scientifically or not, it is a plausible theory with exciting possibilities.

Technique is exact. In strict theory there is one way, and one way alone, of making a given movement correctly; but in fact the exactitude is only approximate and not mathematical, the human elements, both physical and mental, play their part. 'Cet art,' says André Levinson, speaking of the classicism of Trefilova, 'tend vers la formule géometrique, mais, au moment suprême, la brise et s'en évade,'* a perfect summing up. Only the highly trained spectator can gauge the exact departure from the theoretical standard, though at times an audience can sense it. It is just that fraction of difference that reveals the individual. Dancing is so subtle that six ballerinas will perform the same *enchainement* in an almost identical manner and yet create an entirely different impression, and I am talking of a simple sequence of steps here and not of intricate roles where the atmosphere and facial expression are indicated. It is these little differences in execution that underlie personality, and when they become conscious they are the whole basis of acting or 'mime'.

The combination of steps in *L'Oiseau Bleu* for instance, from the same *Sleeping Princess* that is responsible for all this, is a straightforward sequence that might be set in any advanced classroom. But for the 'bird-flight', 'bird-landing' idea to be suggested a special attack is needed. This is the first conscious process of mime. *L'Oiseau Bleu* is not in reality a bird study, and it has no story that develops and comes to a climax like Fokine's *Dying Swan*, where the whole mime becomes more obvious, and further from its roots. Balletic acting, basis of all acting, has endless degrees of intensity. First, there is the question of attack, scarcely removed from mechanical technique; next comes the question of atmosphere, as in the famous *Les Sylphides*, the most difficult problem that can confront the dancer, and where countless fine performers have failed.

In movement *Les Sylphides* is simple, well within reach of the intermediate pupil. The emphasis is on the expression of face and body combined. The only indication the dancer receives is in the music, the scenery, and the few words of the theme; sylphs in a

*'This art tends toward a geometric formula, but at the final, supreme moment breaks away and evades it.'

wood at night. What a test of sensibility and mimetic power, this suite of dances that is so much a complete ballet! The average dancer half closes her eyes and looks just tired or bored, others grin, but they grin sheepishly to indicate romance; the merely technical dancer performs it in a hard, sparkling manner. All are wrong. It is a dream, something brief and fleeting, a little sad perhaps, a landscape by Corot. There are definite moments for which to look; in the Valse there is none of the tempo of the classical adagio; the dancer must float up to her partner, float down to the ground again, without the feeling of a ballet lift. There is a true tender expression of love, as he draws her to him by wing tips, that is echoed in the climax, where she beckons gently, and he responds in an eager leap. One can only write of how it should not be done, which is how it is often done, but there are so many ways that are true. Pavlova was poetry itself; Karsavina a little warmer and more human; while the new dancers all shine – the true measure of their artistry : Toumanova is infinitely sad, with a nostalgia for the world beyond the park, tragically moving; Riabouchinska like gossamer, truly a brush-stroke by Corot; Baronova, my own ideal, joyful, yet a little wistful, profiting from the few moonlit hours in the enchanted garden. A memorable ensemble.

In *Giselle*, great test for the classical dancer, the problem is the reverse. The subject matter is very clearly indicated by a complex scenario, while the banal, tuneful music has nothing whatsoever to do with it and is a definite emotional handicap. When the curtain rises on the village romp, the word *quaint* is in one's mind; if the curtain descends with that impression remaining, the ballerina has failed; yet *Giselle* is ninety per cent conventional gesture to indifferent musical accompaniment, with but ten per cent remaining for individual interpretation. It is that ten per cent that can make it great; without it the first act is intolerable barnstorming, first cousin to the Victorian melodrama *Maria Marten of the Red Barn*, the second act a mere succession of technical exercises. There is an added difficulty, between the acts a total change of atmosphere; act one is the body, act two the spirit. The story belongs to the great romantic period, the romanticism of sighing swains and midnight graveyards, of kilts and Walter Scott, Wilis, werewolves, and the Brocken, very different from the later robust romanticism of a Fokine ballet, though Gautier inspired both *Giselle* and *Le Spectre de la Rose*. It is the difference between Eugène Devéria and Bakst.

The betrayed maiden goes mad. In her madness she repeats mechanically the dance she loved when she was still carefree. In the second act she rises from the grave a Wili, temptress of young men, and so meets her repentant betrayer, whom she still loves.

It is obvious, from this brief description, that there can be no average *Giselle*. The sentiment and the music and story drag it down to the level of a genteel magazine illustration of the period. Olga Spessivtseva is an outstanding Giselle. Pavlova showed more fire and exaltation; Spessivtseva played with tenderness and melancholy, reaching her climax in the scene of madness. Recently Markova has become the only English Giselle in a beautifully balanced performance, with a well-executed mad scene and a more spiritual second act than I could ever have believed possible in anyone whose technical brilliance has at times intruded into the dream of *Les Sylphides*. But in the second act no one can approach the unearthly quality that was Pavlova's. She remains above comparison.

Le Lac des Cygnes, too, is conventional, and does not call for obvious acting. Like *The Sleeping Princess*, it is purely classical; Trefilova's, Spessivtseva's, Nemchinova's, Baronova's, Markova's. Yet, in the version now played, it has its one big moment of drama, when the Swan Princess defends her huddled flock from the hunters, with arms outstretched, protective and regal; a gesture that singled out Trefilova and Spessivtseva from the many who can dance this superbly. The male role in this ballet has always interested me as a problem in mime; it is usually pathetically comical. The dancer must believe in it or fail – a difficult task because in many versions his variation is cut, denying him any dignity of a dancer. Dolin excels as the gallant partner, Lifar through his beautiful walk; Lichine tackles it too impetuously and fails.

Fokine revolutionizes this, mime and dancing become one, as even in the past the great dancer had tried to make them. New problems arise of the type we have already discussed in *Les Sylphides*. In *Le Spectre de la Rose*, gem of the new romanticism, each role calls for consummate acting; the woman stands as a complete contrast to the male virtuoso, who must combine both tenderness and strength; great tenderness, for every movement of the arms, so often reduced to a meaningless weaving motion, is a caress. The supreme moment, though, belongs to the ballerina. It is not the spectacular leap out of the window, but the girl's gradual awakening, where disappointment and happiness are mixed, small sublime moments in ballet, invariably marred by the applause at the leap. Of all those who have danced this, but one has fully succeeded – Tamara Karsavina. She has made it her own for ever.

These then are but a few of the problems that acting within the ballet raises, and that is why without the ability to mime the dancer is uninteresting. 'Tous nos mouvements sont purement automatiques et ne signifient rien, si la face demeure muette en quelque sorte et si elle ne les anime et ne les vivifie,'* said Noverre (1759), most of whose precepts were forgotten until Fokine took command.

Another attribute the dancer requires is a sensitive musical ear, a rarity amongst the rank and file, for the art of mime includes the appreciation of music, since it is so often the music that gives the only real indication of the atmosphere. A musical ear, developed to an unusual degree by a study of the piano, gave Sokolova her first big chance with Stravinsky's *Le Sacre du Printemps* and Ravel's *Daphnis et Chloé*, then so difficult for the dancer to grasp. I have actually seen dancers at rehearsal consulting slips of paper on which the counts were marked, a method not calculated to give a convincing performance. There are such delicate shades of rhythm that, while it might be impossible to accuse an artist of being 'out of time', she has clearly not fully sensed the measure, or is worried by it – just the fraction of difference that distinguishes the best from the second best. The much debated fouetté is dancing when it is in perfect sympathy with the music, a stupid tour de force when it is not.

This is a great chunk of undiluted criticism, but it is the result of a deep artistic experience gained during that one season, and it is doubtless a part of the message that Diaghilev had to convey, and that was not then received. Whether it will be received now, or has already passed into common experience, it is a vital part of my story; the fanatic grown rational, the lover more ardent than ever, but no longer blind. Henceforward every performance becomes a series of studies with the first thrill in no wise impaired, but with the hundredth thrill that counts the most of all.

---

*'All our [ballet] movements are purely automatic and mean nothing if the face remains expressionless and does not succeed in bringing them to life.'

POSTSCRIPT

This chapter stands as my outlook through the forty years since it was written. I do not believe that to have held the same viewpoint for forty years is due to a hardening of the critical arteries or that I am a 'ballet-blimp', though I was considered one even before *Balletomania* first appeared. I have found with experience more and more reason to strengthen my belief in classicism.

Ulanova has shown me new aspects of Giselle; the Maryinsky and the Cuban productions have strengthened the drama. Lifar's Albrecht might have been conceived by Delacroix; Loipa Araujo's Bathilde is exceptional as a dramatic foil to Giselle, instead of the customary lay figure with a picture hat. The very fact that this veteran ballet, considered by its inspirer Théophile Gautier to be a charming anecdote, has survived, not as a museum piece or a coloured lithograph, but as a living drama susceptible of many interpretations – in our time by Karsavina, whose Giselle, alas, I never saw, Pavlova, Spessivtseva, Markova, Chauviré, Ulanova, Bessmertnova, Makarova, Sombert, to name the outstanding ones in my experience – shows the vitality of classicism. I suspect from reading old accounts that it was Petipa and the Russian Anna Andreyanova who first introduced depth into the role, what the Russians call *dousha* (soul). One must be great to bring Giselle to life. It defeats the average good classical ballerina.

This raises another often hotly debated point about classicism. There is always a knowing member of the audience who says, 'Why don't they stick to the original?' As if anyone alive today can recall what the original was. What is really meant is 'Why don't they stick to the version that I first saw?' If the truth were known, many of the original productions, with their corseted ballerinas, might provoke laughter.

New productions of the classics are not only inevitable but welcome in themselves, otherwise the work dates and a living classicism becomes sterile academicism. Carlo Blasis codified the classicism of his own period, but without Petipa, Johannsen, Cecchetti, and Vaganova it would no longer be a living art, an art that fulfilled Paul Valéry's wonderful definition of the dance, 'I am in thee, O movement, beyond and apart from the rest of existence.' No carbon copy of a classic would have any meaning to a contemporary audience. A work is continually modified, even from night to night, by a change of cast. It is this very fact that makes the classics enduring. I can watch six different Auroras in one week, as I so often have at Covent Garden, with intense pleasure. I can think of few modern works that would not send me to the bar after the fifth performance. The important thing is not to tamper with the essentials of the choreography and to retain the romantic element, bearing in mind that true romanticism is not limited in time. To attempt to reproduce period romanticism is to relapse into nostalgic sentimentality. Seen at its best, as in Keith Lester's charming pastiche *Le Pas de Quatre*, it is a slightly tongue-in-cheek affair that brings to life the quaint period lithographs and the Staffordshire figurines. This is deliberate and has succeeded in both the more technical Dolin and Alonso versions so popular today. It would be impossible to tell a moving story in this manner. We smile; if it is badly danced, we laugh but are not moved.

The only period romantic style to remain intact is in the Bournonville ballets so zealously preserved and performed by the Danes. They delight one by their charm and brilliance, and they have sentiment because the Danes believe in what they are doing, but for me they do not have the immediate impact of Petipa. Thanks to the late Vera Volkova, who taught the Petipa idiom, the Danes have become more bilingual, but *aficionados* still treasure the Bournonville inheritance.

I have used the words *classical* and *romantic* as if they meant the same thing, and in ballet, and only in ballet, they are almost interchangeable. *Classical* pertains to the technique that is used to express a romantic emotion. *Classical* is also used to denote Hellenic art and, in yet another sense, to define the well-established repertoire such as *Les Sylphides*, which is neo-romantic. There is strong evidence to suggest that ballet is closer to Greek dancing than certain styles borrowed from Greek vase painting. There are two other words that add to the confusion : *abstract* and *modern*. It is not possible to label works with precision, neither is it desirable. *Abstract* presumably means that there is no story to be interpreted. Are such storyless ballets as *Les Sylphides* and *Symphonic Variations*, each one a masterpiece, abstract for that reason? The word needs some qualification : we may borrow one from painting, *abstract expressionism*. From the moment that we have a pas de deux there is the beginning of a relationship of love, hatred, or indifference. Pure abstraction is geometry or is rhythm for its own sake as in sections of Hindu dancing.

Modern defeats me entirely unless it means contemporary. In ballet *modern*, as in every art, has become an emotive word. *Le Sacre du Printemps* was once called modern and shocked its audience, but it was danced by ballet-trained dancers and had its inspiration in primitive folk rites, whether Slavonic, in Nijinsky's and Massine's versions, or aboriginal, as in Kenneth MacMillan's. Picasso was a modern artist, but he was trained in the rigid classicism of Ingres; the young Matisse was a painstaking copyist of the old masters; Balanchine, a great innovator, traces his descent from Petipa. The great American teacher and choreographer Martha Graham firmly calls her style and technique 'contemporary', and in recent years she has come closer to classicism. Ballet has learned much, in its way, from contemporary dance.

4. Monte Carlo–Paris, 1925

MONTE CARLO, winter headquarters of the Ballet, a paradise for both dancer and balletomane; the little town itself like the carefully planned décor of a not too modern artist, the toy army of uniformed sweepers and attendants, perfect walkers-in in a *ballet bouffe*, and in the very centre the actual theatre, a stage on a stage, ideal in size, the right compromise between grandeur and intimacy. What a saving of energy for the permanently overworked dancers; no bus, tube, or tram, at the worst a walk up the steep flight of steps to Beausoleil, where most of them had flats. It was quite unnecessary ever to fix a rendezvous, impossible not to stumble across dancers in all places; shops, cinemas, cafés, and kiosks, everywhere they were known by sight and record. When one of them quietly arranged to have flowers sent to herself at every performance, we knew of it within the hour and laughed, and sometimes we knew of bouquets from genuine admirers before the recipient. After morning rehearsal the terrace was a veritable news exchange. The occupation of the town was complete. Mothers, aunts, children, all were gathered there to be with their 'family genius' and breadwinner some portion of the year, when theatrical digs could be forgotten and the full privileges of housekeeping enjoyed. This was home. Only the gaming rooms were strictly taboo, and on the rare occasions when dancers had penetrated in disguise, they had come away minus the next month's salary, which meant confronting a stern Grigoriev for an advance, which he did not encourage. The artists of the ballet were employees of the state, and once during that season, when two of them went on strike, they found themselves infringing an imposing bylaw, No. X, and had to answer to the government as well as to Diaghilev. They were promptly deported and no one followed their example.

Chief sign of the occupation was the flock of camp followers, hair sleeked back in severe classical style, complete with ballet shoes and mother, waiting. There was that queer individual, too, who followed the ballet around, in the hopes that the conductor would be suddenly indisposed and that he would be summoned to take his place. He had evidently been reading many biographies. His chance never came, but he himself was an institution.

Cecchetti was fully established in his classroom in a cellar of the Casino, giving his daily class to the company and also numerous private lessons, throwing his little cane at favoured pupils, whose proud privilege it was to replace it when it broke. He spoke in an extraordinary language of his own devising, compound of many that marked his triumphal progress through Europe: 'Quandé la giammbé il va en avante, la tête il va toujours dé la même côté dé où qu'il va la giammbé, ma quandé la giammbé il va en arrière,' etc., very rapidly. I still have it humming in my ears.

It was his pleasure constantly to rail against the horrors and infamies of modern choreography, not unnatural in someone who had danced in a ballet of Katti Lanner's devising in the Empire of the nineties ten years after he had danced Petipa's *L'Oiseau Bleu* for the first time. He said to Diaghilev himself of Nijinsky's *Le Sacre du Printemps*: 'I think the whole thing has been done by four idiots. First: M. Stravinsky, who wrote the music. Second: M. Roerich, who designed the scenery and costumes. Third: M. Nijinsky, who composed the dances. Fourth: M. Diaghilev, who wasted his money on it.'* He was there to repair the ravages of that choreography on his pupils. He was already over eighty, but still leapt into the air, bouncing like the little rubber ball to which the *Times* critic, forty years previously, had compared him. Nor was this his last job, for at the end of the season he was summoned to La Scala, Milan, to take charge of the instruction.

He was born in the dressing room of an Italian theatre, died while in the service of an Italian theatre. His wife, Giuseppina, kindly and patient, who would interpret and soften his ravings to bewildered pupils, was there by his side. Both still danced that season, *maestro* miming brilliantly as the Shopkeeper in *La Boutique Fantasque*, Giuseppina, the duenna of *Les Femmes de Bonne Humeur*, wearing a period wig over her own, both narrowly missing coming off during one performance. Cecchetti, in whose experience almost the entire history of ballet lay, but one generation removed from Vestris, dancing in a Massine ballet, and rubbing shoulders with 'Les six', Picasso and Braque! It was a rare privilege to have watched his classes, to have been even so remotely a pupil.

---

* Quoted from *Enrico Cecchetti*, a memoir by Cyril W. Beaumont, Beaumont, London, 1929.

He was surrounded by young girls of every nationality – private pupils, willing to pay any price to get into the ballet, thrilled already at this first contact. It was as such a camp-follower pupil of *maestro*'s that Romola Nijinsky worked her way into the ballet and won her husband from Diaghilev.

Naturally I found it impossible to stay away from this Mecca. The pilgrimage was indispensable. Here was the opportunity to watch the laboratory at work and to take up friendships constantly interrupted by the hurry and bustle of Paris and London. The seasons were always given in two portions, with a middle period 'out' to put new works into rehearsal. Then the dancers were comparatively free, with six hours' work instead of nine, except some of the non-principals, who were loaned to dance in the opera ballets. It was a chance to earn extra money, especially in the wire-flying ballets, which were considered a little dangerous. Also, under the kindly supervision of Raoul Gunsbourg, instead of Diaghilev, it need not be taken too seriously. There at once one could realize what dancing for Diaghilev meant. Gunsbourg nursed his artists, had cumbersome scenery shifted to suit their movements, while with Diaghilev everything had to be just so, a complete picture in which every element was carefully balanced, and the dancers were clearly just one of the elements.

I arrived straight from the station at the theatre where the first matinée was in progress, meeting Diaghilev on the steps. 'How is Sima [Astafieva]? Is she coming? I have invited her specially to see Dolin and Markova. I am angry. I have just missed *Les Sylphides*, my favourite ballet, for the first time in years. I hope it was danced well. Why couldn't someone have told me what time it began?' In that mood, someone would surely catch it.

1925. His last truly brilliant year, just before the transition period and the gradual waning; Nemchinova and Dolin at the very top of their form, physically and temperamentally ideal partners, dancing in nearly every ballet; Tchernicheva contributing the finish and perfection of the early years; Doubrovska, about to be discovered as the perfect instrument for modernist experiment; Sokolova, most Russian and biggest personality of them all, favoured artist of the great man himself; Leon Woizikovski, always superb, through sheer merit retaining his position with every change of regime, generous colleague, ready to pass on his experience to the new arrival; and Serge Grigoriev, the backbone, with every ballet and lighting cue in his head, a big Russian bear but a hundred per cent efficient. There was young Serge Lifar at the very beginning; he had recently made a success of his first important role, the Shopkeeper's Assistant in *La Boutique Fantasque*, and was rehearsing for his first creation in *Zéphire et Flore*; Markova just thirteen, in socks, but learning her very own Stravinsky ballet and dancing *Le Lac des Cygnes* adagio; and Nikitina and Danilova, the great hopes, whose fate was then being decided at the Hôtel de Paris, where Diaghilev sat with his cabinet : Poulenc and Auric, Boris Kochno, Picasso, Stravinsky, Pruna, Dukelsky, and Edwin Evans.

Evans was musical adviser, and, during the London season, intermediary between Diaghilev and any disgruntled member of the company. No wittier or more kindly person could have been chosen for so arduous a task, and he looked the role. Diaghilev, with no sense of time, would ring him up almost regularly at three o'clock in the morning to discuss some new idea. It was only when Evans suggested that there might be very good reasons why this was inconvenient that Diaghilev gave it up. Any idea so simple as the desire for a good night's rest could not appeal to him. It was understood that no petty annoyance should be allowed to get past Evans, but one day during a season at the Coliseum an angry principal proved too much for him and marched straight into the lion's den, staggering under a load of posters and handbills of a size that only the Coliseum could use.

'Look here, and here, and here' – dumping them down on Diaghilev's desk – 'it is disgraceful. I am a star and my name is here in very small print and under X's, who has never danced any leading roles. What is going to be done about it?'

'This is interesting. I have never seen so many posters. I didn't even know that we had them. Tell me, how did you get hold of them? Who gave them to you?'

'My husband.'

'Your husband? It's a pity, a great pity, that he couldn't give you any other signs of his affection.'

It was in Monte Carlo that I began a form of entertainment that has ever since given me the keenest pleasure : listening to Edwin Evans discuss every conceivable subject, from finance – and he was once the editor of a city journal – to music. He is always better informed than the next man, always magnificently witty. His knowledge of cookery and his discourses are a joy. I believe that he is prouder of having been recognized in France as one of the few English gourmets than of his vast European reputation as a music critic. That year at Monte Carlo he was the only English member of the cabinet, and one of its most active.

Diaghilev's boast at the Monaco première that season, 'If the theatre burned down tonight, all the artistic talent of Europe would perish,' was fully justified.

The members of the company of that year alone have played the leading role in the whole world of ballet, providing prima ballerinas for the de Basil Company, the Kovno Opera, the Vic-Wells, also the *maîtres* de ballet for those theatres, the choreographer and *premier danseur* of the Paris Opéra, the *premier danseur* of the Opéra Comique, and the founder of the School of American Ballet. This is an incomplete list. It honours Diaghilev as nothing else could.

My first *formal* meeting with Alexandra Danilova, after the Astafieva party, was in one of those irritating intervals the French are so fond of having between the reels of a film, in this case *The Orphans of the Storm*, where I had gone with Dolin. He was wearing, I remember, a tie of many bright colours and intricate design, which I rudely criticized. 'Well, it must be all right, it was designed for me by Picasso.' That shut me up completely; then he went on :

'Look, just four rows away in front of us is Danilova – there, you can just see the back of her head. She's divinely beautiful, and a really fine artist. Big things are being planned for her,' then a wild yell across four rows of heads :

'Shoura – SHOURA, turn round a minute. I want Haskell to see you. I've just told him you're very beautiful. There, I thought you wouldn't be disappointed. It's all right, *galoupchik*, he's seen you – you can turn round again.'

Every afternoon after rehearsal we met at Rumpelmayer's, Pat going from tray to tray sampling the chocolates, commenting on them, and offering them to Alicia, toward whom he was very much 'the heavy father'.

'Send that child home to bed at once, she's worn out'; or on one occasion, when she was proudly displaying a new rabbit-wool jumper, 'So they're dressing the child in furs now. Perfectly ridiculous.'

He looked after her wonderfully, like an elder brother who had been in the school a few terms longer.

It was precisely this schoolboy attitude that irritated Diaghilev so profoundly and was the beginning of their quarrel. He had no understanding of the English character. For him, a day's outing on the river was an absurdity, and tennis or a picnic with friends the limit of vulgarity. He expected his favoured artists to live at 'high pitch' the whole time; the first essential, entire subservience to his will, to discuss artistic topics and to visit museums with him. A visit to a museum with Diaghilev was inspiring but utterly exhausting. His great pleasure was in the reactions of his companion, and it was difficult, with his expectant gaze fixed upon one, to react sincerely or intelligently, especially over a period of three hours. He could not sympathize with Pat's very natural desire to escape with less intellectual friends and complained to me bitterly on many occasions about the English and all their ways. He never failed to bring in his great sore point, the river party, as being the very height of imbecility, and the dangers of draughts and open windows.

Nemchinova joined our little company, practising her English on me when she could.

'My foots is all bloody,' was one of her very first efforts.

One day I nearly ruined the whole future of ballet by taking her, Vera Savina, and Alicia out in a motorboat. It was very rough, but they egged me on, and we only just reached the shore in safety, all of us very green. The only casualty was a black coat of Savina's. She had sat on a bag of peppermint creams.

The great event of the season, occupying everyone's time and attention, was the preparation of Massine's *Zéphire et Flore*, the vehicle for Lifar's rise to stardom. He sometimes worked with Cecchetti almost the whole day at a stretch; I can recall periods where he rehearsed uninterruptedly for ten hours. We never saw him at all. This also was to be Alice Nikitina's first big chance. I can never remember having seen anyone who promised more. Angular, a trifle gawky, piquante, everything she did had a strong personal quality; her very faults were the making of future virtues. Unfortunately she has not lived up to that promise. Her failure was due to an attempt to make her into a ballerina quickly and artificially. The Nikitina boom strangled all her immense talent. The faults that should and could have become virtues became glaring –

hard arms in *Les Sylphides* and the like. One could clearly foresee that her lack of technical strength would result in continual small accidents. Less haste could have made Alice Nikitina into something unique.

Diaghilev was amazed at his good fortune. That season he was a truly happy man, with Nikitina, Lifar, and Dukelsky, whose total ages only amounted to sixty. Lifar alone has lived up to, and exceeded, that early promise. Nikitina was forced, and Dukelsky has led a 'double life' as a composer of ballets and as a writer of popular melody for Ziegfeld and others, under the name of Vernon Duke, which has since become the better known of the two.

From the very first this ballet was dogged by ill luck. I remember the first dress rehearsal. It began at nine o'clock and at two we were still sitting there when it was cut short by the first accident. Every detail in each one of the acts was attended to by Diaghilev himself, and one could only be amazed at his immense practical knowledge. The lighting was his great speciality, and some of the effects would take hours to set. He could mix colours like paint on a canvas, and was revealing to us bit by bit all the richness of Braque's fine décor.

Meanwhile the dancers went on and on, while he criticized and called for repeats. The first contretemps was the inevitable one with the orchestra.

'I am sorry, Monsieur Diaghilev, I can do nothing more. The members of the orchestra say that it is well past their time and refuse to stay.'

'They are artists and not factory hands. Tell them that they can have ten minutes' rest' – looking at his watch; 'then they must come back to their places, and play till we have finished, perhaps another four hours, perhaps more. I intend to finish.'

In ten minutes' time they were back, and it began again, movement by movement, another two hours of it, until suddenly Lifar crumpled up and fell. In turning he had touched one of the dancers, and both ankles, tired from overwork, were badly strained. The theatre was cleared in an instant, Diaghilev in tears. 'It was too good, too beautiful to last. I thought the great days had returned again and now this perfection has been spoiled. I should not have boasted; it is my fault.' He was intensely superstitious.

The première in Monte Carlo was put off and the company left for Barcelona. Nemchinova alone remained behind with an acute attack of mumps, unpoetic malady that had made her usually beautiful *Lac des Cygnes* into something grotesque. She had been forced to dance nonetheless, to the horror of the rest of the company.

In Spain, Lifar's ankles showed no signs of mending. He was helpless in bed, and the doctor talked of six weeks at least. 'I am sorry,' Diaghilev told him, 'but by my contract I must give the première in Paris next week. It will not be the same thing but someone else will have to dance it, and I will make it up to you later.'

But Lifar was determined, saw the end of his career before the beginning, and talked of suicide. He was ready on the night, performed admirably but in dreadful pain, with the doctor waiting anxiously in the wings. The day before and the day after he could not walk, but that night he danced. Diaghilev in his joy inscribed a present to him : 'Au plus jeune parmi les premiers, et au premier parmi les jeunes.'*

I have seen such medically inexplicable feats of will power on many occasions. Sokolova and Toumanova both accomplished them; Lifar in London, just before *Lac des Cygnes*, was practising an entrechat in the wings, and, leaping too high, his head hit an iron staircase with great force. He was half-stunned, but when his cue came, he went on to dance, the blood trickling from under his wig. Afterwards the wig was removed with great difficulty, and he was laid up for some time, swathed in bandages.

Lifar's mishap was not the end of the *Zéphire et Flore* ill luck. Nikitina was injured during one of the first Paris performances, and Danilova took her place, a new partner for the still-inexperienced boy. Finally Dolin, the third important member of the cast, left, Tcherkas taking his place.

This ballet did not enjoy a long life or deserve it. Today it would not bear revival, but it played an important part in discovering Lifar. I had once more assisted at the beginnings of a new talent, and a photograph that I have of that date is inscribed : 'To one who assisted at the birth of my art.' This is another case, the most important, where Diaghilev did not see the magnificent progress of the artist in whom he so greatly believed. His Lifar was still technically unformed.

The last week of that Monte Carlo season I fell madly in love and became engaged. Mutual enthusiasm seemed a sufficient reason. It was immediately after a performance of *Thamar*, and we had met on the terrace that very afternoon. Then the Ballet left. We saw

* 'To the youngest among the firsts and the first among the youngest.'

them off at the station together, and when the train disappeared through the toy tunnel everything suddenly changed. Things seemed different, we both regretted it, did not quite like to admit it or to put it into words, and the parting was a horrible anticlimax.

The Ballet did things like that to one. Gambling was not the only or the worst madness of the season. It was sometimes difficult to know what was real, what was illusion. The dancers were saved by their work, their tired muscles, *maestro's* curses; we, quite helpless, living their dreams without effort. In London or Paris escape was possible; in Monte Carlo, 1925, all was pure ballet magic.

Paris that season saw the first revival of *Les Biches*, most perfect of all the 'decadent' ballets and a landmark in history. It remains unique, a satirical literary subject told perfectly in movement alone, a modern *Les Sylphides*, the sylphs still there, an elegant house of pleasure substituted for the woods. It is at the same time a keen analysis of contemporary womanhood in its reactions to the male – represented by the three disturbing athletes who enter into the women's lives – from the flamboyancy of the hostess to the indifference of two friends who ignore them completely in their very own love duet. It is vicious, exceedingly so, but never in any way vulgar. If you ignore its meaning, which is easy to do when it is disguised as the *House Party*, it can still remain a thing of beauty. This avoidance of the obvious is especially noticeable in Nijinska's own dance, 'The Rag Mazurka', where the character must be vulgar. It is a perfect interpretation, but never the real thing. Here, as in the classicism that inspired it, the whole responsibility rests with the dancers. The dancer who excels in *Le Lac des Cygnes* can excel in this. Who can ever forget Vera Nemchinova?

L'entrée de Nemchinova est proprement sublime. Lorsque cette petite dame sort de la coulisse, sur ses pointes, avec de longues jambes, un justaucorps trop court, la main droite gantée en blanc, mise près de la joue comme pour un salut militaire, mon coeur bat plus vite ou s'arrête de battre. En suite, un goût sans fléchissement combine les pas classiques et les gestes neufs.*

---

*'The entrance of Nemchinova is absolutely sublime. When this little lady emerges from the wings, on her pointes, with long legs, her tunic too short, her white-gloved hand placed near her cheek as for a military salute, my heart beats more rapidly or ceases to beat. And then, with unfaltering taste, classical steps and modern gestures are combined.'

When such an experienced balletomane as the poet-artist Jean Cocteau can write in this manner of a dancer in her role, the choreographer has obviously succeeded. Here is modern ballet at its peak. *Les Biches*, too, demonstrates better than anything else Diaghilev's skilful choice of collaborators. Nijinska, Poulenc, and Laurencin become one, each interpreting the same thought in his own particular medium.

Nijinska's whole influence on dancing has been of first-class importance. The only successful woman choreographer in history, great sister of a great brother, she has understood the systematic development of the male dancer. Dolin owes much to her, his first *maître de ballet*, and pays constant tribute to her inspiration; Lifar started as a conscious artist under her regime, as did Lichine in the Ida Rubenstein ballets. Each one bears the unmistakable stamp of her influence. As a dancer she has few equals. She is apart from ordinary standards. She has much of the strength and elevation of her brother, his own particular attack. She is also the only ugly dancer to find fame, ugly but never in any sense plain. There was no incongruity in her assuming the role of the Lilac Fairy, her movement and expression were so in keeping with Perrault's tale.

Her *Les Noces* too was revived at that time. Another truly literary subject treated plastically, another landmark, the return to Russia of the Russian Ballet. When Diaghilev left Russia far behind, as he was bound to do, he lost at least one important asset : the sympathetic and complete understanding of his interpreters. *Petrouchka* could move them and the audience because it was the story of Russia and the universal story of a man's soul. *Les Noces* could do so, too, because it was the life of a Russian woman, counterpart to Petrouchka, and an aspect of a universal institution, marriage. The further the origins of the Ballet were left behind, the less moving could be the performances. While *Les Matelots*, a novelty that season, a modern non-Russian ballet, was easily understandable as broad knockabout pantomime, it was rather much to expect a Russian choreographer and dancers to enter into such a purely local joke as the elaborate Victorian *The Triumph of Neptune*. The Ballets Suédois as a dancing force was thoroughly weakened through losing sight of its origins and becoming the plaything of French artists, for the exploitation of temporary and localized experiment. Diaghilev never made that mistake for long. *Les Noces* and later *Le Pas d'Acier* were healthy signs that the Ballet could flirt with Western Europe and remember where its roots lay.

At this time in Paris I saw much of the Russian painter and decorative artist Constantine Korovin. He was a link with the theatre of the past and had done hundreds of costumes and décors for the Imperial theatres, specializing in Russian costume. His set for *Russlan and Ludmila*, a fine baronial hall, was used by Diaghilev for the divertissement *Festin* in the very first programme. This and the dear old set for *Le Lac des Cygnes*, dignified through age and travel, were their only links. I had been introduced to him with a view to induce him to write about the part he had played and all that he knew of that vanished epoch of Russian art, as brief and brilliant as the literature, music, and ballet of the era, and quite unknown to us, where it did not touch the stage. Although our only common language was a rather shaky French, helped out by Russian and gesticulation, Korovin was so fine a storyteller and an actor that it was possible to catch every word he said, although nearly always impossible to reproduce it in black and white, so rapidly did the stories succeed one another, so much did their point depend upon some vocal inflection, some mime or gesture. Our project of recording the conversations was soon given up, but my enthusiasm for things Russian had touched him, and he decided to adopt me and to pilot me round the Russian colony. Korovin is a superb looking man, deeply impressive, like many of the actors he had dressed magnificently in the make-up of a Boyar, tall and white-bearded. He talked ceaselessly, studying his audience with care, leaving no effect to chance; everything else however was left to take its own course. He was generous to a fault, untidy – I had to wade through piles of drawings and canvases to greet him – and rarely kept an appointment on time. There were many points of resemblance between him and my first Russian friend, Astafieva.

One morning, at the beginning of our friendship, he turned up at my flat early. For once he seemed in a hurry.

'We go to see Chaliapin – now – right away. I have fixed everything; he expects you. Hurry, I have a taxi outside.'

'But Constantine Alexandrovitch, I am in pyjamas; I cannot possibly go like this.'

'Pyjamas? Yes. What does it matter? We are artists; you love our art. Chaliapin will understand; he understands everything.

Anyhow, what do clothes matter?' He burst into song in his favourite imitation of Chaliapin. The argument was irresistible, and the taxi was ticking in agreement. I went to the interview in a makeshift costume, more and more embarrassed as butler passed us on to secretary and so on through the big Trocadero flat. Korovin was right; costume did not seem to matter in the slightest as we talked to the representative Russian artist, the one man who almost alone made the convention of opera possible. He showed us a gallery full of portraits of himself in various roles, a unique collection of work by the leading Russian artists, all inspired by the man in front of us. He should have been conceited – insufferably so – but he was not. 'We great artists are never self-satisfied,' he told me, and I believed him. His pleasure at being world famous was so naïve and so genuine, it resembled that of the little coryphée in her first role – and he had had a full quarter century in which to get used to it. He discussed the pictures naturally and impersonally, as if they had really represented Boris Godounov, Don Quixote, or a mad old miller.

I visited many other museums and galleries with Korovin. Extraordinary and unsettling experiences. In front of any picture that thrilled him, he would suddenly burst into song in a rich bass voice – opera, Russian song, or tsigane, always music that seemed to bear a close relationship to the picture. I had to pacify an occasional guard:

'Voyons, monsieur, on ne chante pas ici.'

But for the most part they seemed to enjoy and understand his enthusiasm. An academician himself, he would enthuse about Picasso. He was a magnificent connoisseur of painting and literally savoured it like fine cooking.

'Ça ce tableau – ça c'est quelque chose. Ah, ça, vrai peinture. Regardez, là et là et là,' and he saluted it, kissing the tips of his fingers.

One day I took a young English painter to see him. Korovin admired the young man's work, saluted it impressively, and then kissed him exuberantly on both cheeks. This accolade terrified my friend, and I had the greatest difficulty in restraining him as he rushed for the door. 'The old codger's crazy. I'm going to get out of here quickly.'

He admired intensely the new ballet of Diaghilev, although he was so much a product of an earlier period. Starting with the somewhat revolutionary upheaval set into motion by the *Mir Isskoustva* [*The World of Art*], he had been left behind, frittering away his fine talent. Alexandre Benois writes of this 'great and delicate talent, rather unbalanced, reaching at many things, but completeing nothing. Korovin is by nature the absolute negation of everything balanced, moderate and dully conventional'. The only big-scale décor of his that we have seen, Pavlova's *Don Quixote*, was a serious disappointment; he cannot be judged by it. When we met he was engaged on new costumes for *Prince Igor*, which the de Basil Opera, parent of the new Ballet, was doing, and painting a portrait of the beautiful Vera Fokina. In his studio I had my first conversations with Fokine, saddened by the recent choreographic developments, especially disgusted by *Les Matelots*, which shocked me too at the time, although now I greatly enjoy it as the frolic it is, properly situated in Massine's creations and not considered as *the* important première of the season. With all the fuss of its presentation forgotten, it survives today, and is well worth its place on the programme.

For me the great treat arranged by Korovin was my meeting with Vera Trefilova and the doyen of ballet critics, Valerian Svetlov, whose career I so greatly envied. His flat had been a gathering-place after first nights where every movement would be fought over and analysed. In his *Ballet Contemporain* he was the first to recognize the successful revolt of Fokine. Today, old, bent, and white-bearded, the ballet is still his great love. He has survived Anna Pavlova, whom he discovered, worshipped, and celebrated in a large critical volume. Our common interest has banished the years, and he has followed my fight for classicism with encouragement. Svetlov, taking his place in the theatre today, gives every performance the grand manner.

I had worshipped Trefilova for four years, measured other dancers by her, and knew her every little movement by heart. I had already written about her at length, so that we met almost as old friends. At once she remembered the timid youth who had haunted the Alhambra corridors, under pretext of seeing Dolin, too impressed to speak to her. At this very meeting I was struck unconscious by her, but she does not know of it yet.

'You admire my dancing. Will you do me a great service? I hate drinking, but my host will be offended if I refuse. Please drink it all up for me, quietly.'

I did so, and my own too. Korovin kept on pouring it out, vodka, wine, brandy. Thank goodness Trefilova left early that night. I could just see her to the door. I came to myself early the next morning, stiff and cold, being shaken by an angry *gendarme*. I had been sleeping on a pile of stones in the Champs Élysées.

Trefilova is quiet, deliberate, calm, and infinitely methodical. She always answers letters promptly. Yet she is as typically Russian as the other better-known type of Astafieva or Korovin, made so popular by literature. The sense of reserve power that is so great a feature of her dancing is there in life. Knowing her calm manner, I once told her how remarkable it was that she never suffered stage fright before her important roles. 'But I do, absolute agonies, only it is nobody's business. I keep it to myself. Many times at the Maryinsky I felt like resigning before a performance, and finishing with it all. Only one never does such things.'

Trefilova was never in love with the stage, and when she retired, early on in her career, to a happy married life, she did so with joy and intended it to be for ever. The death of her husband destroyed that dream, and her return was a struggle. With quiet determination she worked until she was as flawless as ever. With her infinite sense of balance, mental as well as physical, and her common sense, Trefilova has never known jealousy or intrigue. Her admiration for her greatest rival, Anna Pavlova, appointed ballerina the same day as she was, was intense and unstinting. Trefilova sees in the success of one person the success of Russian art as a whole. When staying with me after the death of Anna Pavlova, I took her to visit Ivy House. We could not find it, and I had to ask a policeman to direct us to 'where Pavlova had lived'. Trefilova was crying. 'To think that even a policeman knows where Pavlova, my school friend and the glory of our Russian stage, lived. It is beautiful.' That was one of the rare occasions when she showed her emotions to others. Perhaps never very happy, Trefilova accepts the inevitable and is quietly content. She does not live in the past, but understands the present. She teaches her beloved art to others. The Trefilova I know as a private person is the same that I have loved and admired on the stage.

Recovered from my Monte Carlo madness, I became engaged again, this time for good. To a Russian, of course, but not to a dancer. Immediately all my friends asked what company she was in, what roles she had performed. But I knew dancers too well already, by then, to marry one. Immediately I would have become a partisan, forced to take every little tiff as a personal affront, waiting nightly in the wings for the inevitable scene. I would have been cut off from ballet as the property of *the* dancer. There are a few dancers I love, none with whom I have been in love. I believe myself to be immune.

My wife has suffered during each ballet season. Engagements have been cancelled, and furious acquaintances have had to be pacified. They have not always understood that it is quite impossible to miss a performance.

As a Russian she can diagnose the malady. It comes from her country, and has made me love all that is Russian and understand many things. She loves ballet, too, a little less intensely; about twenty times a season. Still, for nearly ten years now she has been infinitely patient, and I hope that I am grateful.

POSTSCRIPT

I have been re-reading this chapter seated at the Café de Paris in Monte Carlo, or what was once Monte Carlo.

The last time I saw a Ballets Russes company in Monte Carlo was in 1934, when de Basil's company returned from the United States. The gallant René Blum was still his partner. To part company with Monte Carlo meant the death of the 'Ballet Russe' conception of Diaghilev, though the war would certainly have killed it a few years later. It was not the subsidy, which was comparatively small, but the leisure in which to create and repair, the time for rehearsal, and, most important of all, the ambience. Monte Carlo drew the musicians and the painters – the focal point was the Café de Paris – and gave them the opportunity of seeing ballet rehearsals and performances and of meeting choreographers. As I have written, there was no need to make a formal appointment, no telephone interruptions, one just sat down at a table and exchanged ideas that came to fruition in one, two, or three years or were forgotten as unsuitable. Time was the important factor, the time for the idea to take shape, to develop, and to be put into rehearsal. Some of the most successful works had required a gestation period of two years or more.

I can remember seeing a living *Who's Who* of the arts whenever I passed by : Picasso, Cocteau, Stravinsky, Auric, Poulenc, Gontcharova, Larionov, Matisse, Derain, Milhaud, Gershwin – and with them, Nijinska, Massine, Balanchine, Dolin, Lifar. The list could be prolonged indefinitely. The gaming rooms that had first made the name of the Principality occupied the wealthy in the Sporting Club, and the little old ladies eking out their small pensions in the 'cuisine'* as drab as any provincial post office. They were no concern of the international arts cabinet or of Diaghilev, its prime minister. There were no strikes, the very threat of one meant instant expulsion from the Principality, as had happened in the Diaghilev Ballet on one occasion. The Opera House was a miniature, its five hundred and fifty seats mostly occupied by an international public that was informed, critical, and articulate. On the nights when there was no ballet Raoul Gunsbourg directed an opera company equally worthy of its audience. Books have been written on the gambler's Monte Carlo; a history of Monte Carlo as a capital of the artistic world remains to be written. The public was a wealthy one, elegant in the best sense of the word, but living was cheap; there were many inexpensive hotels and restaurants so that the poor intellectual could also survive and be present. The Opera House seats, being subsidised, were well within their reach.

As I write the old Monte Carlo has completely vanished. There is not even a pious and grateful looking-back as in Paris, which, thanks to Serge Lifar, has its Place Diaghilev, outside the Opéra. There is, I wish I could forget it, a particularly ugly bronze bust of Diaghilev that is neither a work of art nor a likeness. The simple commemorative plaque is more appropriate. The Café de Paris, but for the sunshine, might be in Blackpool. Its *consommateurs* pour in by the coach load. The Hôtel de Paris is full of wealthy nonentities who carry on the stock-exchange gossip of their city lives and patronize the galas that once were worthy of the name. Elegance has given way to display. Stars there always were, but now they are as synthetic and mechanical as the electronic devices they use to make themselves audible if not intelligible. Today, if you threw a stone in that area, which I find tempting, it would bounce off the skin of some tycoon bemoaning his poverty. The more staid Hôtel Metropole, the last outpost of Empire, peopled by old ladies with pug dogs, is being gradually hemmed in by skyscrapers that blot out the sun and the mountain views. The marble Greco-Edwardian statues in its lounge – nude yet ever so respectable – and the Palm

---

*The 'cuisine': what Monte Carlo gamblers call the room where the lowest stakes are wagered.

Court orchestra in its restaurant vainly attempt to put back the clock. The Riviera-style villas with their ornate Art-Nouveau decorations are being torn down to give way to vast ill-designed apartment houses that jut into the mountain scenery. There is no one to protect the amenities as in other Riviera resorts. Cement-mixers and bulldozers fill the streets with dust and noise. One can no longer stroll or sit and eat the delectable delicacies at Pasquier's or Rumpelmayer's. To cross the road has become a perilous adventure. Monte Carlo has vanished as completely as the type of creative ballet it nourished so richly for nearly half a century.

My original chapter is full of trivial gossip. I have left it unchanged. It shows the family atmosphere that existed at that time, and also some steps in the education of a balletomane half a century ago. It is often said that a critic should not know the artists of whom he writes. This may be so, but in practice it is an impossible ideal to achieve and, looking back, I cannot think that it influenced my judgement in any way; the tugs worked in so many directions. And I am certain that it added to my understanding and saved me from being a destructive critic. I was in fact far too inclined to praise by the standards of today. The circumstances that existed made it necessary – there were no other critics to strike a fair balance. One thing I never did : take seriously one dancer's opinion of another.

I have mentioned Grigoriev and his wife, the beautiful Lubov Tchernicheva. He was the engineer of the whole Ballets Russes enterprise, arranging rehearsals and travel, and carrying the whole repertoire in his head, a man as solid as the Russian merchants he mimed so admirably. I dedicated my biography of Diaghilev to Benois, Stravinsky, and Grigoriev. The first two were hurt and puzzled in having their names linked to someone who was not a creative artist and 'who took orders'. They never realized what they owed to a craftsman of such complete integrity, a man who kept his head in every emergency. Later, when he performed the same function for de Basil and his wife took the company classes, I became more than ever conscious of the debt that ballet owed to their knowledge, tradition, and discipline. Dancers, choreographers, painters, and musicians came and went. Grigoriev, the rock, remained. The Grigorievs' familiarity with the old repertoire greatly benefited the Royal Ballet. They must occupy an important position in any history of twentieth-century ballet.

5. Anna Pavlova

SEEING Anna Pavlova is one of my very earliest memories, and throughout her London and Paris seasons I rarely missed a performance. My reactions to her dancing were so emotional that it is only now when the beauty of her work has ceased, and there is no possibility of seeing her again, that I can rationalize my feelings, but still I cannot quite fit her into my scheme of things. Anna Pavlova has always been the great exception to every carefully laid down artistic principle, the individual who triumphed over the theory.

Physically she was remarkable; her long, perfectly proportioned arms accentuated the large noble movements of the Russian school, while her well-modelled legs, her strong slender ankles, and her highly developed instep gave to her pointes a unique beauty. Her face was not beautiful; it was more than that. It could assume beauty at will, so that there was not one Pavlova, but many: a gypsy, a dying delirious woman, a coquette. It was this unusual ability to live each role convincingly that made so trivial a sketch as *Christmas* into something so much more than a charming period piece à la *Chauve Souris*. Again and again she rose above her material. What she had to say was so highly concentrated that she never wasted time with frills and embellishments. It is this concentration that is one of her chief characteristics.

When she died, following Diaghilev so closely, there died not only a sublime artist, but a totally different conception of ballet that no one less great than Pavlova could have supported throughout the years of rapidly changing artistic fashion, when yesterday's novelty was old-fashioned and even ridiculous today. That was the mark of her greatness, the most thorough tribute that could be paid her.

When one went to a Diaghilev performance it was to see ballet; to a Pavlova performance, as the very name implies, to see one woman dance. It was a dance concert, a glorious *divertissement* under a slender, unconvincing disguise, but that one woman could convert a *divertissement* into a whole drama. When one lived the performance over again, if under the spell one could think at all clearly, it may possibly have seemed a supreme waste of genius, but it was not, for her pointes were strong enough to carry one along. Her public was not the Diaghilev public; the latter were wrong. She had so very much to give to the highly sophisticated, provided they were true dance lovers, as much as a whole evening of fine music, fine décor, and fine dancing. It was different when Diaghilev died. Ballet of this type did not die with him. Genius he may have been, inspiration he surely had, but ballet of his conception was founded on something logical, on the close collaboration of certain artists. Today and tomorrow such a thing can continue. It will be of the same kind, differing only in quality. Pavlova's ballet died with her. It was as ephemeral as the many roles she interpreted so feelingly : the Dying Swan, the Californian Poppy, the Dragonfly. Pavlova was indeed supreme when representing the life of some frail, beautiful thing, her own great strength completely veiled. I once wrote of her : 'In the Swan this whole aspect of Pavlova's art is summed up; the reaching out as if to struggle for flight, the final quiver, the shudder throughout the whole body and then repose, meant real death.'

In *The Dragonfly* and *The Californian Poppy* she made the dance more intense and joyful, because there was always the suggestion that death was near at hand to put an end to movement, a conscious suggestion she seized upon in her own *Autumn Leaves*, a simple ballet in which she managed to convey a whole philosophy. Without her I doubt whether it could ever have existed. It would have given an impression of intense sentimentality, and Pavlova had too much true sentiment ever to approach the sentimental. It is that cheating of death for an instant, but with the certainty that there was no old age to come, that made the study of youth in *La Fille Mal Gardée*, a ballet conventional enough in every respect, into a personal triumph. No one has ever shown youth on the stage with such purity. *Chopiniana* is another exceptional Pavlova ballet, even in the inferior version she adopted. Composer and dancer are in such absolute sympathy. Here she is as little tangible as a figure lightly sketched on a canvas with but a flick of the brush.

None of these questions concern definite interpretative acting. It is in *Giselle* that she reveals herself as a powerful dramatic actress. It is her greatest role, as it must be with every ballerina who does

not fail, and it reveals in her a totally new aspect. Again the quality
we notice is pathos, but not the gentle pathos of *The Dying Swan*
or *Autumn Leaves*, something incomprehensible and irresistibly
strong, too strong by far for tears. The impression made by Pavlova
during the mad scene literally made one shudder. It was subtle,
very restrained, yet everyone in the theatre could feel it and suffered. The other Giselles I have seen have not nearly approached
this point, and to have seen her in the part was to gain a new conception of her genius. For all my balletomania the word *genius* is
one that I fear to use; with Pavlova there can be no other word.
Talent is so manifestly ridiculous. She took ordinary material and
made of it something extraordinary. We have seen for a season
'The Pavlova Ballet' without her; a pathetic spectacle of good
dancers waiting for someone to come and make them dance, or for
La Pavlova herself to make us forget our little rules of good and
bad choreography. She was associated with mediocrity almost her
whole life – in music, décor, and by comparison in the company
with which she danced – but she herself was never anything but
great. Her genius defies analysis, for on careful consideration a
whole group of negatives makes one astounding, unmistakable
positive – her genius.

There is the Maryinsky Ballet, the Diaghilev Ballet; there was
Anna Pavlova.

In spite of the fact that Pavlova, the name, is a household word
meaning dancing, she herself has never been truly understood save
by her fellow artists. No one yet has given a complete and accurate
portrait of her, either as an artist or as a woman. Perhaps it is a part
of her quality that no one can. I lay no claim to do so. I knew her
scarcely at all – our meetings were five or six at the most; but on
those occasions we discussed some interesting points, and the vision
I have of her is far more plausible, concrete, and certainly flattering
than the inevitable talk of her love of animals and flowers and her
meetings with royalty. Such stories create a certain glamour, but
Pavlova above all had no need of anything so artificial. Her glamour
was blinding even to her intimates. I have questioned many members of her company. They could feel much, but tell me nothing.
In spite of their being on the same side of the curtain, in a position
to see and suffer from her little tantrums or to benefit by her im-
pulsive generosity, she was always, to them as well, the supreme

artist with an invisible barrier of footlights between her and them.

The first time I met her was on the stage at Covent Garden. I arrived early and took up a position in the wings to watch *Bacchanal*. From my novel and notoriously unflattering angle there was no loss of illusion, but a positive gain. It became almost unbearably exciting and real, and it was with the greatest difficulty that I could restrain myself from cheering and making 'noises off'. Added to the glories of the dance itself, one could feel her contact with the audience as a definite, concrete thing, a feeling that I had never experienced to that degree before. Excitement, the sense of her immense power, made Pavlova young and vital. 'Vous avez une ambition dévorante et vos yeux insatiables voudraient embrasser plus de succès qu'il n'y en a sur cette terre,' said Sarah Bernhardt to Anna Pavlova.*

When the curtain fell for the first time, while the applause continued, she still belonged body and soul to her audience. In that beautiful bow, so much a part of her performance, she dedicated herself to them, but when the curtain went down for the last time, the national anthem played, and all echoes of the applause had died down, the contact was suddenly broken, and an immediate transformation took place. A tired middle-aged woman, with only the figure of a very young girl, stood before me, the smallest on a crowded stage, instead of the one, the dominating figure. It was a transformation, a shock even, but not a disillusionment. It made her performance all the greater, and it explained something too. No one has ever reacted to an audience to the same degree as Pavlova. Then she spoke:

'So you are a balletomane? Are you on my side or Diaghilev's?'

It was a quite unanswerable question, but it was perfectly clear what she meant. I was on her side at that moment, so to speak, because against all reason she had compelled me to be. I gave a halting, conventional reply, and, without waiting for a fuller explanation, she went on: 'Please don't tell me I danced *The Swan* well tonight. I know I didn't. One is not a machine. I wasn't in the right mood. Yet the audience applauds just the same. It is kind of them, but so difficult for me, so bad for an artist. In Russia the

---

* 'You have a devouring ambition and your covetous eyes seek more success than there is in the world.'

slightest shade of difference would be noted and commented on. All
the time we had to make a great effort. Here my applause does not
vary. I am grateful of course, but it was not so good tonight. I
know.'

She was dissatisfied – a feeling that every dancer will recognize.
Pavlova may have been, must have been, exceptionally self-centred,
in a sense almost ruthless, in pursuit of her ambition – her whole
career proves that – but she was also intensely self-critical, laying
bare those little faults that others could no longer see. She could not
be deceived by an easy success, was incapable of ever resorting to
bluff. When she said, 'I danced well tonight,' it was true. Pavlova
was above any criticism but her own.

She died while she could still produce perfection; only the Pavlova of ten years before was her bitter rival. In dying she averted a
terrible tragedy – the tragedy of the ballerinas in Vicki Baum's
Grand Hotel or Eleanor Smith's *Ballerina*. She often talked of
settling down quietly at Ivy House, of concentrating on her sculpture or taking up some new career, sometimes with great conviction. Once she even flirted with the idea of starting an hotel. She
could never have done any of these things. Her look of nostalgia
when the curtain went down that night convinced me. To retire
was impossible, to continue with diminished powers equally so.

During her final visit to London I met her at a Sunshine Matinée.
She greatly admired the Ballet Rambert, then a new organization,
in *Capriol Suite*, and saw in Frederick Ashton a possible new
choreographer for herself. There was talk of a new repertoire, of
ballets by Ashton and Balanchine that were modern but not
'modernist'. Then and there I arranged a visit to the studio, so
that she could watch some works in rehearsal. She was both critical
and enthusiastic, asked to see *Capriol Suite* again, and admired
Diana Gould in *Leda* so much that she wished to engage her for a
tour. That was Pavlova's one link with the Ballet Club, a precious
memory.

I saw her but once again, at Golders Green, more magnificently
alive and real than any one of us, her admiring audience. She had
wisely pruned her dances of their greater technicalities and was
showing a restricted repertoire, in which she was still perfection.
With her the technique was always so completely natural that it
defied discernment. She was alone among the great dancers in never

being applauded for any one technical feat. There was none of the hanging knee, the first signs of departing strength, no hint of tragedy. It is from others that I heard how very tired she was.

The news of her death reached me in a cold, empty theatre, during a lighting rehearsal of the Camargo Society. I broke the news to her old friend, partner, and professor, Legat. It seemed so very difficult to believe, especially when heard in a theatre at a ballet rehearsal. Gradually the entire committee turned up, and we held an informal meeting on the spot. Some suggested cancelling the performance, but that would have meant the ruin of the society. We were heavily committed, and finances, as always, were precarious. Then the idea occurred to Stephen Thomas and myself of playing the music of *The Dying Swan*, with curtains raised on the empty stage. Someone objected, 'It wouldn't do at all. Quite lacking in dignity. Too theatrical by far,' which aroused from Lydia Lopokova, in her earnest, carefully enunciated Anglo-Russian : 'A good idea, we will do it. We are *theatrical*, so was Pavlova. It is a word of praise; besides she would have understood and liked it.'

It was the most vivid item of the whole programme. This memory of perfection completely put the living performance in the shade; but it was at the orchestra rehearsal that it was the most impressive, before just a few people, her friends and true admirers, in the intimate workshop atmosphere of the theatre.

Many are the uses to which Pavlova's name will be put. There is even talk of a film of her life. How can such a thing be? What was her life but her art – *Giselle*, *The Dying Swan*, and the rest? Who dares dance them in her name?

Pavlova's name will be heard for long years to come, for it is now synonymous with the dance. Every new talent that arises will be called a 'second Pavlova' by her well-meaning admirers, who in that way will promptly and effectively damn her for ever. I must have seen over a score of such 'second Pavlovas' during the last few years, and I could not see that any of them bore the slightest resemblance to her namesake. If Pavlova herself had been called a 'second Zucchi' when she made her glorious debut, we should never have heard of her today. It was perfectly safe to compare her to Taglioni, for by then 'Taglioni' simply implied ethereality; the name could be assigned no positive personality.

Our new star may well have some of those things that were Pavlova's, but she must have something to give that is essentially her own.

Will it be possible for such a reputation to be made at the present day? That is the way I carefully phrase my query, for I have great enough faith in the art to believe that even such a talent as was Pavlova's can be repeated in quantity but not in quality.

The whole conception of the ballet today seems to be against it; a one-act affair lasting from twenty minutes to an hour at most with a variety of parts rather than one central one. If the dancer makes anything of a name, and is at all discussed, it is usually in a definite character role and not as herself at all. Aesthetically this may be an advantage, but it does prevent her from attaining her full stature as an individual.

At the present day in England ballet is becoming more and more understood, while the dancer herself is almost completely anonymous. She is said to dance 'charmingly', 'brilliantly', or 'lightly', but she is never appreciated critically and never taken to task; that is the tragedy.

During the Covent Garden season of 1934 a ballerina was compared by three newspaper writers to the Australian cricketer Don Bradman, much to my disgust and hers – and perhaps Bradman's! It was obviously intended as praise, very great praise, since Bradman was piling on runs and in very high favour at the time. Not only did it mean nothing, but it revealed how fully the dancer is misunderstood by the very people whose duty it is to interpret her to others. The ballet is rich enough as an art for some comparison or terms of praise to be found from within it.

Another factor that will prevent the dancer from equalling her elders as a personality is the fact that today she is enormously overworked. In the great period of the Imperial Ballet, out of which Pavlova herself was born, nightly performances were an unheard of thing, and the prominent dancer could go into training for her role much as the opera singer or the instrumentalist. This gave not only a physical repose, but also full time in which to work upon an interpretation, and there were always those on hand who could guide the young dancer.

Igor Stravinsky told me only recently that in Russia alone was the dancer regarded as a serious artist, the equal of any piano or violin virtuoso. This spirit still exists today, but too frequent appearances must damage the young dancer both in fact and in the eyes of the public.

It is a cliché in the ballet world that 'a dancer will become as great as her mother allows her to be, provided of course that she herself has the essentials'.

In Russia in the palmy days of the Imperial Ballet the state took on the task of mothering the dancers. Each one received the same education, but personality did not suffer. Or did it? It may have been a question of the survival of the fittest, the triumph of a few exceptional individuals, with the rest as just a decorative pattern in the background. Today we have the interplay of personalities struggling to develop; that, as well as lack of adequate rehearsal time, makes a corps de ballet ragged, a fault that has been found with all young companies recently. It is inherent in the present system because the dancer beginning to develop as an individual cannot express herself in a group. Again, with the new system as with the old, the exceptional personality will triumph, with the difference that in Russia the fight was almost decided from school days and now it goes on in front of us daily on the stage.

With the very young, personality and technique develop rapidly, and especially stage presence. People say, 'How fickle you are; once again you have changed your opinion.' Ridiculous people, as if it were an opinion about some inanimate stationary thing. The dancer develops from season to season, the critic does too, although there are many, including Diaghilev himself, who say that critics alone never learn. Perhaps they are right, though such remarks are usually made by dancers when you have not praised them sufficiently.

In a sense the path of the great Maryinsky dancers was more direct aesthetically than that of today's dancer. She had a definite mission to accomplish. The following statement from Prince Wolkonsky will show what the ballet was like before such a dancer as Pavlova came on the scene:

The first time I went to the ballet I was a child, and it was to see the *Fisherman and the Naiad*. I liked the fairy side of the performance, I liked the corps de ballet, but frankly I disliked the soloists. Even in those early days I felt shocked at their affectation, and the technique, which was stressed to an almost acrobatic extent, left me quite cold. I could grasp neither the difficulty nor the charm of it, so tremendously did the 'untruth' of it offend me. It was true to no convention, illogical,

absurd, unnecessary. You will understand something of it when you
compare early theatrical photos with those of today.

Even at the beginning of my directorship, although by then great
creative dancers had emerged, the atmosphere was much the same. I
remember a new production of *Tannhäuser*. The dances in the first act,
the bacchanal in the Venus grotto, had been staged by the great Petipa
himself. At the dress rehearsal I was horrified, it was just tip-toe, tip-
toe, tip-toe, the whole time. The nymphs were ballerinas, never forgot
it themselves and never let the audience forget it. Think of it: during
the wonderful accord that an invisible chorus sings behind the scenes,
we saw three ballerinas cross the stage on their pointes, grinning sweetly
at the enraptured audience.

I gave orders for the scene to be changed but, even if there had been
time, nobody could understand in the slightest what I wanted. The
dancers had elicited applause, how could there possibly be anything
wrong?

Tannhaüser bacchanal *sur les pointes*, hand on heart, lover's
sighs: that is the atmosphere from which Kchessinska, Trefilova,
and then Pavlova emerged, and it was their task to take ballet out
of the lumber room, to dust away its cobwebs, and give to Fokine
and Diaghilev an instrument with which they could work. By
Wolkonsky's statement we can measure what these great ballerinas
accomplished. But now that the battle has been so handsomely
won, in what direction can the new ballerina develop?

Only by the fullest expression of her own individuality, through
which she will be expressing her age. Individuality is a thing that
can be developed in the classroom itself. Kchessinska, an artist of
tremendous personality who recognized the gifts of Nijinsky and
Karsavina before anyone else and who went out of her way to develop them, believes strongly in the systematic development of
personality. She dances continually to demonstrate, but her pupils
do not imitate her; they are not allowed to.

One day I sat in a class watching a classical mazurka interpreted
by five artist pupils, among the finest dancers of today, each one of
different physique and temperament.

'That is splendid,' said their teacher excitedly, 'each one does it
in an entirely different manner, and each one is perfectly right.'

She stressed a very great truth in dancing, and a little understood one: *If there are thousands of ways of doing a thing wrongly,
there are also thousands of ways of doing it rightly.* She cor-

rected each pupil, but for the inconsistencies in each *individual* version, and not by some imaginary mathematical standard or by what she herself or Pavlova would have done.

Pavlova's name will live because she was unique and unrepeatable, and that too will be the sole condition of the future fame of Baronova, Riabouchinska and Toumanova.

POSTSCRIPT

Today, over forty years after I last saw her dance, the impression of Pavlova remains a vivid one. The banal music that she used gains, by association, a quality it does not truly possess. When people ask me, as they invariably do, 'How great was she? Can you compare her to X, Y, or Z? Is it true that she had but little technique?' it is impossible to reply to anything but the last question. Writing of far greater calibre than mine fails to evoke the presence of a superb dancer of the past. Dance film was in its infancy during her lifetime and does her memory a real disservice, though many studio portraits and her own porcelain figurines hint at her grace and seeming fragility.

Some points have struck me in retrospect. *Don Quixote*, that absurd excursion into fireworks, and its famous, if not *notorious*, pas de deux and variations are now in every ballerina's repertoire. On several occasions, at the Varna and Moscow competitions, I have suffered through it over twenty times in a week, and at each performance I remembered Pavlova's superb interpretation. The miserable thing itself is the type of kitsch known as 'Saint Petersburg-Spanish'. Pavlova concealed its acrobatics and gave it the lightness and wit of a flirtatious interlude. She made her audience smile. Since then only Markova had the elegance and lightness of touch, and Maximova the hint of satire, that could transform it into art; Plisetskaya's technique was so dazzling that it too remains in the memory.

Pavlova's range was tremendous, from the tragedy of *Giselle*, the excitement of the *Bacchanal*, to the puff pastry of *Christmas*, *The Gavotte*, and *The Fairy Doll*.

This answers the question of Pavlova's technique. It was unsurpassed in the sense in which technique should be understood. It served her unobtrusively for all the varied emotions she wished to express. Only the Byronic romanticism in which Karsavina excelled was out of her reach. Pavlova was, I believe, very much an instinctive artist. She could not analyse her roles in depth, her taste in music and décor was bad – she rejected *L'Oiseau de Feu* as too modern. But she felt deeply and was able to convey her emotions to her audience. I could feel this extraordinary rapport when I watched her from the wings; when the curtain cut her off from the audience, one suddenly noticed her age and her tiredness.

In later years when I travelled to Australia with her widower, Victor Dandré, a charming man totally devoid of artistic imagination, he talked to me constantly of 'Madame', as he always called her, revealing in itself. He told me that, if she had not died when she did, she could not have continued dancing – a bone condition would have made it impossible. There was nothing else that she could have done. Teaching was out of the question. The tragedy of her life was that she had no children; she felt this increasingly as her many charities to children showed. A Berlin gynaecologist had told Dandré that an operation might succeed but that in Pavlova's case he did not dare risk it.

The main subject of many of her conversations was always concerned with saving the ballet from Diaghilev's excesses. The interview she had with him, mentioned in the chapter on Diaghilev, page 98, in which he had compared Spessivtseva and Pavlova ungraciously and without truth, wounded her deeply; it was a wound that would remain open for the last ten years of her life. She never discussed other dancers, though she was lavish in her praise of the young. There are many who proudly tell one that Pavlova said they had great talent; they are not lying. It was a polite formula deliberately used, partly to give pleasure, partly to save herself from constant over-exposure to anxious mothers. Hers was a stormy character. She could be merciless with any rival. She was intensely jealous of Nijinsky's fame and especially of Karsavina, who had stepped into her shoes in the Diaghilev Ballet through Pavlova's inability to work with a team. On one occasion in Berlin, when Karsavina was dancing, she walked out when it would be most noticeable. Yet she was self-critical, even humble about the great gift she had received, and infinitely kind to the unfortunate. Throughout the Revolution and Civil War she sent food parcels to her colleagues at the Maryinsky. Her charity was always unobtrusive. She had the most extraordinary courage, fighting in the early years against ill health and a frailty that at one time made it doubtful whether she could remain at school, yet later turning this frailty into a tremendous asset.

In this chapter I asked the question, 'Will it be possible for such a reputation to be made today?' I thought not, giving as my reasons that the dancer no longer received the opportunities to develop her personality in the great classics, and that critics did not take the dancer seriously. Not too long afterwards I was proved wrong. Today the classics have regained their rightful place in the repertoire, and there are many admirable critics on both sides of the Atlantic, professional and amateur, who have sufficient respect for the dancer to draw attention to faults as well as virtues and are no longer content with adjectives such as 'charming', 'brilliant', or 'gossamer light'. Ulanova and Fonteyn have become legends, and Nureyev has joined Nijinsky.

I am interested in this legendary quality. It exists in every sphere of activity: Edmund Kean, Sir Henry Irving, Paganini, Caruso, Chaplin, Garbo, the Beatles, Jack Johnson, Dempsey, Muhammad Ali – their names are known the world over, whether people are interested in their particular field or not. Certainly they possess extraordinary qualities, but there are many others, whom specialists rate equally highly, whose names are not household words. In the first place they must appear at the right moment and fill a void. Sometimes an element of sensation and drama helps to launch the legend: Duncan's loves and her dramatic death, a Greek tragedy; Nijinsky's insanity and his relationship with Diaghilev; Nureyev's dramatic defection. In recent times press and publicity combine to begin the legend, whether it is Garbo's 'I want to be alone' or Ali's 'I am the greatest,' but in any case, unless there is real merit and personality, the result is nothing more than a nine days' wonder.

In the case of three of our legendary figures there is no story even to assist in the growth of the cult. Pavlova created history on the stage with scanty material, Ulanova became an international name with a score of performances in Italy, London, Paris, and New York. Fonteyn came gradually to fame, developing over the years. Both Ulanova and Fonteyn were backed by a strong company and powerful organizations; Anna Pavlova did it on her own and remains unique. The quality required cannot be defined or analysed. One could perhaps call it, in religious parlance, a grace, or, in pre-Christian terms, magic. Movement is more eloquent than words. When I was discussing this very point in a symposium on the arts at Downside (a Benedictine monastery and school in Somerset), one of the monks brought up the example of Bernadette Soubirous, the simple peasant saint of Lourdes. 'It was her movements in genuflecting, in looking up at the apparition of Our Lady, that first convinced the multitudes of her sincerity, long before any investigation by the incredulous Church, who had not been present outside the grotto at Masabielle.'

It is not too far-fetched to suggest that the daily exercises of a dancer, especially those seemingly monotonous ones at the barre, are akin to those adopted by some mystics, and that this highly stylized form of theatrical dance harks back to the mystery religions of Egypt and Greece. All art, and especially the dance, has its origins in magic and religion – Monsignor Ronald Knox talked of the mass as a ballet, and there is still dancing in front of the altar at Easter in Seville Cathedral.

Great dancing has this quality of mystery, and Pavlova is the supreme example of the dancing priestess. Paul Valéry, in his masterpiece *L'Âme et la Danse*, could have been thinking of her when he wrote: 'Elle est divine dans l'instable, elle en fait don à nos regards.'*

Recently two young English balletomanes, John and Roberta Lazzarini, have opened a Pavlova museum in a room at Ivy House. It is full of interesting photographs, relics, and archives, and is well worth a pilgrimage.

* 'She is divine in the Unstable, she offers it as a gift to our eyes.'

6. Serge Diaghilev

EVEN during Diaghilev's lifetime a legend surrounded him; it has now grown to such enormous dimensions that it has become impossible to see the real man, or to form a correct estimate of his achievement and that of his many brilliant collaborators. His work and vast knowledge drew him into so many different circles that each person, almost, has a distorted picture of his particular Diaghilev, coloured through distance – pictures generally impossible to reconcile. I have based this sketch of him on innumerable conversations with his collaborators, friends and enemies, members of his company, and also on my personal knowledge. I knew him but slightly, and he disliked me from the moment I began criticising the Ballet, though he agreed with many of the conclusions I reached. He was always intolerant of any independent criticism, and on one occasion, it is said, visited the journalist André Levinson's editor, demanding his instant dismissal. I had an intense admiration for him, and he was the only person of whom I have ever been a little frightened. This distance has given me the possibility of gaining a true perspective; so overpowering was his personality that anyone at all intimate with him would naturally have biased views. 'I could never talk to him without feeling like crying, and many others were the same,' said a usually well-balanced member of his company to me. That makes any kind of approach very difficult. We are immediately on an emotional plane, whereas it is Diaghilev's intellect we wish to assess.

It is first necessary to destroy some of the legend that gets between us and him. The best-known portrait, now, is that by Romola Nijinsky,* and it is all the more misleading through being nearly accurate on so many points, and always highly plausible. It is of course only natural that the wife of Nijinsky should see in Diaghilev the brilliant villain of the Middle Ages; *her* Diaghilev must have assumed some of those aspects, but her biography cannot be allowed to persist in its entirety as a true portrait. I could balance it with as many clearly established acts of goodness that would, by

*Nijinsky, by Romola Nijinsky, Gollancz, 1933.

substituting Santa Claus for Cesare Borgia, form a portrait equally misleading.

We must first admit his abnormal views on love, an undisputed fact. He had only once, early in life, tried normal relations with a woman, and the occasion must have been unfortunate. It left him with a deep disgust, amounting to terror; he never forgot the incident, and talked of it at times. However, women played a large part in his life, and because of his views, he could meet them as equals, select them for their intelligence, and admire their beauty, coldly, as if they were museum exhibits. Women were attracted to him and helped him from the very start. Some of the most remarkable women of the day were his allies and made his triumphs possible. His homosexuality made of him a lonely man, certain to be constantly disillusioned and disappointed, deliriously happy at one moment, dejected the next. He was only attracted by the virile, normal man, who was certain with maturity to attract and be attracted by the opposite sex, and to prefer the company of some witless little girl to the brilliant Sergei Pavlovitch : situations that one could not expect him to accept. Once that fact is admitted and understood, it is not difficult to imagine his feelings on receiving the brief and unexpected telegraphic announcement of Nijinsky's marriage. To Sergei Pavlovitch, it was obviously quite impossible to retain him in the company, to work and remain in daily contact with him and the intruder, his wife. The dismissal of him at once was no beginning of a dark medieval plot to wipe him out of existence, but merely the very normal reaction of a very abnormal man. Once one admits this conception of love – and it has never been disputed – what other course was open to him? Yet there was much more to it. It had its idealistic aspect.

Nijinsky as a choreographer was Diaghilev's own creation, and it was the opportunities that Diaghilev gave him, the careful nursing, the development of his personality, and the all-important intellectual contacts, that enabled him to compose. Nijinsky was famous in Russia first, but in the old repertoire, and without Sergei Pavlovitch his fame would have remained local – just that of another brilliant dancer among brilliant dancers. Diaghilev must certainly have realized, aside from any feelings of jealousy, that however much Nijinsky was now living the normal life of a normal man, those opportunities would cease and his whole dream of creation would be shattered. Nijinsky was exceptionally receptive material, but needed the constant stimulation that Diaghilev alone could provide. When he left Diaghilev he immediately deteriorated as a dancer, and his choreography also failed, in the opinion of many. Another point that must have weighed with him was the fact – and the whole company knew it – that Nijinsky was highly strung and unbalanced from the very beginning, and that he needed the most extraordinary care and a total freedom from responsibility, a care that Diaghilev had always given him. It would be tragic to see him grow worse before his very eyes, without the means or the right to try to save him.

There is no suggestion that Diaghilev seduced him. Nijinsky was not a child; he had an enormous respect and admiration for Diaghilev and profited both materially and as an artist from the friendship. As events proved, his one hope of sanity lay in remaining with Diaghilev. While his desire to marry was natural, it must not be looked upon as an escape from some ogre, from an entirely unmitigated evil. The balance between the two men was, up to this point, very even; materially Nijinsky had certainly gained the most.

Such a separation, therefore, is totally understandable; anything else was quite out of the question. Then came the demand for the payment of arrears of salary – the first unfriendly act, and from the other side. To a man already suffering, this must have been a heavy blow. It is certain from all sources of evidence that Diaghilev was scrupulously honest; strangely avaricious in small things, generous, even lavish, in large. Many dancers, during the war and after, remained with him for years without ever having felt the need for a signed contract. For at least two of his dancers he deposited money in the bank in addition to their generous salaries, as some compensation for having taken them away from the guaranteed livelihood of the Maryinsky. This was done without any compulsion. Another dancer, who had refused his advances, was threatened with tuberculosis. Diaghilev offered to send him to a sanatorium in Switzerland. When it came to a reckoning between him and Nijinsky, he had looked after all Nijinsky's personal needs, had gratified his slightest wish, and had made him many costly presents. It must surely have been tacitly understood that the large salary was but a 'paper' one, for the sake of appearances and publicity. Diaghilev could not stoop to reckon up all these favours, and here at any rate Nijinsky and his wife were the aggressors. A woman older and more experienced than the headstrong young girl, Romola, who knew so clearly what she wanted, and pursued it through so many difficulties, would have persuaded him to leave matters alone instead of taking the lead. She clearly felt her power, and there was a certain thrill even in the duel with her defeated rival – this great man whom her husband still worshipped. Between the two, Nijinsky, sighing for peace and the opportunity to serve his art, must have been both mystified and unhappy.

As to the tale of subsequent persecutions, one cannot for a moment believe them : they are altogether too fantastic and out of keeping with the whole of Diaghilev's known character. Once his dreams had been shattered he would have been bitter and disillusioned, but he would have let so painful a subject alone. Later stories show this to have been the case. Many times disappointed, he still retained a friendship on a non-emotional basis when the other party made it possible. It was while his dancers were still with him that he fought tooth and nail to retain their affections, was jealous to the extent of having them shadowed by detectives day and night, and adopted all the petty tricks that jealousy inspires even in the greatest minds.

The charge that Fokine sought to prevent Nijinsky from appearing in *Le Spectre de la Rose* in London, or that Diaghilev even tried to influence him to do so, is indignantly denied by Fokine. One cannot conceive of these men as joint conspirators. There does not seem to have been any deliberate plot on Bakst's part to collaborate with Nijinsky in his efforts to rival Diaghilev. Bakst, as a loyal and grateful friend of Diaghilev's, must have resented the whole thing and held back not through fear or compulsion, as is suggested by Madame Nijinsky, but through common decency. The notion that Diaghilev incited two men to drive Nijinsky mad by putting vaguely pseudo-Tolstoyan ideas into his head is the most fantastic of all. Nijinsky himself was already unbalanced, obviously sought the company of other unstable men, and one of these 'conspirators' died insane a little time later. The other, whom I know well, was young, impressionable, and soon threw off such thoughts, which must have come at one time or another to many adolescent Russians, who can ill digest so rich a literature. There is, of course, no doubt that at that time Diaghilev had an axe to grind and enjoyed his influence over Nijinsky. It was not for nothing that he was called 'Nijinsky's Rasputin' by the rest of the company. The thing undoubtedly happened as Romola Nijinsky describes it, but quite spontaneously and without the knowledge of Diaghilev, who, when he heard of it, strongly disapproved.

I have investigated, too, the story of the attempt on Nijinsky's life. It was just one of those frightening episodes that, in spite of all precautions, occur from time to time on the stage. A heavy weight fell just behind Nijinsky and in front of Leon Woizikovski, for whom it might equally well have been intended. I have myself witnessed almost the identical thing – the falling of a huge weight from the flies. Nijinsky may have been unpopular – all successful dancers are; it is part of the game – but the game does not include murder.

We know that, throughout Nijinsky's unfortunate malady, Dia-ghilev showed not remorse but a very natural solicitude. He could be remorseless in pursuit of his aims, extremely jealous, and quite capable of strong hatred – every fault and quality in him was ex-aggerated – but this aimless vendetta is entirely out of keeping with his essentially creative character, and is not supported by anything more than the vague conjectures of a loving imaginative wife and her delicate husband. Diaghilev had his petty side, but it was shown by such things as making it indirectly difficult for someone he did not like to remain in the company, through passport troubles and the like, but he never pursued them or tried to damage their livelihood.

Nijinsky's own action in keeping Diaghilev away from the American tour, and assuming responsibilities for which he was so obviously unfitted, must certainly have damaged the artistic results of the entire enterprise and jeopardized its very existence. The Ballet could live perfectly well without Nijinsky, as events have proved, but without Diaghilev it was aimless. In this whole un-pleasant episode Diaghilev showed the very greatest magnanimity. It was his Ballet, and he need not have consented to the tour. He wished for its success, and it was Nijinsky himself who selected the artists, omitting Grigoriev, whose help would have been invaluable. Apart from any sentiment, Diaghilev would never have tried to bring about a costly failure; it would have been cheaper to put his foot down from the very start.

Once the unfortunate basis that made the Nijinsky-Diaghilev re-lationship delicate from the start has been admitted, it is clear that Diaghilev was more hurt than hurting in this story of friendship and enmity.

His *manie des grandeurs*, another important part of the legend, certainly existed, and with some justification. His superiority was felt and admitted by others, who were themselves by no means toadies. He shone in any society, and it was not unnatural to play up to it at times. On one occasion he told me, after some trouble in the company, 'I can get rid of all these people and have just as good a Ballet within three weeks. Dancers will pay to say they have been with me.' Perhaps this was not strictly accurate at the time, 1925, but it was near enough to the truth. I had heard many of the offers that he turned down.

In one case a very large sum of money was offered him to 'star' a young dancer whom he admired but did not yet think ripe for such responsibility. He badly needed the money, but refused without hesitation and felt himself insulted. He never forgave her. He had largely made the present company, the Maryinsky supply was exhausted, and he could form others, if not in three weeks, then within the year. On another occasion, at supper, I heard him reprimand one of his dancers for eating peas with a knife. 'But, Sergei Pavlovitch, you are doing precisely the same thing.' 'I can, because I am Diaghilev'; which was true, and is a very old story that has always been true.

Lydia Sokolova has told me that apart from England, where each dancer has always had groups of friends and admirers, they always danced for Diaghilev and for Diaghilev alone. I have often heard them debating earnestly, when he had gone on one of his trips, as to what train he would take. 'Ah, the 8.30, then he will have dinner at once and won't be there for the first ballet,' in a tone of relief. His presence made an enormous and obvious difference to the whole quality of the performance. He noticed every single detail of dancing, make-up, and costume, even the placing of a safety pin, and his opinions would reach the dancers via Grigoriev day by day, often in the form of a fine. Diaghilev had a hypersensitive eye. One of his *bêtes noires* was a big head. 'I have a big head and there isn't going to be another one in the company.' He was on that account most particular about the style of hairdressing. Another saying of his was: 'There is nothing uglier in the world than a woman's thighs,' and he never permitted the short revealing classical tutu, except in boyishly slim figures, such as Alice Nikitina's in *Zéphir et Flore*.

This fact, of Diaghilev as an *audience*, can give us a first positive clue to his character; it reveals and is explained by his heredity. Ballet in Russia first took root through the nobles having personal troupes, brought over from the Continent or composed of their own serfs, performing not for profit but for the amusement of themselves and that of their guests. Diaghilev by breeding was such a nobleman. However much a showman he was, educating and cultivating his public, this precedent persisted and formed a part of him. He was Diaghilev the autocrat, and never in any sense an impresario, though he could and did outdistance them all at their own game. His Ballet danced for him, for his gratification and his greater glory. Everyone in the theatre worked for him, even carpenters and electricians. On some occasions the dancers would leave the theatre in the evening and find him still seated there the next morning, worn out, with deep bags under his eyes, surrounded by the technical staff. They earned big sums in overtime, but for no one else would they ever have done the same thing. He graciously shared his pleasure with the public, and with him pleasure largely consisted in watching the reactions of others to anything that moved him deeply. That is the essential picture one must have first of all. Otherwise the position of the man who was not an impresario, and neither dancer, painter, nor musician, but who influenced all three for a quarter of a century, is impossible to understand. We can think of him as a Lorenzo the Magnificent, never a dilettante, but an artist in appreciation, and, in many interpretations of the word, a fully creative mind.

Our view of Diaghilev as a creator depends largely upon the particular period of his career. One of the very best studies is that of A. Benois, his first mentor and collaborator of the early days. He tells how Diaghilev, the young provincial, of good county family, joined their little circle of artists, sponsored by his cousin Filosofov, and of the impressions he made, beginning as the timid outsider on sufferance and soon becoming the dominating force. One episode he recalls in particular, the sudden interruption during a picnic of a long abstract discussion on Wagner:

Lying as I was on my back, looking at the clouds, I could not see what was happening... Serge took advantage of this to creep up to me, seize hold of me, and start pummelling me, laughing heartily all the while. Never before had such a thing happened in our group. We were all quiet and well brought up ... real mother's boys... Also I soon felt that big Serge was much stronger than I, and that, although the eldest, I risked a humiliating defeat. I had recourse to a ruse, screaming lustily so as to persuade him that he had broken my arm. He was impressed, released me with regret at having been unable to follow up his advantage, and even helped me to get up, which I did, groaning and rubbing my arm energetically.

This childish scene has remained fixed in my memory with extraordinary vividness and I think that the reason for it is that suddenly I had a vision of the true nature of Serge, the nature of a fighter. Although we soon became fast friends long before any collaboration, a sort of fight was always mixed up in our relationship, which gave our friendship a particular zest.

Diaghilev, the fighter, was to overcome all the difficulties and intrigues of the twenty years that surrounded his venture. Only a fighter and an absolute autocrat could have succeeded. Diaghilev was born a dictator, but that rare thing, the dictator of discrimination and intelligence.

'Only one thing,' says Benois, 'was lacking in that generation of Russian artists who contributed to the creation of all these fine artistic manifestations – it was just that, the will to create, that same will to create that Diaghilev possessed to the full.'*

In the years immediately before the Ballet, Diaghilev shows magnificent scholarship in a monograph on the Russian painter Levitsky. He dabbles in music, tries his voice as a singer, and is dissuaded by Rimsky-Korsakov from composing, after a first effort had been heard. That is the end of dilettantism. Then comes the organization of art exhibitions, the editing of a review, and the sponsoring of a whole new movement. This means fighting and diplomacy. The young provincial has found himself. The first few years of the ballet are an exploitation of that will, but it is still clearly the Fokine ballet, and we are told that the only suggestion he ever made to Fokine was during a rehearsal of *L'Oiseau de Feu*, when he pointed out that the heart was on the left side. Fokine is fully justified in all that he says: the real Diaghilev was still to appear.

It is with the ripening of the Nijinsky friendship that we first see him. The results of that friendship had deprived him of a permanent headquarters and had made him almost an outlaw. Now he had to rely from season to season on his diplomatic skill. Nijinsky, as an

*Both this and the long quotation above are from A. Benois, *La Revue Musicale*, 1 December 1930.

artist, was the result of the opportunities provided for him by Diaghilev, who did not create his ballets or ever claim to do so, but who surrounded him with the necessary ingredients and waited. When Nijinsky left him he was immediately ready with Massine, a truly brilliant and intelligent dancer who profited by the opportunities given him to the full and soon found his own direction.

Diaghilev was now ready to enhance those creations. Forsaking for ever ready-made music, and the décor of those artists who had started out with him, he reaffirmed the Diaghilev Ballet, and it is of this second period, the Massine period, that he was proudest. Choreography, music, décor, all must be commissioned, and the result must show no gaps. And, however bad any of his rare failures may have been, there never was a gap. Much subsequent ballet has been more important, but there have always been some flaws in its presentation, one of the partners struggling to express something different. While it is quite clear that Diaghilev himself was a man of few ideas or direct suggestions, he could give inspiration to his entourage and then act. It could be said that he created personalities and that, with few exceptions, their creativity diminished when they left him. He himself avoided personal publicity. Never on any occasion did he appear on the stage. All the extravagant claims were made by his over-enthusiastic admirers.

'What exactly do I do? Well, you can say that I superintend the lighting' was his invariable reply. He could play with light like an artist mixing paint on his canvas, and patiently persisted until the crease in the old drop curtain of *Petrouchka* was completely washed away.

It is not true, either, to go to the other extreme and to believe the jibe that painters admired his knowledge of music, musicians his knowledge of painting. 'If you placed twenty scores before him, he would pick out the best, and give his reasons, too,' Auric told me, while Larionov used the identical phrase to describe his knowledge of painting. I have seen him interrupt an orchestra rehearsal to make some criticism, when Stravinsky himself was conducting, and the suggestion was readily accepted. If he appeared to interfere but little in the actual choreography, it was because he had picked his men with the greatest care and had previously influenced their whole minds and manner of thinking. He did not just commission a work as a mere financial transaction. His collaborators stayed with him months at a time at Monte Carlo, and he actually watched the work in progress, criticising it bit by bit. The greatest artists of the day listened to his criticism with respect.

'Creative?' says Larionov, one of his brilliant collaborators. 'In one respect at any rate, admirably so. He created his audiences. For months ahead, before each new departure he arranged for inspired talk to circulate in the salons, and listened carefully to opinions. Even the head waiter in a restaurant was worth influencing. This preliminary "provocation" was part of a deliberate system.'

Did he always believe in his own works? At times that is a little doubtful. Once when asked what he really thought of a new ballet, he replied: 'I cannot tell yet. I haven't read the papers.' A joke, of course, but ever since the scandal over *L'Après-midi d'un Faune* he realized the full value of controversy and enjoyed it. It meant a fight. Such a work as *Romeo et Juliette* was boosted far above its merits through the demonstration and quarrel amongst the *surréalistes*, which Diaghilev definitely anticipated even if he did not foster it. His own personal taste in music was for melody; in Switzerland during the war Stravinsky teased him for his excessive admiration of Tchaikovsky. Stravinsky subsequently revised his opinions; Diaghilev remained firm, though publicly for a time he left Tchaikovsky far behind.

His taste in dancing was for classicism, though he could admire something totally different. I remember his urging me to see the acrobatics of the Gertrude Hoffman girls.* This was a superficial momentary interest of a man whom everything interested. Olga Spessivtseva (renamed Spessiva by him) was his favoured ballerina. He said of her: 'Olga Spessiva and Anna Pavlova are like two halves of an apple, but the Spessiva half has been in the sun.' Unjust, of course, but he never could forgive Pavlova for having made a success away from his influence. The Maryinsky ballerinas he admired wholeheartedly; and he could talk for hours about Kchessinska, her art, charm, and intelligence. He was far less of a revolutionary than Fokine, though the results associated with him were so much more extreme. The failure of *The Sleeping Princess* affected him more than most people realized. It was a return to his own taste, and its rejection appeared in the nature of a personal rebuff. Other failures he could talk of lightheartedly, as 'successful failures' or the reverse. His later, deliberate policy, as he said

* An amazing team of acrobats, performing on ropes, and popular in the 1930s.

shortly before his death, was to sicken the public gradually with the grotesque and the *dernier cri* until he had educated them sufficiently to return to the purity of classicism. Both his choreographers of the ultra-modern period were themselves sickened and longing for the return. He died just before this return to classicism could be realized. Often, too, he tried to induce Kchessinska to return to the stage. The change of direction, which took place after his death, was in a sense due to him. Lifar danced *Giselle* and *L'Oiseau Bleu* with Spessivtseva; to see this would have given him the greatest joy. Massine discovered the new symphonic classicism.

All this shows clearly that Diaghilev could not initiate artistic movements without years of preparation; he seized them at their birth and showed them to the public at large. The era 1909–29 became known as the Diaghilev era because he crystallized what was going on, and not because he actually created it. This does not detract from him; it puts his genius on another plane and at the same time allows full credit to his collaborators.

Diaghilev has been called by many an excellent businessman, and if the keeping alive of an expensive company for so long deserves the description, he was, though in point of detail the artist plus nobleman in him always won. *The Sleeping Princess* would have needed a record run to meet its expenses. Each costume in one brief scene cost over £50, a vast amount then. Others have profited by this lavishness, for today in the 1930s the original costumes, still in admirable condition, continue to be worn in *Petrouchka*, *Prince Igor*, and *Le Tricorne*. Not a penny would be spared either on entertaining or on the smallest detail once an idea had entered into his head. He had no fixed home and very few personal wants. Only in the last few years he collected books, chiefly Pushkiniana, that followed him round in crates. His unique collection of pictures was all given away. He collected deliberately for others. He paid a friend's doctor's bill in the finest Baksts I have ever seen. His business ability would be more correctly summed up as infectious personal charm and enthusiasm. I can never conceive of his balancing a budget or attempting to do so. If his guarantors lost their money, as they invariably did, they found the results well worth the expenditure and were ready to lose and gain once more, the next year:

Enfin, en 1913, pour la saison inaugurale des Champs Élysées, il me

tint la dragée haute et me fit payer ses spectacles un demi-million!
Cette folie, que je n'avais pas le droit de ne pas commettre, permit la
création du *Sacre*, mais coûta la vie à ma direction.*

A remarkable statement from even so enlightened a theatrical
manager as Gabriel Astruc.

He was often tight-fisted even over small expenses. I have seen
him haggling with a chauffeur in Monte Carlo over two francs,
and at times his dinner jacket was sadly frayed. Every penny went
into his dreams. He handled millions and died poor.

For so brilliant a man, Diaghilev was strangely superstitious.
When a black cat crossed his path, I have known him to go ten
minutes out of his way to take another route, and on one occasion,
at the Prince's Theatre, when a black cat jumped on the stage during a rehearsal of *Le Sacre du Printemps*, he was first frantic and
then resigned and miserable. Incidentally that season was one of his
rare failures. A hat on the table meant sorrow; a hat on the bed,
death. He was also frightened of being photographed. He needed
much persuading, and considered it most unlucky. There are few
photographs of him, scarcely any that are posed.

Strangely enough, this fighter, who could face a moral situation
with heroism, was a physical coward. He was terrified of the idea of
pain in himself or in others. Once at the Savoy, when a small boil in
his mouth required lancing, he shrieked so hysterically at the sight
of the instrument that the doctor had to abandon his attempt. It
was agony for him to cross the Channel, especially as a gypsy had
once predicted that he would meet death on the water. He loathed
the very sight of a vast expanse of water and would remain locked
in his cabin; at times he waited days for favourable weather, letting
the company go on ahead. It can be imagined how much he suffered
during a wartime crossing to the United States, when there was
actual danger. Day and night he wore his life jacket. Once during
ship's drill, not satisfied with standing by his station, he clambered
into the lifeboat and was snapped in that undignified position.
Later, when, in a fog, the sirens blew, after shivering in his cabin
he rushed on deck prepared for the worst, but the journey was over,
and they were well past the Statue of Liberty.

* 'Finally in 1913 for the inaugural season at the Théâtre des Champs
Élysées, he became really highhanded and made me pay a half million for
his performances. This act of folly, which I did not have the right not to
commit, allowed *Sacre* to be created but cost me my directorship.'

These anecdotes of weakness are not told to detract from a great man; they are an indisputable part of a true portrait, which must take all such things into account.

His relations with the company are interesting. With a few exceptions none of them knew him. He did not suffer fools gladly, politely, or at all, except where his affections were engaged, and if they were not unusually clever or talented then they were – just dancers. For their part they admired him : it almost amounted to worship; but at the same time they were thoroughly scared. The fear of secessions on an important scale played a large part in these relations. He was constantly on the lookout, and no one was allowed to assume too much power. It was not a question of megalomania, but of solid common sense. Where he recognized brains or unusual talent – and he was always generous in recognizing intelligence in others – there was no service he would not render. He once told Lydia Sokolova, 'Remember I am your friend; if ever for any reason you need me, I will come. You can always rely on my help. Consider me as a father.' These were not just words. When she was dangerously ill in Paris, he brought his own surgeon for her, and on the tour that followed, cabled every few hours. He was frantic and asked the company to pray for her. This is an aspect of him that is little known, but it is very much a part of him, the true friend.

He was always, except with his special favourites, where he was blind, able to separate the individual he liked from the artist who served him. It was quite impossible to ask him for roles, equally impossible to drop a role that had grown wearisome. He disliked intensely any fishing for praise. One artist after an unexpected triumph in a difficult part went up to him expectantly. 'Not at all bad,' he told her, 'but let us hope you will do it much better next time.'

He kept a careful eye on the company's morals from an aesthetic point of view. If any girl went out repeatedly in company that he found common or unsuitable for the Russian Ballet, without saying anything definite he took steps to dismiss her from the company. He was no hypocrite; he did not preach a morality foreign to himself, but the whole tone of these servants of art must be maintained. Nothing could be allowed to interfere with the quality of their work.

Fortunately when the end came it was in Venice, a final wish fulfilled. His almost childish greed and love of sweet things certainly hastened the end – he was a diabetic. I have seen him eat almost a whole box of chocolates, chuckling at this defiance of the doctor's orders – a strange contradiction in one so afraid. He died surrounded by those he loved and who loved him. He, who was so terrified of suffering, went out quietly, all fears calmed by nature's soothing anaesthetic of unconsciousness.

'I feel fuddled, drunk' were his last words.

So passed this superman.

POSTSCRIPT

The year following *Balletomania* I wrote a full-length biography of Serge Diaghilev, greatly assisted by his old friend and colleague Walter Nouvel. I interviewed over two hundred people who had known him at different periods of his life. The sketch in this chapter obviously needed considerable amplification, and now, more than forty years after his death, his stature has grown. In 1968 I wrote a monograph, *Ballet Russe*,* reassessing Diaghilev and the movement he had initiated. I was amazed to find that this was something very much alive and that, though dancing flourished as never before, ballet itself – in relegating Diaghilev to either history or nostalgia – was missing something, was marking time.

I was wrong in my first judgement when I wrote, 'The era 1909-29 became known as the Diaghilev era because he crystallized what was going on, and not because he actually created it.'

The fact that no one since has occupied his role, that there is no word to describe it, and that both 'impresario' and 'artistic director' are completely wide of the mark, show that he was as much the creator of his period as Théophile Gautier had been a century before, more so in many respects since romanticism had seen many precursors: Scott, Heine, and Hugo. De Flers and Caillavet wrote in their famous play *La Bois Sacré* (1910): 'Nous commençons à devenir des gens très bien, à avoir des relations très chic, très pourries, très *ballet-russe*.'† Moreover, Gautier never took ballet very seriously as an art form. Diaghilev in a lighthearted interview once compared himself to a bartender. The ingredients were there,

* Weidenfeld & Nicolson.

† 'We are beginning to become smart people, to have very fashionable friends, very decadent, very *ballet-russe*.'

but he alone had the recipe for the right mixture to create the cock-tail – sweet, bittersweet, or tart. For a considerable time after his death his recipes, more or less diluted, dominated the ballet of Colonel de Basil, the Marquis de Cuevas, Serge Lifar, and, most brilliantly of all, the early Roland Petit at first under the tutelage of Diaghilev's lieutenant, Boris Kochno. Had Diaghilev lived it is doubtful whether economics apart he could have continued with his exciting mixtures, at any rate without a considerable pause. People are no longer shocked now that everything from piano-breaking to covering a mountain with plastic is called art. Dia-ghilev's shocks were never 'happenings', they were carefully planned and rehearsed in meticulous detail. No *art just happens* – that is one of today's greatest fallacies.

The public had become sated with novelty, and Diaghilev him-self had begun to look back with nostalgia at the classicism of the Maryinsky. He was in the process of forming a brilliant classical company with Spessivtseva, Dolin, Lifar, and the young Markova, who after her outstanding success in *La Chatte* and as the supreme Bluebird princess was growing into a gracious maturity.

The public was now ready for *The Sleeping Beauty* that had almost ruined Diaghilev in 1921. The English ballet was formed, and it grew from strength to strength on this Maryinsky classicism. The Royal Ballet was later to revive some of the Diaghilev experi-ments; they had become classics. Among these revivals was *Les Noces*, the ballet that now gave Bronislava Nijinska, Nijinsky's sister, the triumph that had been withheld from her when it was first produced. (In England, H. G. Wells was one of the few to jump to its defence, as Rodin had done years before with another Stravinsky ballet, *Le Sacre du Printemps*.) I was not too much of a 'blimp' to recognize its value.

Diaghilev's growing posthumous fame has been shown in a number of ways: with Richard Buckle's superb Diaghilev exhibi-tion at the Edinburgh Festival in 1954 and later at Forbes House; with the comprehensive exhibition in Strasbourg and the pheno-menal prices brought at the auctions of valuable maquettes and much-worn costumes at Sotheby's.

I found it particularly interesting to watch the growth of Dia-ghilev's fame in the Soviet Union. The first time I visited Moscow I gave a lecture on Russian émigré ballet. Very little was known of Diaghilev and the role he had played other than that he had been an impresario. Later he began to be written about and discussed, versions of his ballets have been introduced into the repertoire, not always with conspicuous success, and his value as the leading spirit behind the *Mir Isskoustva* [*The World of Art*] movement recognized.

Five émigré Russians and one English member of his company, each in his or her own way, have put their stamp on the whole ballet scene: Diaghilev opened it for intellectuals. Pavlova gained for it a vast new public, inspired a whole generation of dancers, and made it a respectable profession for the English young lady. De Basil, with the aid of Hurok, popularized it in Britain and the United States. De Valois established it in England. Lifar reinstated it in France. And, above all, Balanchine planted it firmly in America.

I have maintained a friendship with Nijinsky's wife, Romola, over the years and have admired the manner in which she cared for her sick husband. I saw them together from time to time, on the last occasion at the B.B.C. television studios four days before his death, when he was taken to watch Serge Lifar. Romola treated him with loving respect, always searching for a glimmer of interest and continually being frustrated. The last time I saw her was in Moscow in 1972. She attended all the performances and was interested in every new development, particularly in the male dancers. She was full of sympathy, but alert and critical, living in the past as well as the present. I can only hope that, in spite of press announcements, the Nijinsky film she planned never materializes now that she has died. Without the dancing of Nijinsky it is pointless. The famous de Meyer photographs tell us more than any invention ever could how Nijinsky danced. In any case, if the film is produced, Herbert Ross knows his ballet and it will be saved from the hands of Ken Russell.

Since this was written, Richard Buckle has produced a masterly biography of Diaghilev, surely the definitive work.

7. Four Choreographers:
Nijinsky, Fokine, Massine, Balanchine

MY interest in dancers had always been so strong that, apart from the direct lesson of *The Sleeping Princess* – that ballet, to be good, should show the dancer to the very greatest advantage – I had given little thought to balletic structure. Dancing is certainly the correct angle of approach, but it is only one of many elements, perhaps the most important, and certainly, out of Russia, the most neglected critically. So perfectly did the Fokine ballets, my first, satisfy me that I took choreography very much for granted. It was only later, when I became aware of a certain lack of harmony, that I began to investigate the relationship between choreographer, dancer, composer, and decorative artist. The general public too takes choreography very much for granted, scarcely distinguishing it from the putting together of some small dance or routine. One old lady, wearing a delightfully antiquated hat such as only Bournemouth could still produce, was both amazed and disappointed at the fact that two performances were identical. 'I thought that those clever dancers made them up as they went along' – an extreme view, evidently, but not so far behind the accepted one.

In the whole history of ballet, from Louis XIV to Fokine, there are fewer choreographers of quality than men of value in any other branch of art; not surprisingly, perhaps, as choreography combines the elements of sculpture, painting, music, and the drama. Any experienced dancer can arrange a small but effective solo or a pas de deux for herself by dipping into the large repertoire of ready-made movement; it is the *orchestration* of dancing that is the choreographer's function. Like the sculptor, he is concerned with the organization of the single figure and the group, and like the sculptor, too, he is limited by the particular medium in which he works. Like the painter, he is concerned with problems of foreground, background, and spatial composition. There the parallel ceases and his own particular problem commences. So far he is merely the producer of *tableaux vivants*. His particular problem is concerned with movements and the transition from pose to pose. Many comparative

amateurs can lift successful groups and poses from vases and sarcophagi; it is in the transition that the true talent is revealed.

Next comes his relationship to the drama – how to tell his story
in pantomime in the simplest manner possible, without the need
of extraneous literary explanation. Without resorting to paradox,
there is a very definite ballet-realism. The whole of the theatre is a
convention, and, once the particular convention that life is danced
to music has been accepted, all that happens must be made consistent and plausible. There can be the fantastic ballet or the
grotesque ballet, but each must be a harmonious whole. I remember
Karsavina criticizing *Le Fils Prodigue* on the score of realism. 'It is
a sign of decadence when ballet no longer believes in its own conventions. A low barrier that is used as a gate and carefully opened
and shut is ignored after a few minutes. That is a breach of realism.'
In this particular case the weakness was recognized both by Diaghilev and Balanchine. A good work was spoiled by accessories.
The choreographer is working in the medium of the human body;
thus the extreme distortion permissible in paint is not within his
reach. Exaggeration of a particular pose may show a certain invention, but unless it is used for a definite purpose it is laughable, *unrealistic*, and out of place.

There remains the relationship to music. Each ballet must be in
close contact with both the form and the spirit of the musical score,
so that this medium of the human body is still further restricted in
its use. This implies in the choreographer not merely a sound academic knowledge of music – a good ear is not a sufficient substitute
– but taste, discrimination, and sensitivity. Stravinsky's *L'Oiseau
de Feu* was actually worked out phrase by phrase with Fokine, who
had heard the composer's *Fireworks* and had 'seen flames in the
music'. 'Stravinsky brought him a beautiful cantilena on the entrance of the Tsarevitch into the garden of the girls with the beautiful apples, but Fokine disapproved. "No, no," he said, "you bring
him in like a tenor. Break the phrase, where he merely shows his
head, on his first intrusion. Then make the curious swish of the
magic horse's return, and then, when he shows his head again,
bring in the full swing of the melody." '

These questions bear pondering the next time you see 'Choreography by Ivan' on a programme. They explain the paucity of fine
choreographers; they may also explain why you are pleased or
irritated.

The following three conversations with choreographers will show more thoroughly than I could, from just having seen them at work, their views and their individual methods. Fokine's 'five points', first published in England in *The Times* of 6 July 1914, contain the whole history of the birth of modern ballet. They are the Magna Carta of the choreographer, the whole basis of the art as we see it practised today. They may possibly seem obvious just because we are so used to seeing their results. They are however a very great discovery. Without them ballet would have been dead as an artistic force and could never have become the medium for the finest works of Bakst, Stravinsky, and others. The enduring quality of Fokine's own ballets shows the worth of his dicta.

It is interesting to see that both Massine and Balanchine, after long explorations in the over-sophisticated, are each returning to simplicity and a new-found classicism of their own, a complete triumph for the cause that I championed while it was still unpopular and ballet was out of the control of dancers.

It will be noticed that in each of these dialogues the choreographer definitely denies to Diaghilev creative gifts. However, Larionov, the painter the longest associated with him, affirms them, but cites the example of Nijinsky – of all artists certainly the most Diaghilev's creation – as a process of throwing people together and waiting for the explosion. It is obvious that those who are the chief elements in such an explosion cannot be conscious of the fact. In the case of Fokine, his statements are obviously correct, however biased they may sound. Diaghilev unquestionably treated him with injustice, as I can vouch for from many conversations. Diaghilev's statement, for instance, about the extreme influence of Isadora Duncan is absurd, and of the same quality as his remark on Anna Pavlova. From the very moment that Nijinsky began to show the creative urge, there could be no room for the master choreographer, and his leaving, an instinctive act, had to be justified subsequently in Diaghilev's own mind.

'Of course he made many mistakes,' says Larionov, 'but they were the result of love and can be forgiven today.' In any case, his changes of choreographers greatly benefited the whole art, whatever the motives at the time.

Vaslav Nijinsky. Of Nijinsky's methods of work I can only write by hearsay, but they show such a difference from the usual – a groping in the dark, followed by a sudden inspiration – that it is important to describe them, especially as they had a far greater influence on the future than their number or their intrinsic merit might suggest. Larionov, who was in the Diaghilev cabinet at the time, tells me:

'We would all be seated round the table with a very animated conversation in progress. Someone would perhaps make such a casual remark as, "What an interesting idea if the classical positions were reversed and movements made *en dedans* instead of *en dehors*." The idea would then be discussed and expanded, but all in theory. "That is interesting, Vatza; think about it," said Diaghilev. Nijinsky took no active part in these discussions, and even gave the impression that his thoughts were far away. But all the time he was listening, assimilating things. He would go and lock himself up in a dark room for hours, and let all that he had heard take effect, perhaps in actual images.

'Then began the endless rehearsals, sometimes by the hundred, but not rehearsals in the ordinary sense of the word, to add a touch here and there to a work already conceived, but actual laboratory experiments in movement, attempts at creation. Sometimes after an hour's work only a single movement would be fixed. Like a sculptor or a painter with a lay figure, he took hold of the dancer, moving his limbs in different directions, stepping back to judge the effect. "No use, no use. Wait, hold it; not bad like that. That's right now." Sometimes nothing at all would please him, then suddenly came a pose that seemed interesting; he would retain it and begin to build around it, always experimenting and groping for something that was not quite articulate. It was not a deliberate, highly conscious method at first, but it was in this way he enriched choreography, by adding to the repertoire a new variety of movement, naturally varying greatly in quality. This was one of the ways in which Diaghilev worked, throwing young and impressionable material into the company of the leading thinkers of the day, while remaining ever watchful in the background.'

Michael Fokine: Paris, February 1934. These conversations took place during the time that Fokine was hard at work preparing four new ballets for Ida Rubinstein. I watched some of the early stages. Fokine entered armed with a large portfolio of musical scores and notes. First he sorted his dancers into groups, explaining carefully the setting of the scene, and what each one represented. He told them also the chief characteristics of the period. Then he went ahead of each group, dancing, letting them follow, dancing again. He made them try a few bars a number of times, rejecting and building up again, but always as if he were perfecting a work already in existence. There was nothing tense in the atmosphere, no trace of impatience. The company was good, and he had plenty of time to laugh and joke, while carefully indicating every shade of his intention, explaining by example, skilful parody, and over-emphasis the meaning underlying every movement, splitting it up and analysing it in a manner I have never seen done before, but always allowing a certain individual latitude of expression. He also related the movements of ballet to the natural movements of every-day life. He did not impose himself at all, but worked up a genuine mass enthusiasm. (The good choreographer always welcomes signs of individuality, realizing that a strong personality will carry his work much further than a highly trained automaton. The Svengali attitude does not exist outside the imagination.) He is the easiest *maître de ballet* to follow of any I have ever seen at work.

Today he is nearly bald, Napoleonic in appearance, more striking even than in the early days. He still dances with great fire and the most perfect control.

He greeted me with:

'You are just in time to see me setting a *gaillarde*. It is a beautiful dance. Do you know anything about it? I myself knew little about it till just lately. I have been working from old books. It is the first time I have ever worked like that. I usually "feel" the period from my artistic knowledge of it, and then justify myself afterwards. Sit down; when the rehearsal is over we must have dinner and a long talk.'

Fokine is easy to talk to and immediately finds the right word. This dialogue form, devoid of the frills, makes him appear more dogmatic than he really is. He is fully conscious of his words and his achievement and is naturally eager that certain misunderstandings should be set right. He never takes disagreement with any of his opinions as an affront.

(During dinner.)

FOKINE: Before I reply to your question as to how I actually create, I must tell you of the method that underlies all my work. Early in my career I was so disgusted with the stilted 'unrealistic' side of ballet that I nearly left it altogether, when my memorandum* was shelved by the authorities, to become a painter. I have always been deeply interested in painting, and I took to it again when I was forty-three. I dropped it when I was appointed a teacher in the theatre school. At once I felt happier, and began to put into practice my new ideas about a ballet-realism. From the first, people greeted me with, 'Why do we need this young Fokine, when we have the glorious Petipa?' Petipa himself was more generous, for after the production of my first ballet, *Acis and Galatea*, he sent me a card with the inscription, 'Cher camarade. Enchanté de votre composition. Continuez et vous serez un très grand maître de ballet.' I felt from the very first that no matter how obscure, fantastic, and unrealistic the art form of dancing may seem, to be of any value it must have its truth in life. That was my first urge.

A.L.H.: How deep was the influence of Duncan on you? There is a passage in a letter from Diaghilev, published in Propert's *The Russian Ballet, 1921–1929*, that reads, 'I knew Isadora well at Saint Petersburg and was present with Fokine at her first debut. Fokine was mad about her dancing and the influences of Duncan on him lay at the base of all his creative work.'

FOKINE: That is absurd. Diaghilev could never have believed in such a statement nor made it with the slightest degree of sincerity. He watched my rehearsals and saw me compose. He knew perfectly well the differences between my new Russian Ballet and Duncan's dancing. I remember going to see her with him. I had already been engaged as *maître de ballet* and had by that time carried out considerable reforms on the Russian stage. The reason for my very great enthusiasm was just because I felt that here were so many of the elements that I was practising and preaching. I found naturalness, expressiveness, and real simplicity. There was a similarity in our aims but an enormous and obvious difference in our methods. My Russian and Oriental compositions and my romantic ballets, *Les Sylphides*, *Carnaval*, and *Le Spectre de la Rose*, have nothing in common with her. The resemblance is only in *Daphnis et Chloé*, *Narcisse*, and the bacchanals from *Tannhäuser* and *Cléopâtre*, and that is because our sources were the same; the vases and sarcophagi in the museums. The similarity there only lies in the

---

*This memorandum outlined Fokine's views on the nature of ballet; for example, equality of the arts that composed ballet, expressiveness of the dancer's whole body, interpretation of nature, etc.

static, the design of the poses; the differences are far greater. Her dance is free, mine stylized, and my movements are mechanically highly complex. I was working on dancers with a fixed technique and an old tradition, she for an individual, herself. I am very happy, though, that in the treatment of ancient Greek themes, her speciality, I have something in common with her, just as I am delighted to differ from her in other moods and styles. She stood for freedom of the body from clothes, while I believe in the obedience of the movement to costume and its proper adaptation to period. She had only one plastic conception for all periods and nationalities, while I am essentially interested in the difference of the movements of each individual. She had, for instance, the same form of movement for Wagner, Gluck, Chopin, the Spanish dances of Moskovsky, and the waltzes of Strauss. The national character is absent; only Greece existed for her, as if it could be adapted to all periods. Diaghilev was far too keen an observer not to know all this, especially as his opportunities were better than anyone else's. His statement was made with some purpose.

As you know, early in my career I laid down five main principles for the production of ballet, which are, in brief :

To invent in each case a new form of movement corresponding to the subject and character of the music, instead of merely giving combinations of ready-made steps.

Dancing and gesture have no meaning in ballet unless they serve as an expression of dramatic action.

To admit the use of conventional gesture only when it is required by the style of the ballet, and in all other cases to replace the gestures of the hands by movements of the whole body. Man can and should be expressive from head to foot.

The group is not merely an ornament. The new ballet advances from the expressiveness of the face or the hands to that of the whole body, and from that of the individual body to groups of bodies and the expressiveness of the combined dancing of a crowd.

The alliance of dancing on equal terms with the other arts. The new ballet does not demand 'ballet music' from the composer, nor tutus and pink satin slippers from the artist; it gives complete liberty to their creative powers.

A.L.H. : These artistic principles are so much a part of your whole general outlook that they are no longer consciously to the fore each time. How in detail do you compose?

FOKINE: There are no fixed rules; in various ways, as the mood occurs. Only yesterday, for instance, I sat up in bed all night, surrounded by sheets of music. Once the score has become a part of me images are formed, which I occasionally fix in little drawings. That is the general plan, but the fantasy comes during rehearsals. *Carnaval*, for instance, was literally an improvisation during one rehearsal for a charity performance; two further rehearsals, with some thought in the interval, and it was complete. Today, it takes many more rehearsals than that to put it on again. *Igor* [the 'Polovtsian Dances' from *Prince Igor*], which is to me my most perfect work – there is nothing that I would want changed in it – almost came very easily in about eight rehearsals. It is the most complex of all my ballets to revive without my direct supervision, just as *Les Sylphides* is the easiest. Some of the groups in *Les Sylphides* as it now stands were actually arranged on the stage a few moments before the curtain rose. *The Dying Swan*, too, was done hurriedly for Anna Pavlova at a charity performance, a concert of the artists of the chorus of the Imperial Opera in Saint Petersburg in 1905. Small work as it is, and known and applauded all over the world, it was 'revolutionary' then, and illustrates admirably the transition between the old and the new. In this I make use of the technique of the old dance and the traditional costume; a highly developed technique is necessary, but the purpose of the dance is not to display technique but to create the symbol of the everlasting struggle in this life of all that is mortal. It is a dance of the whole body and not of the limbs only; it appeals not merely to the eye but to the emotions and the imagination.

A.L.H.: How far do your dancers collaborate with you in a production?

FOKINE: Not at all. I never conceive works for particular artists, but the particular artist does lead me to make modifications. I did not create *Le Spectre de la Rose* for Nijinsky, but because of his particular style it became less masculine and quite different from what I myself made of it. *Petrouchka* also I did not compose deliberately for Nijinsky. He left his mark on it, but there are various possible interpretations. That is why these works can be so constantly revived.

A.L.H.: What do you think of recent choreography, beginning with your immediate predecessor Nijinsky? *L'Après-midi d'un Faune*, for instance?

FOKINE: *L'Après-midi d'un Faune* was purely *un succès de scandale*, later becoming *un succès de snobisme*. It is fundamentally a work of no importance. Nijinsky's own role, with its oblique movement, is lifted straight out of the bacchanal from *Tannhäuser*, which I arranged for Nijinsky and Karsavina* – the same archaic poses, only he substituted for the final embrace the act of onanism, which I find most displeasing. Also the music, décor, and choreography are definitely out of sympathy, even hostile to one another. There are moments when the public laughs instinctively, and they are perfectly right; they have felt the error. Notably when the nymphs run in flight, heel to toe. As you know, the correct walking movement is heel to toe, while with running it is precisely the opposite. Nijinsky has therefore adopted a meaningless and unrealistic distortion, which the public has sensed.

Frankly I find that recent choreography has all the faults of the pre-Fokine ballet, only with added pretensions. Style has been completely forgotten; 'pointes' and arms express different things. Such Greek themes as *Apollon Musagète* and *Mercure* should not be danced in ballet shoes, any more than a ballet on a purely Russian theme like *Les Noces*. Also, just as in the old days, too great a reliance is placed on programme notes. Most of the ballets I have seen are not expressive in themselves. They are far too closely involved with literature and consequently appeal only to a small specialized coterie.

A.L.H.: In order then to purify choreography can you conceive of it as an entirely independent art, of dancing alone without music or costume?

FOKINE: No. Absence of music is only justified at some particular point, so as to emphasize and bring out a definite dramatic meaning, Dancing has, from its very beginning, always implied noise, stamping, clapping, singing, drums or percussion of some kind. Today it is no longer interesting to return to such primitive sounds. I prefer therefore to use the more highly developed sounds of music. Yes, music is essential, while décor is of lesser importance, an embellishment that can add much but that cannot disguise unsound work.

Museum study is an essential. I have just been spending several

---

*I have verified this with many dancers and balletomanes who saw both works. It is beyond dispute.

weeks in the Assyrian section of the Louvre for *Semiramis*. That
does not mean a slavish imitation, but one must get soaked in the
art of a period to render the correct style.

A.L.H.: How far was Diaghilev a creative artist?

FOKINE: As far as I can see, not at all. I admire him immensely,
and there is no one in a better position than I to judge the full extent of his achievement. Why lessen it by ridiculous claims? He
was a genius as a propagandist for art and as a businessman. He
was something more besides. But many books have recently given
an entirely false impression, and I hope that you will not per-
petuate these mistakes. No one has ever claimed that he wrote the
music or painted the décor. I cannot remember one single choreographic idea of his. Cocteau, Vaudoyer, Benois, all gave ideas, but
never Diaghilev. I had been a creator before he ever came on the
scene. The whole idea of the one-act ballet, and the other reforms
that made the enterprise possible, were already accomplished. Before I joined him I had already composed *Carnaval*, *Les Sylphides*,
Cléopâtre, and *Le Pavillon d'Armide*, the ballets that established
the first big triumphs. That is in itself a sufficient answer. It is
Alexandre Benois who first wrote to me suggesting that Diaghilev
should take my ballets to Western Europe, and I am deeply grateful to him for all the opportunities he gave me, but the early ballet
was the Fokine Ballet. Diaghilev's creativity, then at any rate, consisted in changing a few names. *Nuit d'Égypt* became *Cléopâtre*;
Chopiniana, *Les Sylphides*. That is the clever businessman. Then
there is the story of *L'Oiseau de Feu*. Music had been commissioned
from Liadov for a ballet to be composed by me around that old
Russian legend. After very many months, when it was long overdue, Diaghilev met Liadov. 'Well, is my ballet ready?' 'It won't be
long now; it is well on the way,' was the reply; 'I have just bought
the ruled paper.' As you know, Stravinsky subsequently wrote the
music and had his first triumph, but meanwhile a new ballet of
that name was awaited. Diaghilev found the solution simple. He
took the old *L'Oiseau Bleu*, not yet known in Paris, and it was
temporarily renamed *L'Oiseau de Feu*.

I have in all created sixty-five ballets, and the majority have been
done either before or after my association with Diaghilev. Without
him my work would not have been universally known, but it exists
just the same. *Orphée* to the music of Gluck is one of the finest
things I have ever done.

A.L.H.: Amongst all the dancers you have seen, is there any one obviously outstanding?

FOKINE: No. It is never possible to say in an unqualified manner that a dancer is incomparable. Nijinsky was incomparable in *Le Spectre de la Rose* and very bad indeed in *Prince Igor*. Pavlova, Karsavina, Fokina were each incomparable in certain roles and types of dancing.

A.L.H.: Is the great dancer a thing of the past?

FOKINE: By no means. There are today so many admirable schools, those of the great ballerinas in Paris and others. There are many young dancers developing rapidly into something big. Today I can assemble a troupe of dancers as fine in quality as at any period. There are some magnificent dancers in America today, waiting for the chance to do important work; there are also our young 'loves' of the Monte Carlo Ballet. Have you seen my pupil Patricia Bowman? There is an absolutely faultless technique.

A.L.H.: What would you save out of the old repertoire?

FOKINE: *Giselle, Le Lac des Cygnes, The Sleeping Princess, La Fille Mal Gardée*, and *Coppélia*. What a delicious ballet, this last. I once put it on in Chicago in the old manner. The only time I have ever worked in that way.

A.L.H.: And now for your views on the New Central European dance of Wigman, Laban, and their followers. It is a sore point with me.

FOKINE: Must we talk about that, and spoil a good meal? You know my views so well. I have often spoken and written to you about it, on the last occasion when poor Simeonov died. As it is important I will just go over some of the points. I was glad to hear from you that England has rejected it, for it is a development of dilettantism unparalleled in the history of the dance, a definite step backward. This so-called innovation is based on a total absence of a real knowledge of the grammar and syntax of dancing, and, in order to revolt against anything, it is essential to know it in close detail, perhaps even more thoroughly than its devotees. Musically it is wretched. I find this association with percussion and undeveloped music highly significant.

It is very typical of the Wigman school to substitute elbow for arm movements. For instance, in the gay happy mood of a gypsy dance, the elbows are moved; for a sad dance they are raised, letting the hands hang down helplessly. But most of all they are used to express energy, the strained energy of trying to force one's way into a crowded subway during the rush hours. I went once to an explanatory lecture by Mary Wigman. Nearly the whole time she gesticulated with clenched fists, and the clenched fist and the elbow seem to be the symbols of this movement. Then someone in the audience asked for the reason for the exaggerated turned-out position of her feet in dancing. She explained that it was for the elasticity of her jumps, to gain elevation. This is, of course, quite inaccurate. Immediately after I had denounced in the Maryinsky Ballet the old-fashioned superstition of turned-out feet (dancing *en dehors*), Nijinsky surprised the entire world by his tremendous elevation without ever turning out his legs either à la Wigman or in the old Italian manner. Incidentally Wigman herself has no elevation.

A.L.H.: But is there anything new in it at all?

FOKINE: Absolutely nothing. I have seen each movement in ballet before, and can always tell you what they are attempting to reproduce. It is all hopelessly old-fashioned. Ballet has already outlived such 'modernism'. The Diaghilev Ballet in its last stages, and the Ballets Suédois of Rolf de Maré became so radical that no German dancers can ever catch up with them. I am in disagreement with much in modern choreography, but that is another matter. It is a disagreement in the same family; fundamentally we think alike and have the same groundwork.

The possibility of creating something really new is unlimited, as unlimited as the experiences of life itself, but only when the dancer has a strong technical foundation. The Germans, through lack of experience, invariably confuse the technical exercises with the real thing. One of them once said, 'The ballet is horrible, look at this fifth position' – which she then made incorrectly. 'How can you do a Greek dance like that?' But there exist a number of ballets in which the pointes and the five positions are not used at all; ballets which are based entirely on natural movement. I illustrated this by saying to her, 'In order to lift their arms, your girls lift first their shoulders, then their elbows, and only after that the entire arm. That is not natural; when I go to take my hat off the peg, I lift my entire arm to reach for it.' 'Perhaps; but, just the same, your movement really comes from here,' she explains, pointing to my solar plexus. 'All movement does; you breathe.' 'Yes, that's true. I always breathe,' I admitted, and we got no further.

The teaching of dancing consists to a large degree in the constant elimination of unnecessary strain.

With them everything is cut and dried, quite remote from reality. The chest caved inward expresses hate or envy, yet when we approach the bed of a sick friend the chest is caved inward to express, not our hate, but our sympathy.

The true and final answer is, of course, that we can do everything that they do, while they in their turn can do nothing of our work. I have noticed that as a teacher. In the classroom it is ten times more convincing than on paper. Pompous words such as 'free impulses', and the whole phraseology that goes with it, cannot give them a mastery over their bodies, which are always tense and strained. Do you notice how their followers always call it 'a sad art' and talk of 'dark souls'? People explain it as a postwar neurosis, the spirit of a defeated nation, but the reason is, doubtless, that the portrayal of sadness calls for very little movement. The more joyful we feel the more we desire to move about. The dance is primarily an expression of joy, though sadness of course may be a subject for the dance, as all the other emotions. Yet it is not for nothing that so many have copied Pavlova's *Dying Swan*, and no one her many fast and joyous dances.

This is not Duncan at all. The great Isadora Duncan has reproduced in her own dancing the entire range of human emotions, but when I think of dancers à la Duncan, I always picture a girl in draperies with her hand on her head in the manner of the funeral processions on a Greek urn.

And so we take leave of the rebel composer of *The Dying Swan*, in a fighting mood that today he rarely shows. Perhaps I have spoiled his dinner. He is still an insurgent, fighting against all standardized formulae save the basic principles that first inspired him. Time cannot make his immortal dramas, *Petrouchka*, *Spectre*, and the like, appear old-fashioned. They have already survived the most rapidly changing of all periods. In New York, 1934, Paris, and London, they are still the certain successes of a programme.

As he takes his coat and goes out into the street, the gestures of the waiters and the passers-by will have taught him something new about movement – something he will store up and translate into the dance, which he has bound so closely to life itself.

*A Conversation with Leonide Massine: On Board M.S. Lafayette –
New York bound, December 1933*. It is always difficult to catch
Massine in a free moment. His work now is incessant, with young
dancers to train, new ballets in mind, old ones in constant rehearsal,
and the necessity of continual practice as a dancer. His last Italian
'holiday' was spent in the creation of *Choreartium*. I had tried in
vain to catch him in London, Bournemouth, Birmingham, Plymouth. My chance finally came on the *Lafayette*, with the boat
too unsteady and many of the company too ill to make serious work
possible. Even then he worked daily in his cabin with his wife,
Delarova, and any survivors, and spent hours listening to Antal
Dorati, the Hungarian conductor, a veritable one-man orchestra,
playing and singing scores that might provide an inspiration for
ballet.

Massine today is at the very height of his powers, both as a
creator and as a dancer. There are obviously greater technical performers, but no one who is even nearly his equal as an artist. It is
in his case that I have felt the same concrete audience contact as
with Pavlova. I once watched *Le Beau Danube* from the wings. At
the moment where Massine stands motionless, centre stage, remembering as he hears the strains of the famous waltz, and then very
slowly raises his arm above his head as the crowd of idlers and
midinettes passes him by in scorn, I looked into the auditorium
by chance. Like some big wave the audience had risen in their seats,
craning forward, as if his hand had pulled some unseen string.
There is no one else who could achieve such a result by standing
almost completely still. It is quite another thing to whip an
audience into excitement by a complicated technical feat.

The mature Massine is the biggest personality I have seen in
ballet, and certainly the most intelligent. Diaghilev once stated that
Massine was the only dancer who was his intellectual equal. Coming from Diaghilev, at a time when Massine was no longer in the
company and was actually promoting a rival ballet, it was the
highest praise possible. Massine's knowledge in every branch of art
is encyclopedic. It is never used for conversational effect. Every re-
production or scrap of information that may be of use he pastes
into a large volume, and several such books accompany him everywhere. He is exceptionally calm, with a quiet, dry humour, and is
a very strong disciplinarian.

I have seen Massine compose and rehearse on many occasions,

sometimes seated quietly on a chair, at others in the front row of the dress circle, armed with a megaphone, shouting in three languages, and actually dancing in the limited space to illustrate some point.

There may be a strong connection between his present dancing form and his bursts of creativity. Most choreographers have created during their own dancing zenith; all have been outstanding performers. In one discussion Marie Rambert advanced the theory that the stimulus to create was the result of an unconscious reaction against the daily grind at purely classical exercise. I have put the question to him, but the fact that it is an unconscious reaction makes it impossible to answer. It would at any rate account for Nijinsky, classical dancer *par excellence*, creating in a manner diametrically opposed to his training. Fokine and Massine are far more deliberate in their manner of work.

I have watched Massine at work for a very long time now, and it has taken me several years and an American tour to get to know him and to penetrate his natural reserve. More and more his particular vision has coloured my own views on dancers and has widened them considerably. I have seen him discover and develop talent that was suspected by no one. He is in his right place in charge of a young company that needs such expert guidance between freedom and tradition.

A.L.H. : How do you create a new work?

MASSINE : The first time I hear the music my mind is a complete blank. I am then conscious of the volume, and the pattern takes shape. I write down what I visualize to fix the actual form, but at the first real contact between music and movement it may well alter.

A.L.H. : Are the interpreters of your roles in any sense collaborators?

MASSINE : No. They alter absolutely nothing in the general scheme of the composition, and the work is never composed with particular persons in view. They may of course alter a step or a detail, but that is unimportant. I first compose, and then look out for the ideal person to interpret. One must not adapt oneself to persons, but fit persons into one's scheme.

There is a very definite system of choreography that should enable anyone understanding it to create sound, if uninspired, works.

English choreography fails because it is not based on any system. One day, when I have the time and have ceased creating, I may perhaps teach it. There are definite laws defining the sequence of movement. Why so many choreographers imitate my works is because they see the finished thing without grasping the mechanics behind it.*

A.L.H. : Is museum study a part of that system?

MASSINE : Of course, intensive museum study. Any choreographer is a fool if he doesn't understand that. Choreography cannot exist without it. Ballet is only three hundred years old, while in the museums of the world there are centuries of plastic genius to draw upon.

A.L.H. : And reading, literary inspiration?

MASSINE : Literature is useful to us only insofar as it induces a plastic reaction, and so helps in a choreographic structure.

A.L.H. : What are the most important works by which your artistic development can be measured?

MASSINE : *Les Femmes de Bonne Humeur, Le Tricorne,* in which I enriched the repertoire of movement in ballet by translating the Spanish folk dance, *Le Sacre du Printemps,* dealing with entirely fresh rhythmic problems, and *Les Présages,* my first symphony, the start of a new development which should bring me back to pure choreography.

Choreography has long followed in the footsteps of music and painting. Now once again it can take the lead and demand a new form of those arts. I aim at something simple, healthy, and purely plastic to take the place of the decadent, over-complex, highly sophisticated work of the late Diaghilev period. The ballet you like so much, *Le Beau Danube,* came as a reaction from the intense seriousness of *Parade* and *Le Sacre du Printemps.* It was an absolute necessity for me to create it. Curiously enough, that was in 1923, during the very strongest period of jazz, before there was any thought of a return to the Vienna waltz.

A.L.H. : And the new dancers?

MASSINE : They are technically very advanced, but still lacking in finish and stagecraft. A dancer who can perform the most astonishing things will not know what to do with his hands in

---

* Massine has now established a choreographic course at the Royal Ballet School.

repose. But they overcome these difficulties very quickly, because they are all the time learning in practice on the stage.

A.L.H.: And that much debated point, the recent German school?

MASSINE: Wigman has shown us some interesting new movements, but her dance is too personal and she fails with a group. The whole connection between dancing and music is weak, especially in the abuse of percussion. They also make use of a type of dancing technique with absolutely no basic knowledge of movement, so that their discoveries are haphazard. It is not necessary or possible to create an entirely new techique. With the old one as a basis there are endless ways of enriching choreography, a vast field of movement that has yet to be translated. It is not necessary to stick to the dance style of Petipa. His was pure choreography, but created with a highly restricted vocabulary.

A.L.H.: How far was Diaghilev creative?

MASSINE: As regards artistic expression, not at all. We were all of us caught up in the violence of the artistic creation in Paris of the period. No escape was possible, and the ballet expressed what the poets, painters, and musicians had to say ahead of its realization by the public at large, but theirs were the ideas and Diaghilev followed.

Ballet, to survive, must be constantly freed from extraneous entanglements.

A Conversation with George Balanchine: New York, January 1934.
I like Balanchine. He is so absolutely honest with himself that conversation is easy. He thinks aloud, and there is plenty of give and take. Also, he is one of those very rare people who can discuss his own work critically and dispassionately and, what is more remarkable, will let his friends do the same without the slightest trace of injured pride. He is still experimenting, less positive of his direction than the more experienced Fokine or Massine. I am convinced that he is one of the few who will not feel slighted, whatever I write of him. In fact, on one occasion when I wrote unfavourably of some of his work, the impresario considered himself an injured party, while Balanchine himself was in thorough and amused agreement with me.

I found him in a bare room, surrounded by pots, paint, and workmen, the headquarters of an important new venture, the School of American Ballet, inspired by the admiration that my friend Lincoln Kirstein, a great balletomane, feels for his work. Here he will train the wonderful raw material that exists in America and will develop a company to show his new ideas. It is magnificent pioneering work, in keeping with his story and generation.

Georgi Balanchivadze was a pupil of the Imperial School at Saint Petersburg, which became the state school before he had completed his education. He was the pupil of Andreyanov, Simeonov, Leontiev, Michael Oboukhov, and also came under the influence of Fokine, whom he admires unreservedly. His first choreographic essay at the age of fifteen was plastic, erotic in subject. 'As I remember it today it would be perfectly suitable for presentation in a young ladies' seminary. I thought it very daring at the time.' His first mature theatrical work was as producer at the Alexandrovsky and Michailovsky theatres, which were under state control, but where some experimentation was allowed. There he produced Shaw's *Caesar and Cleopatra* and a play by Ernst Toller. As dancer-choreographer he appeared once at the Maryinsky in a small work, *Enigma*. It was during the Revolution, but he was hissed off the stage as being too revolutionary, and secured damning notices from the powerful critic Akim Volynsky, who had always taken a kindly interest in him. Next he organized a group of young people and gave a series of recitals under the uncompromising title of 'The Young Ballet. Evolution from Petipa-Fokine to Balanchivadze.' The authorities frowned and the young dancers were forbidden to appear with him, so he was compelled to leave revolutionary Russia in order to have the freedom to express ideas that were subversive to the old order of the dance. He went to Germany with a small group, the Russian State Dancers, consisting of Danilova, Gevergeva (Tamara Geva, whom he later married), and N. Efimov; he then proceeded to the Empire in London, where I first saw him. Diaghilev was attracted by *Enigma*, which had been hissed in Russia, and the group was absorbed into the Ballet. Balanchine, whose name was immediately truncated, created the new version of *Le Chant du Rossignol* for Markova, and so began his regime at the time of my first close association with the Ballet.

BALANCHINE: Yes, I collaborate with my dancers, create particular works for particular persons by drawing out what is in

them, but they are quite unconscious of it and alter nothing deliberately.

I can always invent movement, and sometimes it can be fitted
into the right place, but that is not choreography. It is the music
that dictates the whole shape of the work.*

I do not believe in the permanence of anything in ballet save the
purely classical. Classicism is enduring because it is impersonal.

A.L.H.: And your own works, *La Chatte* or *Barabau*?

BALANCHINE: I can assure you they are quite impossible now.
They were made for another time. I have seen them both since their
creation. They seemed very dull indeed. So many things have happened since.

Museum study? Of course I believe in it, but not in the necessity for academic knowledge. It is a deep-down love that is important; there must be a strong reaction to things seen. Even if they
are ugly things, it doesn't matter. Apathy is the only enemy.

I have always been interested in the possibilities of the film in
rendering ballet. There is a wonderful unexplored field there. I
worked out many ideas with Derain in Paris. Now I am in the land
of films, and there may be practical opportunities.

A.L.H.: But the loss of the third dimension always ruins all my
pleasure in dancing.

BALANCHINE: Of course. I don't mean the mere photography
of ballets we already know. That would give most unsatisfactory
results. There is the exploration of pattern and new angles, with
endless possibilities.

A.L.H.: But that sounds cold and dull. The greatest interest in
ballet for me lies not so much in the pattern as in the exploitation
of the personality both of a group and an individual. Mickey Mouse
seems to provide the ballet need in films; a strong personality artificially created out of a pattern. Musically, too, it would be difficult
to imagine a more perfect screen ballet.

BALANCHINE: I agree with all that, but you still miss my meaning. I can visualize ballet conceived for the screen that would possess everything, both pattern and personality. Imagine a great
dancer in a specially prepared film version of *Les Sylphides*; a close-
up of the face, an arm, a wrist, the pointes, all so arranged that the

---

*Balanchine is a magnificent pianist, who might easily have adopted that
career. His whole musical education is far in advance of anyone else in
ballet.

full significance of the work could be revealed. Imagine the sylphs flying through a wood, the swans landing on the lake, Giselle's haunted tomb. There are countless devices that could be used. In actual ballet, after all, only those sitting close at hand catch any of the detail and expression, and that at the loss of some of the pattern. You have just been telling me of how you watch a work again and again, from the wings, the orchestra-pit, the electrician's box, and the front of the house, concentrating on some detail at each performance. Everyone cannot do that, and the very fact that you have shown the need is an ample justification of cine-ballet and its shifting viewpoint.

A.L.H.: I am still unconvinced, not about its justification – I can see many reasons for that – but of the pleasure that I personally would get from it, and that is my main concern. The whole charm of the thing for the balletomane, who goes nightly, lies in the difference in the performers on various days and their reactions to the ever-varying audience. That is as much my reason as the shifting viewpoint for my many explorations backstage. I do not want to see a Toumanova who is for ever fourteen years, ten months, one week, two days, and so many hours old. The idea appals me. It is altogether too inhuman.

BALANCHINE: But I am not thinking in terms of the balletomane now. You are a part of our family. I am thinking of ballet in a much wider sense, of bringing it back to the masses as the ideal form of entertainment. The average ballet today is too complex and is incomplete without programme notes.

A.L.H.: But does the story always matter so much? And in any case they are usually simple enough. Anyone could understand your *La Chatte* for instance.

BALANCHINE: The story does matter if ballet is to be popularized, also *La Chatte* is definitely too complicated. As a start, it embodies the idea of the transmigration of souls. I aim at a story so logical and so simple that all can understand it and follow its development.

A.L.H.: Then that implies a return to conventional mime, hand on heart, lover's sighs.

BALANCHINE: Not at all. That is quite meaningless now and cannot express real things. It is so comical that it can only provoke the reaction of laughter. There are other ways of holding the interest, by vivid contrast, for instance. Imagine the effect that would be produced by six Negresses dancing on their pointes* and six white girls doing a frenzied jazz!

A.L.H.: How big a role did Diaghilev play in the creation of ballets?

BALANCHINE: Choreographically none at all. *La Chatte* he only saw at its final rehearsals. He was very easy to work for and infinitely understanding. He left me a free hand always. Where he excelled was as a man of affairs. What a wonderful minister of finance he would have made!

As we go out into the street Balanchine looks admiringly at the architecture of his new home and tells me of his pupils and the qualities that young America can bring to the dance. With the paint not yet dry in his classrooms, he is already hard at work creating a repertoire, the first work of which is to be a homage to his beloved classicism. Lincoln Kirstein is proud and happy. Ballet to him is a necessity, so that he has taken practical steps to have it with him always, instead of wandering over Europe an exile. Would that there were more Kirsteins.

Hommage à Fokine, Massine, Balanchine. At nearly every ballet performance I attend, the following scene is sure to take place. I am thoroughly weary of it, and must at all costs get it out of my system.

ELDERLY RUSSIAN GENTLEMAN: Wonderful, the Ballets Russes, truly wonderful. What music, what art, and what dancing. Beautiful women too. You love it, I know. You love our Russian art.

A.L.H.: Yes...

With my growing enthusiasm, he cools off visibly until he seems to become positively indignant. Now he is bristling all over.

E.R.G.: Yes, yes, of course. But what do you know of ballet? For that matter, what does anyone here know of ballet? ... Nothing, absolutely nothing. You should have seen the ballet as it was in Russia in the great days. What lavish décor, what music, what dancers! And the public too; uniforms, jewellery, and beauty. That was the real thing. This is not good, I assure you. It is bad even, very bad. What was the meaning of that last ballet? The

---

*This anticipated by nearly forty years the admirable Dance Theatre of Harlem.

programme said something about toys coming to life. Not at all my idea of toys. I don't know at all why I come, but I can't keep away. It makes me sad to see such decadence !

He then proceeds to revel gently in his sadness and I am sorry for him. I may so easily become that way myself some day, when new names will irritate instead of sending me off on long journeys of investigation. Besides, there are other grave reasons for his sorrow, associations that I must respect. He may or may not have been a balletomane in Russia. If he was, all things can now be forgiven him. If he dreams of Trefilova's arabesque, of Kchessinska's wondrous arms, we are brothers even. But he is entirely and utterly mistaken in everything he says. At the time I only nod sympathetically; any argument would spoil my pleasure for the evening, and *Le Beau Danube* is still to come. There is no reason however why I should act the coward and hypocrite here; besides, it has been simmering for too long.

A.L.H. : My dear sir, we in Western Europe have seen everything that is finest in Russian ballet, everything that is art in a universal sense and not something that is purely local on however grand a scale. And what we have seen has been more truly Russian than what you can remember, with its strong Italian influences. There were magnificent exceptions, but many of your favoured dancers might remind us too closely of acrobats. We too have our series of fouettés, you have seen some tonight, but they are used as the indispensable part of a choreographic and dramatic structure.

How do I know all this? It is not merely hearsay, but from circumstantial evidence as well as from innumerable conversations with former dancers, many of whom agree with me; from actually seeing ballets in the old style that some of them have arranged or approved; from listening to the 'music' of the ballets of the grand epoch, Minkus, pah ! From studying photographs and maquettes of the scenery, which was of a truly incredible magnificence, closely approaching the dreams of Roxy. Your own Alexandre Benois, artist whom you venerate for his work and his learning, deals the bitterest blow. 'We were only interested,' he says, 'in those ballets produced on the Continent after 1909.'

It is Fokine and his successors who have freed us and have given me the right to argue – at this respectful distance – with you. They have honoured your country, that is a consolation surely. In any case, how dare you complain. Tonight you have seen Baronova,

Riabouchinska, and Toumanova. Your country is still unchallenged. You should be happy.

But I fear this will begin all over again tomorrow.

POSTSCRIPT

These dialogues still retain their interest and have often been quoted.

I. There is little to add to Fokine's comments. He was already fully formed with his best work behind him. His rehearsals, which I frequently attended, were intensely fascinating – he mimed and danced each role in turn. His explanations were clear, and he accepted no modifications suggested by his dancers as far as steps were concerned, though he left them free to express their personalities. He enjoyed his own creations with relish, roaring with laughter at any comic touches. Vera, his wife, seated next to him, joined in with appreciative comments. There was always a chip on his shoulder, as can be seen from the interview. He was treated as a classicist when he knew himself to be a revolutionary who had charted the path to a new conception of ballet. He never forgave Diaghilev for passing him over for Nijinsky or for attributing his main inspiration to Isadora Duncan. Diaghilev could neither excuse nor accord any merit to those from whom he had parted company. Fokine's years in America had produced nothing. When I visited him there in his Riverside Drive apartment, surrounded by his own very competent but academic paintings, which now hang in the Leningrad classrooms, he was impressed by the de Basil dancers. He seemed like an elder statesman awaiting a call, which eventually came in his work for Blum, de Basil, and Ballet Theatre. He died in harness, leaving two major new works, *L'Épreuve d'Amour* and *Don Juan*, both of which deserve revival. Unfortunately without him the style and detail of his works have faded, as one has seen all too frequently in revivals of *Petrouchka*, where every member of that milling fairground crowd is no longer the well-defined character he originally intended.

II. Massine, after the first de Basil days, when he created the three symphonic works, *Les Présages*, *Choreartium*, and *La Symphonie Fantastique*, has been seriously under-rated, if not forgotten, by the new generation. Many of his works for the Royal Ballet were failures, with the magnificent exception of *Mam'zelle Angot*. He has busied himself with endless revivals of two charming but minor works, *Le Beau Danube* and *Gaîté Parisienne*; without his noble Hussar and the superb Peruvian as the central characters, they have faded badly. As a mime, Massine could only be compared with Chaplin. His characters were round; they had pathos and humour. The Barman in the otherwise trivial *Union Pacific* was a masterly study, a splendid distillation of the comedy of the silent film. When one adds such varied roles as the Can-Can Dancer in *La Boutique Fantasque* and the Miller in *Le Tricorne*, we have a performer of rare quality, especially in his early days, when the *buffo* dancers were so often stereotypes. For the sake of the record and because of the debt that those of my generation owe him, I am writing this postscript at some length. Massine's own autobiography is modest, dry, and factual.

The young Massine, a product of the Moscow school – and this is important – was on the whole more interested in drama than in ballet. Moscow was the great centre of drama, and the young dancer could meet the more articulate actors and take part in such dramatic performances as Gogol's *The Government Inspector*. He was also something of a musician, a student of the violin with a more than usual knowledge of the theory of music.

It was more or less an accident that threw him suddenly into the midst of the world ballet scene just when he was about to leave ballet for the theatre. He was eighteen years old when he was selected for a leading role in the one creative ballet company of the period.

Serge Diaghilev had long wished to produce a ballet by the great Richard Strauss. The subject finally decided upon was *Joseph's Legend*, with a libretto by the composer's constant collaborator, the Austrian poet Hugo von Hofmannsthal, and Count von Kessler, an outstanding amateur of the arts. The decorative artist was to be the Spanish painter J. M. Sert, husband of Diaghilev's great friend and patron, Misia. The choreographer was Michael Fokine, then at the height of his fame as a neo-romantic. The atmosphere of the production was to be that of the great Venetian masters. The frail-looking Massine, with his dark hair and enormous, appealing, lustrous black eyes, seemed to Diaghilev the ideal Venetian Joseph.

In spite of the careful preparation, the production (Paris, 1914) was a failure. All that remained was the startling new discovery, Leonide Massine. Paris said of him, 'The little Massine looks like a poet and his dancing is poetry,' and London called him 'the Russian wonder boy'. But Massine himself (always a realist), Diaghilev, and *Maestro* Cecchetti knew that he still had a long way to go to merit such praise. He worked hard with the *maestro* to supplement his neglected technique.

Fate was kind to Massine, and he was able to grasp the opportunity. Nijinsky had left the company the previous year. Fokine, who had returned to fill the gap, could no longer keep pace with Diaghilev's insatiable need for novelty and sensation – a need that had increased since 1912 following the creation of Nijinsky's allegedly obscene *L'Après-midi d'un Faune* (so strongly championed by Rodin) and the near riot one year later with Stravinsky's *Le Sacre du Printemps*.

Two posts were now vacant, those of choreographer and *premier danseur*. Massine was to fill them both, the first Muscovite and the first character dancer.

Even the coming of World War I was in Massine's favour. When the main company under Nijinsky made its American tour, Massine remained behind with Diaghilev and a remarkable group of men, 'his geniuses' as he called them: Stravinsky, Ansermet, Picasso and Larionov.

With him was to begin Diaghilev's second phase – Moscow with its verve and daring, as opposed to Saint Petersburg with its heritage of French and Italian elegance, the bridge that was to change the Ballets Russes into the Ballets Franco-Russes. Its influence has lasted until today. It was Massine, educated by such remarkable tutors, who was to translate all this into the dance form. I am convinced – from personal experience and from my acquaintance with many of those concerned – that this has been one of the most powerful influences in ballet and it has overflowed from ballet into the music hall and art gallery. He has enriched the whole vocabulary of movement to such an extent that we tend to take it for granted.

Massine's first ballet, given for a Red Cross benefit at the Paris Opéra in 1915, was *The Midnight Sun*, to the music of Rimsky-Korsakov's *Snegourochka*, with settings by Larionov. It was the first ballet in a new idiom. Fokine had produced such 'Russian' ballets as L'*Oiseau de Feu* and *Thamar*, romantic in the Pushkin period sense; *The Midnight Sun* came straight from the people, from pagan festivals, popular songs and tales told by some old *baboushka* to her grandchildren. This was further developed in *Contes Russes*, 1917, with the unforgettable Kikimora of Lydia Sokolova. Here we have the true stuff of folk dancing translated into ballet, with no loss of the authentic spirit that made the child open his eyes in wonder or hide his head in Granny's comforting lap.

Diaghilev and Massine did not cease to experiment. Three masterpieces resulted. *Les Femmes de Bonne Humeur*, in 1917, brought back the influence of the *commedia dell'arte* and the Venice of Goldoni and Scarlatti. Its revival by the Royal Ballet has not been a success. It is a dance-actor's ballet, a style alien to present trends, and only Sokolova and Alexander Grant, a consummate artist in the genre, brought back the colour of the original.

The next ballet (1919), *La Boutique Fantasque* (Rossini-Respighi), which introduced André Derain to ballet, is the only 'toy' ballet since *Coppélia* to come to life. It is full of minute significant detail in its characterization of the Shopkeeper, his Assistant, the Russians and the Americans, as well as the dolls, the grotesque Melon Vendor, the marvellous Snob, and the incontinent poodles. The Lopokova-Massine can-can remains one of the great events for those of my generation.

I was not altogether correct when I said that *La Boutique Fantasque* is unique. Massine himself produced another remarkable toy ballet for de Basil, *Jeux d'Enfants* (Bizet), in Monte Carlo in 1932. And what a contrast! This is the dream world of surrealism, of the grown-up child.

The third major work, *Le Tricorne*, conceived in the war years, had its first performance in London in 1919. Massine had gained a remarkable mastery of the Spanish dance in Seville. His task was to translate this into ballet, just as de Falla had translated folk music into orchestral music and Picasso folk dress into theatrical costume. This was the most complete collaboration since *Petrouchka*.

We have, perhaps, seen too much 'highly polished' Spanish dancing – I use this phrase to distinguish it from the great art of Pastora Imperio and Escudero – to appreciate *Le Tricorne* to the full today. Moreover, revivals are uniformly a travesty of the original in which Massine himself danced the farucca, followed by that rhythmic genius, the late Leon Woizikovski.

Massine's 1917 *Parade*, with Satie and Picasso, must be mentioned in any account of his work. It was not a success, and doubtless did not deserve to be, since the dancing suffered at the expense of Cocteau's many stage innovations. Yet in many ways it is of outstanding importance, decades ahead of its time. It was the first Cubist ballet, later to be revived by both the Joffrey and the Festival Ballets, and was the beginning of pop art, of which Massine may be considered one of the fathers, or, more correctly from the date, grandfathers.

Massine left Diaghilev in 1920, after mounting a new version of *Le Sacre du Printemps*, the only convincing production of an earthy pagan rite that I have seen. Since my memory may seem suspect, I bring the late Julie Sazonova as a witness (*La Vie de la Danse*): 'It presented a tremendous contrast to the ethereal classical dance... The male dancers underlined their efforts in lifting the inert bodies of the women. The final dance was a frenzy ... that seemed to be carved out of stone, so strongly was it permeated by the sensation of weight – one of the rare occasions that Diaghilev's ballet was a precursor of modern dance technique. It was as if Massine wished to show the expressiveness and the constructive possibilities of the contrast between weight and lightness.' This ballet, and Sokolova's astonishing interpretation of the Chosen Virgin, would be acclaimed by modern dance creators today. Inevitably, it is beyond recall.

It was obvious that at this period (1924) Diaghilev would find little to please him even in *Le Beau Danube*, but he was impressed by *Mercure*, created for Comte Étienne de Beaumont, and convinced that Massine could still march in his direction. The brief period of Massine's return to Diaghilev saw two works of importance, works so original then that they have been copied ever since. The first, *Les Matelots* (1925), to the music of Georges Auric, launched the career of those ubiquitous three sailors on a spree. Not forgetting Jerome Robbins's hilarious *Fancy Free*, the Massine ballet seems to me, in retrospect, more subtle, deeper in characterization – the sailors differed in nationality – and more original as choreography. At the time I thought it frivolous!

Diaghilev, like his pupil Massine, was always an artistic revolutionary, but not one in the Marxist sense of the word. One of the greatest compliments he ever received was when the Russian poet Mayakovsky told him, in my hearing, that his ballets were too revolutionary for the Soviet Union.

In 1927 Massine created for Diaghilev the Soviet-inspired *Le Pas d'Acier*, to the music of Prokofiev. This, though only a partial success, marked the beginning of a whole series of ballets in which dancers turned themselves into machines with stamping feet and piston-like arms. Of its type, it has yet to be bettered in score or choreography.

I must touch briefly on what were then Massine's highly controversial symphonic ballets, *Les Présages* (Tchaikovsky's Fifth Symphony in E minor), *Choreartium* (Brahms's Fourth Symphony in E minor), both created in 1933, and *La Symphonie Fantastique* of Berlioz, created the following year.

The symphonic ballet was not in itself an innovation, since Fokine had already developed a symphonic movement, though not a complete symphony. I do not believe that the style has a future, but these three works, superbly danced by an outstanding company, underlined Massine's mastery of music. He could have no better champion than the great musicologist Ernest Newman, no lover of ballet as an art form, whom I have quoted at length in Chapter 12. His last symphonic ballet, to the Beethoven Seventh, was less successful for obvious reasons. The music is not suited to a programme. It is, to quote Wagner, 'the apotheosis of the dance', but complete in itself without the need of any visual aid. Even so it had some remarkable passages.

Massine has created more than a hundred ballets, excluding his 'commercial' work. Inevitably – as a pioneer – he has had many failures, more than most choreographers. When he fails, the failure tends to be total and irretrievable. He has also taken on much work of a pot-boiling nature, doomed in advance. Many of these failures have been of recent date when he has had no stable company with which to work, a factor that is fatal for choreographers and dancers alike. Yet *Laudes Evangelii*, produced in and for the Church of San Domenico, Perugia, in 1952, and foreshadowed by *Nobilissima Visione* in 1938, ranks in my mind with the master works: it is religious in feeling and scholarly in its understanding of liturgy and of the spirit and movement of the period from which it derives. Massine alone could have created it.

The man whose genius was acclaimed by none other than Ernest Newman clearly has much to hand down.

III. The Balanchine of whom I wrote forty years ago was not then universally known as 'Mr B.', venerated as the founding father of American classic ballet, the supreme interpreter and friend of Igor Stravinsky. He was the first 'defector'. In Russia he had come under the influence of a great innovator, Goleizowsky, for a long time in the shadows and only to come into his own again as a veteran. He had spent a few years with Diaghilev, who had little real influence on him – less, in fact, than on any other choreographer, including Fokine. But with Diaghilev, Balanchine had already stated his creed of neo-classicism, notably in *Apollo*.

Balanchine received a thorough training as a musician. We see him in a new studio in a strange country, already completely at home and excited by the immense possibilities now open to him. By his side is Lincoln Kirstein, a remarkable practical visionary, a great scholar, a connoisseur of painting, and, as a writer, himself an artist of stature. His book on Nijinsky, whom he never saw, is a vivid piece of writing, the best has been written on this legendary figure. I remember Lincoln in London, interested in our Camargo experiment and in the new young Russians, feeling his way cautiously before acting. He was as deeply committed as I was, and sharing our passion was then a strong bond between us. He has written of those early days in his recently published diary, an important record for a future historian.

So far I have only written about events of which I have an intimate knowledge and some personal involvement. I knew Balanchine from the beginning of his career in the West, and it is obvious from the interview that I believed in what he was doing. Alas, I have not had the opportunity to follow his work systematically, and there have been great gaps in my experience. I must however write of him at some length, not only because of his unique gifts but because he is the creator of neo-classic ballet in America, giving it an unmistakable American accent. New York has become the centre of the ballet world; every foreign company visits, but few can match the choreographic output and genius of Balanchine.

Much that has been written about Balanchine in the American press savours of idolatry. Only recently on three separate occasions

I have read the words 'the greatest of all time', a statement that obscures his true achievements. No serious historian can use the word 'greatest' to deal with a living art. Over-praise is the critic's most deadly weapon.

I will first discuss the series of ballets by Balanchine that I watched in process of creation and that illustrate the tremendous scope of his choreographic vocabulary and his creative vitality. He was twenty-one when he started to work with Diaghilev, and he created some ten ballets for him: *Le Chant du Rossignol, Barabau, La Pastorale, Jack in the Box, The Triumph of Neptune, La Chatte, Apollon Musagète* (later called *Apollo*), *The Gods Go A-Begging, Le Fils Prodigue*, and *Le Bal*. He choreographed ballets for Colonel de Basil and for his own company, Les Ballets 1933, among them *Concurrence, Cotillon, Errante, Songes, Mozartiana*, and *Les Sept Péchés Capitaux*. All these works came immediately prior to his great American career and were performed by dancers he had certainly influenced but not formed. They were fully mature and in themselves sufficient to establish a great reputation and to point to a new direction in choreography. They encompass narrative ballet, ballet with a theme, and show the beginning of neo-classicism at a time when classicism itself was a back number, existing only in abbreviated one-act versions of *Swan Lake* and a *divertissement* hastily put together from *The Sleeping Beauty*. It remained to be rehabilitated by Markova.

The key Balanchine ballet of the Diaghilev period was *Apollon Musagète*, representing as it did the choreographer's first collaboration with Stravinsky, who played a major role in his development. Their partnership can only be compared to that of Tchaikovsky and Petipa. *Apollo* is as exciting today as it was in 1928.

Apollon Musagète has as its leading characters Apollo, leader of the Muses, and the three Muses most concerned with the dance: Calliope, representing poetry and rhythm, Polyhymnia, representing mime, and Terpsichore, representing the dance itself. The ballet is a manifesto, if one can use so prosaic a term in connection with so lyrical a work. In it Balanchine returns to the classicism of Petipa, discarding everything but the essentials and blending with it the most convincing interpretation of classical Greece that I have seen on the stage. Previously the Greek setting was merely chosen as a romantic theme. Here the discipline of the music and its understanding by a choreographer, himself a musician, led to the elimination of every unnecessary movement. Balanchine had the gift of making music visible; given the music, his choreographic treatment of it appeared inevitable – the great test of any ballet. Bauchant's naïve décor, charming in itself, did little to add or detract from the movement; Stravinsky had suggested using Chirico. It made the point that Balanchine was so often to follow, that dance is complete in itself. This was certainly the case with *Apollo*. I saw it nearly fifty years later in the open air at the dance competitions at Varna, beautifully revived by Alicia Alonso. It was deeply moving and a revelation to a public ignorant of Balanchine's work.

In April 1927, *La Chatte*, to music by Sauguet, had paved the way for the treatment of a classical theme. It is a work I remember in detail and would like to see again.

The other major ballet of this period, *Le Fils Prodigue*, was a complete contrast, a narrative ballet based on the biblical parable. The problem was to avoid banality in dealing with so familiar a subject. It is a ballet rich in invention. The originality lay in his portrayal of the siren, magnificently danced by Felia Doubrovska. This was no Parisian cocotte or Hollywood vamp but a cool, calculating woman with the power to corrupt mind as well as body, a truly religious conception of evil that I have never seen matched in Western dance. There was a 'Russian-ness' to the part that showed a kinship to the philosophy of Dostoievsky. Rouault's setting – and Rouault was an outstanding religious painter – suited and enhanced the choreography admirably. The score is Prokofiev's finest in this medium. The last time I met Diaghilev he told me that *Le Fils Prodigue* had made him prouder than he had been for many years. I have seen many other attempts to treat this subject. They pale before the original, which remains vivid in my memory.

When Diaghilev died, Balanchine created two ballets for Colonel de Basil: *Concurrence*, which launched the 'Baby Ballerinas' on their multiple fouettés, and *Cotillon*, of which I have written in a later chapter. I saw it many times, each time discovering something fresh. To me it is the most memorable of the de Basil ballets. There is no great innovation in the choreography; what makes it outstanding is the fact that Balanchine recognized the mystery inherent in Chabrier's music – a mystery that was absent before he made it visible in dance.

It was these ballets, and especially the works for Les Ballets 1933, which convinced Lincoln Kirstein that he had discovered the one man capable of fulfilling his dream of creating a truly American ballet. Les Ballets 1933, short-lived as it was, must occupy an important place in the history of ballet, a fact that I did not realize when I wrote my original chapter. It provided some of the repertoire of the new American ballet. I had met Kirstein while I was editing Romola Nijinsky's biography of Vaslav. I remember many long discussions we had and how unlikely it seemed that we would ever see the establishment of national ballets in our countries. Lincoln's problem was far more difficult than mine. There was no real audience for ballet in America, while we in England had a faithful if restricted public, but one that had yet to see anything without a Russian label. Kirstein, Balanchine, and Ninette de Valois solved these problems in record time.

The beginning in America was a modest one, with sufficient money to get off the ground and not so much as to stifle the creative effort. Wisely it started with a school where Balanchine could form his own dancers. The physical material in America is magnificent, as I had realized when assisting at auditions for the de Basil Company.

In 1936 Balanchine proved that ballet within musical comedy could be an art form and could highlight the action. Even in opera it had usually been considered a foreign body. In one night he abolished what was known as 'musical comedy' dancing. The show, by Rodgers and Hart, was called *On Your Toes*, the ballet, *Slaughter on Tenth Avenue*. I saw the première and afterwards the film and was amazed at Balanchine's versatility. It was a work that Diaghilev would have accepted with pride. Balanchine choreographed other musicals and was followed by Jerome Robbins, Agnes de Mille, Michael Kidd, and others, thus fulfilling Molière's great dictum, 'Unissons nous tous les trois,' the demand for words and music, acting and dancing to combine in one harmonious whole.

In America Balanchine was able to mould dancers to interpret his own complex works, completely classical performers with a highly developed sense of line, both physical and musical. I have seen comparatively few of the works in his vast repertoire. The outstanding ones that I know have been *Concerto Barocco*, *Symphony in C*, *Ballet Imperial*, *The Four Temperaments*, *Night Shadow*, *Orpheus*, and *Agon*. Apart from *Orpheus* and *Night Shadow* these ballets cannot be described in words. That is the very essence of Balanchine's visual music. They are neither literary nor abstract. Balanchine's answer to the inevitable question, why set a ballet to music that can stand on its own? is, the better the music, the better the choreography; and if you don't like the choreography, then you can always close your eyes and listen to the music. This has been proved by the number of Petipa ballets that have sunk into oblivion because of their tawdry music. Balanchine's proviso is that with classical music movement must be directly inspired by the music without the intrusion of a literary idea, that in all matters the conductor, representing the composer, must have the final word. For instance, *The Four Temperaments*, 'a ballet without a plot' to music by Paul Hindemith is based on the ancient idea of the four humours, melancholic, sanguine, phlegmatic, and choleric, which were linked by the Greeks with the elements of earth, water, fire, and air. This notion was a point of departure for composer and choreographer, but any attempt by the spectator to work it out in detail would only detract from the fusion of music and movement. It makes considerable demands on its audience but is infinitely rewarding.

I have the greatest admiration for Balanchine's integrity. Unlike so many of his associates he has paid Diaghilev a great and generous tribute:* 'Personally I owe to Diaghilev my growth and development during the second part of my artistic life. The first part I owe to the Russian Imperial Ballet where I was brought up, to its strict discipline, to its classicism, the basis of all ballet.'

During the last Balanchine season in London I had certain reservations. At times the dancers, brilliant as they were, seemed to subdue their personalities and subordinate themselves too completely to Balanchine and the music. This sounds a ridiculous complaint, since surely that is exactly what dancers should do. I agree, to some extent, but the dancer is after all an individual and not a machine. Ten pianists can interpret Chopin, each one in a different manner, yet without betraying Chopin. The fact that I have seen a number of dancers interpret Balanchine yet retain strong personalities (among them Spessivtseva, Markova, and Nikitina in *La Chatte*, and, more recently, Maria and Marjorie Tallchief, Tanaquil LeClerq, and Violette Verdy) proves that the choreography is not at

*See his *Complete Stories of the Great Ballets*, Doubleday, Garden City, New York, 1954.

fault but that the Balanchine ballet is exceedingly difficult to cast. Its sometimes puritanical lack of decoration, though often justified, throws a tremendous burden on the dancer, and programmes need very careful choosing for an audience unfamiliar with the Balanchine style. The balletomane is inclined to measure all dancers by those whose work he knows; he is essentially an arch-chauvinist.

Jerome Robbins must be mentioned in this section. I have seen too little of his work to be able to comment on it in detail – my first acquaintance with it was in 1946, when Ballet Theatre came to London. *Fancy Free* made an instant impression; I was even more interested in *Interplay*. I wrote at the time, 'It is indeed a remarkable piece of craftsmanship. Imagine a transatlantic *Les Rendezvous* with a touch of *Symphonic Variations* and you have *Interplay* ... classicism and jazz are skilfully blended to give a continuous pattern in which there is beauty, wit, humour, virtuosity.' For me Robbins's masterpiece is *Afternoon of a Faun*, a truly musical interpretation of Debussy, and a contemporary retelling of the Nijinsky idea.

My ballet-intoxicated American friends are fond of asking if the current top dancers in the West – Nureyev, Baryshnikov, Kirkland, Makarova, Seymour, Sibley, Farrell, Haydée, and the amazing Dowell – are the equals of the great ones of my youth. It is a question that cannot be answered. It is impossible to place them side by side and compare them as texts, musical scores, or paintings. Even in the other arts, directions are constantly changing, reassessments are made with every fresh generation as they cannot be in the dance. The level today is a very high one, and there are a number of dancers who will set the standards for tomorrow. This is a golden age. There is, however, one great and increasing risk to their full development: overwork, especially at the beginning of their careers. This did not happen with the dancers of the past. Apart from the strain and an accident rate far higher than ever before, there is the question of over-exposure. I recognize that an audience either settles down to watch the familiar with a certain uncritical apathy or expects something novel and exciting and is disappointed when it does not occur.

Since these interviews were written, Britain has seen major choreographers in Ninette de Valois, Sir Frederick Ashton, the late John Cranko, and Kenneth MacMillan whom I find particularly interesting at the present time. As a dance-dramatist he reaches the heights, as a choreographer without a text he often fails. In his *House of Birds* 1955, *The Burrow* 1958, and *Invitation* 1960, his short story ballets, the central theme was as admirably concentrated as in a tale by Maupassant, in whose pages he would certainly find a wealth of subject matter. By way of contrast, Ashton is a Tchekovian. *Anastasia* suffered through being over-expanded so that the story was lost in padding. *Manon*, still over-long, showed a marked improvement and gave admirable opportunities to Seymour and Wall, both very much in sympathy with Macmillan's approach. In *Mayerling*, Macmillan, provided with a superb libretto, gave us a perfect example of *balletic-verismo*, sticking to history as none of the many films have done. The truth was indeed sordid and unromantic, but then so is the subject matter of Greek tragedy. Macmillan has translated the events of history into true tragedy. The characterization was magnificent, and once again the remarkable Seymour and Wall were inspired, in their turn inspiring their choreographer, Christopher Bruce.

Among the moderns, and my experience here is very limited, I have been impressed by the Ballet Rambert's *Ancient Voices of Children*. Unlike so many 'modern' works it is derived from life and not at second-hand from literature. It communicates directly, awakening memories of childhood and experiences with children. Every movement is relevant with nothing added for the sake of appearing clever. Quite an achievement. America has shown us Antony Tudor, Agnes de Mille, Glen Tetley, and Jerome Robbins; Russia in Grigorovitch; and France in Lifar and Roland Petit, a small number in forty years. The finding of choreographers with a classical training and an original outlook will always remain the greatest problem in the development of ballet, especially at a time when a large investment in a promising unknown is no longer possible.

As a footnote to this chapter I must leave the last word to the old master Fyodor Lopokhov, who said to me after a long session of judging at Varna, 'Here we are, eighteen experienced people from all over the world. We can agree without much difficulty on the quality of dancers, but when it comes to choreography we are never able to reach agreement. We are conditioned by our ages, nationality, temperament, and what we have been accustomed to see. When we argue we can present no proof. I have been involved for nearly seventy years as choreographer and teacher, and yet I cannot define good choreography, though I could lay down some guidelines.'

We all have our guidelines, the most important being that the subject must be more perfectly expressed in the dance than in any other medium. There must be communication between artists and audience, but what audience? Here we come to an abrupt end.

8. Tamara Karsavina

IT is a logical transition from the choreographers who freed ballet to the dancer of whom Robert Brussel wrote, 'Vous avez compris, vous la fille la plus exquise du *classique chorégraphique*, que l'union était possible entre une tradition et une révolution artistique.'*

The great dancer is a rare and valuable possession, a national treasure. She is, in fact, a living and progressive museum of plastic art and an entire academy of music; but where the museum is lifeless the dancer is an active and powerful propagandist, and on the many occasions when I am accused of making too much of some young dancer, that is my justification. She may lack the great intelligence of a Karsavina, and, without appreciating her true value to art, concentrate exclusively on personal success. If she has the necessary gifts, she will, in spite of her empty little head, carry the work of musicians and painters around the globe.

When, following the death of Serge Diaghilev, I organized an exhibition of works connected with his Ballet, I was struck by the vast number of works that were intimately associated with Karsavina. It was clear that she had brought to us the glories of Russian music, the wealth of Russian legend, and the bright colour of Leon Bakst. She revealed to Paris a new aspect of its own artists. Where Trefilova represents pure classicism, Karsavina stands for romanticism and the drama in ballet, and with Fokine she brings it closer to life. Where Pavlova is an example of the outstanding individual, the solitary star, Karsavina is the very brilliant part of a very brilliant whole. It is impossible to compare them, so rarely did they stand on common ground. Karsavina has assuredly left the whole art of ballet richer than any other dancer; when I say that she brought these gifts to Western Europe I mean it literally.

The Diaghilev contract of the first few years depended on La Karsavina being in the company, the first and last time that such a thing ever occurred. His whole conception opposed the star system,

* 'You, the most exquisite daughter of the classical choreography, have understood the possibility of uniting tradition and an artistic revolution.'

but Karsavina and Nijinsky were definitely stars. They represent from a dancing point of view the finest period of the ballet, the first, the Russian period, that had carried it the furthest from its Franco-Italian origins; a rich, young, very national manifestation. Fokine, Nijinsky, Karsavina, and Diaghilev were Russian. Stravinsky, their favoured composer, and Bakst, perhaps more than anyone responsible for the popularity of the movement, were Russians too, and, if they did dance to the music of a Chopin, Schumann, or Weber, the dreams they created could not be mistaken for anything but Russian, and the park of the sylphs was the park of a Russian palace.

At the same time as she was dancing for Diaghilev, Karsavina was enjoying a career as ballerina of the Maryinsky, practically taking off her make-up on the train as she journeyed from Saint Petersburg to the West and lived her double life. It required enormous effort of mind and body, only possible in one extremely adaptable. When the change came, as logically it had to, she was ready to help the ballet in its transition from the rule of Fokine, her fellow pupil, with whom she had danced *The Fisherman and the Pearl* at the Maryinsky, to that of Leonide Massine, the brilliant new discovery from Moscow. *Le Tricorne*, *Les Femmes de Bonne Humeur*, *La Boutique Fantasque*, indicated a change of direction, gradual at first; then came *Parade*, the Cubist manifesto, led by a Maryinsky ballerina, who was dancing at home in *Raymonda* and *Paquita*!

Throughout her career Karsavina has shown a versatility unsurpassed by any dramatic actress; from *Le Spectre de la Rose*, the personification of girlish innocence, 'la grace ingénue et tendre', which has no significance without her, to *Thamar*, proud, sadistic Georgian queen, feverishly awaiting yet another victim. The curtain rises with Thamar on her couch, waving to entice the passing stranger, and descends with her waving once again. What has gone on in between – the death of a young warrior prince – has been but an episode that could not quench her passion. Thamar is more than a vicious woman, she is a queen in search of amusement; pride as well as cruelty plays its part. The dancing is of secondary importance, all lies in the acting of this one role, and never did a poem translated into action retain its original spirit more intensely. Here is Lermontov's Thamar, realized in paint by Serov, in human form by Karsavina, yet but a moment ago, in the time it took to put on fresh make-up, she was Gautier's fragile dreamer. In *Petrouchka* she lays bare the simple pattern of all tragedy, the tragedy of the puppet, a *Coppélia* of deeper significance, mysticism instead of childish fun, far nearer to Hoffmann than his own balletized story; Karsavina as the eternal flirt without a heart, she who had been all heart in *Giselle*. Then *L'Oiseau de Feu*, requiring all the elevation and virtuosity of the ballerina, but so much more. To be the legendary bird of Russian folklore lightness is not enough; one must feel the passion of the imprisoned woman. To be all bird or all woman is to make the Fokine-Stravinsky dream into a Christmas pantomime, as it has appeared in so many revivals.

'Une légende,' said Vaudoyer, 'veut que l'oiseau de Paradis, qui passe, devant les yeux aveuglés, comme une gerbe de rubis et de perles, soit privé de pattes, qu'il ne se pose jamais. Légende dont il est impossible de douter lorsque Mademoiselle Karsavina, *Oiseau de Feu*, devant les fantasmagories du décor, obéit aux vols obliques ou circulaires de ses ailes cachées.'*

All the works of this romantic period are fatally easy to spoil – but Karsavina made one believe. They were ballets created for the finest talent, without which they are barren; *Le Spectre de la Rose* becomes sentimentality plus cheap virtuosity; *Schéhérazade*, the Oriental scene from a revue; *Petrouchka*, a small item from Baliev's *Chauve Souris*. The ballet with an emotional subject is always dangerous. Karsavina made it possible.

Then came the Massine ballets in a new key: *Le Tricorne*, a peasant theme from Alarçon, the Spanish dance balletized and incredibly difficult, devoid of all the cheap allure that makes Spanish dancing so easily effective; *Les Femmes de Bonne Humeur*, Goldoni with its lighter note of mischief, a living picture by Longhi; and the fun mixed with sadness of *La Boutique Fantasque* with a difficult change of emotions between the boisterous can-can of the first scene and the romantic reverie of the second.

Each one of these roles can be repeated, but not all again by one interpreter.

During the little season of *divertissement* that I arranged for Karsavina at the Arts Theatre, London, in 1930, I gained an insight into her method of working up a dramatic role, from its early

*'A legend has it that the bird of paradise that flashes past the blinded eyes like a spray of rubies and pearls is deprived of feet so that it can never settle. It is impossible not to believe in this legend when Mademoiselle Karsavina, the Firebird, obeys the circular or darting flight of her hidden wings in front of the fabulous setting.'

plastic suggestion to its complete intellectual justification. I have always been interested in the genesis of any particular dramatic interpretation. In ballet-mime it is easier to grasp; neither the choreographer nor the composer imposes himself on the performer in the manner of the author and producer of a play. The role when it comes to her is more fluid. She may feel it or reason it out. With Karsavina it is a combination of both.

In the Arts Theatre season there was a small *divertissement* that stands out as a little masterpiece, *Mademoiselle de Maupin*, to the romantic music of Liesberg, an unknown pupil of Chopin's, the discovery of Edwin Evans. I watched the evolution of the whole idea. It came vaguely at first through the memory of a black velvet *travesti* riding-habit à la 1830, curls, a black hat with feathers, then the desire to do a dance in that spirit, and a few mimed poses, with the playing over of countless melodies till the one that could extend those poses was found. This was followed by a reading of books and poems of the period till finally dance, story, music, and costume met in this exquisite study. And so it was in the bigger roles. The choreographer found the movement, but he could only indicate the mime, and the problem was hers. *Thamar* was at first the most difficult; neither music nor poetry would reveal it fully, and right up to the time of the dress rehearsal it remained a complete mystery. Then, with the first make-up in front of the mirror, and a suggestion from Diaghilev that the eyebrows should meet in a line, the character stood revealed. What she had read could now be fitted in with what she felt.

It is this sensitivity to plastic form and period, afterwards justified by knowledge and extensive research, that has made Karsavina an actress without equal, who worked parallel with her choreographer. If for the moment we can think of her dancing as a thing apart, which in fact it is not, she would have been equally successful through her fine approach to the problems of acting if she had chosen the legitimate stage early in her life. Fortunately, in choosing the ballet she could speak the language of the whole world.

Karsavina I know perhaps better than any other dancer, but not from the Diaghilev days. Then I was content to worship her from afar. We first met over a scheme to organize a world congress of the dance in London. The scheme itself came to nothing, but it provided me with a delightful friendship. It was through listening to her stories of other days, stories that were not mere gossip but a vivid re-creation of the ballet as it had been, that I first hit upon the idea that she should record it in a book, and then by my wild enthusiasm I rushed her headlong into the adventure of writing, by phone calls, letters, and visits, until finally I had persuaded her, conditionally. She would try, and if it did not please her, she would destroy the manuscript and nothing more would be said. I had blind confidence in her ability to write from the very moment she consented. And so Karsavina became what she described to me as 'a literary bloke'. From time to time she called me over for 'readings', her handwriting making it too laborious to take the work home. Whenever I have had a letter from her I have always been in some doubt as to its contents, until I rang up for confirmation. I heard the whole of that dance classic read by her in almost exactly the form in which it finally appeared. Every line of it was written by her alone, with the aid of one of the biggest dictionaries I have ever seen. She who but a short time ago had boasted about her 'beautiful pork [pigskin] bag', now speaks faultless, almost pedantically correct English, with the very strongest of Russian accents.

When the great work was finished we had a long session to assemble the mass of material and to view the final results, her husband and I suggesting the cutting of a few of those passages 'where she had let herself go'. One in particular I remember; she was so proud of it. It contained the word 'kaleidoscope', and its suppression, on her husband's advice, seemed to rankle for quite a time. Wisely I remained silent; marriage might stand such conduct, friendship never. In my own edition she has added it in longhand; I also possess the original manuscript.

No one was more relieved when the work was finished than Joey, the Sealyham terrier, who tried his best on so many occasions to chew the manuscript to pieces. He had sharp teeth, and as if by instinct had chewed up my hat and a pair of gloves on that very first day when I had entered so full of the book.

I find it difficult to write of Karsavina as a person because it is not possible to gossip about her. 'She was quite different from anyone in the company, aloof but never stand-offish. She seemed herself to be part of the dreams she was enacting,' said Sokolova to me. She herself in *Theatre Street* has only revealed the woman by inference. 'I will write of myself as a child, then when I join the theatre; and it is *the* important thing in my life, I become entirely the artist, and my private affairs can interest no one,' she says in a letter to me, discussing the plan of her book. And in the middle we have a bare statement, 'I was married then.'

She can discuss literature, ballet, painting, and music, but always broadly and objectively. She is full of the give and take of discussion, with a very English sense of humour; she is a great lover of Dickens as well as of the Continental type of wit; she relished an incident that I had overheard at the Coliseum. On the entry of her partner in a Cossack solo, 'Is that Tamara Karsavina, dear?' 'I dunno; thought Karsavina was a woman, but you never do know with these Russians.'

There is nothing in her attitude to remind one that here is one of the most applauded artists of the day. But she has an aloofness that many find frightening. She is certainly difficult to know. It is her guard against a too great sensitivity, the fear of being disappointed in people. She is dignified, a 'blue-stocking beauty' and always an artist. The type of work she created called for an analytical mind. Every triumph was as fully and consciously calculated as her faultless period house. I remember her amused annoyance at a long florid description of herself in which the words 'exotic', 'lotus', and 'orchid' appeared many times. The exciting, remarkable thing about the real Karsavina is the very fact that she has never once imagined herself an exotic, a Thamar in real life. The 'artistic temperament', she once insisted, should be kept for the stage.

It is a very great loss to me that she is no longer in London, and it is a great blow to English dancing. She was our only Maryinsky ballerina.

POSTSCRIPT

There is a little that I can add to this chapter on Karsavina. She remains beyond dispute the most important ballerina of our whole period, the prototype of the modern dancer, able to dance the classics with an extraordinary feeling for style but without being mannered or archaistic, and at the same time to excel in neoromantic works and in character dancing. Among dancers in Soviet Russia today her name arouses the greatest interest, and the albums of photographs in Madame Frangopoulo's museum in the Leningrad Ballet School are the most often studied by the students. It is this museum and the obvious inspiration it gave to the pupils that made me establish a similar one in the Royal Ballet School.

Karsavina is the last dancer I have seen who truly understood classical mime and made it acceptable to a modern audience. It was far removed from the Italian school; it was not assumed as a carefully learnt sign language but came from within. The facial expression, the use of the eyes, the whole body came into play. Today in Russia itself and everywhere else classical mime has vanished beyond any hope of revival, though Fokine, who had banned it in modern works, considered that its rightful place was in the classics and should be left unchanged. He maintained that the dancer should be expressive with her whole body instead of using a stereotyped form of mime language. Karsavina alone among modern dancers was able to convey emotion to this conventional language that had degenerated into an incoherent and embarrassing stammer. It was a lost opportunity on the part of the Royal Ballet not to have used Karsavina's knowledge of mime earlier, although later in her life she did teach them the full mime sequence for the Mother in *Giselle* and guided Ashton in the mime scene for Lise in Act II of his *La Fille Mal Gardée*. Her remarkable lecture-demonstrations brought to life the cobwebbed works abandoned in the lumber rooms of the Maryinsky. On the other hand, it is doubtful whether such a subject could ever have been taught successfully. Even a non-classical work such as *Carnaval*, which makes considerable use of *commedia dell'arte*-derived mime, has remained a closed book to the finest post-Karsavina-Nijinsky dancers. It was not a great work. It had originally been designed as a ballroom *divertissement*, and Diaghilev always had his doubts when it was transferred to the stage. One had to be a Karsavina, with her knowledge of the shades of romanticism, to give it life.

Diaghilev and his entourage admired Karsavina more than any other dancer. The great man listened to her views. She was in the truest sense a colleague, who won tremendous public acclaim but at the same time remained a dancer's dancer, the smallest details of whose work could be discussed and enjoyed by her fellow artists.

No other dancer will ever occupy the same position as Karsavina; she came upon the scene at the right time, the last great artist-ballerina of the old Maryinsky tradition, and raised Fokine's new breakthrough to the peak of perfection. She had exceptional beauty combined with an almost academic knowledge that in no way hindered the spontaneous expression of her emotions.

9. The Two Lydias

Two of the earliest characters in this book, Markova and Dolin, happen to be English, both of them closely identified with the last years of the Diaghilev Ballet and with dancing in England since. They have made and deserved international reputations, but it is admittedly Lydia Sokolova who stands out amongst English dancers in a position all by herself.

Hilda Munnings, famous as Sokolova, a name first honoured in the annals of the Imperial Russian Ballet, made her career in the very greatest days of Diaghilev, at a time when competition was feverish and the supply of dancers from Russia still unlimited. It is from such a background, the richest in the history of the dance, the period of Karsavina, Fokine, and Nijinsky, that she must be judged. Her work has a depth, intensity, and versatility that places her next to Karsavina alone. She is the complete actress-dancer-personality I have always set up as an ideal. She arrived at her summit through a bitter struggle and a rich and early experience of life, added to the ordinary daily grind of the dancer, and she arrived 'consciously', rationalizing the experience and storing up every detail, so that today it is a commonplace to be told, 'Ask Sokolova' for any special information about the ballet. It is these adventures, so very rare for an English girl before the war but now shared by the war-revolution generation of Russians, that have brought out extraordinary qualities – qualities of a kind that one does not expect in the English dancer at all, and only rarely in anyone. She is not frightened of showing her emotions; all natural reserve has been banished, so that she can express the beautiful, sad, grotesque, or terrible with complete freedom. I have 'asked Sokolova', and bit by bit I have pieced together the story of how it all came about.

The start is the same as with everyone in this book and with most children – a keen love of dancing, and improvisation at home; unlike so many, it did not remain there long. The little Hilda Munnings, Sokolova-to-be, was given a very thorough musical education and by the age of twelve had already passed many advanced piano examinations. As her passion for dancing grew, she was sent to Stedman's Academy, where Hilda Butsova and Vera Savina were her fellow pupils, and her first role was that of a lobster in *Alice in Wonderland*, with Butsova as chief lobster.

After she had been learning for six months, Pavlova and Mordkin came to the Palace Theatre, and Pavlova, as always, was the big creative inspiration that made childish dreams into something positive. Little Hilda spent her lunch money in going to the matinées, and her parents stinted themselves to give her a course of private lessons with Mordkin, for which they paid the enormous fee of £5 a lesson! Whether she learnt in proportion to that sum or not, it gave her a first footing in a serious ballet atmosphere and made the great ones conscious of her existence.

Then Pavlova slapped Mordkin in full view of the public! He had lifted her in some manner not to her complete satisfaction; an historic event, that affected at least a hundred careers. The results of that slap can still be felt in England today. It was on account of it that Anna Pavlova filled her company with English girls, whose loyalty she felt she could always count upon in any civil war. An immediate declaration of war followed. Factions were formed, and the strong Polish contingent, with a few Russians, went over in a body to Mordkin, who immediately formed a company to tour the United States in *Le Lac des Cygnes*, *Giselle*, *Coppélia*, and the *Russian Wedding*, taking with him Geltzer, the great Moscow ballerina of the day, then already over thirty, Sedova, Gluck, Kuhn, Morosov, and Volinine, cream of the Pavlova Ballet, together with thirteen-year-old Hilda Munnings and nine other English girls.

The trip on the *President Lincoln* started ominously, Mordkin having to be operated upon suddenly for appendicitis in mid-ocean, which left him weak and depressed the company. Hilda, doubtless feeling a little frightened and homesick, celebrated her fourteenth birthday on board. The tour started at the Metropolitan Opera House, but almost at once Mordkin and Sedova quarrelled with Geltzer, and fresh factions were formed.

In the whole of the first part of her career Sokolova was destined to rise and gain knowledge through the disputes of famous artists. She and her English companions, pawns in this game of foreign quarrels, went on with Volinine and some Polish girls for a long tour of one-night stands. For three months they slept on a train, two in a bunk, dancing nightly. Their salaries were meagre, and

Volinine generously supplemented them by five dollars a week from his own pocket. Then one night in New Orleans they played *Coppélia* to a house empty save for three Negroes in the gallery. They did not get beyond the first act. The Poles struck, and the manager wisely disappeared for a time. They were stranded.

The consul could do nothing but write to New York and hope for the best. Then they decided on their own to send a threatening wire to the impresario. This had an immediate effect. A cart was sent to take their luggage to the docks, and the girls perched themselves on top of the pile. I have seen a snapshot of this. They looked more like schoolgirls from a junior form coming home for the holidays than a hungry and stranded theatrical company. They returned to New York in extreme misery, eight days in a smelly cargo boat. On arrival they decided that they had had more than their share of discomfort, and put up at one of the best hotels, informing the manager, who must have been both sympathetic and an optimist, that they were staying indefinitely. They found the impresario and took it in turns to camp on his doorstep. He arranged, suspiciously quickly, for them to sail back on the *Lapland*, but still managed to give them one final shock by not turning up on the quay until the girls, in absolute despair and looking like nothing on earth, had seen the gang-plank taken up and heard the final siren. Mordkin's own impresario, Mr Mitchell, who was travelling on the boat, gave them every penny he had, and as, surprisingly enough, they were travelling first class this time, they had a thoroughly enjoyable trip. They could not guess the reasons for this luxury, and they were ready to accept it without much thought. This time they were pawns in a game between a businessman, his wife, and H.M. Customs officials. This man's wife was an actress, who was bringing over with her several baskets of very expensive costumes. The task of the English girls was to pass these safely through as their personal property. They were useful and could therefore be allowed the resulting comfort. Had the fellow been a bachelor they might still have been in New York – as far as he was concerned !

All this haphazard training was the prelude to a career. It had naturally made a deep impression that could be used later; meanwhile Hilda was ready to receive a more systematic tuition. The sympathetic Mitchell, exceptional in his profession, had immediately put himself in touch with Pavlova and had arranged an audition. 'Madame' was impressed and agreed to have them trained at Ivy House by her own *maître de ballet*, Cheraiev, an expert in character dancing. It was then that Pavlova 'discovered' Hilda as a coming dancer, a fact that she reminded her about their very last meeting. All through her long career Pavlova sowed these seeds of ambition. When her jealousies and tantrums are brought up against her they are more than balanced.

After Sokolova had been learning for a few months, Theodore Koslov arrived in England to produce *Schéhérazade* at the Coliseum, with Baldina, his wife, Alexis Koslov, Becheharov, who had been in the Diaghilev company, Morosov, Zverev, and others. Again chance helped her, and she was ready to profit by it. Baldina had to be absent for two or three performances, and Koslov was not over-eager to draw attention to the fact. Physically there was some resemblance between the two; both were plump and blonde. Hilda was carefully made up in Baldina's wig and costume, and at the age of fifteen danced this exacting role with Koslov. This lasted long enough to reveal her full merits, so when they went on tour to Vienna and Budapest she was given Brahms's Czardas to dance with Alexis Koslov. It was the success of the programme – in a country where every movement of that dance was known and understood. After the tour they returned to the Coliseum.

Diaghilev meanwhile had come to Covent Garden with Nijinsky for the historic season of 1912, with the production of *Le Sacre du Printemps* in mind. Hilda, two of the English girls, and Zverev went up for an audition before Diaghilev, Fokine, Nijinsky, and Cecchetti – a nightmare audience, especially at a time when there were only Russians in the company. All were accepted, but later the other two dropped out and only Hilda remained. She left the Koslov company at Cheltenham (curious contrast, New Orleans to Cheltenham, as first stages in an artistic education!) and joined Diaghilev at Monte Carlo, where so many careers have started. Her first contract allowed her the magnificent sum of 720 francs a month, which was increased yearly, until it ranked with the very highest.

Chance immediately helped her. One of the lesser soloists was expecting a child, and Hilda stepped straight into all her roles. The first act of *Sacre de Printemps* was already known to the company, but she learnt it in a few rehearsals, her musical training making the difficult rhythms easy. All the time she was busy with

Cecchetti, adding pure dancing technique to her knowledge of music and life.

This is the sum of her achievement in one month, her first: *L'Oiseau de Feu*, in which she was one of the Princesses, was learnt at one dress rehearsal and at one general rehearsal; *Thamar* in two rehearsals. *Prince Igor* had to be learnt while the overture was being played, and the second act of *Giselle* was danced as an impromptu, following as best she could; in *Carnaval* she danced in the 'Valse Noble'. That was not the end. Nijinsky selected her as one of the nymphs for his ballet *L'Après-midi d'un Faune*, with its difficult rhythm, its entirely new technique, and record number of rehearsals.

Naturally she collapsed and lay for days in a fever, dancing all the time in her dreams, memorizing and counting beats. There was work to be done, her chance had really come, and she could not allow herself the luxury of a breakdown.

Fokine selected her and a Polish girl, out of the company of sixty, to perform the dance of the veils in *Daphnis et Chloé*. It was the first time that a subsidiary role was entrusted to two dancers, a system that has since increased the interest for the audience, led to the discovery of new talent, and saved the Ballet in many emergencies. It can be imagined how much jealousy was added to her already great difficulties.

At the *répétition générale* – the fashionable 'invited' première – in Paris before a smart audience, the Polish girl, who was given the first turn, became entangled in the veils, and, on a reprimand from Fokine, promptly answered him back – an unheard-of occurrence. Diaghilev was furious. 'Give the veils to the English girl'; and so through these words she made history and had her first small creation in the Russian Ballet in the glorious days of Michael Fokine.

But Sokolova always helped her luck. That year, for the first and last time, *Maestro* offered two prizes for the greatest technical progress. Hilda won the first – his photo in a silver frame, inscribed to 'Ida', his name for her, and one of the many she was known by until 'Sokolova' was truly created, through character, hard work, and experience born of amazing chance.

All that had happened so far was but the prelude to further adventure and proved to be but a mild acclimatization.

She left on the famous American tour under Nijinsky's artistic direction and witnessed the beginnings of his appalling tragedy. The breach with Diaghilev and the sudden assumption of un-accustomed responsibility undoubtedly hastened the end. It was and is an impossibility for even the most balanced of men to dance, create, manage, and be lionized at the same time. Serge Grigoriev, who could have taken so much of the burden from his shoulders, was left behind at Nijinsky's own request; a bad initial blunder. Then two fanatics began to exert their harmful influence on him, hastening the destruction of a weakened mind, upsetting both his newly married life and his career as an artist. The public wished to see him in his great roles, and him alone, but often he refused to dance at all, or assigned himself some subsidiary part such as the eunuch in *Schéhérazade*, and a distracted Kremnev had to come to his hotel, suffer many difficult scenes, and implore him to dance, where Diaghilev would have simply ordered.

From the first Nijinsky took an interest in Hilda, whom he had previously selected as one of his nymphs, and chose her to dance with him in *Le Spectre de la Rose*. 'It was terrifying; he seemed to have altered so completely; he would throw me high in the air, and became increasingly difficult to follow as performance succeeded performance.'

With the production of *Tyl Eulenspiegel* came the complete fiasco. Extravagant ideas entered into his mind; he selected a group of walkers-on, gathered from hobos and down-and-outs, and ex-pected them to dance a complicated *pas de six*. When the last day arrived only the first portion of the ballet was set, and Kremnev, in complete despair, had to arrange with the company to improvise the remainder during the performance. Highly trained dancers, they got through it, but eventually the work had to be abandoned. Without Diaghilev and his careful tutoring the once creative mind had ceased to work.

On their return to Europe they found *La Boutique Fantasque* in active preparation. The brilliant reign of Leonide Massine had be-gun. Hilda was assigned a Venetian dance with Gavrilov, which later was given up in favour of a tarantella with castanets to be danced with Felix, who became too insane for it ever to be carried out. Finally she created with Woizikovski the tarantella we know so well.

The same Gavrilov shortly afterwards suffered from one of the most curious dancing accidents on record. Dancing in *Les Sylphides* in an antiquated theatre in Saragossa, his leg crashed through a rotten board just before the final leap. He pulled it out and was able to continue. The next week, in another Spanish town, at the very same moment in the dance, there was a loud crack, and he fell in agony to the boards and crawled into the wings. His leg had been wrenched above the ankle, had seen him through the week, but now was completely broken. He was on crutches for a year.

The next tour of the Ballet was in South America. It was wartime, travelling was difficult, and the company was to assemble by groups in Spain. Hilda was alone and struck up a casual friendship with a sympathetic woman on the boat. They travelled together as far as the frontier at Hendaye, when she saw this woman in apparent difficulties at the customs, surrounded by important-looking officials, the contents of her trunk spilled all over the floor. Immediately she went up to offer a helping hand. 'So you know her?' said a gendarme. 'That is interesting'; and she was promptly arrested and locked in a room under a military guard. The woman was a spy, and none of Hilda's protests was believed. Fortunately, by sheer good luck Grigoriev was still in the town and able to vouch for her, but she had had a very narrow escape from spending the rest of the war in a concentration camp.

The South American tour was a fiasco, almost a repetition of the North American venture, but it held many thrills for Hilda. In the meantime she had been married and was expecting a child. One day, in a tunnel on the line between Santos and Sao Paulo, a truckload of scenery caught fire. The men fought valiantly to save it, with only three buckets and their bare hands. They were badly burned but succeeded in salvaging the greater part. The shock, however, upset Hilda, and on 1 September 1917, her little girl, Natasha, was born, a month before her time. It turned out to be a fortunate event, in spite of the serious operation required, for she had planned to sail to Buenos Aires in a boat that proved so derelict and suffered so many delays that, with no doctor present, mother and child might well have been lost. The very day before Natasha's birth, Hilda was teaching the Bacchanal in *Narcisse* to Klementovich!

On their return to Madrid, Spanish 'flu was raging, and the entire company went down with it, Sokolova the last. She was forced to remain behind with Kremnev, her baby, and her nurse. Then, still weak, she travelled to Lisbon to rejoin the troupe. When they arrived at the station all was dark, and they could clearly hear the rattle of machine guns. They had landed in the midst of a revolution; from frying-pan to fire, Spanish 'flu to Portuguese revolution. A porter conducted them through heavy machine-gun fire to a *pension* off the Avenida, the nurse dropping the baby in her panic. No sooner had they arrived in their bedroom, and placed the baby safely on the bed, than the mirror on the wall opposite was smashed to fragments, and bullets ricocheted around the room. They spent a miserable foodless night in a cellar and moved the next day to a quieter place, where they were besieged for five days. It was then that she learnt her first Spanish dancing from Felix, Diaghilev's new discovery.

The revolution over, they danced for three weeks, but were stranded for the rest of the spring. Diaghilev went to Barcelona to try to fix a season, but an imposter had forestalled him and was trying to present a ballet with some of the original dancers. Both the bogus and the genuine engagements fell through. They were able, however, to make a tour through Spain on very bad terms, and returned to Madrid penniless. The company disbanded and lived on their own as best they could. Diaghilev, ever sympathetic, was able to scrape together enough money for Sokolova to take a third-class ticket to Lisbon to fetch her baby, who had been left there, and to return. But Diaghilev was starving, and only the kindness or apathy of the hotel proprietor kept a roof above his head. This is a picture that few who knew him in opulence in London, Paris, or Venice can visualize.

Hilda's baby was ill through lack of nourishment and proper medical attention. She was in despair. One day Diaghilev called her; he was unpacking an old trunk and had come across a collection of coins of various nations. He gave them to her to sell for what she could get, and the baby was saved. Diaghilev went without meals for many days then. They met nightly, and Sokolova helped him as translator in his negotiations with Sir Oswald Stoll. Though both were eager for a contract, wartime regulations proved a hindrance. Once she was wakened at four in the morning by Diaghilev standing at her bedside – how he got into her *pension* she never knew – feverishly waving a telegram that he could not understand. It read, 'Try from your end, impossible from ours', and he went wearily home again. When finally negotiations were complete and an advance had been sent, weakened by hunger he fell across his bed in a faint, sobbing with relief.

London received them with joy and the period of suffering was over, but the memory of those events created a deep and lasting friendship between Diaghilev and Sokolova. She had seen a Diaghilev very different from the unapproachable autocrat whose presence frightened so many of his company. These actions of his must be balanced against all the rest, if we are ever to know the complete Diaghilev: rich and poor, weak and strong, petty and jealous, generous and sympathetic, dangerous enemy and staunch friend.

The rest of Sokolova's career in the Ballet had its difficulties, and more than its fair share of illness, but adventure proper was ended, only artistic adventure remained, and those creations that have built up her name.

During the last two months of the Ballet's lifetime, as if by a presentiment, she was given a new lease of life in the middle of a serious illness, and her performances as the Chosen Virgin in *Le Sacre du Printemps* will be remembered as a magnificent climax to the Russian Ballet, bringing back memories of its greatest days. When the curtain went down at Covent Garden, and a doctor and anxious friends rushed to her aid, a chapter of ballet history ended.

Today she is teaching, giving her fine experience to her pupils, in an attempt to repeat in some other that marvel of another great English dancer-artist-personality. Here then is the opportunity to learn at first hand.

Lydia Sokolova has made the journey from England to Russia; today Lydia Lopokova is making the journey from Russia to England, and from ballet to the legitimate stage. Her story has been less varied, but no less full; it is marked from the very first by a success which she has done her very best on many occasions to destroy, but without avail. Her luck, or more accurately her charm, has fortunately always prevented her in time. The artistic pattern of her career is especially rich: as a dancer, she was a pupil of Fokine; as a conscious artist, the pupil of Massine at a time when he was still learning, beginning to discover, and developing rapidly.

At the age of eight she was sent to the Imperial School, following a brother and sister, and went through easily and uneventfully, but with the beginnings of a reputation;* pink dress, grey dress, the coveted white dress, and graduation with her first important solo, Columbine in *Casse-Noisette*; and Columbine is the *leitmotif* of her career. She was only on the Imperial stage a few months before she was invited to join the Diaghilev Ballet in Paris, then in their second year and at the very height of their popularity. Karsavina, in *Theatre Street*, has given us a delicious description of Lopokova's bewildered arrival in Paris:

Young Lopokova danced this season; it was altogether her first journey abroad. As she was stepping out of the railway carriage, emotion overcame her. She fainted right away on the piles of luggage. It had been her dream to be in Paris, she told the alarmed Bakst, who had rendered her first aid; the lovely sight (of the Gare du Nord) was too much for her. A mere child, she reminded me again of the tiny earnest pupil when, in the demure costume of *Les Sylphides*, she ecstatically and swiftly ran on her toes.

As a pupil of Fokine's she was immediately given small roles, and immediately she attracted attention, even amidst all the brilliant stars of that period. She was different. J. L. Vaudoyer wrote of her with his sure instinct for divining that difference:

Sa virtuosité est ingénue, et l'imperceptible gaucherie de l'âge la tempère. Mademoiselle Lopokova ressuscite les poupées de Hoffmann et de Schwind; et sans doute mordait-elle encore, l'an dernier, dans les tartines que distribue Charlotte.†

Luck soon came her way, for after a few months Karsavina was unable to dance for a time, and Lydia was given Columbine in *Carnaval* and the Bluebird pas de deux from *Festin* with Nijinsky (she was just eighteen). Only the young dancers of today have met with such rapid advancement; then she was alone. When Karsavina re-

* 'One out of the group of small pupils given now into my care was little Lopokova. The extreme emphasis she put into her movements was comic to watch in the tiny child with the face of an earnest cherub. Whether she danced or talked, her whole frame quivered with excitement; she bubbled all over. Her personality was manifest from the first, and very lovable.' – Karsavina in *Theatre Street*.

† 'Her virtuosity is ingenuous and is tempered by the imperceptible awkwardness of her youth. Mademoiselle Lopokova brings to life the dolls of Hoffmann and Schwind; without doubt it was only last year that she munched the bread and jam handed out by Charlotte.'

turned, they shared the roles, which definitely established her, not as an understudy, but as a star in her own right. During a further absence of Karsavina she was given *L'Oiseau de Feu*, and all the time with an increase of salary. She should have been content with this, but success always seemed to bore her, and she went off to seek the customary fortune in America. She was there five years before she rejoined the company again, and her path was made easy, for it was the Ballet that came to America at the time of Nijinsky's famous tour. She danced as ballerina during those difficult days when it was almost impossible not to take sides. Then from 1917 to 1919 she remained as leading ballerina of the company, becoming one of the most popular dancers who ever appeared in London. It was the period of *La Boutique Fantasque* and *Les Femmes de Bonne Humeur*.

Once more success seemed monotonous, and she ran away suddenly, again to America. But 'I was a flop,' she says, 'and thoroughly deserved it.' In 1921 she returned for *The Sleeping Princess*, to dance the Lilac Fairy, and sometimes Princess Aurora herself. Truly Diaghilev must have been long-suffering; it was a rare compliment that he never paid to any other dancer. She had deserted him twice, and yet he let her return as if nothing had happened, and after the first reconciliation he never mentioned it again.

After *The Sleeping Princess* things were difficult. No salaries were forthcoming, and Lopokova joined Massine in a new venture. With the exception of *Le Beau Danube*, in which she created the role of the Street Dancer, the work was singularly uninspired. While Diaghilev was alive, away from him the most brilliant minds seemed dulled, as if he possessed a hypnotic power that could travel over space. She met him during this engagement, and he gave her a halfhearted peck instead of the hearty kiss reserved for a favourite artist. 'Sergei Pavlovitch, why are you so angry with me? Haven't other people the right to produce ballets?' 'No,' he replied, 'I am a bartender, and have invented certain cocktails. Now other people come and steal my recipes; certainly they have not the right.' When, unabashed, she asked for the third time to be taken back once again, he replied rather ungraciously that he did not want grandmothers in the company. But his actions belied his words, and she appeared for him again many times, but only as a guest artist during the London seasons.

Lydia Lopokova has given to ballet a quality all her own, the quality of inspired mischief. To call her a *soubrette*, as is so often done, is an understatement. It may cover her role in *Les Femmes de Bonne Humeur*, but not the memorable *Les Sylphides*, or the deliciously sentimental doll in the second scene of *La Boutique Fantasque*. So shrewd a critic as André Levinson failed to understand the real Lopokova and never did her justice.

It was during her reign in the Diaghilev company that I began the habit of going nightly to the ballet. I still have the photograph, the first one in my collection, for which I waited so anxiously outside the stage door. It shows a red-cheeked doll, the heartless coquette, who played with poor Petrouchka, and if in her performance the mischievous girl was more in evidence than the puppet, and some of the feeling of witchery was absent, it was all the same memorable for its beauty of movement.

In private life Mrs J. M. Keynes is the Lydia Lopokova of the stage, in a series of her most enchanting roles; quick, provocative, intelligent, a trifle sentimental. She has an earnest, at times almost pathetic, manner that can allow her to say the rudest or most argumentative things in such a way that the truth of them only dawns upon one some considerable time later, and then leaves no hurt. She is also that rarity, the dancer who cares so little about criticism, that she will read adverse notices with obvious relish and even sympathize with their author. There is never any coldness in meeting her after a non-adulatory article. In many things she can be highly intolerant, but never about anyone's opinion of herself. She shares with George Balanchine almost complete objectivity of outlook, and it is this gift that makes her experiment so recklessly, and then step aside and coldly judge the result.

Finally, she possesses a quality that could be damaging to reveal about anyone less obviously enchanting (a subtle mode of attack that would leave no possible grounds for a libel action) – simply that she is essentially good and right-thinking. Many times I have discussed the latest ballet scandal with her, only to find her taking both sides in turn, and in a perfectly logical manner. She has always an infinite sympathy and understanding of other people. I have seen outbursts during our Camargo venture and even suffered from them. They always arose through the tolerant desire to be reckless in giving other people a chance to create; a temporary victory of heart over reason.

Yes, I love the real Lopokova, though at times she has driven me mad. I have come to the theatre to admire the artist I know, only not to find her there at all. She has carefully hidden her humanity under a mechanical-doll buffoonery. I hear people laugh and applaud, and I am furious. I hear them say, 'What a clown!' and I am still more furious for the Lydia Lopokova whom I know to be an artist.

To me Lopokova failed the moment she stepped out of her own particular field to undertake a classical ballerina role. *L'Oiseau de Feu* was not for her; its whole tempo, its mood of mystery and legend, left on the stage a little girl who had wandered into the magic garden by accident. This was not her fault; it was a case of miscasting. The failure was an honourable one. But for me, jealous of my memories, it is in English ballet that she has failed conspicuously, and for a very understandable reason: the choreography assigned to her was insufficient in complexity to extend a dancer of such wide experience. She forced her effect and earned applause through overacting, where before she had been subtle and restrained. However naïve she may appear, she is in reality, both by training and temperament, highly sophisticated in her reactions, certainly more sophisticated than those who have recently created parts for her. This mixture of an old tradition with a new development can never succeed. It shows neither in a flattering light. Fokine and Massine put so much wit into their dances, and wedded it so carefully to the movement, wit of a quality that she could understand, that there was never any need to come to the rescue by violent methods. The can-can in *La Boutique Fantasque* was as high-spirited as any of the dances in *Façade*, but so much more complicated in its presentation. Where Lopokova failed in *Façade*, Andrée Howard succeeded admirably because she was part of the thought that produced it. Outside that ballet no one would yet compare her to Lopokova, highly promising artist though she is.

Lately Lydia Lopokova has taken to acting. I managed a brief season for her at the Arts Theatre. The *clou* of the performance was Shakespeare's *Lover's Complaint*, acted with members of the Cambridge University Dramatic Society. She looked right, and moved with a rare distinction. She understood the poetry too, but a strong Russian accent, amid the faultless but lifeless declamation of the University men, resulted in a poor unbalanced performance. Later, at the Old Vic as Olivia in *Twelfth Night*, she earned many critical rebukes. One of them said that it was as daring as if Henry Ainley had taken to pirouettes – a far-fetched statement, for Lopokova by her whole training has the basic material of dramatic acting at her command. Again it was the accident of her foreign birth, and not that she was a dancer, that made the performance an incongruous one, a fact that she fully realized when she decided to leave Shakespeare alone for the future. She was reckless enough to try it, critical enough to let it be for the last time. Later she fully proved her dramatic ability by a fine performance as Nora in Ibsen's *A Doll's House*. It was only natural that someone who could understand the intensity of the drama in *Giselle* should give an unforgettable performance of the tarantella in the second act of *A Doll's House*, but it was not just a dancer's performance and a dancer's climax; the true climax came, as it should, with the quiet seated scene of revolt at the end, where with a beautifully modulated voice she proved conclusively that the highly trained dancer could gauge the tempo of spoken drama. And there, after the first few moments, the accent did not matter.

Lopokova, through her restless nature and her love of experiment, will try many things; she will fail and succeed in many things, but it is her magnificent performances with Diaghilev that rate her such an important position in the history of ballet.

POSTSCRIPT

I. Lydia Sokolova died in 1973. Her last appearance was in the Royal Ballet's revival of *Les Femmes de Bonne Humeur* in the role of the Marquise de Silva, a part that had been created by Giuseppina Cecchetti. It was all that remained of a ballet that demanded a style alien to modern dancers. Her memoirs, so ably edited by Richard Buckle, show that, Karsavina apart, no one understood Diaghilev's varying moods more completely than Sokolova. Hilda Munnings was one of the greatest Russian dancers of them all.

II. When Lydia Lopokova read this chapter she laughed aloud at my remarks about her reading bad notices with indifference. 'Like hell I did. I was most upset.'

10. English Interlude

INTEREST in dancing in England, after the great days of the *pas de quatre*, revived with the success of the Empire Ballet, essentially through the art of one really great personality, Adeline Genée.

I imagine that the Empire Ballet was choreographically, musically, and artistically negligible, just a form of light entertainment, where the tired businessman could drop in late after a good dinner instead of going to the cinema as he would today. I have seen a revival of one of these ballets, *The Débutante*, at the Coliseum. Its presentation was a disaster, especially as it was shown in a burst of patriotic fervour, always a silly mistake in matters of art, as an English work for English dancers. The subject was identical with Massine's *Scuola di Ballo* and Ashton's little *Foyer de Danse*, but where these had, by careful study and a genuine feeling for their respective periods, produced something living that will not easily date, *The Débutante* visualized the Paris Opéra as being somewhere in the English suburbs. Massine's dancing master, interpreted by Woizikovski, was a true figure of the *commedia dell'arte*, Ashton's definitely more realistic, French, true to type and period. In *The Débutante* we had the monstrous incongruity of a Svengali doing classical ballet exercises. This ballet, which may possibly have suffered something in revival, was in any case devoid of all choreographic interest, save for a scarf dance that no parodist, no Nervo and Knox at their most inspired, could have equalled. An audience that might have applauded some thirty years ago just yawned and consulted its programmes anxiously for the next item. It was a certain indication of the development of taste. The coming of the Russians had banished this type of thing once and for all; even without the Russians it would have perished of an old age that the far more ancient *Giselle* has never known. The Empire public was certainly never Diaghilev's. From the first he created a fresh public of his own from the people who understood painting, attended concerts, and loved the theatre. The word *ballet* may even have been something of a handicap, for apart from the Empire it was associated with the light relief of an evening at the opera, the jam in the powder, that made so many swallow 'the art' without undue complaint. There is still, as a survival of those days, the fixed superstition that opera is something educational that should be subsidized by the self-respecting state, and that it is a crying scandal to have no permanent opera. Why opera should be a necessity and ballet a luxury is difficult to understand – each one is essential in a civilized community.

Theoretically in their composition the two arts are very closely related, in opera the voice taking the place of the dance, but opera needs both movement and mime, so that what in theory is logical, in actual practice becomes an impossibility. How can one ever find a Melba-Pavlova, when each one is such a rarity? The very intensity of the training required would make it impossible. Pavlova was the complete artist in what she undertook; Melba a voice. When we have acknowledged Chaliapin as a magnificent exception, we are left with the undoubted fact that on the stage there is little true opera-realism. One of the most comical and crudest theatrical sights I can remember was Melba as Mimi, slowly dying of consumption, her muff piled on top of her, with a widely gesticulating Caruso, in appearance the perfect *maître d'hôtel*, lamenting by her bedside. When I closed my eyes it was truly glorious, but they had undertaken to *show* me something, as well as to let me *hear* it, and my complaint was fully justified.

This is not a quarrel on a petty point. *Madame Butterfly* is definitely unrealistic from the Japanese point of view; the whole musical idiom is different, the costumes, décor, and make-up far from the actual truth, but, when it is well acted and produced, it has a truth of its own outside of Japan and is complete. Before the spectacle begins one concedes two things: the general one, that everything in life is sung; the particular one, that this is a Western interpretation of Japan; just as one concedes in *La Bohème* or *La Traviata* that the many unpleasant medical details of phthisis are hidden and that stage consumption is something really poetical. One can easily believe all that, but one cannot credit a fat and ungainly stage consumptive, even though in life the hospitals must be full of them.

The ballet available immediately before 1909 was not sufficiently complete in itself to make this truth self-evident. The opera at any rate was one up on it, in having good music. With the arrival of Diaghilev that truth was made clear, and the word *ballet* assumed a new significance, something the composer and the painter realized even sooner than the public at large. They transferred their allegiance and have since produced their most significant work for ballet. Diaghilev himself experimented in the reform of opera in his famous production of *Le Coq d'Or*, where he found the only possible solution, the leading dancers of the day to act and mime, the leading singers as voices. The programme was divided logically into a *partie chorégraphique* and a *partie vocale*, with a double cast: La Reine de Chemâkhan, Karsavina in body, Dobrovolska in voice. To take an extreme case, this is the only manner in which Strauss's *Salome* can ever be performed successfully.*

This failure of ballet to point out such an obvious truth was the case in Russia too, to a much lesser degree, and in our own experience with Anna Pavlova's company. It kills completely the dancer of small talent, leaving the true ballerina to shine alone. One may talk of wasted talent, but the ballerina will transform the work of the inferior choreographer into something intensely personal, and at any rate so reveal herself.

Adeline Genée, judged by any standards, is a very great artist, as well as a great dancer, which we can take for granted. Without both attributes she could scarcely have survived. Her training and environment in Denmark were much the same as in Russia, and the traditions of that country are parallel to Russia; the tradition of the Bournonvilles that gave Johannsen and Legat to the Maryinsky. Genée is the sister of the great Russian ballerinas, a fact that Diaghilev instantly recognized when he told Karsavina how much he coveted her for the company.

The Genée that I can remember so well belongs to the Coliseum and not to the Empire: the Coliseum, significant for English dancing, the Mecca of schoolchildren home for the holidays, future audiences, future dancers. I can remember her every movement, but nothing of her corps de ballet, décor, or choreography. People have called her cold; she was nothing of the kind. She added to the aristocracy of movement that makes her as regal in private life as on the stage a rare and sparkling quality of wit, very fine and subtle. She was not only commanding on the stage,† her movement appealed

---

*Today I have been proved completely wrong. Opera singers not only look the part, but they can act.

†'What dominion in that face, what assurance of supreme power' – *The Journal of Arnold Bennett.*

to one's reason as well as to the emotions. It was the revelation of a very brilliant personality. She retired while this was still a precious, exciting memory, while she could go on dancing in our imagination for ever. The public clamoured for her, but she possessed a strong enough sense of proportion to halt in time.

Then in 1932 she made a reappearance at the Coliseum in the same programme as the unfortunate *Débutante*. One feared a tragedy; it was a triumph. She was the true debutante, the Genée of old with something different, a new tenderness added to the sparkle. With amazing skill she had chosen a suite of the old French dances, conventional but artfully arranged. She danced with the young Dolin, but their styles blended admirably. The uninitiated might have said that it was all so easy, well within the reach of anyone, but it appeared easy only because a great artist made it so.

Only three of us actually watched the true world-farewell performance of this very great dancer. That is not quite correct, however, because I am told that there were many thousands, but they were invisible, and there were only three of us in the room.

An execution must be very like this; cables and wires everywhere, the constant hum of electric motors, a warning signal, and silence. Beams of light leap out of a little box, and then a flickery signboard appears, gradually getting steadier – FAREWELL OF MADAME ADELINE GENÉE. A black-out, and another blaze of light, gradually dimming down, until a small speck takes shape. That is Adeline Genée, first like a passport photo that has been left overnight in the rain, then, as the details of her costume can be distinguished, like some old and faded family portrait. As she dances, the image takes on some meaning, perhaps because we know and love what it represents. We think we can see the fine carriage, the grace and precision of movement, and we realize that she is in the B.B.C. building with us.

I dash down a long flight of steps, along a corridor and into the studio, just in time to see the real Genée, and the finishing movements of her dance, cut up by the beams of light, black-and-white flickers – no, still not the real Genée. Then the flickering ceases, and there is applause, but the greatest part of the ovation cannot be heard. Genée approaches, and a close friend exclaims: 'Genée, but with the face of Grock'. For it is not yet the real Genée; there is a heavy black make-up still between us.

It is imperfect, but it has been a beautiful, impressive farewell.

The great artist, who paved the way for the vogue of ballet, once again a pioneer, paving the way for this new invention that must in a very few years find perfection and play a big part in spreading the knowledge and cult of dancing. The wireless and gramophone have brought nothing to the dancer; television can; and Captain Robb, its enthusiastic director, has followed the dance with keen interest. He has already shown us Lydia Sokolova, Dolin, and Vera Zorina, Alicia Markova, Penelope Spencer, and others. Very soon every home will have its evening of ballet.

Later, I saw the principals of the Monte Carlo Ballet in the same studio. Still the imperfection, the irritating suggestions of something beautiful not quite within reach, but the compensation of the thoughts – that Hélène Kirsova's mother in Denmark was watching her daughter, and of the difference that a few years must bring.

A wonderful ending to a great record, and a wonderful beginning to new careers.

The whole development of dancing depends not upon the teachers alone but on the choreographers who will use the material that is given them. When Diaghilev died, followed so shortly by Anna Pavlova, we realized that this mass of well-trained machinery would be wasted if something were not done quickly. Both troupes had found use for English dancers, and the vague hope of being received there some day was their only inspiration and incentive. We ourselves had never attempted to make use of them. With Diaghilev alive, such competition as we might offer would have been comical. Indeed, the fact that there ever could be such a thing as English ballet had never occurred to me, not through any snobbery, but because I was well satisfied with the situation as it was. The most important thing seemed to be that there was a large permanent audience ready to welcome the best, and amongst the best were many English dancers, though their nationality was of minor importance. Today, with Russian dancing so firmly re-established, that is once again my feeling. It is impossible to think of such matters in terms of nationality; Diaghilev himself never did, as the list of his collaborators proves.

Then, the need was urgent. There was a gap that the Russians themselves seemed too stunned to fill, and the reaction of their English admirers, too, was that ballet itself had died with Diaghilev, a belief that I never at any time shared. Immediately the dancers split into small factions and were swallowed up by their own jealousies or the commercial theatre. Two or three abortive attempts were made, and contracts were drawn up by optimists, crooks, or lunatics. One in particular, a self-styled Dutch million-aire, raised great hopes, gathered the whole company together, made a few speeches, and then waited. The dancers waited too, but no engagements or money were forthcoming. The gentleman van-ished, and the company melted away. We did not know that de Basil, surrounded by a few children, was soon to prepare to fill that gap – fortunately perhaps, for our efforts saw the birth of English choreography and gave our dancers a self-confidence that has had results that will only be fully revealed in the future.

I was discussing this situation one day with the editor of the *Dancing Times*, P. J. S. Richardson, in a restaurant appropriately enough called Taglioni. Richardson and I invariably disagree on almost every point in our assessment of dancers, choreographers, and artists, but as we agree wholeheartedly on the importance of ballet in general, we have always got on surprisingly well. He has done invaluable pioneer work both through the *Dancing Times* and the Royal Academy of Dancing and is a remarkably fine or-ganizer, the rare practical man in this crazy world of charming but difficult people. An academic discussion immediately took a practi-cal form. 'Why not form a society for the production of ballet, and use our own talent?' said Richardson. Why not, indeed? It seemed easy, and even if it came to nothing it was always a consolation to have tried something. We jotted down a score of names on the back of an envelope, and the Camargo Society was conceived. We in-vited a chosen few to a preliminary meeting in a Soho restaurant, and the response was promising.

Gathered there together, everyone talked at once in a variety of languages, but the general impression was that such a society could and should be formed. I talked with one guest in particular, who was more quiet and practical than the rest. We had in common an intense admiration for Trefilova. He seemed unusually well in-formed, and I could not quite place him. Whenever I tried to nail him down to a definite branch of art, he always escaped. After-wards I found it was J. M. Keynes,* who practises, of course, the most fantastic of them all.

*The future Lord Keynes.

At a second meeting, when the noisier ones had talked themselves out, we proceeded to elect a committee under the chairmanship of Edwin Evans, who had hit upon La Camargo of the shapely legs as our patron saint. The name has since been misspelt in a quantity of different manners, from the usual Carmargo to the deliberate 'Ca Margot', sign of our success. There were many eager candidates for the committee, but Lydia Lopokova, whom we wanted in particular, took a great deal of persuading; she had never belonged to a committee before; one could not do such a thing at once; perhaps she had better be a kindly spectator; after all it was a serious step, 'like parting with one's virginity'. She finally capitulated, and we now had enough of the 'old gang' with us to give our venture a sporting chance. All that remained was to find the necessary money and to agree upon a programme. Both were common difficulties throughout our existence. After a few committee meetings we could usually agree as to the ideal programme, but when came the treasurer's turn to speak, it would be whittled down, the number of dancers employed cut in half, cloth substituted for silk, and a hundred and one small things changed.

LYDIA LOPOKOVA (always very correct, once the great decision of joining a committee had been made): I propose, Mr Chairman, that we put on *Casse-Noisette* on a grand scale, as it was done in Russia.

CONSTANT LAMBERT: Yes, and with a really fine orchestra . . .

A.L.H.: We must get Benois or Doboujinsky to do the costumes.

THE TREASURER: I can allow you exactly £57 3s. 4d. Will that be enough?

We would go on discussing the scheme with all its tempting possibilities, relying on the intervention of some mythical millionaire, till the calendar reminded us that we had to be practical. The whole system of occasional production was extremely wasteful. Each performance cost somewhere around £500, the majority of the expenses being the same as for a long run. The dancers, as usual, gave their services, and I believe that ultimately they benefited. It is a miracle how Alfred Tysser, and later J. M. Keynes, steered us clear of debt. Theirs was the task of curbing us without throwing too much cold water on our efforts. Keynes was unfailingly optimistic. When things were at their very worst, he found a good reason why people should subscribe; when things improved, a still better reason, and thanks to his own efforts he was usually right. An hour on the telephone, and a few tea-parties, always produced the necessary guarantee. He was at times dictatorial in his methods. A very quick thinker, he could not suffer elaborate discussion and acted at times while things were still being debated. That he acted wisely one cannot now deny, but at the time some of us were a little irritated at being kept in the dark about so many things.

Our secretary was M. Montagu-Nathan, author of several volumes of Russian music history and criticism, and a man of exceptionally wide general culture, who could turn his mind from musical scores to box-office arrangements, and, at his most inspired, to the resurrection of a dish in honour of our patron – *La Bombe Camargo* at the Savoy. Montagu-Nathan practically *was* the society, the one tangible person with a definite telephone number. He strongly believed in a utopia where artists in different media would find a common enthusiasm in ballet and our society. Today he still believes in it, but he truly knows it to be utopia. He received the complaints, while the praise was given to the large and elastic committee. Montagu-Nathan can organize anything. He is meticulously exact, and his schedules, agendas, and minutes terrified some of our dancers, and were in comical contrast to the actual conduct of most of the meetings, where separate conversations that often wandered very far from the point were carried on. His actual record of telephone conversations was a constant source of amusement: 12:51, Miss Jones rang up to say that her shoes had been dyed purple instead of blue; what should be done? 1:28, Baroness Y complained that her seats were not good enough, also she wished particularly to be near Lady X. 1:30, Lady X wished on no account to be anywhere near Baroness Y. 1:40, Mrs J would resign unless the society revived *Schéhérazade* at once. 1:45, So-and-so read a long scenario based on an old Indian legend and thought it would be a good ballet for Lifar to produce. 1:55, Miss Jones-Smith considered that Madame Lopokova had treated her with insufficient respect. She must protest energetically. (She did for ten minutes that day, and for very many days after.)

The inaugural event was a large banquet presided over by Adeline Genée, during which Lopokova made an admirable and impassioned appeal in English, and at which a characteristic letter from Bernard Shaw was read, which naturally monopolized the press reports. The dinner brought us good results that more than offset the many complaints from offended people who had not been sufficiently well placed. Montagu-Nathan was already a master of the soft answer.

In summing up the results of all our work I will not plead a lack of money. It is a grave handicap with which nearly every organizer of ballet, from Diaghilev himself, has had to contend.

One of the inherent weaknesses lay in having a committee – perhaps the very best that could be obtained, but nevertheless a committee – instead of a dictator with advisers. No one had the time or the inclination to take the post, so that money finally ruled and our policy was one of compromise. It was impossible to operate on any one clear path.

The other weakness was the lack of a permanent company; without it the difficulty of rehearsals is always too great. Artists who are giving their services cannot be disciplined, and choreographers have no ready material at their beck and call. During the summer season, when the company was paid and stable, this difficulty was less in evidence. We suffered too from a lack of harsh criticism, perhaps because all those who could have spoken with authority were members of the committee. We met with kindness and indulgence everywhere. The press talked of ballets worthy of Diaghilev; we knew quite well that they were nothing of the kind, but this may have made us take matters a little too easily.

The society wound up magnificently with two gala performances at Covent Garden for the edification of the members of the Economic Conference. It solved our own immediate economic problems by turning a large deficit into a small balance, now the nucleus of a fund for the Vic-Wells. J. M. Keynes was our inspired chancellor.

On the positive side we accomplished much. We overcame a national inferiority complex and also paved the way for the triumphs of the Monte Carlo Ballet the following year. Many of the works presented were economy scraps and are best forgotten; a few found their way into ballet history, if only locally, and are fortunately preserved in the Vic-Wells repertoire.

Obviously our choreography today is still immature, as is most of our dancing, and it is quite impossible to judge it by the same critical standards as those we adopt for the Russians. We have no choreographers sufficiently inspired themselves to inspire a company, or with sufficient authority to discipline them perfectly.

Most important of all, those choreographers we do have have not yet a full knowledge of the actual possibilities of movement, either physical or academic, so that the vocabulary in use is an extremely limited one, and the performance of any work is apt to depend on one brilliant dancer alone. Markova and Dolin have enhanced the face value of English choreography a hundredfold, but English choreography could never have given them either the initial experience or a name, and is therefore greatly in their debt. It has not yet reached the formative stage. At present, aided by dancers of experience, it can provide adequate theatrical entertainment – a very great stride, bringing it rapidly toward this second stage. Its ultimate development should now become the concern of painters and musicians, who must realize its vast propaganda value, as the Russians and the French have done. No Exhibition of British Art in Burlington House can have the same effect as one world tour of a really fine national ballet, which is not praised on patriotic grounds but on account of its intrinsic merit.

The pioneers of this 'new art' in England are Ninette de Valois and Frederick Ashton.

Ninette de Valois was a valuable soloist with the Diaghilev Ballet and a favourite pupil of Cecchetti's. When she left the Ballet she took charge of the dancing at the Abbey Theatre, Dublin, and the Festival, Cambridge. This entailed work with amateurs and novices, with a consequent concentration on group effect rather than movement. Her big chance came with the Camargo Society, and in Vaughan-Williams's *Job*, an outstanding example of collaboration in the arts, she created the most important English ballet, a work that can be appraised by any standards. It is big in conception, simple in the grand manner, and the story is told with astonishing style and economy of means. Here is the true dance drama toward which Wigman and Laban have been so vainly striving. There is one virtuoso role that stands apart from the pattern, dominates it, and makes the masque into a ballet proper – that of Satan. Dolin was Satan, superb in the powerful conception of the part, a Miltonic interpretation of the fallen angel, replacing the customary demon king of pantomime. Dolin was able to forget completely that he was a *premier danseur classique* in his surrender to that conception.

I remember well the many meetings we had to decide the delicate point of how to name the Deity in the programme. A bald Mr

X as God would have been out of place, and the censor of *Green Pastures* would certainly have intervened. Finally we compromised on Job's Spiritual Self. When the ballet was performed in Denmark, P. J. S. Richardson showed his height and editorial authority to full advantage in this, his first part, and has never appeared since. Any lesser role would be an anticlimax.

De Valois's choreography to Milhaud's *Création du Monde*, with Edward Wolfe's beautiful scenery and costumes, was also an outstanding success. In her treatment she made the extremely wise choice of retaining a Negro conception of Genesis, the only manner in which she could make it anthropomorphic and moving. Again she excelled in pattern, starting with an intricate group, unravelling it bit by bit as the trees and animals found life, and winding up with a dance in celebration of the birth of Man and Woman. A really superb piece of craftsmanship.

In these heroic canvases, where details of dancing are not paramount, de Valois has found herself and has given a valuable contribution to our ballet. In her lesser works, where the individual dances are the main point, she seems to me to be musically sound but finicky, boring, and uninspired. She is not even saved theatrically by any display of elegance. Such a ballet as *Douanes* (Geoffrey Toye) reveals a lack of originality and some poverty of movement. Round just such a simple frolic Massine created his *Les Matelots*, valuable only because it reveals dancers and finds new uses for their limbs. Most classical of dancers herself, she must leave classical sources far behind and seek inspiration in themes that are in themselves of value. The *ballet bouffe* is not yet for England. More than anything it needs a great directing mind in the background to solder its elements together. I value her work very highly because, when she does succeed, she owes nothing to prevailing fashion and can strike out on a line of her own. In this way schools are made and traditions founded.

Our other choreographer is Frederick Ashton, a man both prolific and versatile, who may influence the whole of English dancing. His story is an interesting one. A public-school boy – the term is always used when anyone takes to crime or dancing – he started late by taking weekly lessons with Massine, who has greatly influenced him. Then he went to Marie Rambert, who made him into a competent and interesting dancer, discovered and encouraged his gifts, and turned him from a love of the chic to more serious things.

For a time he danced with Ida Rubinstein and came under the powerful personality of Nijinska, a valuable way of making up for lost time.

He has usually excellent taste, a good sense of atmosphere and of the stage. His limitation is the general one of an insufficient experience in movement, and the personal one of an enormous facility for producing temporarily effective work that has hampered the creative struggle. Ashton's work as a whole is not yet truly personal and inventive; it has still to bear a definite unmistakable signature. If he can avoid commercial work and handle one group of dancers for any length of time, I have faith in his future. Pavlova believed in him; inspired by her and cut off for the moment from the prevailing fashions that he so readily assimilates, he would have found himself and international importance. Now who knows.*

Constant Lambert's *Pomona*, in our very first programme, was of an extremely high standard, and in it Ashton showed his gift of being able to produce his dancers to full theatrical advantage. Anna Ludmila had appeared in London under a grave handicap. As Dolin's partner she had stepped straight into Nemchinova's classical shoes, and the contrast of types was so striking that Ludmila was found wanting. A beautiful American blonde, she should have been a Follies girl, but, unfortunately for her pocket, she happened to be born an artist who might have fitted into certain of the roles made famous by Lopokova, but who was lost without careful treatment. Ludmila translated sex-appeal into terms of ballet. In *Pomona*, Ashton made full use of this and showed an adorable and very human little goddess who could move with immense charm and softness.

Ashton's other important contribution was Constant Lambert's *Rio Grande*, in which he chose for his interpretation an *étude de moeurs* of the ladies of the port. Logically enough this displeased many, as it clashed with the original poem and the words that were being sung during the action, but the composer himself was satisfied, and Edward Burra's scenery and costumes echoed Ashton's intentions. Choreographically it was weak, but theatrically admirable. His best-liked work for the Camargo was a suite of dances to William Walton's witty *Façade*, a blend of vulgarity, satire, and humour, in which he made excellent use of popular dance idioms.

*I certainly do not! - A.L.H.

Again, if he did not enrich choreography, it was first-class entertainment that amused one, cabaret fashion; the incongruity of a classically flawless Markova in a cheeky straw hat, removing her short skirt to dance a skittish rag polka, was in itself almost a discovery. *The Lord of Burleigh*, to music by Mendelssohn, skilfully sewn together and wedded to Tennyson by Edwin Evans, was an attempt to achieve one of those difficult feats of harmony – between a living choreographer and a dead composer – that a Fokine, Massine, or Balanchine alone can do. Only the finest dancing could have saved it from tedium. Ashton's other work in a more restricted field belongs to the Ballet Club.

A producer of one work, *Adam and Eve*, was Antony Tudor, whose most interesting activities belong to the smaller stage of the Ballet Club. He has yet to arrive, but his method of tackling material, his struggles, and even his failures, point to him as a potential leader in English ballet.

One small *divertissement*, *A Willow Grows Aslant a Brook* (Frank Bridge), was infinitely fresh and charming. Wendy Toye, its arranger and principal dancer, unspoiled heroine of a hundred charity matinées, and everyone's pupil in turn, has yet to find a home. Hers is one of the real talents that we have. She is infinitely musical, with a personality far beyond her years. Her versatility of interest is too great. She dabbles where she should concentrate. She must make a name, but probably it will be outside ballet. A year or so with a big company, and plenty of rivalry, and we should see the real Wendy, who I know exists.

All this activity, and the talent of de Valois, made the Vic-Wells into a permanent home for ballet. There, at cinema prices, an audience can enjoy a whole evening of dancing. It is always full, always appreciated by indulgent audiences. It has yet to prove itself by creating its own ballerina. So far it is an encouraging local phenomenon, a plucky prelude to bigger things. Its much-stressed financial difficulties should not be an insurmountable hindrance. The Monte Carlo Ballet, with no permanent home, has had to go through far worse times before its final success, and the need for funds can sometimes be made to cover too much. The revival of *Carnaval* in brand-new costumes, when the work was devised as a whole – Schumann-Fokine-Bakst – is a disquieting mistake that indicates a whole wrong manner of thinking. Before building up, it is necessary to have an infinite respect for traditions, that are in this case the result of the careful collaboration of the finest creative minds of their day. The revival of *Casse-Noisette* was also a mistake of taste, more debatable this time. Unlike *Giselle*, which depends on one fine dancer who was at hand in Markova, Ivanov's ballet is a spectacle that needs a lavish Maryinsky presentation and a whole body of flawless classical dancers, as well as a fine mime to play the part of Clara. Without such a company the Snowflake interlude becomes cheap provincial pantomime, unbearable at the present day. Hedley Briggs's pleasing costumes cannot turn a small and comparatively inexperienced company into a Russian corps de ballet at its most inspired. The Vic-Wells has vast opportunities, and it would be an unfriendly act to damn it with faint praise, or even just to be grateful for what it gives. It can do so much better, and I like to believe that it will.

The formation of the Ballet Club was altogether an easier venture. It had no committee, but was the child of Marie Rambert and Ashley Dukes, child of her artistry and his theatrical sense, organization, and industry. Ashley possesses a passion for building theatres, his wife a passion for building dancers. Their union had to result in the Ballet Club.

Marie Rambert was first engaged by Diaghilev to analyse for his dancers, especially Nijinsky, the principles of Dalcroze Eurhythmics. The whole trend of Nijinsky's development, and the use of new and complicated music, made this important. Whether she taught them anything or not I do not know, but she herself learnt their secrets from Cecchetti. We first met at the exhibition I had organized in memory of Diaghilev and, squatting on the floor, discussed the whole situation. We both agreed that the only solution was a return to the classics. She told me that her girls could dance Petipa variations. I listened, the talk was good, but I did not for a moment believe her, though now I always believe what she says. She is at times honest almost to the point of rudeness. Later I assisted at a lecture she gave on Petipa that was absorbing for the future that it promised. The hall was disgustingly draughty and uncomfortable, and her pupils performed in practice costumes to a tinkling piano on a dangerously rickety platform.

The effect was admirable. They came across as promising dancers and real personalities. They showed that luxury presentation was no longer necessary. They even had that vague glamour previously so lacking in our dancers.

There was a gloriously beautiful and serene Pearl Argyle, an outstanding dancer anywhere, who still awaits the choreographer who will reveal her to herself and to us; Prudence Hyman, vital and mischievous, with a lovely long line; the stately Diana Gould, perfect in poise and balance, today a really fine artist, who awaits discovery, and Andrée Howard, a stylist who reminded one of a hundred old prints; also the boy, Harold Turner, a fine athletic young animal. One in particular, Maud Lloyd, was quite in a class of her own. She lent distinction to everything that she did, and promised something really good. She is teaching in South Africa when she should be dancing the whole time. These gifted dancers still had a long way to go, but they were magnificent material on which to build. I went to the class almost daily; I had found a new headquarters. Marie Rambert treated each one as an individual problem, moulding character as well as body. She had to master the reserve of Pearl, harness the vitality of Prue, give Andrée self-confidence. She praised and cursed them all, each in a different manner. She tried to give them an awareness of the theatre as well as efficient machinery. She devoted herself to them the entire day. In Ashton she fostered the creative urge, in William Chappell his fine natural gifts as a designer. There were children also, who were being nursed and developed. It is a tragedy for our many fine dancers that English choreography has not kept pace with them. It is always a story of 'not yet discovered'. She took me in hand too, and polished up my rusty technical knowledge. Today Marie Rambert is one of my dearest friends, whose frank opinion I can always trust and value, whose standards are high and invariably unbiased. Her vitality is a tonic. After a busy day at the theatre, when others were irritable and depressed, I have seen her turn cartwheels in the street, to the amazement of the police, and then stop for a careful analysis of their mechanics.

The first matinées at the Lyric, Hammersmith, followed by seasons at which Karsavina danced, showed not pupils, but a young and inexperienced company that knew how to behave in front of an audience and that continued to improve. It seemed a shame to scatter this little band, and so the Ballet Club was formed as a permanent home and as a workshop where chamber ballet could be presented.

They invited me to become a founding director, and I gladly accepted. I have yet to discover my duties; so far it has been a one-

Galina Ulanova and Constantine Sergeev in *Giselle*, Act I

Isadora Duncan by Leon Bakst

Olga Preobrajenska

St.Pétersbourg
Gr. Morskaïa H. Rentz & F. Schrader
· 30 ·

Egorova   Kchessinska   Preobrajenska

Tamara Karsavina and Michael Fokine in *The Fisherman and the Pearl*

Anna Pavlova and Maestro Cecchetti

Kchessinska as Esmeralda

Vera Trefilova in *Swan Lake*

Tamara Karsavina as The Doll
in *Petrouchka*

Nijinsky as the Golden Slave in *Schéhérazade*

Serge Diaghilev and Serge Lifar

Pavlova with Mary Pickford (*National Film Archive*)

Michael Fokine

George Balanchine

Serge Lifar in *Alexander* (Photo Lipnitzki)

Yvette Chauviré in Lifar's
Dying Swan
(*Jacques Mairesse*)

Alexandra Danilova and
Leonide Massine in
La Boutique Fantasque

Beryl Grey

Riabouchinska in *Coq d'Or*

Alicia Markova, Bluebird, *Sleeping Beauty* (*Maurice Seymour*)

Ram Gopal (*Mike & Jesse Davis*)

Shanto Rao

Tamara Toumanova

Natalia Bessmertnova (Bolshoi Ballet)

Roland Petit, Colette Marchand and Orson Welles rehearsing *Lady in the Ice*, Théâtre de l'Empire, Paris (*Photo Lipnitzki*)

Maya Plisetskaya and Nicolai Fadeyechev in the *Firebird* (*Novosti Press Agency*)

Alicia Alonso and Azari Plizetski in *Giselle* (Ballet National, Cuba)

Dame Marie Rambert rehearsing Ballet Rambert production of *Les Sylphides* (*Mike & Jesse Davis*)

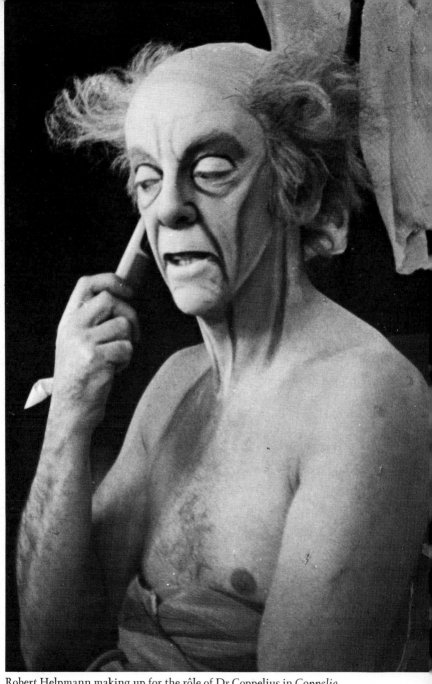
Robert Helpmann making up for the rôle of Dr Coppelius in *Coppelia*
(*Mike & Jesse Davis*)

Kenneth Macmillan rehearsing Rudolf Nureyev (*Mike & Jesse Davis*)

Sir Frederick Ashton rehearsing Margot Fonteyn and Michael Somes for the Royal Ballet's *Ondine* (*Mike & Jesse Davis*)

'Madame's Class'. Dame Ninette de Valois takes class at the Royal Ballet School (*Mike & Jesse Davis*)

Fonteyn and Nureyev in the last act of the Royal Ballet's *Romeo and Juliet*
(*Mike & Jesse Davis*)

Sonia Callero – greatest exponent of the Rumba (Cuba) (*Luis Castaneda*)

Claire Sombert (*Studio Liseg*)

Mikhail Baryshnikov, *Sleeping Beauty*, Kirov (formerly Kirov Ballet, Leningrad)
(*Mike & Jesse Davis*)

Lynn Seymour and David Wall in *Mayerling* (Mike & Jesse Davis)

Nadia Nerina, Ninette de Valois, Yvette Chauviré, Arnold Haskell, Alicia
Alonso, Galina Ulanova, Alicia Markova. Arnold Haskell's 70th birthday party
(*Swaebe*)

sided arrangement, with no risks, no hard work, only continual pleasure in the society of these fine friends and artists. I have criticised, offered advice, and my applause may have counted for something on the sad occasion when I was one-fourteenth of the audience; that is all. I intend to hang on to that directorship, to have at any rate a nominal responsibility for the Pearls and Dianas, and the rest of 'Marie Rambert's jewels'.

The first season was only survived through the invincible optimism of Ashley. 'How many in front tonight?' – (Fifteen and no paper!) 'Not at all bad, a decided improvement.' I called him 'the mad King of Bavaria', as he sat in his almost empty theatre enjoying the performance with no apparent thought of the box office. Meanwhile the church next door, a tabernacle of the Four Square Gospel, was playing, as we should say, to crowded houses, the 'House Full' boards up nightly. They could afford a poster campaign and dramatic floodlighting effects denied to us. They looked like the prosperous opera house, we like the small chapel.

We persisted, till all of a sudden the Ballet Club became fashionable and people began to be turned away nightly. A few faithful friends came throughout the season. Then we suffered from our success. Various managers took our girls from us and offered them important engagements. They danced some absurdly simple steps for five minutes at anything up to fifteen times the salary they received for the complicated work they gave us. Not one manager has yet known how to use them, but the engagements showed at any rate that the work had been thorough and effective. But it meant closing down on week-days. Now on Sunday the whole company is united again, save the fortunate ones who have joined the Russian Ballet. Serious dancers never rest.

It is necessary to keep a sense of proportion, and the achievements must be judged on the same small scale on which they are presented. At times, on that scale, they have reached real perfection. The Ballet Club has been the main recruiting ground for English dancers. None of them can be called great as yet, but they are soloists who must be treated seriously by any standards, and even amongst the Russians they are at home both in class and on the stage. Pearl Argyle, Prudence Hyman, Betty Cuff, and Diana Gould were valuable aids in the difficult season of Les Ballets 1933, taking their places at short notice. Later, when three of them joined de Basil on tour, they went straight from the station onto the stage, a striking tribute to their training. They have danced in miniature revivals of important works before hypercritical audiences who, in the tiny theatre, could see every mistake; they have produced their own choreographers and scene designers.

The revivals have been *Le Lac des Cygnes* and dances from *Le Mariage d'Aurore, Carnaval,* and *Le Spectre de la Rose,* with a delightful Prudence Hyman in Karsavina's roles; *Les Sylphides* and *L'Après-midi d'un Faune;* daring ventures all of them, but fully justified by the results. The company has been assisted by Alicia Markova, not as a solo star but as a guest artist, naturally the most brilliant dancer, but each one has given a positive contribution to the result.

The most interesting creations are Frederick Ashton's *Foyer de Danse* (Berners) and *La Péri* (Dukas), the truly Pre-Raphaelite *Lady of Shalott* (Sibelius), a genuine English ballet, and, the finest of his works, the early *Capriol Suite* (Warlock), a perfect translation of country dances.

Antony Tudor, the other choreographer, has a great deal to say and sometimes a little difficulty in saying it; he strikes dull patches where he cannot get himself out of musical difficulties, but these very mistakes, and the manner in which they are made, show the essential honesty of his purpose. He will not bluff his way out just to satisfy the non-critical in the audience. His first work, *Cross-Garter'd* (Frescobaldi), earned praise from Massine; his second and best, *Lysistrata,* from Prokofiev, both of whom recognized the workings of an original mind. Tudor's last work, *Atalanta of the East,* is a striking example of research into entirely new material, not yet fully assimilated and translated into ballet. Poses are there, the style is fine, but it is heavy and lacking in movement. For all that, I find these three works amongst the most interesting yet produced by an Englishman.

Susan Salaman, one of the most ingenious people I have ever met in the theatre, who can create scenery out of nothing, carpenter, electrician, designer, and artist, has produced three small sporting sketches, *Rugby, Boxing,* and *Cricket,* excellent examples of English humour in dancing, that are based on sound, elementary movement. She has been working with La Compagnie des Quinze, and it is in applying movement to drama that her real future lies.

Andrée Howard is the most recent choreographer; *Mermaid* is a small work, full of feeling and real style. She has used Pearl Argyle too, as no one else, and penetrated her reserve.

This entry of ballet into the little-theatre movement, which has already been imitated in Rome, would be valuable in every country, and especially in America, home of the little theatre. It is the one manner in which choreographers can be trained, and even if it is only regarded as a means to an end, our results have proved that it is a hundred times justified.

Fortunately these organizations are working in perfect harmony, each realizing that the other is concentrating on a different aspect of the same thing. There is an interchange of artists that helps to broaden the outlook and prevent parochialism.

If, in this survey of ballet in England, I have been cautious in my praise it is because I am viewing these achievements from the absolute standards of the main tradition. The progress made, remarkable in three years, has placed these activities far beyond the need of any charity. There is still only one Lydia Sokolova, a glorious bewildering phenomenon, one Markova, one Dolin, but, in these three years, our machinery has been given personality, and the old catch phrase – that English dancers have no temperament or charm – now belongs to the past, just as leadership in the arts may possibly belong to the future.

Meanwhile the cause of the ballet in England is safe in the hands of such fine connoisseurs as Mrs Edward Grenfell and Captain Bruce Ottley, to name but the leading spirits among our ever-growing, active audiences. We owe to them at least one season of unforgettable memories, the opportunity of learning from the finest, and doubtless the ability to keep something for ourselves.

POSTSCRIPT

Today the history of our ballet has been written so many times that we tend to take it for granted. I remember de Valois warning me in the early days that such rapid progress could not be maintained. 'We have the machine, but at certain periods there must be a marking of time, as there has so often been in the Paris Opéra Ballet.' The English school can compete with the Russian on equal terms. It still seems interesting to see its beginnings through the eyes of someone deeply involved, even though he often could not distinguish the wood from the trees and jumped to the hasty conclusions of an enthusiast.

My chapter was written five years after the death of Diaghilev, and three years after the true beginning of our own ballet. This must be remembered or everything that I wrote will seem patronizing and pessimistic. It shows, more than any writing after the event, the rapid rise of our ballet, which could, within thirteen years of my writing, produce a triumphant *Sleeping Beauty** at Covent Garden, with Fonteyn and Helpmann, and pack the Opera House for a three months' season, develop its own school in the grand tradition, and start a second company that discovered the great gifts of John Cranko and Kenneth MacMillan.

There was one all-important fact that I could not foresee: the war. It turned the company that performed twice weekly at Sadler's Wells into a thoroughly professional body with a permanent home at the New Theatre in the West End, under the able management of Donald Albery, who, years later, was responsible for the rescue operation of the London Festival Ballet. It gave audiences the opportunity to see English dancers without the glamorous competition of the Ballets Russes de Monte Carlo (whose glamour had persisted after the quality had declined). Dancers and audience gained in self-confidence. The state became involved through the formation of CEMA, the Council for the Encouragement of Music and the Arts, later to become the Arts Council. The Sadler's Wells Ballet had become a national asset. None of this would have happened if the company had not always had the necessary quality, but the war was the hothouse that speeded growth.

Certain phrases that may seem incomprehensible to modern readers jump out of the text.

'Obviously our choreography today is still immature, as is most of our dancing, and it is quite impossible to judge it by the same critical standards as those we adopt for the Russians.'

'I am viewing these achievements from the absolute standards of the main tradition. The progress made, remarkable in three years, has placed these achievements far beyond the need of any charity.'

This sounded patronizing at the time and to many of our dancers I was 'that Mr Haskell', qualified, no doubt, by an adjective. I was not alone in my reserves. Richard Hughes, in a generous review

*Diaghilev called his 1921 production *The Sleeping Princess*.

of *Balletomania* in the *Spectator*, wrote: 'English Ballet has been treated far more generously than it deserves and there is certainly a considerable body of opinion which does not regard Mlle Ninette de Valois as wholly an apostle of light.'

The essentially realistic Ninette de Valois appreciated my point of view and, as she has written, not only took it as an incentive but later decided to entrust me with the development of her school. She knew my personal involvement through the Camargo Society, the formation of the Benevolent Fund, and my Five-Year Plan for the training of dancers. Lilian Baylis had also fully accepted me as 'one of us' and included me in the company by presenting me with a sprig of rosemary for remembrance at her last end-of-season performance, a memory I treasure. I was proud to unveil her portrait head at the Sadler's Wells Theatre. She was an extraordinary woman, the subject of innumerable legends and books, continually expanding her activities when there was no money available and the pennies seemed to drop from heaven. The Old Vic was the first national theatre, her Opera has become the national Opera, and it is not generally known that there was talk before the war of installing her at Covent Garden. I can still see her in her much-worn cap and gown, with her crooked smile, standing on the stage, like an evangelist, exhorting her audience to greater efforts on behalf of her theatres. Like John Brown, her soul goes marching on. She was the true founder both of the national dramatic and national lyric theatre. Her name should surely have been given to one of the theatres on the South Bank.

Our choreography was not as immature as I have suggested, but it lacked the opportunity of deploying itself with a large company on a large stage. Ashton had already created some miniature masterpieces in *Les Masques*, *La Péri*, *Capriol Suite*, and *Façade*, which I then underrated. He excelled in the pas de deux. His first ballet exploiting the full potential of a corps de ballet, *Les Rendez-vous*, was being choreographed as this book was being written. It has never been quite the same without Markova. Antony Tudor had shown his original approach in *Jardin aux Lilas* and *Dark Elegies*, but his association with American Ballet Theatre and other American influences were to bring about his full development. Wendy Toye has made her name as a producer outside ballet, as I predicted.

The most significant thing I wrote was: 'It [the Vic-Wells] has yet to prove itself by creating its own ballerina.' I considered Markova to be a Russian dancer; her training, experience, and prestige had fully justified the adoption of a Russian name. Her role in the development of our ballet cannot be exaggerated. She made possible the revival of the great classics, she inspired the dancers and the young choreographers, and she packed the theatre as no other dancer could have done. She was in the right place at the right time, but in a sense she was the permanent guest artist, the solitary star, and a company cannot be founded on stars.

This book started with the child Alicia Markova and the great influence she had on my career through injecting a personal element. She later tends to disappear from the book, and I must make a seeming digression on her extraordinary career – or, rather, careers. Until 1929, when Diaghilev died, her future seemed secure. After that everything had to be started all over again. She threw in her lot with the Camargo Society and the Ballet Club, neither of which could pay more than a pittance. She was forced to dance in cinema presentations, probably a valuable experience at the time but certainly a bleak outlook for someone who had worked with Balanchine, Nijinska, and Massine and who took her art seriously. Then came her big opportunity at Sadler's Wells, still not very lucrative but deeply satisfying, the chance to make history as the first English Giselle and one of the greatest names in that select order of Wilis. Then in 1935 she left the Wells to form her own company with Anton Dolin. This company did valuable pioneering work, although any company based on individual dancers not only lacks permanence but ultimately does not benefit the dancers themselves. They must make decisions not in their province, and they lack the essential competition. In 1938 Markova joined Les Ballets Russes de Monte Carlo and returned to her natural environment. When the war broke out she was offered a contract in America. She was hesitant about accepting, feeling that her place was in this country. She consulted de Valois and myself, and we persuaded her, rightly, that she could do more good for English prestige in America, and that proved the case (though she remained steadfastly British, a fact that was recognized when, in 1958, she was awarded a C.B.E., followed, in 1963, by a D.B.E.) during her great years in America, first with Denham's Ballet Russe de Monte Carlo, then with Ballet Theatre. She completely won over the sceptical John Martin, all-powerful critic of *The New York Times*, who, until then, had eyes only for Martha Graham. Alas, I never saw her greatest creations and cannot write at second hand.

On her return to England, Markova danced as guest artist at Covent Garden and made a series of spectacular appearances at Harringay Arena and the Empress Hall, where she astonished those who had seen her before by her extraordinary command over an enormous audience. Then, in 1950, once again with her gallant partner Anton Dolin, she founded yet another company, London Festival Ballet (named by her at the time of the Festival of Britain), which still flourishes. On her retirement, she took up the post of Director of the Metropolitan Opera Ballet Company, but the Met had no formal ballet policy, and the ballet was completely subservient to the opera. It was a frustrating experience, but it proved to Markova that she had the vocation and the gift for teaching. In 1970 the Met appointment was followed by a professorship at the University of Cincinnati, where she held the position of Professor of Ballet and Performing Arts with the College-Conservatory of Music.

One is forced to ask why the services of someone such as Markova, who has worked with all the great choreographers, has a phenomenal memory for detail and a true vocation for teaching, have not been used in a professional ballet company, preferably one of ours. It is this that constitutes one of the greatest assets of the Soviet ballet, where such outstanding ballerinas as Semenova and Ulanova are an essential part of the establishment.

The important point in this hasty summary of a great career is the fact that Markova left Sadler's Wells in 1935. In the original text I wrote, 'The Wells has yet to prove itself by creating its own ballerina.' There is no mention of Margot Fonteyn in the original book, yet two years later, in the autumn of 1935, she was being hailed as a successor to Markova, and from then on her opportunities, her artistry, and her fame grew. Markova had left her imprint on her successor just as she was to do later, in America, on her namesake – Alicia Alonso, whose remarkable contribution to ballet, both as dancer and artistic director, I was to see during two long visits to Havana. Though the dancer's art is so ephemeral, it is handed down from generation to generation, as I have witnessed in my own short experience. Camargo, Sallé, Guimard, Taglioni, Elssler, and Zucchi are not just names in the annals of the dance – their spirit still haunts the stage. This was the whole point of de

Valois's calculated gamble; by moving to an unfashionable theatre on the wrong side of the river, she had a school that could develop its own artists, a fact which led to the establishment of the Royal Ballet and eventually secured its future. De Valois was always conscious of what she was doing, and of its eventual outcome, even in the days when she was only allowed a permanent company of six with the backing of typists and shop girls, who were part-time dancers. I did not of course realize this in the *Balletomania* days, and I doubt whether anyone else did save de Valois herself, and possibly her able and devoted lieutenants, my colleagues, the late Ursula Moreton and Ailne Phillips.

My main attention was focused on Marie Rambert, a remarkable woman of dynamic energy, and one who was able to communicate that energy to others, notably Frederick Ashton and Antony Tudor. Rambert worked on a small scale but with rapid and spectacular results, and it was inevitable that, in time, the larger stage and the opportunities provided would absorb much of the talent she had launched.

The first English dancer to reveal to many sceptics that it was possible for a girl with an English name and background to project herself was Pearl Argyle. She was gifted with exceptional beauty and was at the time more emotionally mature than the flawless Markova or the emerging Fonteyn. She had started comparatively late and her technique was small. No one who saw her will ever forget her matchless Pre-Raphaelite grace in Ashton's *Lady of Shalott*. She died early in 1947 in Hollywood in retirement. Her name is unknown to the present generation, but, in writing this commentary on the English interlude, I am certain that she must occupy an assured position in our ballet history.

Another dancer who had that particular quality of innocence was the South African Patricia Miller. In Cranko's sensitive *Beauty and the Beast* there was an echo of Pearl Argyle that I found particularly moving.

Already our very young tradition has spread beyond the Opera House and Sadler's Wells – Beryl Grey was the first English ballerina to dance in the Soviet Union and China and now directs the London Festival Ballet. I remember her first memorable Odette-Odile at the age of fifteen, when she rushed round to the dressing rooms asking the older girls how to be wicked as Odile. Peggy van Praagh has founded the National Ballet of Australia, Celia Franca the National Ballet of Canada, companies of international standing whose soloists were prizewinners in Moscow. And of course there is the indefatigable de Valois herself. She has formed Turkey's National Ballet and always seems to me to be getting on or getting off a plane to or from Ankara. Working with her has been a joy. She has no use for 'yes men'. She revels in argument which is never personal, and she is totally unselfish. It is the work alone that matters. Truly a wise woman – and what fun.

11. Balletomane in Waiting

IN these long years of waiting we saw many manifestations of dancing, some of them called ballet, others frankly dance concerts.

The most ambitious was the season of Madame Ida Rubinstein at Covent Garden. She had spared no expense. She recognized the finest creative minds of the day and promptly bought them. Unfortunately she always insisted on dancing herself, in a manner that even in her youth was unfamiliar to her. She had been famous as a mime, but here she was showing us an extensive repertoire that only a Karsavina could have carried, from the cold classicism of *Princesse Cygne* to the warmth of Spanish dancing in Ravel's *Bolero*. So many near-masterpieces were presented that season one lamented the fact that their inspirer was not content to play the role of super-impresario. Nijinska's *Valse* will long remain in the memory, with its impressions of a whirling mass of couples in an enfilade of brightly lit and mirrored rooms; Massine's *David* had a simplicity and grandeur that gave one a taste of his new development. This magnificent failure was valuable as a nursery for the new and the real thing. There, under Nijinska, Lichine was first disciplined, Frederick Ashton learnt early lessons in choreography, and Nina Verchinina danced in the perfectly trained corps de ballet; also, sad reversal of things, there was a Saint Petersburg star, Ludmila Schollar, who had delighted us in *The Sleeping Princess*. Even though generally in the background, she was a menace to the star, a reminder of the value of a sense of proportion, and of the value of money too. This was so nearly the real thing that, *faute de mieux*, we were grateful and went nightly to applaud.

The dance recital, so much an institution in Paris and New York, has never become popular in this country, where dancing is best loved and understood. In truth, the dance concert is usually a piece of monstrous impudence on the part of its giver, the sole motive being to follow the lines of least resistance. When we consider that Anna Pavlova, for all her art and personality, never appeared unsupported, and that her famous solos, *The Dying Swan*, *The Dragonfly*, or *The Californian Poppy*, lasted but two minutes each, what can we think of those who ask us to watch them for an entire evening in the triple role of artists, dancers, and choreographers? The usual pretext is that it gives ample opportunity to display personality and full freedom for self-expression. Actually the true reason is that the performer is not sufficiently good to appear with any company but is aching to be seen, if only by her family and friends – a form of exhibitionism – so that we have a whole class of 'inspiration' dancers, expressionist dancers, and exotics, whom Nijinsky so happily labelled 'mushroom' dancers. Isadora Duncan is their goddess, but they have not understood her, for Isadora alone was the great exception. Even in her case one cannot help feeling that had she possessed a background of orthodox technical training we should never have seen the pathetic spectacle of a prematurely aged woman, unable to control her body, forcing an inspiration she could no longer completely command. In her prime, her art and her message shone through all these self-imposed handicaps.

While in New York in 1933, I had an interesting conversation with Maurice Goldberg, amazing photographer of dancers and keen balletomane, on the technique of the solo dancer. He has advanced the theory, after many photographic investigations, that the success of the solo dancer depends on kinaesthetic memory, the ability in an executant to feel exactly the last position she was in and to take up the new one in complete harmony with it. The audience, he claims, can sense this without being able to express it. The solo dancer must compensate for the deficiency of standing alone by making out of herself a complete harmonious company. I have seen his photographic results. He takes the first pose; then, still with the same plate, tells the dancer to move, and touch with the tips of her fingers where her outstretched arms have been, and so on till a complete frieze has been made by one woman. The results of this memory test are amazing. In some cases they are so accurate that it is difficult to imagine that one person has made the intricate pattern just by dancing with herself. I have no doubt at all that it is the possession of this gift that explains so many questions of failure or success, that makes one performance seem thin while the other fills the entire stage.

By far the finest dancer-*diseuse* I have seen is the American, Agnes de Mille, niece of Cecil B. I believe that she has been greatly handicapped by her relationship to that illustrious man. Agnes is not a wealthy dilettante who felt that she had to practise some art or other, but a very thorough and hard-working professional, whose inspiration and technique are very sophisticated. She could step straight into a ballet company today and find herself fully competent. In that respect she is unique. De Mille has understood her medium and expresses herself completely in movement, so that all programme notes are unnecessary; and all the time she dances. Her range is wide, from the brutal realism of *The Ouled Naïl*, the satire of *The Audition*, to the white ecstasy of *Hymn*. Her two Degas sketches, fatally easy pitfalls for the merely artistic, show an extraordinary assimilation of material. The one is the painter, the other the sculptor, and they are not just period pieces with a snatched pose or so; they are pure Degas throughout. Gifted with a mobile and expressive face, she usually resists the temptation to gain easy applause by clowning. The *Burghermaster's Bransle* is genuine mime of a very high order. De Mille is really important, not just another wordless Ruth Draper.

We have one such dancer in England, Penelope Spencer, who has also failed to reach the summits, only through a lack of technique. She is definitely an artist, but her inspiration is more developed than her muscles. She is beautifully built, and it is a pleasure to watch her in that little masterpiece *Laideronette* (from Ravel's *Ma Mère L'Oie*), where she portrays a timid Javanese bathing by moonlight. This is far more effective than her famous *Funeral March on the Death of a Rich Aunt*, which depends so much on a joke and a mask, excellent though they are.

These things could not long compensate us for ballet, which contains the possibility of everything. The finest theatrical Spanish dancers I have seen are Karsavina and Massine; the finest light comedy jazz, Dolin in *Le Train Bleu* and Irina Baronova in *Plage*; the finest character mime, Cecchetti in *La Boutique Fantasque*; dramatic mime in recent times, Toumanova in *Cotillon* and Baronova in *Les Présages*; the finest tragedy of all, Nijinsky in *Petrouchka*; and there is all the rest they have to give so lavishly. It was hard to have to wait, snatch feverishly at substitutes, and to praise them exaggeratedly at times, because one wanted so hard to believe.

The English experiment had been definitely worthwhile. It was honest. It had kept together the nucleus of an enthusiastic public, had given opportunities to young dancers to perform serious work, and so provided a stimulus to the dancing schools and organizations, from whom come the expert section of the public, the old guard, who cheer enthusiastically from pit and gallery. It had done more than that: it had shown works that could really be classed as choreography, instead of the usual depressing 'dances arranged by Miss X', or the exceptionally daring and exotic 'Madame X'. But in spite of all our enthusiasm we realized that so far all this was of local importance, a pleasant, colourful backwater, apart from the main stream of ballet tradition. Ballet had settled in France, Italy, and Russia. In England it was welcome, understood, but not yet indigenous. There could as yet be no question of an English school, with characteristics that eventually become distinguishing virtues.

Strangely enough, while London was a hum of ballet activity, so much so that the late André Levinson, writing in the Paris *Comoedia*, could acclaim it as the ballet centre of the world, his own Paris, of late always completely indifferent to the finer points of dancing or anything that was not a startling novelty, was preparing dancers and inspiring choreographers, painters, and musicians to take up the great tradition where Diaghilev had left off. Whether Paris is vitally interested or not, France has again and again reaped the reward of her hospitality to foreign emigrations by keeping unchallenged her supremacy in the plastic arts. Jongkind, van Gogh, Picasso, Larionov, and the many Russians assimilated into Parisian life have given to French art, without swamping it, a fresh point of view and a new vitality. Ballet is a true synthesis of the arts, and the French, above all nations, have never kept their arts in watertight compartments. Their poets have been in the vanguard of plastic development, sympathetic to and often practising another art, as in the case of Victor Hugo and Baudelaire; their authors of repute are critics and fervent collectors of pictures; both collaborate with the musicians in opera, ballet, and now in films. Chaplin inaugurates a style, René Clair makes it into a school. It would not be surprising to see France, within very few years, gain complete superiority in the film world, if the financiers will forget their superstitions about the box office and give the artists a free hand. Already Jean Cocteau, poet, artist, inspirer of ballet, has made one important experiment.

It is not French originality that counts, but the whole conception of parallelism in the arts. Every period of French art underlines this. In the great romantic movement, Delacroix, Berlioz, and

Hugo made the same discoveries at the same time, and, up to a certain point, from English sources: Constable, Bonington, Walter Scott, the rediscovery of Shakespeare. It is only with such a parallel outlook that ballet can achieve its full expression. France has never in modern times provided dancers of genius; England has done so once and can do so again, but in England the dancers are not a part of the general artistic activity. They remain in the atmosphere of the classroom and are thought of mainly in terms of the light musical show. In France perhaps this interchange of ideas between artists in different media takes place in the café. Impressionism, the *fauve*, Cubist, and *surréaliste* movements in literature, painting, and music are born round a table laden with hock, liqueurs, and wine. No club can ever replace the informal, free and easy interchange of ideas that takes place in the café. Certainly no committee of artists, solemnly convened to meet, complete with secretary and minutes, can ever fuse the various artistic elements. In England, while this is so, we shall continue to provide the raw material for fine artists; occasionally one, such as Sokolova, will escape into the main stream; but it is always others who will provide the ideas. The very essence of any ballet that is of more than local importance is a permanent touring company with its roots in Paris.

The balletomane began to come to life in the season of 1933 with the announcement of four visiting companies: Ballets Jooss, Les Ballets 1933, Serge Lifar, and Les Ballets Russes de Monte Carlo, each one with its different aesthetic. Discussion and rivalry would take place once again, and that, both between companies and within a company, means life and creation. The only fear was that with the box-office competition they would all fail, and failure meant another long wait, the gradual fading away of the small public, and the rise of 'mushroom dancers' and exotics, with hundreds of English girls waiting desolately at the barre with no potential artistic home. It was a question of an immediate decision as to which company was in the true line of succession. When the choice came, the public had no difficulty at all in deciding.

The first arrivals, and fortunately for them, were the Ballets Jooss, fresh from a victory in a choreographic competition organized in Paris by the Archives Internationales de la Danse. They made an undoubted success of the kind where nearly everyone

spoke well of them, very well, and then stayed away. I find it difficult to write of them, or even to think of them as a fully established
ballet company. They have still to prove themselves. They are the
creators of one successful work, *The Green Table*, a political satire
effective up to a point the first time it is seen : it varies from an
original angle of thought, more literary than plastic, to a complete
banality that is not saved by richness and beauty of movement or
execution. In the first tableau, where the performers are hampered
by dress clothes and masks, they succeed admirably. These artificial
limitations suit their style by concealing shortcomings, and the
effect is marvellous theatre. Later in the action one has the vivid
impression that an extra element, that of poetry, is missing. La
Compagnie des Quinze had expressed the same thing so completely and powerfully in André Obey's *Bataille de la Marne*. They
have created an entirely new medium, a successful marriage between ballet and the theatre, by resorting to the old method of
writing the play for the actors actually in the theatre, under the
guidance of a producer-choreographer of genius. In *Noë*, *Lucrèce*,
Don Juan, and especially *La Loire*, they have made admirable use
of this near-ballet technique, incorporating into it the added element of declamation. Saint Denis, Marie-Hélène Dasté, inspired designer of costumes and magnificent actress, and André Obey have
found the perfect Diaghilev method of collaboration, without a
gap between the media. There are moments in *La Loire*, where the
river is shown in flood, that are pure ballet at its finest, but, because of the limitations of the movement, they never make the
mistake of believing that it is enough in itself. By resorting to art
and artifice, they have produced the most realistic drama of war
that I have seen.

Technically, the Ballets Jooss are a compromise between ballet
and the German school, but nearer to ballet. This compromise
leaves them unable to express vital ideas – and they so clearly have
ideas. It also places an immense onus on the choreographer never
to be able to allow an interval between ideas, since the dance itself
cannot hold the audience. This well-disciplined troupe is like a
picture that contains a vast expanse of admirably painted background with no clear focal point of interest. There is none of the
glamour of outstanding personality. Usually, after nightly visits
to the ballet, I recognize each member of the corps de ballet as an
individual artist with something of her own to express. Here names

mean nothing. It is not a question of stars, who are created film fashion with an eye on the box office, but of individuals picked out by the public because of their work. In ballet, with the exception of Anna Pavlova, the public has never been attracted or kept away by a name, but by names, and the choreographer has been the main attraction. The true ballet company solves the whole 'star system' controversy in an admirably logical fashion. It is led by dancers who, because of their attributes, are better qualified to be in the foreground, but it contains a corps de ballet any member of which is able technically to assume a leading role at a moment's notice. With Jooss all are good, but none outstanding. The preliminary ballets are but a prelude to the main attraction, *The Green Table*, so far their whole *raison d'être*. A *Ball in Old Vienna* can be dismissed as 'charming'. Massine, using the same material, has created in *Le Beau Danube* a work that has been revived after ten years, one that is a fine vehicle for his own genius as a dancer and for such artists as Danilova, Riabouchinska, Baronova, and Lichine, whom it helped to create. In this lies the true difference between the ballet proper and the group of dancers. In an interview, Jooss outlined certain principles for his method of working, but all of them were principles that had been discovered and worked with by Fokine and his successors, who were using material that enabled them to be exploited to the full. His main point was that mime did not exist apart from dancing and that every portion of the body should be expressive. Today that is a truism.

I believe that Jooss has the makings of an important choreographer, but only after additional study in the classroom with some Maryinsky teacher who has a rich repertoire of *enchaînements*. At present he is like a pianist deliberately limiting himself to one hand but playing brilliantly in spite of his self-imposed handicap.

Tilly Losch and Les Ballets 1933. This first taste of ballet left us more eager than ever to welcome the next arrivals. Here there would be less of a surprise, for Balanchine, Derain, and Milhaud had proved themselves in the great days.

In its origin Les Ballets 1933 was a fragment of the Monte Carlo Ballet, the result of one of those quarrels unfortunately possible at any moment in the dancing world.

Diaghilev had always foreseen this, and, rather than risk the wreck of his enterprise, had kept such a hold on his company that it was an impossibility. Anyone he suspected of wanting to defect would be speedily thrust into the background. He was as expert at unmaking reputations as at making them. On one occasion a secession on a very large scale nearly occurred, when the majority of his company tried to fix up an engagement without him. He waited till their plans were well advanced, then let them know that all the music copyrights were in his possession. The revolt promptly ended. There is never room for more than one such company at a time, and the individual shines only as one of its members. The best proof is the tragic case of Nijinsky, inside the ballet a popular hero, but afterwards alone, pathetic, and homeless. I imagine that dancers will never learn this, and it is a constant threat to any organization when things are going too well. If the head of a company is called a slave driver and plays one element against the other, he has all my sympathy. He is protecting the interests of everyone, as well as his own.

The disagreement between de Basil and Balanchine must have been a bitter one; there was a constant drifting of dancers from one company to the other, and for a time it was difficult, without the very latest news, to know where anyone belonged. At mid-day one of the artists could not tell me where she was going to dance that night ! What an opportunity too for the mothers to play one manager against the other for roles and money. To increase the animosity, Balanchine played in Paris at the same time as de Basil, and reached London first with a clear field and a hungry public.

Les Ballets 1933 ! A name that did not imply any permanence or stability, the first presage of misfortune; and if only it had reflected 1933 ! A real title to attract the snob, the amateur of the *dernier cri*, with the brightest, newest, and *funniest* artists. This venture was doomed from the first by the nature of its composition. Born of a quarrel, it was called into being by Edward James, a young Englishman of taste, culture, and wealth, but with absolutely no experience, a man certainly not born to command, as an offering to his wife, a Viennese dancer, who had never worked with Russians. There was a remarkable but still inexperienced child prodigy, and a thin corps de ballet, the whole to be set into motion by a highly sophisticated choreographer, who, more than anyone, needed ideal conditions under which to work.

Tilly Losch, the reason for the whole venture, is an artist of taste, talent, beauty, and positive personality, whom I have always greatly admired in her own sphere. I was perhaps the first, in our little world, to acclaim her and have always had a strong belief in her future. An early success in a small Gothic *divertissement* in a Cochran revue, an admirable number within its limitations, led her to forsake ballet half-heartedly for a Gothic-plastic form of the dance of her own imagining, the possibilities of whose expression are exhausted after a few moments. Her Nun in *The Miracle* was a success and served to confirm her in that direction. She was beautifully, deeply moving, aided by a physique perfect for the role, but there was no question of great miming. The whole surroundings were a colossal bluff that was sufficient to bring her to the fore and obscure the real talent of such a proven artist as Leonide Massine. In fact, given the requisite physique, it was well within the reach of many. In truth this part, like that of the Madonna, is practically foolproof. The whole subject of Roman Catholic ritual, treated in the direct manner, is quite out of reach of the choreographer; it is already so dramatic and moving as a spectacle, traditionally so much older than ballet, that there remains nothing for him to say. The wedding in *Les Noces* was a genuine creation, as Nijinska and Gontcharova, wiser than Reinhardt, transferred it from the religious ritual to find its deeper, underlying significance. Saint Denis with his Compagnie des Quinze could have made a masterpiece of this simple legend. It is quite impossible, given such treatment as *The Miracle* received, not to achieve something superficially effective, but it will not bear close investigation, and I saw it several times with lessening effect. By this, I do not wish to imply that Tilly Losch is one of many. At any rate there is no reason at all why she should be. I remember well when she first arrived in England, ravishingly fresh and beautiful like some young girl just out of a finishing school, and very full of interesting ideas. One in particular that she elaborated for me – the composition of a baroque ballet – still remains an exciting possibility for a Sitwell to devise. Since this first success, so rapid and complete, she has taken the line of least resistance, till a technique grown thin through disuse has had to be replaced by dresses, lighting, and literary conceits; a losing struggle for a choreographer with something to express.

The results: *Anna-Anna* [later called *The Seven Deadly Sins*], the main attraction and the very latest novelty. German masquerading as American, just as Berlin sometimes plays at being New

York, with Kurt Weill, composer of talent, trying to do 'Frankie and Johnnie' all over again in a Louisiana setting that could have meant very little to him. The novelty lay in the fact that Lotte Lenya sang Anna, and Tilly Losch danced Anna, an expression of dual personality by no means novel, being the subject of the original *Le Lac des Cygnes*, where Odette and Odile, two aspects of the same person, were danced by different ballerinas. No ballet, no trace of Balanchine anywhere. The fact that the role gave no opportunity for real dancing does not mean that it gave any opportunity for mime, which must have been its whole object. Those would-be erotic movements from the hip, so abused by the plastic dancer and so cheaply effective, become monotonous and meaningless through constant repetition.

And then there was *Errante*, the story of the wanderings of a lost soul in search of something or other – I have mislaid my programme – with Losch manipulating a gigantic train, show-girl fashion, amidst scenery reminiscent of a big 'white sale'. She certainly manipulated it very well, never once got caught up in anything or anyone, but then Loie Fuller had done precisely the same thing, twenty, thirty, forty years before; and Losch has real talent, and it is 1933 on programme, poster, and in fact! Then, the worst of all, *Waltzes from Beethoven*, with the crudest décor I have ever seen in ballet, the pathetic showing up of a neglected technique by a thin and uninspired corps de ballet. Still no trace of Balanchine, who had succeeded with the finest artists of all, who had succeeded for Cochran and Sir Oswald Stoll with a troupe of girls. He appeared twice only that season, working with congenial material, and he has left two real memories : *Mozartiana* and *Songes*.

For me the whole point of the season was the first appearance in London of one of the major artists of modern ballet, Tamara Toumanova, a first appearance that was nearly a disaster, for her childish weight hid the true extent of her artistry from the uninitiated. She saved the season from complete artistic collapse, and from the very first performance had a following of applauding, bravo'ing people, the good old guard.

For years I had read of this Russian child with as much scepticism as when I had been told of little Alicia Marks, heightened in the interval through having seen one much talked-of and thorougly mediocre Russian girl. The minute Toumanova stood on the stage I knew a great artist had appeared once again; already I felt a strong personal interest, and already I feared for her future career. Those few moments of Toumanova were painful. I knew that she did not belong there. I recognized in her the beginnings of a new chapter in the history of the dance. This fourteen-year-old could play with her audiences, make them infinitely sad, and then banish that sadness with a smile that was all the more effective through being used so sparingly. She could soothe them with a dream, and then whip them into excitement by the thrill of some technical feat.

Two minutes in particular gave a thrill of such pain-pleasure, the real aim of fine ballet; in *Songes*, the fantastic toy ballet of Derain-Milhaud-Balanchine, where the child, Tamara, already on her pointes in the dance, has to indicate that she is tiptoeing gently, quietly out of the nursery. A subtle effect that is a tour de force of balletic acting, and that compelled one from the first to take her seriously.

Mozartiana and *Songes* may survive, in spite of what Balanchine said to me in the wings after the première : 'I am no longer interested in these works, they already belong to yesterday. Only the classical lives.'

So far the balletomane could with the best will in the world – and since the deaths of Diaghilev and Pavlova he had the best will in the world, and was no longer hypercritical – return night after night, looking for something worthwhile, and finding it only in those few minutes of Toumanova, the fine presence of Jasinsky, or in some odd movements of Losch.

After Toumanova's very first performance, I went to see her, tumbling headlong up a flight of stairs in my excitement. I told her what I had seen in her dancing. She cried. I now know that Tamara usually cries when she is happy (and sometimes when she is sad). She asked eagerly for a list of her mistakes, and, when I hesitated, herself provided the answers, promising better next time. At last I had found someone to whom I could safely entrust a series of letters I had from Elssler and the great dancers of the past. She was of their breed and would understand. Of course she cried again. At that time she was just three months over fourteen.

Sandwiched in the middle of this unhappy season was not a ballet, but a concert ensemble centred around the virtuosity and personality of Serge Lifar : Jooss had been all background; this was the very opposite. Lifar must not be judged by these performances, of which an American critic wrote with some bitterness, 'Serge Lifar has done nothing since the death of Diaghilev than to appear as best man at the Mdvani-Hutton wedding.' This *bon mot* is less than just, as Lifar's main work has been at the Paris Opéra, which in spite of its heritage has been of purely local importance. Lifar is bringing it once again into the great tradition, a curious position for a young Russian, follower of the rebel Diaghilev. There his work has earned the highest approval of André Levinson, greatest of all ballet critics. In London he showed us a dance so very near greatness that the failure was all the more evident.

It was his first visit as a great classical dancer, and he revelled in his virtuosity sometimes at the expense of the art. He danced like a god, yet shattered the delicate romantic dream of *Le Spectre de la Rose*. Since then, I have seen him dance it at the Paris Opéra, where he is sure of his audience, in a performance as near perfection as we deserve to see. This time in London it was not the nymphless Faun, strange unsatisfactory experiment, that showed us something new, but *L'Oiseau Bleu* danced with an effortless brilliance that would have delighted Diaghilev, and that crowned Cecchetti's tireless work. Serge Lifar today has found himself completely, technically; only the accident of imagining that that is the end will prevent us from seeing male dancing at its finest. But Diaghilev is dead, Cecchetti is dead, and there is danger.

Unfortunately I have not had an opportunity to study Lifar's work as choreographer. Recently he outlined to me, in movement, design, and description, a new ballet that showed an interesting point of view. I believe in Lifar's ultimate triumph because of the supple intelligence that has made him a collector and connoisseur of pictures and has led him to the best in poetry and music. He is a fine product of Diaghilev's training, but he has had to fend for himself before his education was complete.

1933. A sharpened appetite; the meal is yet to come.

POSTSCRIPT

This is the only chapter in the original in which I have made drastic cuts, deleting references, frequently hostile, to a number of concert dancers, especially Alexandre and Clotilde Sakharov. The writing in that chapter was uncritical and laboured, and I was ashamed to let it stand. The Sakharovs, however, warrant some mention here. I came to know their work well; they were serious artists, outside the main stream. She was a highly trained ballerina, a great beauty; his inspiration came from beyond the field of ballet. As a student, Alexandre had seen Sarah Bernhardt and, without understanding French, had been so moved by her mime that he had envisioned new possibilities for the dance – one notices a parallel here with Noverre's being inspired by David Garrick. Alexandre Sakharov was a musician and a remarkable costume designer, specializing in the Renaissance period. Alas, the Sakharovs' researches have been lost beyond trace, but they did have something of importance to contribute to the ballet. They taught for a considerable time in Rome; had their headquarters been in Paris, Alexandre might have become that rare thing, an artistic director of distinction.

I was completely wrong in my estimate of Kurt Jooss, as I realized shortly after this chapter was written and I had been given the chance to see his original programme several times. It is only too relevant at present; Jooss's Germanic conception of Death has not been bettered. It was the brilliant opening and closing scenes of the masked diplomats that blinded me to the skilled choreography in between. A *Ball in Old Vienna*, refined but not stylized, I long to see again. Later I compared this ballet to *Le Beau Danube* and *Graduation Ball* and recognized that it was the real thing perfectly translated for the stage.

The Big City seems to me to have been not only Jooss's masterpiece but a masterpiece without qualification. How could I have been so blind as to have written of the lack of poetry? It was more expressive of the struggle between innocence and corruption than any of the massive balletic works that deal with this subject in a romantic manner. There is a circle of light in which children dance, anxious mothers hovering in the background, and outside, the darkness of some slum that sets the imagination working: there lurks the world of Georg Grosz and *The Threepenny Opera*. It has the tremendous impact of Edvard Munch's *The Cry*. It would be as relevant today as *The Green Table*. Its extraordinary economy is a lesson to the modern sociological-psychoanalytical school so prevalent in America, a lesson for Maurice Béjart, who has so much to say, but says it without selection and at such inordinate length. There is no strain, no shouting, no ground-grovelling. Jooss was a master of light and shade, one of the few choreographers for whom scenery was totally superfluous. And his company had superb dancers in Elsa Kahl, Hans Zullig, Noelle de Mosa, and Atty van Berg. What did I mean by that advertising copywriter's word *glamour*? These dancers had outstanding personalities. I must have been thinking of fouettés and their immediate impact. In 1933 we were as besotted by multiple fouettés as the Maryinsky balletomanes at at the beginning of the century. Today I find them a meaningless intrusion, even when brilliantly performed, which is a rare occurrence.

Unfortunately Kurt Jooss never surpassed that original programme. In a sense the world-wide acclaim of *The Green Table* seems to have inhibited him. He occupied a middle position, caught between classical ballet and the modernism of Wigman and, later, of Martha Graham.

I came to know Jooss well. In spite of my narrow balletomane's strictures, which I recognize as unfair, he invited me to write the foreword to his souvenir programme. Jooss is a man of exceptional integrity. When the Nazis came, he and his company walked across the border from Germany rather than part with his Jewish colleague, the pianist-composer Fritz Cohen. He settled in Dartington Hall in Devon, England, a privately subsidized arts centre, during World War II, becoming a British citizen. It made me very happy when, at the end of the war, the British Council sent me to Essen to be present at his first performance in the new Opera House. His personal triumph was undoubted, but he had been outdistanced by the new ballet scene.

After the war we met once again, at the request of the Netherlands government, to write a report on the foundation of a state-supported Netherlands ballet. We had a difficult time. I never realized that the Dutch, whom I had considered a placid people, could prove so temperamental. We visited a number of schools, one more depressing than the other. The only one we really wanted to see was that of Sonia Gaskell, and she flatly refused to see us. She said that she had been on her own for so long, had produced results, had been given promises, and had been so often disappointed that she felt the only thing we could do was to produce yet another disappointment. We got as far as coffee at the Hôtel d'Europe. We promised nothing but asked to see her work. Finally we were admitted. That evening we wrote a joint report. Sonia Gaskell was the one person, a combination of Rambert and de Valois, capable of founding a Dutch national ballet. The report was accepted.

Later I came over for the first auditions. Some of the press was hostile, noting the similarity of the names Gaskell and Haskell. The theatre was picketed; there were posters and catcalls. It was a demonstration, mild by today's standards, and we crept in by the stage door.

The Netherlands Ballet is now completely established. I was invited once again when Sonia Gaskell retired after receiving the highest awards the state could offer. I thought of those stormy scenes as she made her farewell speech, and I was even given a round of applause on my own. Jooss unfortunately could not be present.

In after years I met Sonia Gaskell on the jury at Varna. She died in 1974 and Jooss has died since this postscript was written.

12. Home Again—
Les Ballets Russes de Monte Carlo

ON 4 July 1933, came the long-awaited première of Les Ballets Russes de Monte Carlo at the Alhambra, home of the greatest memory of all, *The Sleeping Princess*. They were the last of the four invaders, and our final chance. Already well known on the Continent, they were called the 'Baby Ballet', the principals being anywhere between thirteen and seventeen years old. Little Tamara Toumanova, one of the original members and now in the rival show at the Savoy, had already taught us that extreme youth was no longer a handicap, and could, indeed, be a help, but we should take nothing for granted. They had to convince us here in London, where, since Diaghilev, we had given our allegiance to no company, even if we had admired and applauded individuals.

Les Sylphides, first ballet and greatest test, challenging comparisons, awaking memories. It had been murdered for so many years now that one despaired of ever seeing it again. I was conscious only of two things through the jarring new orchestration that cut into the dream, like pain through morphia: Danilova at the very top of her form and the incredible lightness, charm, and racehorse aristocracy of Tatiana Riabouchinska, whom I had seen as a child two years before in *La Chauve Souris*, and who had made no impression at all. Dolin, too, was back in his right place, the *danseur noble*. Nothing had altered; Fokine's masterpiece still hurt with its beauty. Already I was sad at the thought that the season must come to an end, and I was making vague plans to follow the company, anywhere, everywhere.

Then *Les Présages* and the revelation that was Irina Baronova.

So God in His wisdom, through Olga Preobrajenska, had made two of them: Irina and Tamara, each of whom would dance the better, for the rest of her life, through the very knowledge that the other existed, rivals who met at some points and in some parts, yet each dissimilar and incomparable. I could foresee the fierce partisanship: Taglioni and Elssler, Pavlova and Karsavina, all over again.

Perhaps I too had already taken sides; but now that I know the minute details that go to the making of each of their roles, I can see that preference becomes a matter of temperament. Tamara has a dramatic fire and a dominating personality that at its worst turns into overacting and a too keen awareness of the public; Irina has a serenity and reserve that may mean a loss of contact. Tamara is grave, tragic, and dark, Irina gay and fair; between them they divide the emotions, with each one supple enough to challenge the other on her own terrain. Theirs are the big names in ballet today.

Something of all this flashed through my mind a few moments after Baronova's unforgettable entrance with Lichine in *Les Présages*, so beautifully, poetically tender, the finest interpretation of young love that I had seen on the stage.

Finally *Le Beau Danube*; Leonide Massine with his contrasting partners: Riabouchinska, light, delicate, a true maiden whom the spectre of the rose might visit, and Danilova, the beautiful shrew; then Baronova again, a subtle mime this time, in the light, almost insignificant role of the Midinette, which she has made memorable. In it she was the very synthesis of the *soubrette*, a vast jump from the destiny-haunted maiden of *Les Présages*. No contrast could have shown her to greater advantage. She was a part of the music, expressing every shade in face and body.

There was enough that night to set one's head in a whirl: Massine choreographer, Massine dancer; the glorious reappearance of Danilova, Woizikovski, and Dolin; Nina Verchinina, by herself the complete answer to the Central European school; the bounding, fiery Lichine, triumphant hero of *Les Présages*; and the others. To me, however, as to so many, this night was Baronova's, the second great revelation in one month of the fact that the Maryinsky principle was alive and situated in Paris. Great dancers who were artists, too, could still be formed. Both girls had their faults. I was never blind to them, but they were superficial and could be remedied.

This was a greater surprise than the first Diaghilev visit, and because of that a greater triumph too, for it was Diaghilev who had formed our tastes, taught us all the finer points, and the great fact that he himself so clearly realized: *memory magnifies impressions of the past*. People arrived at the Alhambra on the defensive – 'We shall never see another X again,' 'I wish, dear, that you could have seen Y in *Les Sylphides*; nothing can ever be the same.' In spite of the fact that X and Y would have been the first to disagree with these opinions, the new company had to struggle against an exaggerated sentimental memory. X and Y were young then, and so were their beholders; income tax was a shilling in the pound, and life was worth living – for the few. When the curtain went down that night no one said anything of the sort. It was all forgotten. They applauded without reserve – not the smart, frightened-to-split-new-kid-gloves sort of thing, but the wholehearted enthusiasm of people who are supposed to take their pleasures quietly and sadly. The ground was unprepared, most of the names quite unknown, and the material difficulties had been enormous. Yet it was no feat of divination on the part of the audience, so obvious and abundant were the merits. At last the growing superstition that the dancer was only in her prime after thirty had gone for ever. Already that night they were no longer *de Monte Carlo*, but *Les Ballets Russes tout court*. They now had the full allegiance of the faithful old public, so constantly disappointed, and of a larger new public of their own.

'Bravo – bravo – *bis – bis* – hurrah!' Stamp – stamp – stamp. 'Speech! Speech!' ...

De Basil came toward me smiling and slapped me on the back.

'Well, have I learned now? You wouldn't say rotten any more? But I shall go on learning. This will be better soon, much better. There are still many mistakes.'

He resumed an argument of years ago. I had only met him once before in an interval at the Lyceum after his first night of ballet, during the Russian opera season.

'Well, and what do you think of it?'

'Rotten,' I told him. 'We can do much better than that in England.'

'Perhaps,' he beamed at me. 'Perhaps. I have only just begun. But I will learn, certainly I will learn. We shall see – you will see. Good-bye.'

I was as impressed by his long memory as by the definite manner in which he had got the better of me in this long-delayed discussion.

Colonel de Basil is a remarkable man, as his achievement after the failure of so many others clearly proves, but I very much doubt whether anyone will ever give him full credit. (The memory of Diaghilev will prevent that.) He will not mind in the slightest, but just go on smiling, learning, and showing concrete results.

He has in no sense modelled himself on Diaghilev or attempted the comparison. He has taste, but none of the vast erudition of his predecessor. How then does this many times war-wounded Cossack come to be involved in ballet at all, and what is his particular contribution? De Basil is a man of action, and a keen businessman, whose great interest lies in the handling of difficult people. Where Diaghilev maintained discipline through aloofness and fear, de Basil seems to court trouble through an intimacy with his company, and then to avoid it at the very last moment. He smiles, never raises his voice, and generally gets his own way. He is popular or unpopular in the company at any given moment as he himself wills. I have seen a dancer come in to him furious, only to come out again and tell me how wrong she was in judging him, and how sympathetically he spoke to her – an opinion she kept, until she had had a little conversation with her mother. His problems are endless in a company whose leading dancers are schoolchildren, spoiled at times, backed up by their querulous mothers, ever on the lookout for trouble. He is expert at gaining results from these jealousies, by setting one against the other. No one could have kept the company alive by any other method. For a year before the London triumph there was a terrible struggle for existence; one-night stands in Holland and Belgium, where only the generosity of a friend, in lending motor coaches for the journeys, made the venture possible. It speaks a great deal for the dancers that under such financial conditions they did not desert him for better-paid engagements, but it is essentially a tribute to his manner of handling them. I can well imagine him at work, betraying no excitement at all: 'All right, of course you must go if you are dissatisfied. In any case X dances your roles more brilliantly, so everyone will be satisfied. You with five times the salary, X with the roles, and myself and the public with her success.' And then a phrase that I have heard him repeat so often, 'But come and see us. I like you personally very much, and such a business disagreement cannot be allowed to interfere in personal matters.'

No one of any consequence left, and now they can be grateful to him. A story I heard in the company may or may not be true; I hope it is. One of the male dancers flatly refused to take on a part as being too unimportant and therefore beneath his dignity. De Basil left him alone, but summoned his wife, whom he had recently married. 'It is a great pity that you should put such exaggerated ideas into his head. Now on account of that I shall have to lose a very excellent dancer. His career will be ruined, and it will be all your fault.'

That same evening the young man performed, and nothing more was said about it.

Undoubtedly de Basil is a master psychologist, but such moves take time, and this is only one phase of his work; there is much business to be done and the reactions of the public to be gauged.

De Basil has had many important decisions to make, and each time any hesitation or compromise would have wrecked the affair. He is a clear thinker of immense courage. The first example of this was when he turned his activities from opera and occasional ballet to ballet alone. From that very day the fortunes of the opera declined. Next came the question of the composition of that ballet. He immediately decided on a new young company under the guidance of experts. During the negotiations with Monte Carlo they naturally wished for famous names and established favourites. He temporized, and started the season, saying that the well-known dancers would join them later. By that time, as he foresaw, his unknowns had established themselves, and the question of the others was not even raised. With certain exceptions, from the very first he was opposed to mixing the old and the new, which would have involved so many cruel comparisons in both directions. Then during the difficult year came a brilliant offer from London, better financially than the one that he later accepted. He refused it, fortunately for our Camargo season, realizing that his company was not yet fit for our critical audiences, and remembering, perhaps, 'We can do better in England,' and his reply.

At last, when, after nearly four months at the Alhambra, success was really his, he decided to risk all on a large expenditure in the final week – a new ballet, *Choreartium*. 'I must end,' he told me, 'on a new note that will prepare for next year, and leave people with a memory. Already I have stayed the whole hot summer against all advice and have succeeded. Now people will remember the ballet that came for three weeks and stayed four months.'

Those were big decisions, and they reveal a big man. So far he has concentrated on dancing rather than the embellishments. Soon he will learn still more, and, with a rapidly improving company, we shall have the annual treat of ballet, perfect in all its details, music, and décor, together with dancing. Unlike Diaghilev, he may not directly inspire the artists, but he can use them so that they give of their very best. His work may be carried on quietly, but, as the non-dancing member of his company, I know that his influence is to be felt everywhere.*

I. *The Choreography*. The company was first formed around the work and personality of Balanchine, who was always ready to search for new talent, and with him lies the credit of discovering Baronova and Toumanova in Preobrajenska's studio.

Balanchine in all his work has a dual outlook that produces remarkable results, so long as he is interested. More than anyone he requires the inspiration of fine material. He is enamoured of classicism, and at the same time passionately interested in contemporary life and thought, so that he gives to his work a twist that attempts to reconcile the two. He is a poet, and it is fantasy that appeals to him, the curious results that modern thought can give when dressed in the garb of what has gone before. His *Cotillon* is a dream and not a fairy tale. It is a commentary on life, in which the incongruous happens in the most logical sequence, all bound together by the dreamlike presence of the young girl, who, Alice-like, fits so very logically into the life of the ballet, if not into the printed synopsis of the humorous little story.

In the conventional setting of a ball, amidst dance and gaiety, there is the ominous feeling that something is happening involving the fate of all the revellers, and that they are powerless to understand or to intervene. Like a dream, when transcribed on paper it is vague; during the dreaming all seems so straightforward, but it leaves a vague, disturbing impression in the mind. When the curtain goes down on the lighthearted fun of the *Cotillon*, one asks oneself, Has it all happened? What exactly has happened?

This ballet and, to a lesser degree, *Concurrence* show the true Balanchine. In them, instead of giving rein to the facile and witty diversion of one season, his great self-confessed temptation, and so often his fault, he has created something permanent.

From the dancing point of view, Balanchine's distortions, typified in such a work as *Mozartiana*, bear the same relationship to clas-

*This was de Basil as I knew him during the first two years.

sicism as new wine does to old; an analogy that can even be followed up quite closely. The new wine is made of the same grape,
is exhilarating, rapidly intoxicating, but does not produce the full
satisfying effect. Balanchine has been greatly copied by young
choreographers, and it is a mistake. He is not essentially the *chef
d'école*.* His vision is too intensely personal, and his movements
are an interpretation of that vision and not part of some system that
can be learned. Balanchine without doubt possesses a brilliant mind
together with a rare choreographic talent, but of the hit-or-miss
variety. If, and when, he fails, he does not produce a sound and
uninspired school piece, but something that is complex to dance in
and tortuous to follow, but that has a strong justification in his own
mind, and almost certainly musical truth. In the past I imagined
that he was insincere; now I know that that has never been the case.
When he is complex and appears to exaggerate, it is on the contrary
his sincerity in following through a conviction. His whole method
of creation depends on a spontaneous inspiration at the very start,
without which it is no good continuing. With all his experience
he has remained unsettled, still the revolutionary, not always quite
sure what cause he is supporting.

With Balanchine's departure Massine was the ideal man to lead
and mould the young company. It is for them that he has done
much of his finest work, and they bear unmistakably the imprint of
his personality. Were I writing of Massine a little time ago, I would
have referred to his past achievement and then would have mentioned a decided falling off in inspiration, a feverish hunting after
sensationalism. His exaggerated movement, that, as in the later
Raphael, so often destroyed the unity of a composition, gave to his
work a lack of that repose every great work must show. It developed
into the *tic* that his imitators have seized upon. All the praise would
have belonged to the past, his early years. After his Roxy interlude
I regarded him as finished, a brilliant man trying to make up for his
brilliance by earning a comfortable pittance before retiring. In fact,
even in dealing with his ballet achievements, in a past work I have
done him less than justice. I would not now acclaim *Les Matelots*
as a masterpiece; to do so would be to lose sight of the essential
Massine who created *Le Tricorne*. It is an agreeable novelty that
has worn remarkably well, but it is worth far more than I originally
found, when to my shame I accused him of *épatisme*. I could not

* How wrong can one be?

know how much he was wishing to escape from the current artistic formulae, waiting patiently for time and opportunity. My criticism must have echoed his thoughts. Then, thinking of his best, I called him a fine choreographer of unusual intelligence; today I know him to be an inspired leader.

There are three well-defined Massines: the satiric, the period, and the symphonic. *Le Beau Danube* is pure period. Here the creator of the highly sophisticated *Jeux d'Enfants* is not afraid of sentimentality, and the ballet succeeds admirably on that account. He underlines it and treats it quite frankly as something artificial. By his own dancing in it he sets the whole tone. It is a period piece, as is *Scuola di Ballo*, which is in such perfect harmony with the music and thought of the time. Neither is pastiche. They are original creations in the correct atmosphere, a gift that Massine possesses to an unusual degree. He never makes the common mistake of taking his poses directly from pictures, but conceives the action as a whole in the first place. These two ballets are immense favourites with the company, so natural are they to dance, and to dance with the maximum of effect. *Jeux d'Enfants* is the first truly *surréaliste* ballet, the expression of a former theme, *La Boutique Fantasque*, which was treated in a more direct and conventional manner. Once again, for the hundredth time, toys come to life, not as they actually appear, but as they seem to the subconscious of the little girl.

In all these different works, with their varying moods and intentions, there is invention and richness, but no forcing of effects and not the slightest taint of eccentricity. Moreover, the dancer is left with a latitude of interpretation that is rare in contemporary ballet, so that when the roles are taken by different dancers the work as a whole does not suffer. That is a sign of their essential classical foundation and their permanence.

The true greatness of Massine lies in his very latest phase, the choreographic translation of symphonic works. *Les Présages*, to Tchaikovsky's Fifth Symphony, is the first step. The music is still close to conventional ballet music and suggests a definite programme, so that it is possible to conceive of a theme – destiny and the final triumph of the individual – and to coordinate the development of that theme logically with the development of the music. Choreographically the weakest portion, the third, coincides with the weakest in the music, but throughout the two are so close together that it seems possible to see the music and hear the dancers. The Central Europeans have aimed at just such expressive mass-movement drama. Massine has utilized the classical training to arrive at a result that is technically complex, theatrically effective, and yet simple in the grand manner. The German school goes after mass movement for the simple reason that it cannot develop the soloist, or that, when it does, she is merely a concert dancer, incapable of being inserted into a complicated ensemble. Here is a work with some of the most effective mass movement I have ever seen on the stage because that mass is composed of individuals who are treated as such; in addition, the ballet is enriched by five solo dancers of the front rank. Stamping, gesticulating machine-emulating groups grow wearisome in a very short time, however impressive they are on the rise of the curtain. In conception the role of Fate is as banal as that of Death in *The Green Table*, with the difference that the movements are varied and enjoyable in themselves apart from the conception. For into this classicism has been imported and skilfully woven a whole fresh field of dancing – the alliance between Isadora Duncan and classicism in the first movement and the tribal dance of natives at the moment when Fate leads his triumphal procession, before the victory of the Hero.

The use of abstract, *surréaliste* scenery in ballet is entirely logical, as the music itself is abstract, and, now that symphonic ballet is taking the stage, it is the décor of the future. In *Les Présages* the backcloth echoes the movement, and the colour is admirable, if some of the costumes are a trifle too rigid. Abstract scenery implies the triumph of music in ballet. From now on there will be less 'literature', the element that marred the last few years of the Diaghilev Ballet.

In *Choreartium*, his masterpiece, Massine goes still further. Brahms's Fourth Symphony contains no obvious theme. It is definitely abstract and not programme music. To translate it into choreography needs a sculptor of the heroic, a Michelangelo working with human material. The result is forty minutes of individual and group movement, always beautiful, logical, and yet surprising, with every member of the huge cast an individual and at the same time part of a fresco. There is repose in plenty. The eye has time to wander from group to group and to dwell on their contours. There is a remarkable series of entries and exits, and a variety of moods that makes the absence of subject no loss, and proves once again, as did *Les Sylphides* in the past, that the scenario is only necessary for the uninspired. Such a feat on this scale has never before been attempted in choreography. It is the birth and the triumph of pure dancing and shows that in the hands of a master its possibilities are inexhaustible. Now no music is beyond the reach of ballet. It is the furthest point of evolution from Minkus and Pugni.

As so much here depends on musical interpretation, I will quote from that great music critic Ernest Newman (*Sunday Times*, 29 October 1933). He is in no sense a balletomane, and was not present, as I was, to see the latest Massine, but to hold a watching brief for Brahms:

Massine showed the common sense we might have expected of him when he put aside all thought of reading a story into Brahms's symphony and decided to approach it as music pure and simple ... If music is to be ruled out from ballet when it is 'pure' music, what justification is there for *Les Sylphides*, for example? There is no more programme in Chopin's music than there is in Brahms's; yet the enduring success of *Les Sylphides* proves that choreographic figures can be devised that are felt to be not in the least alien to the spirit and the build of this music. We are bound to grant, I think, that there is nothing *a priori* incongruous in the mating of 'pure' music, whether that of Brahms or of any other composer, with the lines and masses and movements of the ballet ... The only question is to what extent the choreographer has succeeded.

After an interesting discussion on nationality, in which he justifies Massine for a non-German interpretation, he goes on to say:

What has Massine done with the remainder of the symphony? Here I can only wonder at the lack of imagination that prevents some people from seeing the points of genius with which Massine's choreographic score, so to call it, positively bristles. There can, of course, be no question of a translation of the 'meaning' of this music as a whole into terms of another art: this kind of music is just itself, the expression of something to which there is no real equivalent in any other art. But if there is no equivalent, surely there can be parallelisms; surely certain elements in the musical design, certain gestures of the music, certain softenings and hardenings of the colours, can be suggested quite well in the more objective medium. I found myself profoundly interested in watching these correspondences, many of which gave me a fresh respect for Massine's genius. Unfortunately, as I have remarked before in a similar connection, there is no way of making these correspondences clear to the reader without quoting the musical passages in question side by side with photographs of the particular moments of the ballet with which they are associated. But how any musical listener in the audience who knows the Brahms score and has any imagination at all could fail to perceive these extraordinary parallelisms I confess myself unable to understand.

The opening entry of these two figures for instance, with their curious gliding, undulating motion, seemed to me as perfect a translation into visible motion of the well-known dip and rise of the first phrase in the violins as could possibly be conceived. I could cite similar felicities of parallelism by the hundred; the sense of the musical design conveyed for instance by the entry of the same two figures each time the first subject of the symphony assumed a leading part in the structure, the subtle distinctions invariably made in choreography between the basic elements in the music and the transitional passages – between the bones as it were and the cartilages – the curious correspondence between harshness in the harmonies and musical colours and angularities or violences in the gestures, and so on. In the finale, which, as the reader no doubt knows, is in passacaglia form – a series of variations upon a ground fugue – Massine seems to me to have done wonders. He typifies the commanding main theme by six black figures that persist through the whole movement as the ground bass itself persists in the music; and he intensifies or thins out the action and the groupings in accordance with the changing texture of the variations.

II. *The Company.* To have achieved these things, more especially *Choreartium*, in so short a time calls for a company of extraordinary training and versatility, and, from that point of view at least, it is the finest and the most complete I have ever seen. Wisely it has been entrusted to Serge Grigoriev, who was Diaghilev's stage manager from the beginning. He graduated from the Imperial School in 1900 and performed for twelve years at the Maryinsky as dancer-mime. For four years he learned dramatic technique from Davidov and Sanine. Then he worked for Fokine in private performances and joined Diaghilev in 1909, finally severing his connection with Russia in 1912 after two years' leave. No critic has ever given full credit to Grigoriev for his immense work and experience. The smooth running of each performance, with its correct lighting and complicated cues, is due to him. He carries the entire old repertoire in his head. Grigoriev is a strict disciplinarian, even a martinet at times, but he never loses a grim sense of humour. He represents tradition.

His wife, the beautiful Tchernicheva, takes the classes, and there is a young Grigoriev, Vsevolod, educated at an English university, ready to carry on the tradition and to cope with the worries. It is the most difficult and thankless task of all.

It is only in the Monte Carlo Ballet that Woizikovski, still another Polish dancer and a pillar of the old regime, has truly revealed himself in a succession of strong roles. Previously it had always been his misfortune to assume, like a younger brother, the cast-off parts created by others, to assume them with brilliance as a dancer but with the inevitable sacrifice of personality. He inherited *Prince Igor* from Bolm, *L'Après-midi d'un Faune*, *Petrouchka*, and *Carnaval* from Massine. These were his outstanding Diaghilev performances, as a dancer, no whit inferior to the originals. His vitality and clean work have always been the signal for enthusiastic applause, but till recently Woizikovski has been underrated. The first role he could call his own was in *Les Matelots*; in the last Diaghilev creation and Lifar's first, *Le Renard*, he carried the entire weight on his shoulders. After that a long and sad interruption. One of my most painful memories is of seeing him with Pavlova's company after her death, dancing as brilliantly as ever, but completely lost. One sat waiting for the climax that never came, and suddenly realized more vividly than ever the death of the two gigantic figures.

Then at a loose end, Woizikovski gave some of his knowledge to the English dance by putting on *Carnaval* and *L'Après-midi d'un Faune* for the Ballet Club and dancing with them for a season.

Woizikovski is the most essentially sane of all the dancers. 'It may be fashionable for dancers to go mad,' I have heard him say, 'but I have not the slightest intention of doing so.' Perhaps just because he is so reliable, and does not 'play at madness', he has never had his real due, save from the applause of the moment. His memory is prodigious. It is thanks to him that many of the ballets we see are alive today.

From the very beginning of the Monte Carlo Ballet he comes into his own. In *Cotillon* as the Master of Ceremonies, in *Concurrence* as the lousy, unwashed Beggar, in *Les Présages* as the centrepiece, Fate, in *Scuola di Ballo* as the Master – he is always the strong and experienced dancer in a young and talented company, never snatching his effect by over-emphasis. Technically a good classical dancer, he is by temperament a 'baritone', whose extraordinary range allows him to go from the delicate *commedia dell'arte* of *Scuola di*

Ballo to the vigorous national dancing of Spain and Russia. A company fortunate enough to possess Woizikovski has in him five strong dancers and five fine artists.

The next 'old timer' is Alexandra Danilova, last ballerina of the Diaghilev company. Young as she is, and now in her prime as a dancer, she just belongs to the old tradition in Russia. She is especially brilliant in light, mischievous roles, as in *Le Beau Danube*, but she is by no means limited to these. Her classical work has real nobility. Danilova is a dancer of such a type that the performance she gives is, as a whole, far more brilliant than the details that go into its making. The better her audience, the better her dancing. To see Danilova at a gala performance, a first or last night, is to see her at her very best, when there are few who can equal her today. The outstanding feature of her work is the tautness of her magnificently straight knees, a natural foundation that is rare indeed. This alone makes her *Lac des Cygnes*, a ballet where every line is revealed, outstanding. Danilova stands almost alone amongst the already experienced dancers who could have fitted so happily into this brilliant young group. She is still supple enough to make progress and to accept the challenge they offer her.

Those fine artists Natalia Branitska, pure classical stylist, L. Obidennya, Tatiana Chamié, Jan Hoyer, and Maryan Ladre complete the survivors from Diaghilev's group. In these early days their responsibility has been heavy. Perhaps at times they sigh for the old days and think sadly of Big Serge, but they have been loyal to the new.

The Russian emigration of great ballerinas from the Maryinsky Theatre has now lasted long enough to take effect on the generation born during the first years of the Revolution. Whether the Russians are physically or temperamentally better suited to make dancers than other nationalities is an interesting but unsatisfactory subject for discussion. From experience I believe that they are, and I have put it to the test more than once by picking out two or three of the best pupils from a crowded classroom, without exception always Russians. I cannot explain the reason either to my own satisfaction or anyone else's.

Too much may easily be made of the youth of the new dancers, especially in England, where we are apt to take to our hearts those foreign artists who are long past their prime and no longer welcome at home. It must also be remembered that when we saw Russian dancers for the first time in Western Europe, young as they were, they had already appeared sufficiently long on the Imperial stage to be thoroughly established. This is our first real opportunity of watching the actual creation of the ballerina. These dancers are at the most three years younger than usual, and they have experienced a life that was denied to their carefully cloistered predecessors. Although the older dancers have a *school* and a finish missing in these children, youth is a quality in dancing that has been too rarely seen. The dancer is at her prime between twenty-five and thirty, and these years of formation, which we are now privileged to see, are the most absorbing of all, especially treasured by the Russian balletomane. Now we too can emulate Valerian Svetlov, doyen of critics, who once wrote that a small debutante, Anna Pavlova by name, seemed destined for very great things.

It is also argued, by those who exaggerate this whole question of youth, that the young dancer is easily spoilt by too much praise, applause, and critical attention. Rubbish, complete and utter; by the lack of it perhaps. Praise can never change the genuine artist. At the most my remarks will cause a *mauvais quart d'heure* to my poor friend de Basil. He and Madame Tchernicheva, at her morning class, will soon readjust things. With daily classes there can be no conceited dancer – exception made for a few males.

A few depressing souls, of the type of my elderly Russian gentleman, say, 'That is all very well, but this is no return to the old days: they are not classical, the big role would lose them.' That is not so. At present they are mainly concentrating on the new repertoire, and the emphasis is there. Equally careful guidance in the old would produce great results in people who have already brought *Les Sylphides* back from the dead. Once again I deny the inferiority of the modern dancer, and the dancers of yesterday are solidly on my side.*

As I saw the company at work and enjoyed their success, I became jealous and frightened for Tamara. This was so clearly her home, and the Savoy was playing to empty houses. We went together to a performance one day, and it was infinitely sad to see her part being danced by others. She was brave, but I regretted having brought her. Then, when her own company disbanded, she went back to Paris to work and get thin. I received constant bulletins of the progress: 'J'ai perdu neuf kilos ! Mais je ne danse pas et

*More than forty years later, I still believe in the dancers of today.

je suis triste.' So daily I pestered the good-natured de Basil. 'Without Tamara you are incomplete. She and Irina must be in the same company. With both of them you will conquer the world.' 'Peut-être; nous verrons,' and the smile, but he did not commit himself. At last I received an excited letter: 'J'arrive mardi,' and on the next afternoon she was dancing as if she had never been away, but it was only later that I saw the perfect Toumanova, thinner, lighter, more certain and restrained.

Her real comeback, the appearance in *Choreartium*, was an exciting event, routine at the beginning with endless long rehearsals – and then the first night. If she was nervous, I was terrified. It is always an agony for me to watch the first performance of anyone of whom I am especially fond, and whose reactions and difficulties I can follow through the smile, the make-up, and the costume. Almost from the first I could see that she was in pain, although she danced superbly, making her entrance like 'a big black sun'. When I went round afterwards her foot was swollen, and she could scarcely walk. She had been dropped from three or four feet onto her toes!

The next morning I took her round to a famous orthopaedist, promising her immediate and miraculous results – 'just a click and you will be dancing again' – but he shook his head and would not proceed without an X-ray examination. We waited impatiently, going over the whole occurrence, each one with a different diagnosis, more cheerful than we really felt. He came in looking grim. 'I am afraid there is a fracture in a small but important bone. It will come all right, but it is a nasty business: two months at least.' Tamara and her mother cried, while I was completely sick, and, like Diaghilev on another occasion, felt like saying, 'It was all to beautiful to last.' He bound it up in plaster of Paris and told us to come back the next day.

However upset we may have felt, that next day started as a farce. The doctor's room was completely invaded by an excited, sympathetic crowd; Delarova, Massine, de Basil, all asking questions in Russian, calming poor Tamara, and at the same time happy and excited by the fine reception of *Choreartium*. I imagine that the doctor will long remember this. He took another series of X-rays, and Madame Toumanova, completely out of control, against all orders followed him into the developing room. She returned in a few minutes laughing hysterically, and tried to tell us something.

We were frightened. Then the doctor came back. 'I have never be-fore been so ashamed of myself. There is no fracture at all, but a small supplementary bone of most unusual shape, that I have only seen now that I compare the two feet. You have torn some liga-ments and will be well within a week. Here are the photos. Every dancer should be X-rayed in a normal state.' Tamara slid off the bench onto both feet, without noticing the pain, and we proceeded to dance round the doctor, who unexpectedly found himself a principal in a strange, very Russian, ballet.

After the excitement I took a giggling and very happy school-girl, hopping on one foot, home to the calm of a nursery tea.

There can be no escape from the fact that the whole story of Toumanova, in essence the story of all the émigré dancers, is ex-tremely sentimental. Let us revel in it; there is no escape.

The daughter of a Russian colonel and a young Caucasian girl, she was born in a cattle-wagon occupied by seventeen officers, dur-ing the cold and hardship of a retreat into Siberia. Her father had been badly wounded in the civil war, and her mother also had suf-fered a fractured jaw. After many wanderings they settled in Shanghai, where the Colonel found work of a sort. Then Anna Pavlova arrived on tour and upset the plans of the whole family, as she habitually upset family plans. Little Tamara had always been fond of acting her own tragedies in front of the mirror, and warning off any grown-up who interrupted, with a 'Go away, you don't understand.' Once she had seen Pavlova she determined to be-come a dancer, and even wrote a letter to God asking Him to make her one, and quickly, too. Shanghai offered no opportunities, but the family had found security there, and it was difficult to move. The mother believed so strongly in her child that finally she per-suaded her husband to risk the great adventure of Paris, staking everything on Tamara's wish and her faith. They went straight to Olga Preobrajenska. They could just pay for the first few lessons, and then it became increasingly difficult, but the great ballerina realized that here was exceptional material and helped them to live. Tamara quickly developed and was equally brilliant in her lessons and at the piano, but soon she had to devote all her energies to dancing.

Pavlova came to the school, saw Tamara, and was moved to tears; this is one of the rare cases, of the many that are reported, where she predicted a brilliant future.

Tamara made her debut with Pavlova at the Trocadero. I remember the occasion well. Not because she danced brilliantly, and made me into a successful prophet, but because her first appearance was greeted with laughter and applause. She was the smallest person I have ever seen in ballet skirts, and, to accentuate this, her hair was done up in an enormous top-heavy bow. Everyone in the entire theatre became intensely maternal, and to my shame I remarked, 'Much too young. She ought to have been in bed long ago.' After the performance she was handed over the footlights, embraced, and fed with chocolates. I did not see her again till the Savoy.

Meanwhile she began to work hard to pay the rent and food bills. With private parties and receptions her reputation grew, the fashion in baby dancers started, and young Russians flocked to the studios. An offer from the Casino de Paris at a dazzling salary was refused, and she even felt a little hurt. Critics praised her, and then wrote gravely about cruelty and exploitation. It was natural, but it amuses me now that I know of her parents' loving tenderness and their attitude throughout. At the age of eleven she appeared as a guest artist at the Paris Opéra in L'*Eventail de Jeanne*, the joint work of Ravel, Ferroud, Ibert, Manuel, Roussel, Milhaud, Poulenc, Auric, Schmitt; nearly a composer for each year of her age !

Then, after a further period of recitals, when she was thirteen, Balanchine, who was recruiting the Ballets Russes de Monte Carlo, saw her and she became a star. He created *Cotillon* and *Concurrence* for her, and she danced in the revivals of *Petrouchka*, *Le Lac des Cygnes*, and *Les Sylphides*.

André Levinson, always grudging in his praise where the classics were concerned, wrote of her :

Tamara, qui porte le même prénom que son illustre ainée, Karsavina, partage avec elle une certaine langeur orientale et ce don poétique si rare, pénétrant chaque mouvement d'un fluide lyrisme élégiaque. Mais les airs penchés, les mines dolentes que les chorégraphes s'accordent pour attribuer à la suave Caucasienne avec son teint mat et ses grands yeux pleins d'un étonnement mélancholique, cache un méchanisme d'une vigueur et d'une perfection que ne possédait aucune des Sylphides 'Impériales' de 1909. (*Candide*, 16 June 1932)*

* 'Tamara, who shares the same name as her illustrious elder, Karsavina, has like her a certain oriental languor and that very rare poetic gift which imbues each movement with a flowing elegiac lyricism. But the languid air and the sorrowful expression that the critics agree to attribute to the

This great critic, whose word could make a reputation, had acclaimed a thirteen-year-old dancer without reserve. Tamara had 'arrived'. Her struggle had been intense but concentrated. In another form it still continues, in that quest for perfection which it has been my greatest joy to watch.

This unusual beauty, technique, dramatic and musical ability in one person are attributes that spell *Giselle*, and if she can last the pace, always a debatable question with that type of temperament, she may well be one of the greatest Giselles in history; then so may Baronova. They are reaching greatness from different angles. At present Tamara is Act I, Irina Act II.

Irina Baronova too, today my ideal classical dancer from the same school, had the privilege of Levinson's seal, unfortunately for every dancer and balletomane now a thing of the past, at her very first performance in *Orphée* at the Mogador:

Mais ce fut une variation du ballet des Nymphes qui nous réserva la surprise sensationelle de la soirée. Elle mit en vedette Mlle Baronova, toute jeune fillette, qui enleva son galop, culminant en un tourbillon vertigineux avec un naturel ingénu et une sûreté magistrale . . .*

What a pleasure it is to quote from Levinson. How many dancers will live again through his writings. A *Russian* ballet and art critic, pupil of Volynsky, after the Revolution he became one of the leading *French* writers on music, painting, literature, and the drama, and a superb stylist in the language of Voltaire. On ballet he stood supreme.

I have already written of the first vivid impression Baronova's beautiful artistry made upon me.

Each one is fortunate in her only rival. I was right when I told de Basil that together they would conquer the world.

The third prodigy is Tatiana Riabouchinska, daughter of a dancer and a wealthy Moscow merchant, patron of the arts. She possesses a lightness that I have rarely seen equalled, and an elevation that the others have yet to discover. At present her field seems restricted

---

suave Caucasian, together with her matt complexion and those great eyes filled with melancholy astonishment, hide a mechanism, a vigour, and a perfection that not one of the 'Imperial' Sylphides of 1909 possessed.'

* 'But it was a variation from the ballet of the nymphs that was the sensation of the evening. It revealed a star in Mlle Baronova, almost a child, whose gallop ended in a breathtaking whirlwind accomplished with complete simplicity and a masterly assurance.'

to a composer's lighter moods, to the third movements of Tchaikovsky's Fifth Symphony and of Brahms's Fourth. She has a quiet personality and charm that grows on one, and a strongly developed sense of atmosphere, without being a great actress. Her finest role is that of the Child in *Jeux d'Enfants*, with its gawkish movements that must never be overstressed, a perfect synthesis of character. She also has a feylike quality that makes of her the ideal Sylphide, but greatest of all gifts are her arms, a present from her teacher Kchessinska. They make everything she undertakes into poetry, and they will make a complicated Russian name into a household word for those who understand the dance.

Nina Verchinina, more than anyone, carries in her the new symphonic conception of the dance, and it was only natural that Massine should discover her at the very beginning of his new choreographic period and make full use of her in the first two ballets.

She has, to begin with, an unusually sensitive understanding of symphonic music, which she feels plastically rather than in the rigid classicism of her upbringing. She has at her command a strength usually denied the plastic dancer, so that her supple movements are under the most perfect control. Verchinina, as used by Massine, is the union of the essentials of ballet and Duncanism. Who can forget her entrance in *Les Présages*? In it she reconciles so many seeming opposites: the use of the pointes with the plastic dance, enormous strength with fluid movement. What so many others have stressed in the past, she conceals. Her second movement in *Choreartium* gives the instant effect of simplicity with energy in reserve. It is never redundant, always immediately effective. Without such a dancer as Verchinina one might well say that some symphonic movements cannot be danced. The union in her of these mental and physical attributes coming so directly through music, something different and more abstract than the ability to mime, shows the enormous range that ballet, when properly understood, can possess.

To delve deeper into those riches: there is Hélène Kirsova, the compatriot of Genée, so many of whose gifts she shares, elusive in personality, flawless in technique, with her back of finely tempered steel; Tarakanova, from a picture by Botticelli; the beautiful Rostova of the lovely arabesque; Delarova, one of the finest light mimes of today, who adds distinction to roles as small as a nurse in *Pet-*

rouchka or as large as the Bad Pupil in *Scuola di Ballo*; the witty Semenova; tall, distinctive Sidorenko with her keen musical ear; Tchinarova, later to make a big name in Australia; and others, each a distinct personality.

Amongst the men David Lichine is outstanding, a new type of male dancer whose virility can never be questioned. He is fiery, dominating, irresistible. Sketchy in detail, he excels in some striking climax – the leap over the box in *Cotillon*, the struggle and victory in *Les Présages*, the dive offstage in *Plage*. He is neither a classical nor a character dancer *tout court*, but a *jeune premier* with character and personality, and the first of his kind. The choreographer is the most important member of a company, and Lichine is, as yet, the only one of the new generation to show real promise in that line. His debut with *Nocturne* paralleled both his gifts and faults as a dancer: it was untidy, ill-organized, yet strong in climax. He understood his own body remarkably well and created the finest dance, Puck, for himself, always a weakness in the inexperienced; not a sign of conceit, but the very natural result of conceiving movement in terms of the thing one knows the best, one's own body. This strong dance was near to the Faun in spirit, but always slightly different. When we discount what was derivative, and the novice's desire for movement just for the sake of movement, something very hopeful remains. Already in his second work, *Les Imaginaires*, there is more discipline, and one complete success in the adagio. In this ballet again there is the conflict between his fine original idea and something romantic and personal. His whole attitude and approach is sound. He will certainly achieve big things – in time.*

There is Yurek Shabelevsky, maintaining the Polish tradition, a beautifully finished dancer in every field, and André Eglevsky, truly classical *premier danseur* of the immediate future. He is large, ungainly, all hands and feet in repose, but in movement long in line and graceful, with a strong technique and the gift of turning slowly and deliberately that I have never seen equalled. He takes everything with astonishing ease. When the young colt – he is sixteen years old – grows up he will surely be a record-breaking racehorse. The male dancer takes longer to mature, and unfortunately lasts but half the years.

* Alas, there was no Diaghilev to guide him. Only his *Graduation Ball* survives.

Nothing would give me greater pleasure than to portray the whole corps de ballet, all of whom are individual artists, if only for the subsequent satisfaction of saying 'I told you so.' With Massine in charge, always free from preconceived ideas, anyone may suddenly be taken up to create a leading role.

From within this company as it is now composed should come the important work of the next twenty-five years. My future has been assured. I am at home once again.

POSTSCRIPT

Reading this chapter after an interval of forty years I wondered whether it would have any meaning for today's balletomane. For a number of reasons I have decided to leave it intact.

The arrival of de Basil's company was the driving force behind *Balletomania*, coming as it did at a moment when the old Diaghilev public had given up all hope of seeing their kind of ballet again. It proved not only that the machinery for producing great dancers of the Russian school still existed, but that their technique was in fact far in advance of the latter-day Diaghilev dancers, where it was almost impossible to assemble a company that could deal with the complexities of *Aurora's Wedding*, the truncated version of *The Sleeping Beauty*.

De Basil's company had the largest public of any in history until that time, giving the Alhambra Theatre a four months' reprieve and keeping Covent Garden open long after the London season had ended, something unheard of till then. It proved a grave threat to our own very young company, which had just emerged from its Camargo Society chrysalis. This was, as I would have realized had I known Ninette de Valois better, an invaluable challenge. There exists no history of the Ballets Russes's Indian summer. My impressions of that first London season (unfortunately, later seasons did not live up to the promise of the initial one) are of value, in spite of my rose-coloured opera glasses. De Basil remains a man of mystery. I know that his real name was Voskresensky, but I never ran across anyone who had met him in Russia. He used to tell us hair-raising stories of his activities in the civil war, and carried in his lapel some kind of medal for courage; knowing him I can well believe that he had earned it.

To the new ballet public this 'Baby Ballerina' period is more remote than the days of Pavlova, Karsavina, and Nijinsky. If in some respects I went overboard in my enthusiasm, I was not too far wrong. In July 1933 I could not dream of the rapid decay its very success would bring.

From a purely personal point of view – and this book is a personal record – it turned me from a dilettante into a professional. I travelled with the company to the United States on those gruelling one-night stands and twice visited Australia. I studied the human problems, the management side, the composition of programmes, and the public's reaction. I witnessed the beginnings of an American tradition and the early efforts of that practical aesthete Lincoln Kirstein, a truly remarkable man, to launch and establish Balanchine, with whom he was to found a vigorous native school. It was a greater struggle than in England, since ballet itself at that time was suspect. It took Markova, some years later, to convince the all-powerful John Martin that there was merit in the classics. I saw the success of Kirsova in Australia and the groundwork laid by Edouard Borovansky, the Czech dancer formerly with de Basil, for the Australian Ballet.

Without de Basil none of these things would have happened. He remains an underrated figure whose name scarcely figures in any history of ballet. It was in some ways his own fault, as I was to learn in the years that followed. He had the most tremendous drive, great courage, both physical and moral, but very limited artistic knowledge. Except in England, where he was guided by the businessman balletomane Bruce Ottley, a wise man of exceptional taste, he trusted the wrong people and gathered round him a junta of adventurers devoid of foresight and intensely jealous of one another. He ruled his company as if it had been a banana republic, with the constant intrigue and revolutions that were inevitable.

In *Balletomania* there is no mention of the company's co-founder in Monte Carlo, René Blum; Blum later reproached me for this. His name remained hidden, completely obscured by de Basil's bravura attitudes. René Blum was gentle, a man of great culture, the brother of Prime Minister Léon Blum, littérateur as well as politician. Blum had secured the company for Monte Carlo, knew the French artistic and social world, and the two together should in theory have proved an ideal partnership, but de Basil could never have supported a partner, even one as self-effacing as Blum. René Blum was murdered at Auschwitz during World War II, by the Germans, after gallantly surrendering his freedom for another man at the Drancy camp. His son was killed in the Resistance.

De Basil revelled in secret diplomacy, as if anything could be 'secret' in that setup, or as if he himself were ever diplomatic. He enjoyed getting into difficulties and extricating himself at the last moment. He was jealous of his choreographers and frightened of the too-great success of any of his dancers. Where Diaghilev for many years kept his name out of the programmes, de Basil would be in the forefront of all the press photographs with the idea that dancers may come and go, but the company carries on, and 'I am the company.' Off duty with close friends, especially when he was cooking a complicated meal, he was an excellent host.

The war and the economic situation would have finally destroyed the company; de Basil did it more rapidly. The brief interlude lasted from 1933 until 1939, but the company was already crippled by 1936. This period of balletomania was celebrated by almost nightly parties, some of them intimate affairs in the Savoy Grill, others at private houses to which the whole company was often invited. At first the hostesses were mainly Diaghilev faithfuls, headed by Lady St Just, then the idea of a ballet party spread. Nine times out of ten no one knew who was giving the party; the dancers would make a beeline for the food and then retire into corners to chat with one another. Especially welcome were the weekend parties at Lord Burnham's home, Hall Barn, where everyone was free to swim, play tennis, or saunter through the superb grounds, or at the Oswald Birleys at Shoreham, where Rhoda, the beautiful hostess, might have walked straight out of *Schéhérazade*. At one never-to-be-forgotten party at the Oswald Birleys' house in Wellington Road, Colonel de Basil cooked a lamb in a charcoal pit, *à la Caucasienne*.

The ballet was fashionable during those six pre-war years, and popular as well. The faithful gallery fans gave parties for their favourites at Lyons's Corner House. These constant parties may have been overtiring for the young dancers, and Grigoriev kept them hard at work, but they gave of their very best to an audience of friends. The parties continued during the two Australian tours; there were splendid affairs on the beaches, or picnics, when a whole convoy of cars would call at the stage door to take us to some wooded retreat. Rehearsals were somewhat curtailed because of the heat, and the sunbathing sylphs showed scarlet or brick-brown in their moonlit glade, something strictly forbidden in Diaghilev days. Holidays were always spent in the South of France, where many Russian refugees kept boarding houses. After a week of complete relaxation, spent mostly in the water, boredom set in as the daily routine was missed. 'Was there the possibility of a class anywhere along the coast?' One or two of the dancers had bought small houses – Jan Hoyer and his wife, Branitska, with money they had won in a state lottery. They kept their own chickens, each one named after a ballerina, and it was with great glee that they announced, 'We are serving X for supper tonight,' naming some unpopular member of the company.

The last party I remember at which some fifteen different nationalities were represented was at the end of the 1939 season, a sad morning – I might have written *mourning* – affair at the Arts Theatre Club. Most of the party-giving balletomanes had left for their holidays. War was imminent, parents were anxious, and it looked like the end of all seasons, which in a sense it was.

De Basil survived in South America during the war, suffering incredible hardships, and returned to Covent Garden shortly after. The glamour had vanished; the season was a pathetic anticlimax. Our own ballet was going from strength to strength, and even the Ballets Russes diehards were finding their way, a trifle apologetically, to Covent Garden and Sadler's Wells; Ashton and the late John Cranko, Fonteyn and Helpmann were the names they discussed. For a time the Marquis de Cuevas maintained a company paid for and supported by his Rockefeller wife's money. It was elegant, *très snob*, but not in the Diaghilev sense of the word, where elegance and intelligence went hand in hand. It produced some memorable works – John Taras's *Piège de Lumière* and George Skibine's beautiful *Idylle* and *Annabel Lee*, which he danced with his wife, Marjorie Tallchief, to my mind one of the most lyrical of American dancers, and a revival of Balanchine's *Night Shadow*. But the company was a rich man's hobby and had no staying power. The era of cosmopolitan ballet with no permanent base in a capital city has disappeared for ever; nevertheless, the loss was a great one for the art of ballet.

13. To America with the Ballet

It was in Bournemouth after the final performance, and all the excitement of the fire that had so nearly ended in tragedy, that I announced to my friends in the company that this was my hundredth performance.

'But of course you are coming to America with us,' said Delarova, and, without a moment's thought, I replied, 'Of course. When exactly are you leaving, and on what boat?' No one was in the slightest bit surprised. Here my 'obsession' was normal and perfectly understood by those who had given their whole lives to dancing. There could be nothing strange in someone willing to give up his evenings, and part of his mornings and afternoons, too, in watching them and receiving what they gave.

I have realized from the very first, without making any plans, that it would be quite impossible, now that I was safely 'at home' once again, to leave it all behind for a number of months, especially during the most exciting adventure of all. I had followed them to Golders Green, Streatham Hill, and Bournemouth; America was not so far away! By now I was a definite part of the company, their travelling audience and friend, and the hundred performances had far from satisfied me, for there was always some improvement to look forward to in this history of rapid artistic development. On tour, too, I had just begun to know individuals and to get interested in them. I was absolutely starved after all these years. I wanted to talk of ballet, live in its atmosphere, and to go on learning. I wanted especially to witness the amazement of an audience who had known no true ballet since 1916 and the disastrous Nijinsky venture.

I left for London, going straight to Thomas Cook's from the station. The decision was taken, but it was distinctly difficult to explain. My wife, of course, understood, and urged me to go from the first, with the plea that it was so rare that anyone got such positive joy from anything in life that it would be foolish to miss the opportunity. Most people, however, pitied her demonstratively and thought me completely mad, though they themselves were always willing to set a few weeks aside every year to go to winter sports and the like. An elderly relative prided himself on his deep knowledge of human nature at having discovered the true reason. 'There's a woman in the case of course.' (He probably said, 'Cherchez la femme.') 'There always is, and he's following her to America. It's perfectly simple. He's in love.' It was too simple. He was so very nearly right. I was in love, but with an art and an entire company. I am sure that he is still quite unconvinced, still the clever man of the world who found out the true reason.

I left for Plymouth to see the final performances. The company had made it like Monte Carlo in atmosphere. At every street corner there were animated conversations in Russian, Woolworth's was the great shopping centre for the little ballerinas, and the whole town had become ballet-conscious. Surely small girls were worrying their mothers to let them dance, mothers were worrying their husbands, and all were dreaming dreams. Thank heaven that so many will be courting or married before they can put them to the test.

It was the beginning of the cold snap, and the theatre was like an icebox. 'I see that *Aladdin's* the next performance,' Algeranov told the stage manager. 'If you don't get the theatre warmer, the oil will freeze in his lamp.' Many London friends had come down to see us off; the excitement and confusion were amazing. Some of the girls were terrified at the prospect, convinced that the ship would sink, while one had mislaid her mother and no one seemed to know whether she would join the ship in England or in France, if at all. Young Grigoriev must have had an especially difficult task in tracing them all, since in the majority of cases stage names differed from those on the passports, which came as a revelation even to their owners. Who is Khacidovitch? Why, Tamara Toumanova. Ellen Wittrup? Kirsova, of course.

No one was lost. We got on board at midnight and were ushered into the dining room. Immediately it was obvious that everything was ballet, and the ship belonged to us. One unfortunate gentleman, a total stranger with a Russian name, was almost forcibly detained in our party until final orders were given by Grigoriev, amazed why he could not go quietly to bed. The missing mother had been sighted from the tender and was greeted with loud and startling cries of 'Mama' by the entire company.

It was rough from the first day out, and many of the company disappeared and were seen no more. De Basil made daily tours of the cabins and shouted words of encouragement. Sometimes he went into the wrong ones, but it did not seem to worry him at all; just a smile. 'Eh bien, comment ça va – oh, pardon.' Finally he decided that no one in his company should be allowed to be sick any longer, and together we carried Verchinina and Kirsova, the worst offenders, on deck, very much against their will and followed by the reproaches of a fat and intensely motherly stewardess. But de Basil was right; they were cured within a few hours and were playing deck games the next morning. There was one unfortunate relapse, when, during a talking film, the music of *Les Présages* was played. Its suggestion of violent movement was too much for many.

I had proved myself abundantly. I could still believe that girls I had seen with hair bedraggled and a wild look in their eyes, being very unpoetical in sound and look, were truly sylphs. Crossings may have wrecked honeymoons; they could not disturb the balleto-mane.

Soon a routine was established; Massine worked daily in his cabin, Dorati memorized musical scores and played Hungarian melodies for us by the hour, Toumanova and Baronova found fresh rivalry at deck tennis, de Basil sent telegrams, Algeranov and Tresahar told of their travels in out-of-the-way places with Pavlova, and Grigoriev marched the deck, for once not captain.

One night, in mid-Atlantic, Tarakanova came of age, and we celebrated the event. Twenty-one; the Ballets Russes de Monte Carlo are growing up! There were three christenings too. Our Ballet Club girls became Russian; Prudence Hyman as Polina Strogova; Betty Cuff, Olga Nelidova; Elizabeth Ruxton, Lisa Serova. The names soon passed into common usage and only their owners were still a little dazed from time to time. Then there was the ship's concert, a grand *Gala des Ballets Russes* followed by a supper and dance. The ship rolled badly, in spite of engines specially stopped; outside there was a regular blizzard. I have seen better performances of *Les Sylphides*, but never under more curious circumstances.

I had many long talks with de Basil.

'Sometimes I feel like giving this all up; truly the strain isn't worth it. I have been through the war, so that I know what strain means. It's those mothers. I have to take them along to look after the children, but instead of providing a good home atmosphere, they provide nothing but trouble, putting all sorts of ideas into their daughters' heads. Every small event is immediately magnified into a conspiracy. Why can't they see that their interests and mine are identical? Success is the common aim. Of course, if the girls themselves were not naturally jealous, they wouldn't care enough to be artists; there is always that consolation. I have received letters from aggrieved fathers too. I can even understand that, but when I receive a letter from a sister-in-law the limit has been reached. Look at this.'

Once, I think, I have seen something extra in his usual smile, almost a wink. He has just been to visit a very sick and sorry mother, one of the most troublesome.

Blessed jealousy, constructive jealousy, a virtue in all dancers! Each one performs the better for knowing that her rival in the wings is watching every movement, and will dance the role better if she can, and at the very next performance. It is an incentive, the certain great inspiration. What has killed so much talent in England is that fine public school attempt to stamp it out. 'Jane came to the school first; she must have the leading role at the school performance.' Heavens, if Jane is no good and Jill, the newcomer, is brilliant, can there be any doubt? Jane's feelings in seeing Jill dance may stir up that something in her. Once a *maître de ballet* told me with pride, 'There is no jealousy here, we are all one big happy family,' and I believed it at once, for I had just seen the performance. A dancer need no longer be jealous only when she has bought her very last pair of shoes, or settled down to a comfortable suburban existence. Till then long live jealousy, say I, and its results. Only the outsider, who knows but one dancer in a company and does not yet fully understand the game, must watch his step or he will easily believe the worst of everyone, and many illusions will be speedily shattered.

Just when we had settled down into a comfortable routine, made doubly so by the French ship's company, whose honoured guests we had felt from the very start, the journey ended. Journalists besieged the ship, and the great adventure had begun.

'Say, is the great Dye-aghilev with you?' someone asked. 'Dead; no, you don't say that? Well, if it isn't just too bad, and he was the greatest dancer ever.'

'Now, girls, bunch up together, show plenty of leg; you're dancers, aren't you? Well, what are you waiting for? Hey, you, you're a good looker; step right in front and smile; that's right.'

This lasted for some two hours. A paternal-looking man, our impresario, Hurok, came on board, followed by two men holding out bread and salt – a beautiful old Russian ceremony of welcome, cheapened by its obvious publicity use and the careful photographic poses. If it served its purpose, well and good.

At last we get off the ship. It is pouring, and the famous skyline has come out blurred but still impressive – it gives me a tremendous thrill. At the customs we get a really bad reception from a crowd of ill-mannered, quarrelsome petty officials, who must give many a traveller a totally false idea of the warmth of American hospitality. There is immediate trouble about the ballet shoes found in every trunk. 'Six pairs; you'll have to pay on those.' Everyone shouts at once. I translate for a little group. 'These shoes are already darned and ready for use. They are purely personal property, and without them the dancers could not perform. At the most they will last ten days, and then they will all buy American shoes.' 'I don't know anything about that. You come along with me, and pay up quick.' I do not attempt to translate further; no one could possibly hear me. The bewildered official is now surrounded by four furious and voluble mothers (they do have their uses); all speak in Russian together, their anxious daughters chirping in from time to time. 'Say, they're plumb crazy, that's what they are. I'll leave them to cool down a bit.' Just as he is walking away, a more important official turns up. 'Let 'em all through.' With relief he scribbles on the baggage. First great and complete victory for the mothers, how complete I only learned later. The English girls, with an unquestioning belief in law and order, had paid the sum demanded after a little polite argument. Their money was promptly and apologetically refunded. With such tactics free trade would soon be an established fact. We have been given lists of hotels and go off in groups. The seventeen-year-old Riabouchinska, who has been here before with Baliev, constitutes herself our guide. We greatly admire her knowledge, as she points out, 'This is Broadway; that's the Roxy; there's a cafeteria,' and excitedly, 'there's Woolworth's,' which makes us feel at home. We know we are completely safe in her hands.

A brief visit to our theatre, and surprisingly enough we are free for what remains of the day to unpack and find our equilibrium.

Some of the girls are a little scared. A few days before we had seen a James Cagney roughneck picture, with plenty of shootings and beatings up, and Dolotine, a hundred per cent disguised American, had told them that it was a pretty accurate picture of daily life in New York, especially around Broadway. The happenings at the customs had not helped to dispel the illusion.

The following day is given over entirely to rehearsal. Everyone has recovered, and there is immense joy at being back at work once again. Dancers resent an enforced holiday. Also, a good sign, there is a revival of some feuds temporarily suspended. In the Green Room, Madame Karinska is in complete control, trying on costumes and superintending a whole company of tailors. I feel that she should be on the stage and not under it; as beautiful as any of our dancers, during the journey she earned the name 'Princess'. No matter how rough, there was the Princess at eleven each morning, walking up and down the deck as calm and elegant as if she had been in the Bois. This businesswoman-artist from Russia has stormed the city of dressmakers and won. The work of the great decorative artists of the day is entrusted to her; they admire her beauty, enjoy the wit of her conversation, and trust her completely.

A charming friend who travelled with us, Mrs de Mille, mother of Agnes, had asked me to tea with some of the leading dancers of New York, among them Martha Graham, most famous exponent of the modern dance, whose link with ballet had been a performance of *Le Sacre du Printemps* directed by Massine. The account of an angry debate with Fokine had greatly prejudiced me against her. On first sight I found her a plain, earnest, rather grim-looking person, who, apart from her expressive hands, might have been a New England 'schoolmarm'. She was different from any dancer I had ever seen, but as she talked and became animated I discovered in her a real beauty and a quiet, pleasing strength. She was so entirely reasonable, too, as I immediately and tactlessly questioned her on the famous debate and on her attitude toward ballet in general. She did not deny ballet, she had studied it and realized that it was not for her; also she had no intense admiration for German dancing, which she found too cerebral. She was sorry that her views had been so misrepresented. She never said that only Pavlova's bow was interesting, but the very opposite, that with such a dancer as Pavlova *even* her bow was interesting. I felt I should see her if possible, though it was more than likely that I would not approve. To my regret the opportunity never came. I was left with the impression of an utterly sincere artist of strong personality, who can, when her interest is aroused, *make* herself beautiful.

I still do not know why the exponents of the 'modern dance' despise feminine thrills and fashions. Not one of them has ever given me the idea that any man has ever waited for her at the stage door. It may well be a reaction against artificiality, but it is in itself terrifyingly artificial. There is nothing more natural than for a woman, and especially an actress, to wish to appear at her most beautiful. When she becomes a missionary for a new cause, a rabid enthusiast, then her cause would be all the more advanced by a little propaganda offstage. Without resorting to the extremes of the 'show a little leg, girls' of our reporter friend, a fine appearance offstage is at any rate a guarantee that something beautiful will be seen onstage. This first denial of beauty is in itself the sign not of revolt, as they imagine, but of something utterly out of contact with the realities of life, the very charge that is so often ignorantly made about ballet. It is part of the dancer's education to know how to wear the costume of all periods becomingly. It should be second nature. Only when one is a Lydia Lopokova, with an amazing record of beautiful creation, can one afford to be seen walking down Bond Street in Wellington boots and a knitted tam-o'-shanter – and even that seems a pity.

I also met John Martin, the leading dance critic of America. We disagreed on many points and found little common ground at that first meeting, but we belonged to the same party, only to different branches, which made our quarrel a family affair. Martin has done big things for the dance in America, the most important being the difficult task of driving home the fact that it is an art, not a light entertainment. Like every conscientious critic, he has troubled to learn, so that his standards are high. For the rest, we both think each other a little misguided, a trifle narrow-minded, and enjoy the friendly rows that ensue.

The first night was almost a repetition of London – the same crowded house, the same shouts and applause, but *Concurrence* and then *Le Beau Danube* drew it all, and *Les Présages*, the ballet that had kept the company for so long in London, the meat of the programme, was obviously not greatly liked.

The Americans were exactly in the same position as Western Europe before 1909, only prejudiced against the very name *ballet*, and no wonder. Mr Roxy's efforts at entertainment under that sacred name were sufficient to bewilder any intelligent person with a sense of the theatre. He provided girls by the hundred, pretty ones too, elephants whenever possible, dazzling lights and costumes; and all on a stage the size of Waterloo Station. Personality was out of the question; even sex-appeal, America's gift to the theatre, was not strong enough to break through these methods of the wholesaler in his warehouse. It is a current joke that a man up from the country, seeing elephants in one of these ballets, turned to his neighbour and said, 'I never did like performing mice.' To make matters worse, these 'ballets' were given the names of standard works, so that to-day *Schéhérazade* means elephants and girls instead of the pantherine leaps of Nijinsky. It is true that Massine worked there for two years, but, while he could make the pattern richer, he could not do the impossible and create a weekly masterpiece. Also this had undoubtedly damaged his prestige. It was all that they knew of him. The rest was hearsay, and New York takes nothing on trust.

Against that was the memory of the one creative American dancer, Isadora Duncan, who had made her reputation in Europe. If ballet meant Roxy, then she was clearly justified in all that she said against it. Her sayings were cherished, even more than the memory of her performances. At some time she had said that it was not possible to dance to symphonic music, although she did so herself. The ballet, then, could enjoy success when it did the lighter things, but it must not attempt to be too serious; that was the province of the concert dancer. Also it was unforgivable for those serious things to be demonstrated by young and very pretty girls. Against all advice, de Basil took another big decision, persisted with *Les Présages*, and so made the final triumph possible. The Americans, sensibly enough, were not prepared to take European success as a hallmark. They were less *au courant* of ballet than we, but all the more critical. It was a magnificent test for the dancers, and it matured them. They saw in it a challenge and excelled themselves. Never had Toumanova given more significance to *Concurrence*, Baronova more poetry to *Les Sylphides*, or Lichine danced with greater fire. And they won handsomely, so that Europe will be the poorer for several months a year.

This victory has now also made it possible for America to use her own dancers. Hundreds are trained every year, the schools are popular, but then they disappear, absorbed into the dance factories and films. There is Harriet Hoctor, light as a feather, with a dignity that triumphs over surroundings and audience; Patricia Bowman, superb technician, who has worked with Massine, but not long enough to be 'discovered'; and Paul Haakon, worthy pupil of Fokine, all being used as trick machines in vaudeville. Under Russian guidance they can bring a new contribution to ballet, the American spirit of the sheer, effortless joy of movement. The Camargo Society had already revealed a fine talent in Anna Ludmila (of Chicago), the perfect blend of classicism and American sex-appeal. They can regenerate the name of ballet and expose the untheatrical and anaemic group concerts that have been forced into prominence *faute de mieux*. Curiously enough, the forms of dancing that are indigenous do not come straight from Isadora Duncan, in spite of the power of her name, but from Ruth St Denis and Ted Shawn, veritable chameleons who have dabbled in the dances of the entire world. I saw some of the groups arranged by one of their most successful pupils, Charles Weidman. To me, they were weak and unconvincing. 'Art comes to the cabaret,' wrote the critics, but a form of art was already there, awaiting their interest. Fred Astaire is an American artist, the troupes of girls express a phase of life – as a machine, it is true – and such Negroes as Bill Robinson provide a quality that is unique. There is tremendous wealth awaiting artistic development, and to be added to the ballet movement and expression of the future. There is a richness of theme, legend, history, and daily life that could inspire all those limbs to beauty, if it takes a Frenchman to conceive of it as a school, and a Russian to set it in motion. A start has been made with the Russo-American *Union Pacific*.

One day on my way to rehearsal I took a taxi.

'St James's Theatre.'

'Where's that? Oh, I know; 44th and Broadway. What's on there now? Russian ballet. Well, you're lucky, I'll say you are. You'll see real women, not little painted dolls with platinum blonde tops to them. There's nothing to touch Russian women; real flesh and blood, plenty of temperament. I must go to that show; haven't seen a Russian ballet for years; ah, the good old days. I speak with feeling? You bet I do. Was born in Russia, Tobolsk, forty-five years ago.' So spoke my hundred per cent American driver. He was irresistible, and naturally I treated him to the show.

Before I left, the scenery and costumes of the Diaghilev Ballet were once more with their rightful owners; the Polovtsian warriors seemed more savage in Roerich's fine setting, the Russian crowd more animated in Benois's original décor. The link with tradition, too, meant something to these young dancers, thrilled at discovering a historic name in a faded blouse. *Le Tricorne* was in active rehearsal. As I saw Toumanova learning, with Tchernicheva, Massine and Woizikovski stamping in a corner, Picasso's bridge, and the twinkling stars, I thought of the tragedy connected with its first presentation. As it has so often been used in various fantastic ways against Diaghilev, and linked to the tragedy of Nijinsky, I will tell the true story .

When in Spain Diaghilev, ever on the lookout for unusual talent, discovered a cabaret dancer, a foundling and thoroughly rough diamond, Felix by name, who was exceptionally gifted in the dances of his country. Sokolova remembers going with a party to see the gypsy dancers of Seville. One after another performed in intense rivalry, Felix, who was seated at their table, growing paler and paler, more and more anxious, until finally Diaghilev told him, 'Now you show us what you can do.' No one will ever forget how he danced that night; he excelled them all.

With *Le Tricorne* in view, Felix was taken on to teach Massine, Woizikovski, Sokolova, and later Karsavina, his native dances. He was always a little strange, being known by his friends at home as 'Felix loco', but in London he became stranger still. He imagined that he was to be launched as a great dancer and that *Tricorne* and all the preparations were for him. He was haunted too by the rhythm of his native dance. When friends visited him in his lodgings, they found him in front of a metronome, tic-tac-tic-tac, taking mouthfuls of food to the rhythm, finally chewing his fork in a feverish endeavour to keep up with it ... tic-tac-tic-tac-tic-tac. Then one day the truth dawned on him, and he disappeared from the theatre and was lost.

A few days after, a policeman on his beat heard strange noises in a church – tic-tac-tic-tac. He entered, and there was a man dancing, leaping, stamping on the altar, a modern *jongleur de Notre Dame* performing his greatest role before his invisible audience.

The body of Felix is still alive today, well cared for in an asylum near London. Part of him lives in the work I saw in preparation, the Spanish dance that had haunted him.

*

Meanwhile, in the present on Broadway, the crowds came to the box office; they had discovered the ballet for themselves.

POSTSCRIPT

I. For Russian ballet, émigré style, this was the beginning of the end, and in many ways it was damaging to ballet as a whole, not because the country was America, but through the wear and tear on the dancers and the lack of leisure in which to create. The one-night stands, the proud records of a hundred cities in a six-month tour rapidly took their toll. The audiences outside the big cities had no critical standards. Today the major companies have abandoned such stands, but, on the other hand, the speed of air travel gives no time for relaxation. In Russia dancers rehearsed continually but gave comparatively few performances; today both our own and the Soviet companies are over-exposed, the accident rate has greatly increased, and the wastage in the corps de ballet is too great. Diaghilev valued his older dancers; they gave tradition and stability to a company.

There is a single mention in *Balletomania* of Sol Hurok. His role had only just started with the docking of the M.S. *Lafayette* in New York harbour. The first thing Sol Hurok told de Basil the very day we landed was, 'Why don't you get rid of some of these old girls?' I must write a few more recent words about him, a great character and the last of the grand impresarios who were stars in their own right. He had launched Anna Pavlova in the United States, but when I first met him at the Alhambra in 1933, he had little knowledge of ballet and to the end he knew what the public wanted rather than what was good in itself. He told me on that first occasion he felt *Carnaval* was too short and trivial and 'needed some meat added to it'. He thought in terms of stars and of how his superb publicity machine could build them up. He was in fact the very reverse of Diaghilev, and they could never have worked together. De Basil was easily influenced. He sought to gain his way by intrigue, and in that he was no match for Hurok, who invariably gained his point whenever it came to a question of casting, a vital function in the running of any company. It sowed disruption, a disruption that gave him the temporary benefit of shifting his stars from one company to another. Russian émigré companies split amoeba-like, and each time the original strain was diluted.

For all that he was a great man, larger than life. 'Hurok proudly presents' was a slogan for half a century, from Anna Pavlova to the Soviet ballet. In addition to his high distinctions from the British and French governments, he received the accolade of a 'Hurok story' film, *Tonight We Dance*, in which David Wayne played an unrecognizable Hurok. Sol alone could have played it himself. He was a shrewd businessman with very generous instincts, a champion of the underdog but ruthless in his dealings with management – all combined with a wonderful sense of humour in the traditional Jewish manner. In his dealings with the Royal Ballet, he met his match in Ninette de Valois and David Webster, acting as their agent rather than impresario. They rapidly gained an understanding of one another's role, an understanding that grew into respect and friendship.

The last time I saw Hurok was in Moscow in 1973, where he was received as a plenipotentiary. He was a sick man, badly shaken by the terrorist bombing of his offices, an incident in which a valued assistant had been killed. My last glimpse of him was talking to Khachaturian and Chagall, and I knew it would be for the last time, that it was the passing of an era. He had made the American public ballet-conscious, paved the way for American ballet, and deserves a conspicuous place in any twentieth-century history of the art.

II. There is a brief mention here of Martha Graham and the modern dance movement, of which she was, and still is, the high priestess. I was, I must admit, prejudiced from the start by the devotees of the modern school, who were almost religious in their fervour, puritanical in outlook, and humourless to a degree. They were intellectuals who would discuss at great length works that should have been self-explanatory, in an extraordinary jargon of Freudian psychoanalysis and sociology, intermixed with a new technical language that discussed space, tension, relaxation, and so on and so forth. We were of course familiar with the German expressionism of Wigman and others, which had extraordinary vitality mixed with its morbidity, especially in the choice of subject. It was born of the defeat of the German Empire.

The American school was a different thing, though it had its Germanic influences. It came partly from the fact that Isadora Duncan had set an example of revolt, and that Ruth St Denis and

Ted Shawn had dabbled – the word is not meant too unkindly – in a number of different dance idioms. The impact of Diaghilev in America was negligible, so that the words *modern* and *ballet* seemed to be in direct opposition. If modern ideas must be stressed in a young country, then surely, the argument went, you need a new language in which to express them. In 1933, when I first visited America, *modern* and *ballet* were in bitter opposition. Today this is no longer the case. What I did not see was that the modern dance, most especially that of Martha Graham, could make a great contribution to ballet, just as the discoveries of Isadora Duncan had been absorbed into ballet.

Isadora Duncan was altogether the exceptional case of someone who was a born dancer and who would not have fitted into the ballet scene or into any ready-made technique. One is tempted to say that, had she known discipline in her private life and carried it onto the stage, she would have been the greatest artist; on reflection, she would not have been Duncan. She remains in magnificent isolation. When I saw her she was no longer in her prime – one could see the remains of a superb Greek statue that had been eroded by time and damaged by vandalism, her own. She had followers, a band of devoted disciples, but they never amounted to anything. Her art was completely personal, and when she tried to express it in words she failed completely. There was no theory or thought behind it; it was its own justification. She came at a time when ballet was rapidly degenerating into 'toe-dancing', and her use of good music and the freedom her costumes gave to the body awoke the more critical public, especially in Russia, to the great possibilities of the dance. Fokine, in fact, was working along the same lines, but within the discipline of ballet.

The last time I saw Isadora Duncan was in the lift of the Adlon Hotel in Berlin. She was on her honeymoon with the great poet Esenin, and they were having the first of the stormy scenes that led to their expulsion from the hotel. It was a pathetic sight. It is a shame that television, the films, and many books, including her own, should have seen fit to indulge in muck-raking. The true Isadora Duncan lives in the inspiration she gave to Rodin and especially to Rodin's colleague Émile Bourdelle. No other dancer, with the possible exception of Nijinsky, has had so much to contribute to sculpture. What the modernists did not understand was that the best ballet was not a degenerate academicism but a classical discipline out of which something modern in outlook had already emerged in *Le Sacre du Printemps* and was to come later in Massine's superb *Nobilissima Visione*.

I must confess Martha Graham's creations are not for me; I find that many of her ideas cannot be expressed in movement alone. However, I am no longer completely blind to her importance in the history of the dance, to the fact that she has devised a true technique that will be absorbed in ballet and is completely professional in outlook. Gone are the days when I could see no salvation outside ballet or national dancing.

It was not, however, the same with the vast majority of other 'modern' dancers I saw then and have seen since. I remember a case in point when de Valois went around in the interval to see a much-publicized dance recitalist and was greeted with the remark, 'I am afraid I completely lost my concentration when some people came in late and made a clatter. I could not regain it after that.' De Valois's reaction was summed up in one word: 'amateur'.

That year, 1933, was an exciting period for American dance, the beginning of a national identity. It was composed of Graham with her small and ardent band of helpers and admirers, Balanchine with his neo-classicism, so suited to the built-in rhythm and fine physique of his young American dancers, and the Americana that came from jazz and the national folklore. Agnes de Mille, whom I had greatly admired as a soloist in England, was then unknown in her own country. As I have shown, I believed in her potential. She later became one of those who revolutionized dancing in musicals, combining the ballet she had absorbed from Rambert in England and American folk themes. Then came Michael Kidd and a figure of world stature in Jerome Robbins. His *West Side Story* is outstanding.

In those early days the struggle was a hard one financially, as it was in England. Choreographers supported ballet by the money they made from musicals and films, gaining valuable experience at the same time. On the stage Fred Astaire turned the tap-dance drill of the comedian into an art, earning the unlimited admiration of Diaghilev. His imagination, his freedom of movement, and his wit have earned him a place among the great dancers of the twentieth century. Dancers and choreographers would do well to study his films. Cinema and television in particular have remained bogged down in the dim past of the pre-Astairian period.

There is still little state support for ballet, but a number of private foundations have come to the rescue. There is patronage from private enterprise for a vast number of local, semi-amateur ballet companies, which include several professional members in their ranks. They may possibly have something to contribute; that remains to be proved.

III. I must mention one great experience given me by American Ballet Theatre, and the impact returns whenever I hear the music, Schoenberg's *Verklärte Nacht*. This was Antony Tudor's *Pillar of Fire*. There is only a brief mention of Tudor in my original text. It was years later, in the United States, that he developed his great gifts and became something of a cult figure.

I will quote from what I wrote when I first saw this remarkable ballet:

Antony Tudor left this country seven years ago with a growing reputation and the certainty that he had something original to express in the dance. He had given a foretaste of his quality for Marie Rambert in *Jardin aux Lilas* and *Dark Elegies*. In America he rapidly established an outstanding reputation, first with *Jardin aux Lilas* expanded on a large stage and next with *Pillar of Fire*.

Much has been made of its subtle psychological content and on paper it would seem that Tudor was attempting the impossible, a wordless Chekhov play. Has Tudor succeeded? Could Tudor succeed? If success lies in making his story abundantly clear in every detail at a first seeing, then he has clearly failed, as Chekhov would fail in drama where a lack of communication between the characters is the very essence. A prominent critic dismissed Tudor's ballet as 'the descent into obscurity of meaning' and 'a pack of solemn nonsense'.

I resent obscurity especially in many modern works that only have a meaning for the creator and his immediate circle. Such works are sheer self-indulgence. This is not at all the case in *Pillar of Fire*. Narrative apart, the characterisation is so fine that the theme is crystal clear and the atmosphere established from the beginning, even if at first sight its detail is lost in a Carrière-like mist.

The music was written in 1900, the period in which the ballet is set. The scene, admirably designed by Jo Mielziner, gives us the impression of a small market town in which everyone's business is known and discussed by the neighbours. All the movement flows directly from the music, and is beautiful and expressive; Tudor has taken from classical ballet just what he requires to discipline a very keen observation of natural movement. It is such a ballet that reinforces my insistence on classical discipline. His three sisters are as living as if one had known them : the spiteful, jealous, pleasure-loving kid, favoured and protected by the oldest straitlaced spinster, and the unfortunate middle sister, passionate and thwarted at every turn.

Once these three characters are clearly established – the fact that this is written after a first visit, and with no detailed synopsis, proves the point – then the ensuing conflict in the mind of Hagar, the middle sister, proceeds entirely naturally. Her meeting with the right man, his temporary loss and her giving of herself to the wrong man, followed by her reflections on the nature of love all arise out of her character and environment. We are watching a woman on the verge of a nervous breakdown, and here we can see Tudor's keen clinical observation magnificently translated into terms of choreography.

I have since seen this ballet on repeated occasions and with enhanced pleasure as its subtleties reveal themselves. No one, however, has ever interpreted the role of Hagar with such passionate intensity as Nora Kaye, 'the Duse of the Dance'.

14. Contrasts

IT is necessary for a time both for the dancer and the choreographer to get away from the atmosphere of the classroom and the stage in their search for perfection. Noverre, centuries ago, urged the choreographer to study nature closely. 'Watch the jealous man, observe the shades and differences of expression on his face.' The old-fashioned *maître de ballet* had stayed too long in the school if 'ballet is nature embellished with all the charms of art'; he had forgotten the meaning of nature, and could only put into his ballets steps, steps, and yet more steps. Massine in his Spanish travels had brought from the cabarets and corridas movement that has enriched the whole of the dance.

I too found that it was profitable to tear myself away from the theatre to investigate movement by which I could measure the truth of choreography, lest by sitting there night after night I came to attach too great importance to the actual execution of the pirouette, lose myself in its technical enchantments, and, by forgetting the whole, reduce myself to the condition of the crossword-puzzle fiend.

It may well be this whole question of outside experience that has given the young dancer of today her particular qualities and her early development. Where the Imperial School gives an academic and technical knowledge, the life of the émigré with its wanderings, hardships, and vivid contrasts provides a depth of feeling to draw upon. In New York, city of contrasts, I learnt three such lessons in ballet.

I. *Harlem Heaven*. A favourite haunt of mine after the ballet was Harlem, and in particular the Savoy in Lenox Avenue. It provided a powerful contrast to the classicism I had just witnessed and gave me a greater pleasure in each. There could really be seen the American contribution to the popular dance and music of the world. The latest steps performed in the smartest restaurants and music halls of London and Paris, both by the duchess and her gigolo, the orchestra to which they danced, and the greatest rage of all, the 'crooner', have all originated in some such place in Lenox Avenue. The Pullman porter and bell hop are blissfully unaware of this and perform purely for their own pleasure, so that here at its actual source it is full of meaning, but by the time it has been commercialized and canned, and has had all the native taken away from it, it is anaemic and empty as a spectacle.

So few of those who hate jazz, or make a fetish of it, have ever seen the real thing.

One Tuesday night – the best, for it is the meeting of the Four Hundred Club – daringly I took Lubov Tchernicheva and Grigoriev to show them something absolutely new in dancing. They were sceptical, and it takes something really new to impress Sergei Leoniditch, who has seen so many generations of dancers, but from the moment we entered I could see that I had succeeded. They were dancing the Lindy Hop, but it was not ordinary ballroom dancing in the sense that we understand it. There was a strong feeling of rivalry amongst the couples, and each one was not a self-contained unit of gloom. They improvised and separated, men and women performing intricate steps in front of one another and then coming together again. But such was the bond between dancers and orchestra, like one big heart beating for them all, that there was no impression of separate couples, but of one huge Afro-American ballet, danced by some five hundred principals, or corps de ballet, as you will. I saw couples twenty feet or more apart, dancing in unison, as if controlled by invisible wires. All were grinning, their eyes rolling, just as I had noticed in a religious revival ceremony in New Orleans: that was the very apotheosis of jazz. Now New York, Pullman cars, and elevators were completely forgotten. They had, too, an extraordinary feeling for décor; a semi-darkened room arranged like some Southern grove, with lighting effects of angry thunderclouds rolling by; a scene that became convincingly real, just because they believed in it, but that a bright light or a lack of sympathy could have destroyed in an instant. No Parisian artist could have improved upon their sense of style. If they were physically grotesque, then they accentuated that grotesquerie up to a point where it became beautiful. Squat, fat, thick-lipped women wore diminutive Paris hats, perched at an angle on top of their fuzzy African heads, till all that could be seen was a hat, a hank of hair, and a broad toothy grin. If they were beautiful – and many were – they gave that beauty a worthy setting. I shall never forget one tall slim Negro Venus, coal black, in a low-cut white satin *robe de style*, with long white openwork gloves. It was perhaps obvious, but no one else there had thought of it, and she was the certain envy of all, her nearest rival wearing a canary-yellow jumper with a high-rolled round collar. They improvised on the fashion, never becoming slaves to it, and obviously gave it the greatest thought. The rhythm of colour is highly developed in them; Negro Baksts, they blend the impossible and create beauty.

On this night new members were initiated into the club with all the horseplay of the elderly stockbroker becoming an Elk and a great deal less self-consciousness. First there is a parade of all the members around the hall – an excellent opportunity to watch types and costumes. They walk magnificently, lightly caressing the floor, and take an obvious pride in their footwear, the men in patent leather with cream cloth tops, the women in the very highest of Louis heels. The parade over, intending members remain on the floor. The men form a long line, while the initiate must run rapidly through their legs, receiving a good hard hit as he passes. With the women it is a kind of dervish dance. Each one is given a small stick, which she must point downwards at the floor; then she is spun around it by three strong men, the audience chanting the number of her turns. When she has done some fifteen she either falls, amidst laughter, with a loud crash to the ground, or staggers drunkenly across the floor to hand her stick to the M.C.

Then follows the 'floor show', the same type of thing as in the ordinary cabaret, but performed before an audience each one of whom is an expert, to a loud commentary of approval or otherwise. Gradually, as the evening wears on, the excitement grows greater and greater. When the band plays some slow sad blues, they surrender themselves to the point of tears; when gay, they swing in and out dervish fashion with never a collision. That night a man lightly touched the white-gowned Venus. Like a flash her partner hit him on the jaw and sent him spinning. The women disappeared from the centre of the floor and a running fight followed, as clean and beautiful as the dance. (Razors are getting out of date in the North. It is all a part of the ballet, a little masterpiece of unconscious choreography, a male *pas de huit* centre stage, with a gesticulating, shouting chorus, and an accompaniment of drums and trombone. One or two are knocked down, only to get up and bolt into the crowd like rabbits. The fight ceases, the *pas de huit* is swallowed amongst the whirling, dazzling, dancing blacks, and there is nothing to tell it has not been a dream, for, fighting or dancing, there is no pause, no change of tempo. The whole evening has an extraordinary dreamlike quality. Then, as morning comes, the dancers creep home to the drudgery of elevators and dustbins, to exist until the glorious freedom of the following Tuesday night, when each one can be drugged by the ritual of the dance once again.

Whether we can call this spontaneous Negro dancing an art or not depends very much on our definition of art. If we belong to those who associate creation with the free play of the child, then the Negro dance is at any rate the stuff of which art is made.

> And what would I do in heaven, pray,
> Me with my dancing feet
> And limbs like apple boughs that sway
> When the gusty rain winds beat?

asks the little coloured girl.

It is the most interesting thing by far that can be seen in dancing in America today, and America is foremost in its creation. It is far more expressive of the rhythm of the country than the dreary, self-conscious groups of dancers influenced by German post-war neuroses.

During the past twenty years or more, Harlem influence upon all branches of art and life has been as great as the Diaghilev influence and has been felt even in the ballet, stronghold of tradition itself. *The Blackbirds* was one of the most important manifestations of theatrical art we have ever seen in London. London enjoyed it thoroughly, but Paris realized it more consciously and made capital from it. The French, with their essentially logical outlook, invariably make a school out of every individual manifestation and in a few years naturalize it. The Negro entered the ballet first through the plastic arts. Picasso, Derain, Vlaminck, and Modigliani, backed up by the poet Apollinaire, and the entire *fauve* school have looked to primitive African sculpture, just as their immediate predecessors were influenced by the Japanese colour print. Then the man of letters justified this and glorified the Negro, who was as unconscious of this art of his ancestors as any suburban dweller in England.

The entire modern school, who looked upon Blaise Cendrars's *Anthologie Nègre* as a divine revelation, has been swayed and almost dominated by the Negro. The same influence, but to a very much lesser degree, is noticeable in the theatre with the success of such plays as *Porgy and Bess*, *The Emperor Jones*, *All God's Chillun*, and *Green Pastures*.

Such influence has been developed consciously by the astute colonial officials in France, where it serves as excellent colonial propaganda; and its climax was reached at the time of the Colonial Exhibition. If the American is unwilling to admit indebtedness to the Negro, the French have no such scruples, and what the black man under the French flag produces all goes to the greater glory of France. There are two ways of regarding this; the one draws a strong artistic colour line and deplores the fact that the white races should owe anything to 'savages', whose ancestors were 'anthropophagi and men whose heads do grow beneath their shoulders', while the other welcomes any new blood, says that the white man is over-civilized, artistically sterile, and that Greek culture has been worked to death. Both are very wide of the mark. People in talking of the Negro always lose all sense of proportion.

It is important to know what is this *jazz* that the Negro has given us, a blessing or a curse.

We are told that poverty compelled the music-loving Negro to evolve instruments of his own, and, for reasons practical as well as atavistic, these instruments were chiefly percussion, bones and the like. One W. C. Handy, unknown today, but whose influence is felt more than that of Wagner or any other Aryan composer, brought up in this atmosphere of improvised sound, wrote the first piece of music proper, *Memphis Blues*, which was performed by a coloured Chicago cabaret artist, Jasbo Brown, who owed his popularity to some startling discoveries. He found that by placing his bowler hat over his trombone he could make it laugh and cry. Already something more complex to add to the simple background of percussion. 'More Jasbo, More Jasbo, More Jas' ', his listeners yelled, and so jazz was born, the results of a necessity for rhythm, poverty, and invention. Once the drums were throbbing and the trombone bleating – wah – wah – wah – the dance could not remain behind, so Shelton Brooks, a Negro comedian, popularized a new strut, 'Walkin' the dog', and added his name to those of Handy and Brown to the classics of this new 'art'; and it is perhaps just at that point that it

becomes an art, if ever it does. Previously it had been purely improvised and unconscious. The step-dance came from the cotton
buyers of Lancashire imported into the South, and with its new
home underwent a change : it was superimposed upon the dances
of Africa, though how much Africa is in all this one can only wonder. It is faster, gayer; it has banished much of the feeling of witch
doctory and fear. Also there is still another element, the missionary
and *Hymns Ancient and Modern*. Gradually the life of America is
shutting out the jungle. The motor horn is more strident than the
tom-tom, the revivalist's hallelujah more blatant than the mumbo
jumbo of the medicine man.

The Lancashire man regarded his dance more as a sport for a
wake or special occasion, while the Negro promptly attached it to
his everyday life. He would dance when washing, dance when
cleaning boots. Every movement had a real significance, which to
this day marks the entire difference between the step-dance of the
white man and the black. Where with the white it is a complicated
technical exercise that means precisely nothing at all because both
musically and plastically it is barren, with the Negro it is a means
of conveying joy or sadness, with all the endless different shades of
meaning in between. It has become a living and growing folk dance.
The true Negro dance obeys one of Fokine's fundamental laws; it is
closely related to life itself. It is that reason, and not so much the
fact of the special physique of the Negro and his markedly finer
sense of rhythm, that makes this dance quite meaningless when
performed by the white. The white man invariably draws attention
to its difficulties, while the whole basis of Negro dancing is the
fact that it is natural and not acrobatic : it is free, an expression of
the feelings of a certain person at a certain moment. Frederick Ashton, who has had the unique experience, amongst serious choreographers, of working with Negro dancers, tells me that if they do
not approve of a certain movement they will all rub it away imperceptibly during rehearsal and revert to what seems really
natural to them.

Its essence lies in its artlessness; but both music and dance have
followed the usual path of folk music and dancing to a more
sophisticated form of expression. The 'jazz' of the modern composer
is something very different, sentimentalized beyond recognition.
The majority of these composers are Jews, far too sophisticated ever
to collaborate with the Negro, their very opposite in every respect,

and they have brought into it entirely new elements. The 'mammy singer', too, is a Jew, and he is clearly thinking of a 'Yiddisher momma'. Gershwin alone approaches the real thing at times. Paul Whiteman's band is different; Duke Ellington's is far removed, but of the same kind as Jasbo Brown's. Serious composers, in Paris of course, Auric, Milhaud, Satie, and others, have understood this far more clearly than the writers of popular music. The Negro is sensual. He is not all the time wanting to go back to some place or other. He revels in a glorious mixture of sex and religion, without any false sense of shame; once shame is imported it becomes disgusting. The Negro revivalist and Aimée Semple MacPherson are poles apart. The white has tried to clean it all up, put it on a European basis, and has succeeded in making it into a highly paying proposition. All this material for creation is still awaiting someone who can translate it into our own conception of music and dancing, and make use of it as all folk movement has been utilized : to translate it just as the Negro translated clog dances and the hymnbook, and not imitate it.

The Negro himself, through social reasons, is a grave offender in that respect. The first 'Negro' song and dance act to gain popularity was our old friend the minstrel show,* still surviving in the halls and with a new lease of life on the wireless – a white man with a cork-blackened face, dressed to ape the Negro. He would use the Negro dialect more or less correctly, but his voice and his movements were different, and he raised his laughs through the attitude. 'I'll show you how darn funny these blacks can be. They're a rum lot – yes, sir.' Then followed the first coloured entertainers, but in this very same tradition. It was a proved success and was expected of them. It would have been lacking in respect and business acumen to do anything else. The white man must be made to feel his superiority the entire time. So the Negro imitated the white man imitating the Negro, and laughed *at* the Negro instead of *with* him. He didn't cry at all. It would never have done to be so human. To this day that attitude has persisted with a large number of coloured artists.

If we look at jazz other than historically, and try to find its

*The minstrel, who performed in a singing and joke-cracking group, was a time-honoured feature of the Edwardian music hall. The tradition survives today on British television in the 'Black and White Minstrel Show'.

universal meaning rather than its local and national interpretation, we can immediately see how difficult it is to transpose into choreography, which is the ordered orchestration of dancing. Jazz is the very opposite : spontaneity; David dancing before the ark; the revolutionary *carmagnole*; a Jewish wedding dance. It implies noise, lack of restraint, anarchy, escape.

Balanchine, now on the spot, with his extraordinary feeling for musical rhythm, and his sympathy with vivid contrasts, may be the first to achieve a real success in this fascinating field.

All this becomes clear, not so much through a visit to the music halls and cabarets, in spite of such a superb dancer as Bill Robinson, who certainly improvises, for I have never seen a dance of his repeated identically, but through those visits to the Negro ball. Once one has seen that, it is impossible to applaud imitation. It is the great unconscious ballet with music, décor, lighting, all a perfect unity – the natural result of some four hundred people all out for a good time.

II. *Ideals of Masculinity*. One night, again in pursuit of contrasts, I left the theatre after the first ballet, *Les Sylphides*, and went to Madison Square Garden to watch a wrestling match, billed as for the World's Championship. Immediately I found my contrast, for in the ring were two misshapen, sweating, grunting men, sprawling on the floor in an embrace, one of them sitting on the other, clutching tightly to his thumb and bending it back until his unfortunate victim yelled out in pain. Finally he managed to break loose, get up, seize his opponent by the hips, and throw him over his shoulder so that he landed on his cannonball head with a loud thud. This was repeated four times in quick succession, the man-missile growing dizzier until his legs crumpled under him, and he collapsed, crosseyed, in a heap on the floor. It was by no means over yet; more sprawling, hugs, and yells, with an occasional cuff on the side of the head. This sorry performance lasted for an hour and a half, watched by eager thousands, who would scorn the corrida as a degrading spectacle. My neighbour seemed to be echoing my thoughts :

'Disgusting, I call it, disgusting. Why, in Dallas, where I come from, they wouldn't stand for this; no, sir, they'd have 'em right out of that ring in a jiffy... Hi, lay off, you big pansy ... Sissy stuff, that's what I call it; there's no action at all. They're not trying. Why, in Dallas I've seen 'em gouge eyes out, and we don't even have top-liners.'

In disgust and boredom I left. Afterwards those in the know told me that my horror was wasted, as this was all as carefully rehearsed as the ballet itself. At any rate it had made me enjoy *Les Sylphides* all the more in retrospect, and this, together with an experience I had had in Spain, also in search of contrasts, taught me a great deal about the functions and quality of the male dancer.

I had gone to my first corrida with Markova and Dolin. There, from the first mad entrance of that superb character dancer, the bull, we understood what we were seeing, and our natural repugnance was overcome by our interest. Here was a ballet and not a sport, for the outcome was inevitable – a twenty-minute religious ballet in three acts; the parade, various forms of the dance, cloak play, entrée comique of the picadors, the pure classicism of the banderilleros, and the grand *pas de sacrifice* as a climax, where the matador is the complete dancer and never a butcher. *Religious* and *sacrifice* are the exact words : when Saint Theresa was canonized three hundred bulls were worked in her honour. There is a definite choreography, varied only slightly in each particular case by the exigencies of the one unconscious dancer, the bull. There are also distinct schools of tauromachy : the classical, the romantic, and the modern. The great Juan Belmonte, Fokine of the corrida, had imposed his methods throughout the bull-ring. It is entirely from this, our dancer's angle, that the Spanish crowd approaches the corrida, a running of bulls mistranslated as a fight. The *aficionado* is blood brother to the balletomane. His first interest is in the beauty of the 'dancing', and of the execution of such definite steps and moves as the *veronica*, *navarra*, or *mariposa*. He will criticize it in detail right up to the final bow, when the matador is receiving the plaudits of the crowd, which is a definite part of the whole ballet. ('X is too much the clown. His bows to the applauding arena are lacking in the dignity that is the first essential of the serious artist.' – Account of corrida in *La Petite Gironde*, August 1932.)

Théophile Gautier, balletomane, who has left us so many exquisite impressions of contemporary dancers, noted this attitude. He says in his *Voyages en Espagne* :

Because they behold, unmoved, scenes of carnage which would cause our sensitive Parisian beauties to faint, it must not be inferred that they are cruel or deficient in tenderness of soul... The sanguinary side of a bull fight, which is what strikes foreigners the most forcibly, is exactly what least interests Spaniards, who devote their whole attention to the amount of address . . .

Courage, the *aficionado* will admire, also a clean quick kill, but reckless courage will be condemned if it is too showy and obvious, and the kill must be done according to strict rules. Even the bull is criticized as if he were a conscious protagonist and his footwork carefully noted. A bull who will not do the orthodox thing is called *criminal*. Costume, too, plays an important role and is subject to criticism.

Martial Lalanda was one of the finest and most classical dancers we had ever seen. In writing an article for the Spanish press I fell quite naturally into the point of view and even the jargon of the *aficionado*, but without being able to go at all deeply into detail.

The wrestler and the matador, two different ideals of masculinity; more vivid still, the wrestler and the male dancer.

To those who hold that the unpleasant and witless display in Madison Square Garden* is a glorification of masculinity, the torero (and more especially the male dancer in *Les Sylphides*, with his long hair, white tights, and velvet jacket) must certainly appear effeminate. The two conceptions are far apart; they have as their respective champions the fist and the sword. D'Artagnan, for all his grace as a fencer – and grace means reasoned movement – his long hair, and his ornate costume, is surely very much more the ideal of manhood than a Primo Carnera or the sweating monstrosities of the wrestling ring. It is a sad confusion of ideas, not man against effeminate man, but stupid primitive man against sophisticated man. Also it is a confusion between what is effeminate and what belongs to a romantic period. In truth the effeminate dancer – and there are many, especially in England today – is without exception a worthless dancer. The very *raison d'être* of the male in ballet is to stand as a strong mental and physical contrast to the woman. His body is different, his movements are different. One of the great beauties of the classical system lies in the fact that it can bring out the characteristics of both man and woman. When the man apes the woman, that whole contrast is lost, and he has no longer any place in ballet. It is for this reason, the need for the mature male, that we do not hear of many men infant prodigies in ballet. A

---

* British television has led to a revival of these unsavoury acrobatics with their faked ferocity.

striking example of such contrast occurred in Nijinska's *Les Fâcheux*, where Anton Dolin was given a dance on the pointes, a technique that is by tradition exclusively reserved for women, though very many male dancers are able to perform it quite naturally. There was an immediate protest from the audience. It looked all wrong, although in this case there was a very sound literary reason for it. Dolin was representing a fop, *L'Élégant*, and it was an essential part of the character. The public however had felt the truth, that this natural balance was lacking.

In his use of one man in *Les Sylphides*, Fokine gave a striking example of his genius. The man has little actual dancing to do, but one cannot conceive of the ballet without him. Not only does he lift his partner, but his contrasting line is indispensable to the design, and his presence to the whole idea and atmosphere of the ballet. He brings into it a definite feeling of love, although the word is too strong for anything so ethereal.

Le Spectre de la Rose is another example of the effect that is gained by the orchestration of male and female movement and personality. The idea of the spirit of a rose is in itself banal. Thousands of producers would have adopted it, thought no further, and used a woman : unconscious Lesbianism to their mind being safer than the experiment of a male rose.

The whole conception of the effeminacy of the male dancer has arisen through Nijinsky in these roles. In *Le Spectre de la Rose* he was not there to exploit his masculinity, for he succeeded in conveying the sexless spirit itself, but had he been in any sense effeminate, acting opposite Karsavina's young girl, the very essence of femininity, the ballet would have been an unpleasant failure from the first. In *Schéhérazade* there was the embodiment of masculinity, expressed with so little restraint that it shocked many by its brutality, while the Faun was the excited male animal itself. The whole notion of Nijinsky's effeminacy, even admitted by some of his most fervent admirers, with a pathetic, 'But then he was so beautiful,' is utterly absurd. The classical dancer must be a far finer athlete than anyone in the world of sport. Remember the mighty feats of elevation in *Le Spectre de la Rose* and *Schéhérazade*, records perhaps in height, certainly in the beauty that disguised their prowess.

The *danseur noble*, in his self-effacing role as a partner, is displaying perfect gallantry, formerly recognized as a male characteristic. He is the eternal Raleigh, making easier the passage of his queen. If he sweated and groaned when carrying his ballerina around the stage, instead of showing how very light she was, he would immediately be proclaimed the hundred per cent male – a revolting creature, if he exists outside the films, for it is through the films, where every man worth his salt must throw the villain down a flight of stairs before the climax, that such an ideal has been most advertised.

In Samoa the gallantry of the male dancer is carried to such extremes that the men appearing with a girl of real merit will assume grotesque and clumsy postures to underline her grace.

The male dancer is the lover in every movement, a conception of masculinity that may be difficult to understand in countries where, by a strange paradox, it is considered so essentially masculine for men to be happiest in the company of their own sex.

The male dancer in the Russian Ballet was the first feature that astounded Paris audiences in 1909, not merely for the reason that they had never seen such virtuosity, but because without such strong contrast they had never seen perfect ballet and could not measure their own ballerinas. Diaghilev, because of his particular outlook, gave a greater importance to the male than had been done previously, though this has been exaggerated, since *Les Sylphides* was created before his reign, but he never could tolerate the effeminate man. A Fokine, Bolm, or Nijinsky not only made his own reputation, he enhanced those of Pavlova and Karsavina, as Dolin did with Markova.

It is so often said as a recognized fact that all male dancers are perverts that this must be contradicted at once. The obvious freaks who flocked to the ballet at a certain period were attracted by the dancer in exactly the same way as the gallery girl by the matinée idol. One of my friends receives several letters a day from amorous men, usually signed in full. He throws away this potential fortune in blackmail in amused disgust. No man can be held responsible for his admirers. Of the outstanding male dancers that I know, and I know them all, not one is effeminate in manner, and comparatively few indeed are not thoroughly normal.

'But you must be wrong. It is so unnatural for a man to be graceful at all,' says the respectable married woman, hankering after a little dirt, and thinking of her husband, the table he knocked over in the drawing room, and his old golfing shoes.

But why, I cannot see. Grace means efficiency; it is an attribute

of both sexes, and *she* has no monopoly there. The runner is graceful, the tennis player is graceful, and so is her husband, in his role
as a golfer, if he is any good at all.

III. *From Virtuosity to Art.* On my very last night in New York
came my third contrast, a totally unpremeditated one this time,
and most vivid of all.

With Massine I went to Carnegie Hall to see the Maryinsky
Soviet dancers, Veceslova and Chabukiani, in their programme of
dances from the *new* Soviet ballets: *Le Corsaire, Don Quixote, Le
Petit Cheval Bossu*! This phrasing alone was sufficient to convict
them of active anti-revolutionary propaganda, but they enjoyed a
very big reputation in Russia, and their teachers were the same as
my friends'. Danilova could remember the little Veceslova as a
promising pupil.

From the very first dance, an acrobatic waltz of cabaret type, we
knew that we should see no revolutionary fire, no *carmagnole*, but
the oldest of dances to the cheap ballet music of our friend Minkus,
performed in a manner so vulgar, the usual permanent smirk with
behind sticking out, and an acrobatic approach so deliberate and
insistent that it could not dazzle anyone who knew the art of a
Trefilova or Pavlova in these selfsame dances. It seemed aimed as a
direct appeal to everything that was most bourgeois, smug, and self-
satisfied. It was as crudely applause-inviting as the sentimental
singer who removes his hat and pauses as the last note of his song
fades away.

'There,' said Massine, 'you have the worst of the pre-Fokine
ballet, and danced without any of the nobility of the pre-Fokine
ballerina, yet the man is perfect in build and a wonderful performer. A few months' work could transform him completely. That
is the tragedy.'

It was a step into the past, the result of a whole generation who
knew neither Fokine nor Massine, who had forgotten Kchessinska,
save in a political sense. The reactionaries had won in the end, and
this was the measure of their victory.

The famous *Red Poppy*, from the excerpts I have seen, is nothing
more than a conventional and well-arranged series of exercises that
might have come from Petipa at his least inspired. Judging from this
couple and the Messerers, who were on much the same level, Russia
is continuing to produce good, even brilliant material, and is now

waiting for a revolutionary leader – strange paradox. Balanchine, who might have filled the role, was forced to leave at the very height of the Revolution in order to find the freedom to produce his revolutionary ideas, just as twenty years before, under the tsarist regime, Fokine had left the Maryinsky to make a name abroad.

Choreography apart, the very spirit of Russian dancing, with its large free movements, had vanished. I am taking a risk in generalizing from these few examples and in judging a whole well-organized school, but it is justifiable from the very fact that these are the dancers who have been chosen to come abroad, and who have been so widely advertised as from the Maryinsky.

Hurriedly we returned to the theatre, each one to our respective jobs – Massine to dance in *Le Beau Danube* and I to watch him. As I saw once again the exquisite finish of this ballet to old-fashioned music and an old-fashioned theme, apparently as counter-revolutionary as the doings at Carnegie Hall, I lived in one evening the whole of the ballet development of the last thirty years. I needed no such extreme contrasts as *Le Sacre du Printemps* or *Le Pas d'Acier*. In thirty years, from virtuosity to art.

There was Baronova doing the same fouettés as Veceslova, but they had a real meaning both musically and dramatically. They were an expression of the joy of living of the little Viennese *soubrette*, and she performed them with exactly the same simplicity and apparent ease as that mimed flirtation scene where she is having her portrait painted – one of her many little masterpieces. There was an absolute lack of tension, or rather the illusion of it, for I have watched her prepare in the wings and knew perfectly well what she felt; only she had left all that strain behind her. The Soviet dancers had given one a constant feeling of actual physical discomfort, so that there was never a climax, just repose, then excitement, the constant device of such a choreographer as Balanchine. There too was Massine moving his audience more by standing still, his arm raised, than could Chabukiani in spinning through the air. 'No artist,' people say, 'but a fine technique, nevertheless.' Not at all, for it is Massine who has the fine technique. With the Maryinsky couple every *préparation* was made visibly on the stage, this obvious bracing up for an effort. The Negro is actually spontaneous; the technique of the Massine type of artist is to appear so. Both give pleasure. *Only when one movement blends into the other does dancing begin and acrobacy cease.*

The margin between the two is very small indeed, lying first in the intention. *Acrobacy is the making of a movement for the sake of the movement itself, the solution of a problem; dancing, the making of a movement, it may be the identical one, for what it can express.* Nine out of ten acrobatic 'dancers' are not dancers at all. It is only when the impression received has nothing to do with the danger involved or the difficulty of the trick, when neither is signalled out by obvious preparation or underlined by special music, when the movement expresses the music, that they can be called dancers, and then the word acrobatic has no relevance at all.

The supporters of Greek and natural movement claim that all ballet is acrobatic. They themselves illogically make an enormous sacrifice to convention by using, because they are forced to, music that has nothing whatsoever to do with Greek civilization. Like us, they can only hint at Greece and convey the atmosphere as best they can. If either succeeds, it is not a proof of authenticity, but because the audience too does not know the music of Greece. Where they generally fail is through being untrue to the laws of the sequence of movement. Their original source, the vase or sarcophagus, is dead, and they themselves must devise the transition from one pose that they know to the next; that transition and not the pose is the dancing.

The late Cecil Sharp, a real expert and enthusiast on his own subject of folk dancing, once made the ridiculous statement that dancing *sur les pointes* was laborious to acquire, exceedingly painful, and not without danger even. This is of course quite inaccurate. To many it comes perfectly naturally, as soon as the rudiments of movement have been learned; by most it is acquired in a few months. Dolin, for instance, was able to dance on his pointes without a single lesson. It is painful perhaps for a very short time, as all unaccustomed movement – riding, swimming, or running – till the bones and muscles are properly educated; dangerous never, unless imposed by an idiot teacher on a child with an unusual toe formation, just in the same way as a voice can be ruined by incompetence. It is no more *unnatural* than Cecil Sharp's folk dancing, now that it has been resurrected by learned professors, dressed up and brought with pomp and ceremony from where the village green once stood to the Royal Albert Hall.

The pointe is mistakenly considered the mainstay of ballet, hence the term 'toe dancing', the sure betrayal of the complete tyro. Actually this 'toe dancing' only occupies some ten minutes of an hour's class. Its aesthetic justification is the impression of lightness that it creates – a bird about to leave the ground. Its mechanical justification is the facility that it gives in turning. Actually it only develops an inch more of the foot than is used by the 'naturalists' themselves. Another objection to the use of pointes is based on the use of blocked shoes, but the male dancer, who does not dance on his toes at all, also requires slippers, for the friction of a series of turns would tear the feet to pieces. Isadora Duncan uses the misleading argument, 'Shoes on a dancer are as ridiculous as gloves on a pianist.' But Isadora, from her own magnificent work, clearly realized that the feet alone are not the dancer's instrument, but the whole body. To be thoroughly consistent, why wear clothes at all? In any case, the piano analogy is an unfortunate one to advance in an argument for naturalism. Is it *natural* for a man in dress clothes to sit down at an instrument manufactured in a factory of wood, ivory, and wire, and to hit the ivories with his fingers, bang the pedals with his feet in an attempt to reproduce something that is in itself the result of a highly complex and artificial system? 'Dancing is an art because it is subject to rules,' said Voltaire, the French balletomane, in an anticipatory reply.

I am not in the slightest interested in the health and curative effects of dancing, but, since they are always stressed by the other side, it is worth mentioning that Alicia Markova, who has legs and feet that any 'natural' dancer might envy, originally took up dancing to cure a bad case of knock-knees. Nemchinova's bare feet are the most beautiful that I have seen, naturally so, but embellished by their fine training. 'The ballet dancer's back is rigid,' said one 'naturalist', in a controversy we had. Perhaps she had never seen the astonishing back bend in the last few bars of *Les Sylphides* or the dance of the odalisques in *Schéhérazade*, where rigid backs would have snapped in an instant. 'But ballet is remote from life, an exotic, a luxury.' She had forgotten the moving tragedy of *Petrouchka*, which is the tragedy of us all, or the vast primitive *Le Sacre du Printemps*, which is the infancy of us all. In any case this whole stressing of the word *natural* is a fallacy that has gained ground through laziness and *dilettantism*. It can only ever be used in a very qualified sense, modified by the theatrical convention, as the *ballet-naturalism* of Noverre and Fokine. Little that we do today is natural : poetry is unnatural, so are music and painting, while the films spend much time and vast sums of money daily to give, by the most unnatural mechanical methods, the natural impression of a man walking down the street, in itself a most unnatural thing.

Yet all these things are a logical development of the natural resources in man, and the doing of them alone distinguishes him from the monkey, who knows not the use of fire or instruments.

Isadora Duncan tells of how she was watching a small child dancing on the seashore in perfect unconscious tune with the waves and the clouds, the sun and the shadows. She thought, as all people of the theatre should, of how to transport onto the stage, not only the unaffected grace of the child, but also the suggestion of the harmony with the waves and the clouds, the sun and the shadows. As a great artist she must have solved the problem for herself; she certainly realized that to put the child on the stage behind the footlights and proscenium was no solution, and that even her own grace would be lost and appear unnatural, for in order to appear natural a definite translation is necessary. Diaghilev illustrated this vividly when he turned his great mind to the problem. In *Contes Russes* there arose the question of bringing a horse onto the stage. Once there, he discovered what is now a theatrical truism, that away from its own surroundings the horse looked grotesque, not like a horse at all. It was necessary to find its stage equivalent – in this instance, a painted wooden horse.

This seems far away from an evening of dancing at Carnegie Hall, but, if ballet does not provoke such an investigation, then the Greeks were wrong in assigning it a muse. It is as an art that it must be seen and studied, and not as something that is good or bad for the health, natural or unnatural. I have never understood why of all arts dancing should be considered thus. Singing, also a natural gift, is never subjected to such cant.

On my way home in the boat, by contrast, I learned still a further lesson, one that I really knew all along : for me, life without ballet was really not worth living. Every minute I was being carried further and further away from the small group of inspiring artists, my friends. The sea was calm, the company deadly, and I felt sick – at heart.

POSTSCRIPT

I. The fact that in 1933 one could spend an enjoyable evening in Harlem denotes the lapse of time. Although I was and am completely unconscious of colour, I can now understand that these visits must have been an irritating intrusion, a sort of slumming. On re-reading this section it sounds patronizing. I am fortunate indeed to have heard the early Duke Ellington and to have seen what the dance could mean to an underprivileged people. The Dance Theatre of Harlem, which visited London in 1974, is a great achievement, artistically and sociologically.

I was aware of the Afro-American as a conscious artist when that remarkable woman Katharine Dunham, scholar, dancer, choreographer, and producer, brought her company to London in 1948. It remains in my memory as one of the great dance companies. In later days only Moiseyev combined ballet and folklore with such consummate skill, and his task was an easier one, more readily accepted since the dances he translated were of the stuff of which ballet is made and his dancers already trained in the idiom. Dunham's scenery, costumes, and lighting put most ballet in the shade, the music was superbly orchestrated, and the dancing was a perfect fusion of Africa and Europe. Years later when I saw an actual voodoo ceremony in Cuba, I realized Dunham's extraordinary skill. The real thing was excitingly urgent, since one was a part of the scene; it was also scruffy, with long intervals in which nothing much seemed to be happening. This was very raw material indeed. We have seen what the Americans call ethnic dance, sometimes bogus, sometimes over-realistic; the drumming and intensity often seem unsuited to the stage despite the beauty of glistening black bodies. The slogan 'black is beautiful' does apply. It remained for Dunham to make the perfect translation, to be realistic rather than naturalistic through her finely evolved technique, which used the stage to its best advantage and exploited the physique of her dancers to the full. Her classes were partly balletic, partly folklore, piano-cum-tom-tom. She was at the same time a woman of the theatre and a distinguished academic anthropologist with many papers to her credit. Once when I heard her lecture to a learned society, some of the more elderly members of her audience were astonished to hear that she was a distinguished stage personality.

She painted as a hobby, but her painting was in no sense the work of an amateur. Everything about her was professional. She was a perfectionist and something of a martinet in the drilling of her company, a member of which was Eartha Kitt. She always instilled in them the idea that each evening's performance was the most important of all, even when that audience consisted of a group of Indians in a mountain-top South American village. Possibly because her performances were such superb entertainment, her art has never been given the importance it deserves. Markova was quick to realize it when she commissioned Dunham to do the choreography for Aïda at the Metropolitan Opera House. Dunham deserved the financial backing that the American Ballet Theatre and Martha Graham have since received. She was an innovator and a great ambassador for the United States.

The last time I saw her dance was in Hamburg. I was staying with our Land Commissioner, the virtual ruler of the district after the war. Afterwards he invited her to the Officers' Club and asked her to dance with him. Some of the American brass seemed a trifle startled. They danced an old-fashioned Viennese waltz to perfection. At the end of the evening he asked her if there was anything he could do for her in Hamburg. 'Take me to the notorious Reeperbahn,' she said. 'I could pick up some material there.' 'That is the only thing I cannot do,' he replied. 'With your fame and my position it would provide a feast for the popular press; Haskell will take you.' I could see his point of view as we drove off in his Rolls bearing his personal pennant. Ellington, Dunham, and our own Cleo Laine have done more for the dignity of their race than any other coloured performers I have seen.

II. The prejudice against male dancers, in this country at any rate, has largely vanished. In the United States it was a reason for not being inducted into the armed forces; a strange reason since military valour and homosexuality have so often been associated. However in the case of ballet it is not sexual habits that are relevant, but the appearance of virility. An effeminate dancer is a bad dancer. The arguments set out in this section are still valid though they may not convince the average golfing male, who in any case is probably blind to ballet and may himself have hidden homosexual tendencies.

The bad name given to male dancers in non-Slavic countries came in part through the romantic idealization of women, which caused the almost total disappearance of the male, and partly through the Diaghilev-Nijinsky relationship, so greatly publicised. If there was anything that Diaghilev loathed it was an effeminate male, whom he would describe in a rude phrase. Nijinsky was a superb athlete. When the big ballet boom started in the Western world, it was an unfamiliar profession; there were few people able to teach boys, so that the occasional boy, who followed his sister to dancing class, adopted feminine attitudes just through copying what he saw around him. It was as simple as that, with no need of complex psychological explanations. Moreover the English boy matures more slowly than the Latin or the Slav. During the war when our ballet began to become completely professional, the male dancers were immature for the simple reason that the moment they became men they were whisked off into the services. Their record was an admirable one because of their physical fitness, which was probably above average. Today the situation has altered : the promising male dancer is no longer a freak; the eye has become accustomed to male dancers as it once had to become accustomed to women dancers and actresses. Nureyev, Dowell, Wall, Villella, and Baryshnikov now all have an immense popular following.

There is one point worth mentioning. The recognition of the male dancer has been delayed by the ridiculous costumes they are often made to wear, frilled and beribboned like so many gift-wrapped packages.

III. This section deals with my first exposure to Soviet ballet, which has played such a major role in my subsequent balletomania.

Russian ballet meant the Diaghilev tradition; Soviet ballet and the great school of Vaganova were completely unknown to us. They represented something that was paradoxically both reactionary and left-wing propagandist. This had an element of truth. The dancers we saw were shockingly badly presented as music-hall turns, the acrobatic side of their technique being flamboyantly stressed. I admit to making a sweeping generalization, but I should never have jumped to conclusions from such out-of-context concert performances; they likewise should never have been exposed in this manner. When later I saw these same dancers in their proper setting they made a totally different impression.

The first Soviet ballerina I saw in an appropriate setting was at the Paris Opéra, when Marina Semenova, the first great Soviet ballerina, danced *Giselle* with Serge Lifar. She gave a flawless performance technically, but it was not a role in which she excelled. Moreover she was completely cut off from the rest of the company and was not even allowed to take a curtain call with her partner. I had to wait until the revelation of 1956 and my many visits to the Soviet Union to realize the true value of the Soviet school, its background, technique and general outlook. That belongs in a separate chapter.

15. The Artistic Background of Ballet

IN MOSCOW one night, thirty years ago, after a concert given in honour of Debussy, Diaghilev met young Michael Larionov leaving the hall and asked to be shown some works by Natalia Gontcharova, whose painting had caused a sensation in various group exhibitions. It was late, but both men were enthusiasts, and Diaghilev's visits were brief, almost a halt between two train journeys, with discoveries to be made and contacts taken up. Diaghilev refused a lift in Debussy's smart car; he was timid of new inventions, unless they were artistic, and took the usual cab that followed him around – carefully closed, of course, so that he could catch no sort of infection from the horse; even such slow travelling had its hidden dangers. The studio was in complete darkness, and with the aid of a candle they examined canvas after canvas. Diaghilev was at once excited, exclaimed that it was the painting of a genius, and commissioned an important décor, his first by a young artist with a career unmade. (One of the pictures they saw that night is in my study, a gift from Gontcharova. It is a still life depicting the window of the artist's flat. And in the corner there is a mask of Diaghilev.) The following year in Paris when the curtain went up on Le Coq d'Or, the audience gasped, and a whole new school of decorative art was born, distinct from that of Leon Bakst and, to my mind, more characteristically Russian.

The audience gasped because they felt the brilliance and the novelty, but without quite knowing how to place it or where it was leading.

Most of us have been content to accept and to enjoy the decorative art that the ballet has shown us, without any curiosity as to its origins. Like the audience that night, we have applauded from the first moment the curtain rose, but what we have seen has been either something brilliant and entertaining on its own, or a background for our favourite dancers. The loss is ours, for it illuminates the whole genesis of the Russian ballet and shows it quite clearly to be not an isolated theatrical undertaking, but something that has been given life by the finest minds of a whole nation, at a time of unparalleled artistic renaissance. The Russian artist has interested himself in the theatre, the music, and the literature of his period. It is characteristic that the portraits that predominate in the work of such great artists as Serov, son of the famous composer, are not of society beauties, provincial officials, or even wealthy patrons, but of brother artists. Moreover books were not illustrated by a special caste of hack-workers termed book illustrators but by the finest creative minds; even the covers of musical scores were rich in fine designs.

The fame of Russian art has suffered through our lack of curiosity. It does not consist of ikons, Ilya Repine, and then straight on to Bakst, painted peasant dolls, or the artists made known through the *Chauve Souris*, who mistakenly appear to so many to be its standard-bearers. It is more complete and more logical.

The whole history of the ballet is so closely bound up with the social and artistic movements of the last century in Russia that it is essential to give a brief sketch of them in order to understand why the Russian artist was so eager to welcome ballet as a medium, and in that sense give a lead to the modern French masters, who finally took his place. The whole development has been so rapid that I have been able to meet and talk with many of its leading practitioners in each successive stage.

The nineteenth century in Russian art is summed up by the successful assaults of two groups on official academicism, the decay of the first, and the emergence of the second into world importance, led by Serge Diaghilev, Alexandre Benois, and others.

The first group was foreshadowed in 1855 by an important manifesto of Tchernichevsky's, *The Relationship between Art and Reality*, in which he denies 'art as an end in itself' and sees in it 'an instrument for popular education' – the professed attitude of a modern cinema tsar at his most hypocritical, except that Tchernichevsky was in deadly earnest. This was the period immediately before the freedom of the serfs, and agitation was at its height. Many of the artists were themselves serfs, and active sympathy with democracy, reality, and popular education was only natural. Politics have always played a bigger role in art history than many will allow; in Russia the expression of this was cruder, more sudden, and more evident.

In 1863 came the actual secession from the Academy in what is known as the Revolt of the Thirteen Competitors, who refused to participate in the subject set for examination, *Odin in Valhalla*, as being too non-Russian and remote from reality. Out of this was born the *Perejvidniki* movement, seven years later. The name, which means 'The Ambulants', outlines an entire programme. Its members stood for the representation of something national and not for Saint Petersburg alone. As all the important commissions were in the hands of the official world, the artists had at first to live a communistic life, pooling their resources, but they soon found their Maecenas in the Moscow millionaire collector Tretiakov, and their victory was then speedy and complete. The subject triumphed over technique, and many acres of pictures were turned out with a sound moral and an appropriate historical background. It was the great era of advertising democracy, with 'Every picture tells a story' for a slogan. The dominating figure was Ilya Repine, with his grandiose and often inspiring illustrations, but obviously the most interesting legacy is its crude and vigorous portraits, and the reaction away from the movement itself. 'The Ambulants' were extremely hostile to the great movement that was going on in France, and Repine himself wrote deploring the high prices fetched by Degas and Delacroix in public sales and extolling certain tenth-rate German artists.

It did not take long for the new movement to become solidly and immovably academic. It had reached the furthest point from what we know of Russian art. The swing of the pendulum brought the whole school of art associated with the ballet. It was centred round *The World of Art* [*Mir Isskoustva*], a magazine of which Diaghilev was the editor; and if his story ended there, in the beginning of the century, he would already have created history. It must be stressed that he did not merely bring the work of others to Western Europe, as any brilliant opportunist might have done, but the fruits of his own inspiration.

The World of Art threw aside the mediocrities of German painting and welcomed wholeheartedly an alliance with France. It was recruited too for the most part from a higher social class, from those with more leisure who had travelled and were conscious of other cultures. Alexandre Benois, its most articulate member, helped by his pen as much as by his brush. His ancestry gave him a leaning both toward France and the theatre. He had been impressed with Versailles and could see Saint Petersburg in a new light. It was just at this period that the beauties of Russian rococo and the Empire style were beginning to be understood, as against the more Oriental glamour of Moscow.

The whole difference in outlook between the two great cities is important. It can only be traced here in the broadest possible manner, as there are so many other influences at work. Saint Petersburg was more formal, Moscow experimental, so that where the first city viewed the ikon archaeologically, the second saw in it an important phase of art that could have a living message to the artist. Saint Petersburg turned to the French eighteenth century; Moscow, with its rich independent merchant collectors of peasant stock, to contemporary France, and recognized the *fauves* almost before Paris itself. In ballet, Saint Petersburg was well ahead, rich in great dancers, but, when the time came for a new note to be struck, it was a Moscow dancer, Leonide Massine, who took the lead, and that perhaps is typical of the relationship between the cities. Benois in his orientation is definitely Saint Petersburg.

There are many reasons, apart from Benois's tastes, that turned this group to ballet and made theatrical decoration to them what the fresco was to the Italian of the Quattrocentro; reasons psychological and economic. The Russian liked the immediate and glamorous effect of this medium, and there was at the time a dearth of Russian collectors of Russian pictures; the fashion was solidly for French. Here in their midst was this wonderful institution, the ballet. It was only natural therefore to embellish it and to let it carry their names across the world. Prince Serge Wolkonsky and his successor, Teliakovsky, were responsible for bringing *Mir Isskoustva* to the theatre. For the first time in history, Russian art became international, revolutionizing not only the entire conception of stage decoration, but fashions, fabrics, shop displays, and furnishings. I remember Diaghilev's excitement at the Paris Exhibition of Decorative Arts, when this was so obvious in the pavilions of every nation that it was commented on by the entire press.

The great figure behind the reform of theatrical décor was M. A. Vrubel, a painter, sculptor, architect, and designer. He was at once the most complete yet the most incomplete and tragic figure in the whole history of Russian art; a giant, the result of whose labours has reached us nightly since 1909, but who is completely unknown outside Russia. Always he was bitterly disappointed at his own impotence. 'Is there anything,' he wrote in his youth, 'more tragic than to feel the infinite beauty around one, to see God everywhere, and feel one's incapacity to express the great things?' That was the refrain of his life, as he struggled with the Demon. He died a madman, but the glowing visions of colour that he left behind him were seized upon by Bakst and others, and given to us. It is time the world acknowledged this truly remarkable man.

Bakst's fame is world-wide, and deservedly so, but he must not be allowed to eclipse the other artists; he is but a brilliant colour in a complex, glowing scheme. It was an essential policy of Diaghilev's to change his artists before the public had an opportunity to weary of them. It was consistent after Bakst to leave the Oriental style for the logic of Cubism, to avoid direct comparison at all costs. Diaghilev brought the French easel artists, Braque, Derain, Matisse, and others, into the theatre. They were a direct continuation of the Russian school from whom they learnt their métier, but although they created masterpieces, they have always lacked the inventiveness of their predecessors. In the later days painters such as Rouault, Utrillo, and Chirico produced typical fine Rouaults, Utrillos, and Chiricos on a larger scale, but they can never be said to have added one jot to theatrical art, which is so much more than the enlargement of a canvas. Of the non-Russians, Picasso alone has pointed a new direction in *Le Tricorne* and *Pulcinella*, which was closely seized upon by Pruna and others. Where Bakst exploited colour, Picasso showed the effectiveness of angles.

Only two artists, Russians – Gontcharova and Larionov – have made the whole journey with Diaghilev, from the first days of Massine till the very end.

Larionov is the biggest of all Diaghilev's artist-collaborators: where Bakst represents emotion, Benois erudition, Larionov is the perfect blend of both. His success in ballet lies in the fact that he conceives choreographically from the start, sees his costumes, shapes, and colours in movement. He can initiate ideas and collaborate with the dancers. He is master of the grotesque – not the morbid German importation, but the buffoonery that has its origins in the people. His own education makes an interesting story that covers the whole period of Russian art.

He was born in 1881 in Tiraspol, a small village near Odessa. His father was the local chemist, and his earliest memories are of eating cough candy and lozenges in the store. From the first he drew every scene that interested him. Then the family moved to Moscow. It was intended to make of him an explosives chemist, but he took the law into his own hands and, unknown to his parents, presented himself before the Moscow Academy of Arts instead of sitting for the chemical examinations. There were one hundred and sixty competitors and twenty-eight places. He came out thirty-first, through never having drawn from casts. Fortunately three of the candidates were rejected for other subjects, and he was received, the last. Amongst his professors were Serov, Levitan, and my friend Korovin.

The actual school did not interest Larionov a great deal. He was fonder of discussing art in the common-room, on occasions so heatedly that he would come to blows with other students over a canvas of Levitan's.

He exhibited some landscapes with the *Perejvidniki*, and at the school exhibition some erotic illustrations to the *Arabian Nights* that did not pass the censor. When the *Mir Isskoustva* started, he threw himself wholeheartedly into the movement.

A minor artistic scandal saw him rusticated for a year, during which he painted a landscape which Serov bought for the Tretiakov Collection. On his return, Makovsky, a mediocre genre painter on the governing body, maintained that his work was so poor that he must be sent away for good. Serov took his part and agreed to a compromise. He must either win the annual gold medal or leave. He won the medal.

This entitled him to a shorter term of army service, but the army was a turning-point in his career. Its vivid contrasts – the brutality of the soldiers, the dandyism of the officers – interested him, and he was attracted by what he calls 'the water-closet school of art', a form of *surréalisme*, and the only place where the soldier could express himself. Stravinsky's *Tale of a Soldier* owes something to Larionov's army experiences.

Free of the army, Larionov became president of the annual school exhibition, changed its whole character, and devoted a room to the works of a young animal sculptor, Natalia Gontcharova. Diaghilev was immediately attracted by him, and he was sent to Paris with Diaghilev's first continental venture, the Exhibition of Russian Art in the Grand Palais.

He soon became a wholehearted propagandist for French art, though he stayed only for a fortnight, having spent all his grant buying books and prints. The pictures that he bought were donated to the Stchoukine Collection, where they are at present. Amused and understanding, Diaghilev advanced him the money to return home. Moscow never seemed more gloomy than after 'la ville lumière', but he organized a whole series of exhibitions that turned Russian art in a new direction. Once, when a critic accused him of deliberate *épatisme* and said, 'What will your next medium be – grass?' Larionov answered, 'No, my face,' and went through the crowded Moscow streets with a facial fresco. But he had learned a lesson, and his next exhibition was entirely anonymous.

He asked himself, 'Why should certain pictures be called art and placed in museums, while others, such as signboards, are not taken seriously?' He could not answer the question and turned more and more to popular subjects and freer methods. It was in this mood that he met Diaghilev again. It is not surprising that the great discoverer valued this man and turned to him for advice and, later, active help.

The first result was Gontcharova's *Le Coq d'Or*, with Larionov in Paris once again, as Diaghilev's guest.

We have left the curtain up on *Le Coq d'Or*, with the effect made all the more dazzling by what was then a new theatrical device of Gontcharova's, its raising during a black-out, so that the whole set could be seen at once.

In *Le Coq d'Or* Gontcharova went to popular Russian art for her inspiration. The subject lent itself to that treatment, and the singers were grouped on stairs at the side of the stage, in a manner suggested by religious paintings, but that was at the same time intensely practical, leaving freedom for action.

This method led to immediate trouble and illustrates Diaghilev's manner of working throughout his whole career. No one, save he and the artist, realized what the finished result would be. Each actor knew his own small role. If there were any disappointments, Diaghilev preferred them at the very last moment. A leading opera singer asked Gontcharova what the astrologer's costume would be like, and she, thinking of the costume for the dancer's part, gave him a glowing description. Imagine his rage when he was issued with a cerise cloak, the same as all the other singers ! He flatly refused to sing, but, after a short talk with Diaghilev, changed his mind.

'That was genius,' says Larionov, and Diaghilev truly was a genius at avoiding last-moment difficulties. Once when Nijinsky, dissatisfied with his shoes, refused to appear half an hour before a performance, Diaghilev entered the dressing room and came out shortly afterwards with his hat bashed over his head, in a very dishevelled state. What exactly happened no one knew, but Nijinsky danced.

The popular style of *Le Coq d'Or* gave birth to that whole pseudo-folk-school of the *Chauve Souris*; Gontcharova herself abandoned it for the religious motives of *Liturgie* and the mysticism of *Les Noces*. Later an exhibition in Berlin led to the 'Caligari style', and a whole series of new film angles. That too she abandoned as soon as it became popular. Like Diaghilev, she was eager for exploration.

The war cut short the partnership. Larionov served for a fortnight on the Russian front, was wounded, spent six months in hospital, and was invalided out. Diaghilev in Italy bombarded him with telegrams, and he and Gontcharova left for Florence, where Diaghilev was living in a house so small that, when more than three persons sat down to dine, it was necessary to open the door. He was served by an amiable rascal, Beppe, about whom he said, 'I know he is dishonest, but I like dishonest people at times. You don't have to be particular about what you ask them to do.' Shortly afterwards Beppe decamped with whatever he could lay hands on. Fokine, the last link with the old Russia, had left; Massine was being formed along with the real Diaghilev Ballet.

The first work to be devised was *Chout*, with music by Prokofiev. Larionov himself undertook the choreography, with Slavinsky as a technical aid. He had greatly wished to start Sokolova as choreographer and felt certain that she had the gift, but Sergei Pavlovitch did not then like the idea of a woman in charge, and it came to nothing. Woizikovski was his next choice, but the idea did not appeal to him. Then Diaghilev urged Larionov himself to dance, but he suffered from stage fright and refused.

He utilized many innovations for this ballet, not all of which were adopted at once; objects not in actual use were painted on the cloth, tables were slanted at an angle, and the objects hooked onto them. This was a crazy house, the home of buffoons. Many of the constructivist ideas popular in the modern Soviet theatre were first conceived here. The work, however, proved too complex for hurried presentation and was given years later. In the meantime Larionov prepared *Le Soleil de Minuit*, Massine's first work, and a photograph from that time bears the inscription, 'Your grateful pupil'.

At this time also Respighi, a pupil of Rimsky-Korsakov, proposed to Larionov a ballet made up of some small pieces by Rossini, composed for the entertainment of his guests. Massine and Diaghilev were enchanted, and Larionov prepared a series of designs. He thought of it in an impressionistic manner, the scene laid in a country fair. However he did not progress any further, and suggested Bakst, who also made designs.* Finally Diaghilev proposed it to Derain, who was greatly impressed by a recently published history of playing cards and saw it as a game of cards. The work was rediscussed with Larionov, and the ballet that we know and love – *La Boutique Fantasque* – is an amalgamation of these ideas, which is typical of ballet creation.

At the same time, in Italy, Massine created *Les Femmes de Bonne Humeur*, influenced by Hogarth at the instance of Bakst, Jacques Callot at the instance of Larionov. Massine's unique ability to assimilate plastic knowledge is the foundation of his great career. More than anyone he has profited from the Diaghilev circle.

The Larionov-Massine *Contes Russes* is in many respects the most truly Russian of all the repertoire, an attempt to see folklore not through the eyes of the professor or even the poet but as the people see it; for that reason it is the most moving, living fairy tale ever presented on the stage; Kikimora, Baba Yaga, and the rest are grotesques that are bigger than life. This is not a children's fairy tale, but the tale of a primitive people, and it is in that original angle that its genius lies.

The two versions of *Le Renard* further illustrate Larionov's original approach; they are entirely conceived by him, an expression of the army experience that moved him so deeply. Enchanting colours are left behind, replaced by harsh browns and reds, ornamented by scribbles instead of arabesques.

In the first version the Cock is a dashing hussar, the Fox a ballerina in nun's clothing, while the other farmyard characters are yokels; it is, however, the second version, Lifar's first choreographic essay and Diaghilev's swan song, that has survived in the memory. Here Larionov's passion for popular art and the circus gave him the idea of exploiting dance and acrobatic movement simultaneously,

---

*These were recently exhibited in London by the Fine Art Society. The magnificent set would have dwarfed the action. Diaghilev made a wise decision.

with a double cast of similarly costumed characters. Its execution was difficult. The first troupe of acrobats engaged did not appreciate Stravinsky and would not be browbeaten into accepting his music. They, too, had an old tradition and insisted on making their preparations in their own tempi – clearly impossible here. The actual troupe who performed was less brilliant, and some of the ideas had to be sacrificed. The experiment was magnificent but incomplete, and still remains to be carried out. Lifar, like Massine, started under Larionov's guiding influence.

Today, in an historic building in the rue Jacques Callot, four cruel flights up a wooden staircase in Larionov's studio, is one of the finest theatrical museums in the world, kept in such disorder, so constantly added to, that, after several long visits, I have only just skimmed the surface. It is my great ambition to work on a systematic arrangement of the hundreds of portfolios containing sketches, maquettes, letters, photographs, and working notes of all the choreographers from Petipa to Lifar. This is not in any sense a sentimental collection; every item has its practical value that traces the journey from Saint Petersburg and Moscow to Paris. The loss or disposal of these works would be a tragedy. But when we meet there is so much to be said that we talk the whole night, each picture or document suggesting a new exciting train of thought, so that perhaps the work may never get done.

In these portfolios, too, is the proof that Gontcharova and Larionov have anticipated many of the major artistic movements since 1900, and the disorder in which they lie is contradicted by the extremely scientific nature of the researches. There are whole series of subjects, each treated in hundreds of drawings, realistically, as caricatures, studies in form, colour, abstractly and finally theatrically. It is an exciting event to watch the development and variations of a theme, if and when Larionov can find the right portfolio. They are carried out in every type of medium, painted and drawn on paper ranging from thick parchment and rare Japanese vellum to a brand of toilet paper, the possibilities of which delighted him. Larionov realizes their value as documentation. He is continually increasing his knowledge, but he makes little effort to make himself more generally known as an easel painter in a city where it is necessary to help genius by an occasional shout.

He is fully accepted by a small group of brother artists, and has been acclaimed by the two finest critical minds of his generation,

Diaghilev and Apollinaire. His ultimate fame is certain, but probably he will never enjoy it. He does not complain, but I do. It is largely his own doing that he is not as universally recognized as Picasso, whom he has influenced as he influenced the whole Diaghilev circle, and whose equal he is, at any rate, as an artist-investigator.

One afternoon he had a very narrow escape from prosperity. Paul Guillaume brought the Philadelphia collector Albert Barnes to visit him with a view to the purchase of some of his works and Gontcharova's. Barnes eagerly selected various pictures and was prepared to pay a good price for them, but Larionov refused to sell those particular ones. He had given them to Gontcharova, and she was attached to them. The millionaire, cheque book in hand, was disgruntled and amazed. He walked out, missing the opportunity of adding some further masterpieces to his collection and of discovering an artist of world importance, while Larionov lost the material benefits of such a discovery. He was most certainly amused by the whole affair and was soon consoled by the discovery of some dancing print on the quays.

Some day I must, however, make that catalogue.

Gontcharova on the Essence of Theatre Costume. 'When an artist says to one of his friends : "I have created dresses for such a firm," or "I have created costumes for such a play," the reply will always be the same. "It is very interesting (thrilling) to create dresses (in the first case), costumes (in the second)."

'For the friend, dresses and costumes are identical.

'Perhaps there is no difference; perhaps the theatrical costumier is only more *decorative*. There is another word with no clear meaning.

'The everyday dress is conceived to cover, decorate, hide, embellish, to keep warm; in fact to make life bearable and even agreeable amongst one's fellow creatures. Everyday wear dresses a person !

'The reason and aims of the theatrical costume seem to me to be different. While they, too, cover the actor, they create the impression of an imaginary person, his character and type. When a dress serves this purpose in everyday life, it is theatrical, destined to give the illusion of an imaginary person conceived by the wearer – fancy dress, wedding dress, and the like.'

POSTSCRIPT

At long last Larionov and Gontcharova have been recognized at their true value as painters, in sale rooms and museums as well as critically. Important books are devoted to their work, and they are no longer judged solely in connection with their contribution to ballet.

Their story has a sad ending. The valuable collection of paintings and drawings of the *école de Paris* they kept stacked in the rue Jacques Callot in bundles under the bed was raided and dispersed by 'friends' when Larionov was in hospital. They represented a fortune.

16. The End Is the Beginning

I WAS introduced to La Kchessinska, most famous of all Russian dancers, by Diaghilev in Monte Carlo, while he was making every effort to induce her to return to the stage. He failed, and the loss was enormous. Kchessinska would have dazzled us then, just as she could dazzle us today. She thought otherwise and would not risk the memories of those days, when she stood, more than Pavlova even, for the Imperial Russian Ballet and its great traditions. I still feel sore at having lost that season; without it my collection of memories is sadly incomplete.

By way of compensation I was taken to visit her, in her school, by Prince Serge Wolkonsky, former director of the Imperial Theatres, a fact that greatly pleased me, for it was through her, in one of the greatest balletic comedies in history, that he had lost his difficult post, and the happy ending was artistically correct in this case.

Today, Prince Wolkonsky is a leading critic on all branches of the theatre and an expert on dramatic declamation. Handsome, with the face of a sane Don Quixote, he is the very opposite of my 'elderly Russian gentleman'. However much he may regret the things of the past, joyfully he welcomes the present and the future.

'I am seventy, the reference books say so, but I don't believe it. I have never lost my zest for the theatre, and, when the curtain rises, I still get the old thrill of expectation. How wonderful to see the perfection of these young dancers today.'

He has gone much further than I have in his welcome of today. He has even become an enthusiastic film fan and has made a close study of the technique, relating it to his knowledge of the great actresses of the past. All memory of his struggles in the theatre has vanished. Now he is a staunch admirer of Sergei Pavlovitch, and there is no one more welcome in Kchessinska's studio, where the pupils dance especially well for his benefit. But his brief reign in Russia was a stormy one.

At the very beginning of his regime he had trouble, through his official recognition of Diaghilev, then beginning to be known as the revolutionary editor of *The World of Art*. He was entrusted by Wolkonsky with the editorship of the *Annual of the Imperial Theatres*, hitherto a dull official publication. He made of it 'a landmark in Russian book production ... the first of a whole series of works that mark an epoch for the Russian book'.

But Diaghilev had a genius for raising opposition, and his sponsor suffered. However, Wolkonsky had the greatest faith in Diaghilev and entrusted to him a new production of *Sylvia*. The diehards would not stand for this; a yearbook was one thing, but a production by an upstart on those sacred boards! The order was retracted, and Diaghilev resigned. The very same people who had first fought against him turned on the unfortunate director, and by devious routes the case reached the Tsar, who confirmed Wolkonsky in his action. That was the beginning, but there was never a time when the barometer read 'set fair'. The middle period was stormy, the climax a gale.

Prince Wolkonsky has described the episode in his memoirs, under the appropriate title 'Farthingales'.

Kchessinska was to dance in a revival of the celebrated ballet *Camargo*, and for the Russian dance (a Russian dance was inserted into every ballet, wherever the action lay; a point that I might have used in my argument with the elderly Russian gentleman) a special costume was designed, the counterpart of one worn by Catherine the Great at a ball she gave in honour of the Emperor Joseph II.

About two weeks before the performance I heard rumours that Kchessinska did not want to wear the farthingale. The nearer the day approached the more persistent the rumours became. At that time society was very much interested in all questions connected with the ballet; they were even capable of agitating it. Every trifling occurrence behind the scenes became the subject of town gossip, and, as by an electric wire, the excitement was transmitted from place to place... The question of the farthingale assumed the proportions of something great and important.

The day of the performance arrived. The theatre was filled to the last place, and quite half the audience was occupied with the question: 'Well, what will it be? In a farthingale or without a farthingale? ...'

The curtain rose, and to the sounds of the Russian dance Kchessinska appeared – without the farthingale. The next day there was published in the journal of the directorate the following order: 'The Director of the Imperial Theatres has imposed a fine on the ballerina, Kchessinska, for wilfully changing the appointed costume in the ballet *Camargo*.' ...

This was the beginning of a costume comedy that had nearly as far-reaching effects as Nijinsky's refusal to wear the customary trunks over his tights in *Giselle*, only with the reverse ending: the director left. Strings were pulled energetically, the whole Court was interested, and, one morning early, Wolkonsky was summoned by a minister, who requested him to remit the fine. He decided to do nothing of the kind, and, delighted with the pretext, resigned from his complicated post. To have held it longer might have killed that zest in the theatre. In his place I could never have stuck so determinedly to my resolve. Duty, principles, and the rest are small things besides Kchessinska's incomparable charm. I have yet to meet a more remarkable woman. I cannot say if she is beautiful; on reflection, I doubt it. But there is about her a harmony that is enhanced by something exciting – wit, intelligence, character – that breaks up the monotony of harmony and makes her perfect, the complete artist. Kchessinska is the artist in life as well as on the stage. To watch her at ease, let alone dancing in her classroom, is to learn something new about the possibilities of movement. Beside her the word *graceful*, that we so often use, has absolutely no meaning.

It is useless; I am completely defeated, I cannot translate Kchessinska into words. A small pupil in her class recently paid her a greater, simpler tribute.

For two weeks the new arrival, an eight-year-old, would not attempt to make a movement or to join in with the others. She stood apart and watched. Then one day, coming up to the great ballerina, she said: 'I like your dancing. Now I will try.' And she tried, with conspicuous success.

The class is one of the finest I have ever seen: very personal, stimulating and a definite artistic experience. Kchessinska has given herself to the work with intense enthusiasm, working and dancing with her pupils, sometimes for eight hours a day.

Yesterday and Today. A.L.H.: How do the dancers of your time compare with the young people today? No one can give more valuable information on that point.

KCHESSINSKA: It is a curious thing, when I think over the great reputations of the past, first those of my schooldays. Many who were then greatly applauded would make one laugh today just for their style. Gerdt, for instance, was a great dancer, but I cannot for a moment imagine him on the stage now. There are others, however, who could triumph, today just as yesterday. Virginia Zucchi, for instance, was one of the greatest artists I have ever seen. There are some dancers whose performance excites you at the time, but who leave you with nothing. After all these years I can still see Zucchi.

The dancers of this time are technically very far advanced, more so than even Legnani, whose name at one time stood for technique. In the development of the artistic personality it is a different, more complicated matter.

A.L.H.: Can artistry be learnt?

KCHESSINSKA: Up to a point, it can be developed. The innate artistry of our great Anna Pavlova is a different matter, but I can think of many notable dancers who learned to be artists gradually.

The time factor is the important thing in answering all these questions. This works in many directions. We studied longer before tackling difficult roles, and though technique today justifies a shorter apprenticeship, the mind is not yet always ready. It is in watching great artists that we can eventually become great artists ourselves. In those days we had plenty of time to watch. I remember when I was twenty, asking Petipa to let me dance *Esmeralda*. 'Not yet,' he told me, 'you are not sufficiently ripe.' And he was right. Those old ballets may have had many ridiculous features, but to interpret them emotionally was an enormous test. I felt *Esmeralda* so strongly when finally I did dance it that often I had to fight with tears before I went on. Here again time plays a part. These ballets were long and sustained. One could develop a role or learn by watching its development.

I am amazed at these young artists, but I often ask myself, will they last as long as we have done? Will they be as fresh as Anna Pavlova in middle age? It is the time factor again. They dance nightly, we only at intervals. It is impossible to be in the right mood every night, and to force one's inclinations may be dangerous for the young; but time again will show.

A.L.H.: Your class differs from any that I have seen in many respects. Have you any special method of teaching?

KCHESSINSKA: I try to make every class new and exciting. I want to teach dancing as well as the isolated movement that is part of it. I try to place the orthodox, routine steps into a context that will stimulate the imagination. In this way the dancers will, when the time comes, be able to assimilate choreography rapidly. You will notice that I never count aloud. It ruins a class as much as it does a performance. Before beginning to dance the pupils must get the rhythm into their heads. It is useless to begin until then.

A.L.H.: How do you prevent them becoming small imitation Kchessinskas?

KCHESSINSKA: By studying them as individuals. While each one must learn the general technique, when they are sufficiently advanced I give them exercises to which they are especially well suited.

I do not believe in Cecchetti's methods for a long period of training. I find they stifle the imagination by making the class too stereotyped, where it should be an artistic adventure. It is admirable to develop strength and confidence in someone already trained. He taught me the fouetté, and I shall always be grateful for what he did for me. It is Johannsen whom I consider the greatest of all teachers, and the creator of the Russian ballerina. He was one of the very few men who could teach a woman how to dance.

I agree with you, in spite of these small reservations, that the ballet today is remarkable, and anyhow the dancers will continue to develop on the stage. In my own case complete mastery came at about the age of thirty. How easy it was to dance then, quite effortless. Before then, and after, one had sometimes to make a little effort to be in the right mood. Now, maturity will come early. The three little girls, Riabouchinska, Toumanova, and Baronova, should play a very big part in the future history of our art. They have also ensured the supremacy for Russians for some time to come.

The first Russian dancer to gain supremacy for Russia over the Italian school, Kchessinska, is teaching those who will maintain the Russian name. These ideas have already produced Riabouchinska, Rostova, Semenova, Tarakanova, Lichine, and others. This is a proof of their wisdom. When you applaud them, you applaud her.

My final pilgrimage is to the class of Olga Preobrajenska, great Maryinsky dancer, famed for her wit; and it is my final pilgrimage, for there Toumanova and Baronova received their first lessons. The Ballet is in Paris, and they are back once again under Preobrajenska's eagle eye. What the audiences of Paris, London, and New York have applauded, she will appraise critically; the faults they have missed she will correct. Mesdemoiselles Toumanova and Baronova are no more, only the two small pupils – Tamara and Irina.

It is a curious thing, although I have now been with the company a year, it was not until their return from America, when I started attending classes with regularity, that I noticed Irina Baronova's outstanding technique, to me the most *complete* that can be found at the present day. I knew from the first that she had those pure Russian-school movements that flow one into the other, and that nobility of line that seems to reach into infinity. I knew she was an exceptional mime, able to render the most subtle shades of expression with a range that extended from the passionate drama of *Les Présages* to the jealousy of the Top in *Jeux d'Enfants* and the fine light comedy of *Le Beau Danube* and *Scuola di Ballo*. All these things I knew well, but somehow I had never thought of her as a technical dancer, and that is her triumph. It also explains so many things about English dancing, and perhaps finally answers the troublesome question of the reason for the marked superiority of Russian dancers. It is, of course, possible for us to produce Baronova's technical equal, but in that case both the dancer and we, her public, would be so very excited about it, that we would cry out loudly in our triumph and forget all those other things that turn the dancer from the acrobat into the artist. The Russians talk less about technique than we do. They work for it hard in class and then leave it at that. Actually their standards are far more exacting. They have had so many years in which to grow accustomed to technical prowess, while we, as newcomers, are still too thrilled with the possibilities of technical achievement. It all comes back, then, to the question of tradition with which I started this book. Added to this the Russian has by nature a deep humility – not modesty, which is a social attribute – a humility in front of the immensity of art itself, so that he will never imagine that a flawless pirouette in itself means attainment. Karsavina in her praise of our superb Sokolova stresses that 'religious fervour gave her the same attitude towards our work as we had'.

I have also this season been taking lessons in make-up from Baronova, in return for some English lessons. Like all dancers she turns up at the theatre at seven o'clock for nine : one hour in advance would be considered running things dangerously close. Gifted with an exceedingly mobile and plastic face, she has experimented in the one short year since she has been making-up by herself until she can perform wonders. Now she has with infinite patience given herself a new nose. The charming little Russian snub becomes Grecian, the schoolgirl looks more completely the loving heroine of *Les Présages*, or the film-vamp, Lady Gay of *Union Pacific*; then with three minutes' work and some cold cream she is ready to go on again as the soubrette in *Le Beau Danube*, where the snub is so completely a part of the picture. Like Karsavina she too finds inspiration in the make-up box, bringing one plastic art to the aid of the other in her quest for perfection. Yet in spite of all this conscious effort, this intelligent prelude to success, I believe it was an accident that played the biggest part in turning a great dancer into a great artist with such rapidity. Playing in the snow in Saint Louis, Irina fractured a small bone in her leg. For a few days she took it lightheartedly, until one day in bed she plugged in the wireless. It played Tchaikovsky's Fifth Symphony, the music of her very own *Les Présages*, which she should have been dancing at that moment. She broke down and cried for hours. Then two months later, when she could dance again, we saw Baronova the incomparable, of whom I have been writing.

POSTSCRIPT

Kchessinska lived on for nearly forty years after this last chapter was written, dying in her ninety-ninth year. I came to know her very well, with increasing admiration and affection. She wrote to me, 'It is strange that our unshakable friendship came about through the offices of Serge Diaghilev and Prince Wolkonsky, with whom I had formerly the severest conflicts in my career.' She spoke very freely about her past life with the Tsar, and I finally persuaded her to write her memoirs, which I translated from the French. In her life this remarkable woman only had three loves, an emperor and two grand dukes, and it was said that the Imperial family called her *notre Tilde* in place of *Matilde*. Her complete acceptance into the Imperial family is an extraordinary tribute to her character, as was her ability to allow the *grande dame* and the ballerina to coexist. Her love affair with the Emperor developed into a firm friendship after his marriage. It went far deeper than a passing affair.

Certain episodes stand out in my memory : Kchessinska dancing a mazurka with the young Lifar. 'It's simple to do as long as you have Polish ancestry'; Kchessinska as hostess at a Christmas party at which Rachmaninov played for the children and Chaliapin sang; Kchessinska in her seventies, having broken her hip falling off a ladder, jumping across the room from chair to chair and laughing; Kchessinska saying to me before my first visit to Russia – 'Be sure to visit my palace. I believe it's some kind of revolutionary museum, but if you mention my name they will show you my private apartments' – needless to say I did nothing of the kind; the Soviet Union regarded her as the du Barry of the old regime. Kchessinska applauding the Bolshoi : 'They have kept up the standard and bettered it. Go round and tell Ulanova how wonderful I thought her; it might embarrass her if I went.' In her later days this ex-ballerina, wife of the Grand Duke André, and Imperial favourite, corresponded with the curator of the Tchaikovsky museum in Klin and sent them some of her costumes.

She told me she had had so many jewels and furs that she kept a card index to keep track of them, yet in her Paris studio she and Grand Duke André would clean the floor with evident enjoyment. In her great days of power she was certainly domineering and given to intrigue, as is very clear from her book, *Dancing in Saint Petersburg.* Yet she was kind to the young aspirant Karsavina, who remembers her with deep affection. I saw traces of the old Kchessinska in her continued rivalry with Preobrajenska, even when the two old ladies were in their nineties. The rivalry was between the school shows and the progress of their respective pupils. Kchessinska attracted more foreigners and debutantes, though she produced such dancers as Riabouchinska, Lichine, and Tarakanova. She had an extraordinary rapport with the young and was able to understand their problems not only as dancers. One of them, Diana Gould, the future Mrs Yehudi Menuhin, remained a devoted friend till the end. Preobrajenska had the majority of the de Basil 'babies', headed by Baronova and Toumanova.

Kchessinska's studio was in an elegant apartment in Auteuil; Preobrajenska taught in a rather dingy and dusty rented room in the Salle Wacker, a place of pilgrimage to all dancers. Alas, it has been pulled down. She was something of a recluse, living with her elderly friend Count Zubov. I remember a room full of parrots that flew around freely, squawking and flapping their wings. The third great Maryinsky teacher, Lubov Egorova, who had married into the nobility through a close friend of Kchessinska's, kept the peace.

These three great women dominated the ballet world at that time, not only taking the young émigré talent without payment, but subsidising their parents whenever necessary. Later when I went to the Soviet Union, I saw many other former ballerinas teaching in very much the same way. I realized that the strength of the Russian school lay in the fact that ballet was a vocation for life, because no one really retired and the tradition was never broken.

PART II

Balletomania Now

*

This second part belongs to Galina Ulanova, 'the miracle woman', who in 1956 rekindled my dormant balletomania.

17. Where I Left Off

I TAKE up where I left off in 1933, when I was so certain that everything in ballet was wonderful and would continue that way. As a result of the success of *Balletomania*, I became the first dance critic to be employed by an English newspaper, the *Daily Telegraph*. It was wonderful discipline, but to a certain extent it spoilt my pleasure in the performance. As the only specialist I was obsessed by the desire to be scrupulously fair, though fortunately I realized from the first that objective criticism was an impossibility. Much of what I wrote stirred controversy; dancers seemed more touchy in those days.

I do not believe the old cliché that critics are invariably disappointed artists, unproductive eunuchs. They have an especially valuable service to perform for ballet in an age where there are no artistic directors and the dancer is in sole control. In the beginning they may have let themselves be guided by the opinions of dancers. (It is always an uncomfortable experience to go to the ballet with a dancer, quite apart from the danger of being nudged and hacked as she tries to restrain herself from responding to the music.) With a few magnificent exceptions among whom Ulanova is outstanding, I find dancers and choreographers bad judges of ballet. If they did not have one-track minds that convinced them their way was the right and only one, they would not be artists of great personality. They are deeply involved in the minutiae of technique at the expense of the performance as a whole. They are aware of background conditions that do not concern the critic, who is giving his reaction to one particular performance. I have been often enough on the receiving end of criticism both to realize its value and to have been irritated by it. Beware of those who proudly announce that they never read their press notices. It has yet to happen. What was wrong when I started was that I was working in isolation, and what I wrote received too much attention. The same thing existed in the United States in John Martin's heyday, and is still more the case today, with Clive Barnes's virtual monopoly of dance and drama in New York. I can sympathize with his heavy and responsible burden and am not amazed at the hostility he so often arouses. He can only express what he feels, and he does so with feeling tempered by knowledge. The critic is usually disliked, not because of his strictures on any one dancer, but for the praise he gives to another. To say that X's Giselle lacks a certain quality may be forgiven, but to praise Y's interpretation upsets X and all her admirers.

Today in England there are a number of exceptionally well-informed critics who write with devotion to the art and with the elegance it merits. They are constructive, and if one gets to know their prejudices, and we all have prejudices, the sum total of their work is as valuable to the ballet as it is to the public, and serves as a record for the historian.

I abandoned criticism in the English press in 1936 and paid two long visits to Australia, where I found myself reviewing the same performances for three or four different newspapers and magazines. I could see that the ballet company which had sparked my original enthusiasm was breaking up. I became bored by the hundredth performance of *Schéhérazade* and *Les Sylphides* and more and more interested in the country and its people. I took time off to write about them in *Waltzing Matilda*, which many people thought was a book about Kchessinska! I also learnt a great deal about management that left me even more disillusioned.

On my return I turned lecturer, talking on dancing in general and trying to turn my experience into an aesthetic of the dance. I have lectured all over the world and greatly enjoyed the experience. I still do, especially when it comes to question time. There is always something new to learn.

Immediately before World War II, and for its duration, my enthusiasm was rekindled by the rapidly developing Sadler's Wells company, performing at the New Theatre in London, and by the wonderful partnership of Margot Fonteyn and Robert Helpmann. I had already acclaimed her first performances in *Swan Lake* in 1935. Week by week she grew in stature. She was infinitely musical, and the detail in her work never detracted from the whole. I cannot hope to see a finer Aurora; I shall never forget Fonteyn's first run down the stage as the happy, carefree birthday girl, or how the Rose Adagio, so often a painful acrobatic exercise, gained its true significance as a testing of suitors. She danced not only to the audience but to her parents seated on the throne and usually left in isolation as a part of the scenery. The climax of the needle prick, when the spoilt darling suddenly realizes that there is such a thing as suffering and is helpless to resist, I have never seen equalled. There were wonderful romantic performances in Ashton's *Apparitions* and *Nocturne*, and later at Covent Garden in *Ondine* and the perfect revival of *The Firebird*. She has earned her legendary fame.

Helpmann was extraordinary; he is the only man I know who was an indifferent dancer from a purely classical point of view, but who could act the role of a *danseur noble* so perfectly that he carried conviction from the moment he appeared on the stage. 'He walked on as a conqueror,' Bridges Adams once said to me. 'I have not seen such a walk since Irving's time.' The success of his many drolls and grotesques, which have put him in a class of his own alongside Massine, have obscured the amazing bluff of those classical performances.

As a choreographer he does not rate so high. He was more a brilliant producer of dance-drama, extremely intelligent and with something original to say; two of his works were outstanding and bore repeated visits, *Hamlet* and *Miracle in the Gorbals*.

He did not tell the story of *Hamlet*, but gave a Freudian-based description of Hamlet's state of mind – the first time, in my experience, that such a dance-translation has been accomplished. There has been no other Shakespearian drama treated in this indirect manner. It could, and should, be revived. It also brought Leslie Hurry to the fore as a stage designer.

Miracle in the Gorbals, to Arthur Bliss's most dramatic and concise score, depicted what would happen in a big city slum if Christ reappeared and performed a miracle; a trite subject in literature but moving in a ballet that characterized holiness, evil, and indifference. I well remember a meeting where the possible effect of this ballet on the various denominations was discussed. When it came to the Church of Scotland, Lord Waverley, chairman of the Covent Garden Governors, gave it his instant imprimatur. He was an elder of the Scottish Kirk.

With what rapidity we saw the emergence of June Brae and Pamela May; followed by Beryl Grey, the first of our dancers to appear in Russia, so far the only one to dance in China and today the artistic director of the Festival Ballet. Then Ann Heaton; and the sparkling, Russian-backed Nadia Nerina who made her great impact in *La Fille Mal Gardée*; Beriosova splendidly lyrical; and then follows a long list of those dancers formed in the Royal Ballet School: Sibley, Seymour, and Park, as well as the men, Dowell and Wall – all in the great tradition which has taken generations to produce in Europe.

I will leave the subject of English ballet, which has been so much written about and is there for all my readers to see – it is second to none in the world today – to turn to other experiences that have enriched my life and rekindled my balletomania when at times it came perilously close to extinction. As this is a personal record I have omitted many dancers and companies I have not seen in spite of extensive travels. Moreover I can only write of companies that I have known for an extended period at school, in rehearsal, and on the stage. I will avoid chronology.

This is no dull history – the experiences still live and must come tumbling out if they are to retain the sense of excitement that was and is mine.

The only danger to the advancement of ballet in England today is an economic one. Neither ballet nor opera has room to economise if either is to be worthy of subsidies at all. V.A.T. (Value Added Tax) is proving an iniquitous burden on the theatre, and the admirable work and foresight shown by that remarkable minister Jennie Lee are being rapidly squandered. We must recognize that art is a national investment; the French, essentially a practical people, have long realized this.

18. Danceomania

I. *Folk Dance*. As time went on I became more and more interested in dancing in general. *Balletomania* became *Danceomania*, as it should have been from the start. I drew the line at morris dancing and the like, worthy pastimes that bored me to extinction. This was not entirely due to prejudice, since its revival was artificial and only where a true peasantry still exists or has recently existed has national dancing any meaning. Curiously enough, even then it is often more real, if not more authentic, on the stage than in the village. Folk costumes are not only expensive to make; few people have the time or the knowledge needed, and when a costume that has been handed down through many generations wears out, it is no longer replaced. I have seen folk and tribal dances performed all over the world in the most incongruous mixture of beautiful costumes and store-bought clothes, including cloth caps and bowler hats, a symbol of a rapidly changing world and the extreme fragility of the social dance. Even the aboriginal dances of Australia and New Guinea will soon be lost, though the instinct to dance is so strong that the natives have devised new dances showing the flight of aeroplanes. Many governments, especially in Central Europe, Russia, and Spain, have done excellent work in preserving national dances, something totally different from merely resurrecting them. National dancing, which originally contained the seeds of ballet, still nourishes it.

The most pathetic thing I witnessed was the degeneration of the dancing of the native tribes in the mine compounds outside Johannesburg. I saw them twice, in 1939 and 1969. The contrast was devastating. These dances had developed spontaneously, so it is said, for the enjoyment of the participants, one of the last forms of self-expression remaining to them after the breakdown of the tribal system. They had originally been associated with war, hunting, and witchcraft. In 1939 the Zulus in particular gave a display that was frightening in its intensity. Brought up like most boys of my period on Rider Haggard, they carried me right back to the world of Umslopagaas. There was pride and dignity of movement; for a brief time the natives could forget their semi-slavery in the compound and in the dark depths underground. Yet even then, though they obviously danced for their own pleasure, the performance had become a big tourist attraction. Thirty years later the dance was for the most part a tawdry and lackadaisical affair, with only an occasional flash of involvement. There was a complete loss of identity. Should that identity return, it would be a poor outlook for the white population, who have not found the means to replace it or to compensate for its loss. This is not the place to draw any political conclusions. The economic situation alone has had its influence on all forms of social dancing.

There are certain sporting events so closely related to dancing in style, grace and the emotions they inspire, that they belong here: gymnastics with the classical Turischeva, the demi-caractère Korbut and the dramatic Saady; figure skating with such exponents as Rodnina and Zaitsev. Paradoxically I find the dancing section the least interesting and I marvel at the inconsistency and lack of sensitivity of the judges in marking for artistic achievement. There is never such a discrepancy in marking our ballet competitions and as Vice-President both in Varna and Moscow I have scrutinized all the ballot papers. Athletics, lawn tennis, cricket and football are all dance-related. The connection between sport and dancing has become more obvious now that ballet is included in so many training schedules. I would include the art of the matador as the closest of all in grace, drama and emotion, were it not for the brutally ugly moments that intrude. The *aficionados* have said that the maiming of the horses provides a comic element. Black comedy? Certainly not, the broken hacks look grotesque but the episodes are too raw to possess any artistry, pathos gives way to indignation. Ballroom dancing as a sport I find compulsive viewing, if only for the high comedy that it provides especially in the allegedly Latin American section, as far removed from the original as Balham from Buenos Aires and Coventry from Cuba.

II. *The Indian Dance*. As a lover of classicism I found myself more and more interested, and then moved, by the Indian classical dances, especially the Bharata Natyam of South India. They have been rediscovered and fostered by Anna Pavlova after having degenerated into what we popularly called nautch dancing. They were seen from time to time in cabaret, often performed by Europeans in a provocative style close to that of the belly dance. Unfortunately the Indians themselves have out-distanced Hollywood-Oriental in their films. There were still teachers of the traditional dance, especially in South India, but it was not considered a suitable profession for a well-bred girl.

The first time I saw such dancing in India was with Pavlova's husband, Victor Dandré. Pavlova herself had at one time danced with Uday Shankar, who preceded Gopal. Menaka, the wife of a distinguished physician, had been one of the earliest dancers to be encouraged by Pavlova. She put on a display for us in the courtyard of her school, and it was a revelation. Afterwards the dancers of East and West met and compared notes, explaining their techniques; there was a complete rapport, and it was an inspiring occasion. Later, Ram Gopal, a bronze god, came to England and not only danced but lectured on the technique and the origin of this, the oldest surviving classical dance form in the world. He, the pioneer, gained a small and enthusiastic public, and was followed by a number of others, notably Mrinalini Sarabhai, who became a close friend. We had met in Cambridge when I was lecturing on classical ballet and where I had been chased down a corridor by an infuriated woman devotee of modern dance armed with an umbrella. Mrinalini was in complete sympathy with my point of view; she told me that she was a dancer, and she and her scientist husband, Vikram, spent the evening discussing the dance with me. I encouraged her to give a season in London. She was greatly concerned with translating her dances into theatrical terms without impairing their technique. Her dancers and musicians were as thoroughly disciplined as any Western company, but they had been apprenticed from early childhood to a guru whose word was law. Mrinalini had started a school of dance, music, and drama in Ahmedabad, and members of her company visited the villages reviving the traditional art and gathering material to develop it.

All too often we in England had seen brilliant dancers in some unsuitable hall with poor lighting and no organization. The Indian is as strong an individualist as the Spaniard, and so highly organized an ensemble was something rare. I begged Nehru to send over a large and superbly presented group from all over India; he was sympathetic, but pleaded the extreme poverty existing in the villages and emphasized the need for priorities. My old friend Krishna Menon, when he was High Commissioner, did everything he could to further the cause of Indian dance and music, and kept me in constant touch with Indian dancers in Europe, usually asking me to find a West End theatre 'in three days' time'. Dr Anghadi of the Asian Music Circle was a staunch pioneer, helped in particular by Yehudi Menuhin. Where music is concerned the Indians have met with considerable success; even the 'electric-guitar boys' have heard of the veena, and, alas, some Indians have fallen in love with the microphone – an object totally unnecessary for their needs, as it should be for anyone save a politician at a mass meeting, and often he would be better unheard.

At the beginning my knowledge of Indian dancing was very limited. I found to my great interest that by applying the same standards of judgement as for Western dancers I could distinguish the very good from the adequate, and that it was not really important to understand the technique in order to be carried away by the dance. I have always told this to would-be balletgoers who are frightened that they 'do not know enough to enjoy it', a refrain I hear constantly. You can enjoy roast lamb or crêpes suzette without reading a cookery book, you can enjoy ballet without reading any of mine. Olives are an acquired taste – you can only acquire it by repeated tastings. It is exposure to any art that is the important thing. My driver in Bulgaria, who had watched the ballet competitions for several years, could give an admirable forecast of the result.

I still know only the fringes of a subject that requires a lifelong study of history, religion, music, and Sanscrit literature. I have seen enough, however, to convince me that at its best this is the most complete and expressive of all dance systems, for it contains all, and more, that the modern dance school so often tries to express. It is 'abstract' – movement to meaningless syllabic sounds – and it contains sections of narrative described in the inexhaustible language of mime, beautiful in itself and deeply expressive. It is as religious and subtly erotic as the Song of Songs. There is no physical contact between the dancers; the movement is highly disciplined, but within its framework the dancer has freedom to improvise. At one moment the musicians are in control, at another they follow the dancer in her variations. Indian dancing poses the most complex rhythmic problems, and the time element involved is extraordinary. In ballet a pas de deux lasting ten minutes is a marathon for dancers and audience, a five-minute classical variation is exceptional. A solo in the Bharata Natyam dance can last for two hours or more in

India; in Europe it is usually cut to twenty minutes. When perfectly performed it has an almost hypnotic effect; the passage of time becomes forgotten. The dancer's breath control is fantastic: one always has the feeling of power exerted and power held in reserve, a quality that enhances all dancing. The feeling of inevitability is strongly present, as it must be in all good choreography. 'This is how it happened, there can be no other solution.'

To the Indian dancer the mysticism and the symbols of their religion remain a living culture. In the Kathakali school the gods come alive and make the earth tremble, positive good and positive evil are continually locked in combat. In Western culture only Wagner's *Ring* can carry one into a world of gods and monsters, and by the music alone, since the ideal production defies the theatrical medium. The Kathakali dances can move any audience because of the conviction with which they are performed, but they are not for export and can only be danced by Indians themselves.

One of my greatest dance experiences was provided by Shanta Rao. The connoisseur-impresarios John and Luce Coast had brought her over, and had summoned me to watch a rehearsal. Amongst the small audience was that redoubtable woman Beryl de Zoete, who, well in her late seventies, had wandered through India and Ceylon studying Eastern dancing. The rehearsal was held in most unpromising surroundings – the private reception room of a not very glamorous hotel; the sort given over to Rotarian revels or masonic junketings. One could almost hear Gilbert and Sullivan bouncing off the cream walls or the conjuror asking his victim to choose a card.

There were a dozen or so of us muffled in great coats and seated on those ridiculously uncomfortable gilded cane chairs reserved for festive occasions. Three musicians squatted on the floor tuning their instruments. Shanta Rao sat in the far corner of the room, looking very small but, even when motionless, very much in command, with her proud head held like that of some Spanish flamenco dancer painted by Manet.

Then she started to dance; a mixture of silk and steel, rippling water and sledgehammer blows. Every movement was crystal clear in a school of dance that combines as none other the mathematical and the dramatic, the abstract and the emotional. And this first impact, tremendous as it was, grew with a cumulative effect that became completely hypnotic.

I am told that the dance lasted half an hour. I was not conscious of it; the dancer had abolished time just as she had wiped out the drab surroundings, creating her own bright atmosphere.

Years later I saw Shanta Rao in a packed Festival Hall, a building equally ill-suited to dancing. She has absolute concentration, an almost masculine strength that can turn to tenderness and seductive femininity. One woman filled the stage with an Ajanta fresco of movement.

The dance in India is the gateway to all the arts, closely related to sculpture. Both arts express the same attitude toward worship. Shiva created the world through movement, rhythm keeps the world spinning and the body functioning. Dancing is truly a gift of the gods.

III. Spanish Dancing. Spanish dancing, especially gypsy dancing, which I have greatly enjoyed, has on the whole never been really at home on the stage. The dancers have inherited rather than learnt their technique. It is essentially an art involving audience participation. When it is staged the setting is usually an inn with a crowd gathered together for a fiesta from which we are barred entrance by the footlights. It is difficult in Spain today to see the real thing unless some wealthy landowner arranges a special party. It was Gautier who said, 'La Danse espagnole est une invention bien parisienne.' I could see the great difference underlined when a Spanish company performed *Le Tricorne*. In the original, two Spaniards, de Falla and Picasso, and a Russian, Leonide Massine, had made a perfect stage *translation* of the Spanish scene, one that was highly appreciated in Spain, while the Spaniards' attempt had no reality. During my student days in Paris, the music halls would show whole evenings of Spanish dancing, with performers gathered from all over Spain. I remember a party given in Spain for Diaghilev where the great Pastora Imperio danced. It was magic; Chaliapin knelt to kiss the hem of her dress. I saw her once again at a party, when she had become too fat and old to dance. She sat on a stool and danced with her arms, and the magic still remained. When Spanish troupes appeared in London, the cultural attaché Xavier de Salas and Richard Buckle sometimes gave parties for them; the guests sat on the floor. Here was Spanish dancing at its best, full of the spontaneity that had been simulated on the stage.

Amongst the gypsies only Carmen Amaya seemed able to banish

the footlights and carry me with her. The whole Amaya tribe were from Barcelona, and appeared completely untamed. I remember seeing them one Sunday morning, children and veterans, dressed in the most motley attire, and kicking a football around in Hyde Park. No one could imagine that they were filling a London theatre. In their lodgings it was the same; they cooked their food over a brazier in the middle of the floor, leaving behind a heavy bill for damages. I watched them for numerous performances, each one different, and it was clear that they danced for their own amusement and would have done the same with or without an audience.

There were some magnificent exceptions, dancers who had successfully made the transition from cabaret and *cave* to the theatre. Argentina, Argentinita, Mariemma, Pilar Lopez, and the Mexicans Teresa and Luisillo immediately come to mind. Antonio, the most famous of all, never really moved me once he had separated from his cousin and partner, Rosario. He seemed too slick, a marvellous performer of steps that one applauded for their extreme difficulty : his rhythmic heel taps, at first positive and loud, gradually becoming more and more rapid until they faded almost imperceptibly into a tremble, the body held proudly erect and motionless, were certainly sensational. The first time I could not believe my eyes and ears, and then I felt the whole thing become as meaningless as an attempt at a world record of those accursed fouettés. The great Escudero and the Mexican Luisillo had less precision, but there were beauty and mystery in all their movements.

19. French Ballet

I. *Serge Lifar*. I first met Lifar as a raw recruit in 1924 at Astafieva's studio, when Alicia Markova gave her sensational audition. He was wearing his first dinner jacket and was pointed out to me by many of the dancers as a potential star. He sat unobtrusively in a corner absorbing everything that was happening. It was after 1934 that I came to know him really well, making frequent trips to Paris to see his wonderful partnership with Spessivtseva in *Giselle*, and to attend the first nights of his own ballets.

In a surprisingly short time he had revolutionized the Paris Opéra Ballet, which had lain dormant for so long. The school taught a brilliant, somewhat brittle technique devised from Blasis via Lepri via Zambelli, but for a long time the dancers had been interested only in the wealthy connections they could make. It was the done thing for a banker or aspiring politician to keep a little dancer as a pet, and the wife of one such referred with great pride to 'notre maîtresse'. The dancer was badly paid, but if she grumbled the director told her, 'Look at the opportunities this gives you.' When I first saw the Opéra Ballet, there were very few male dancers, and the Walpurgis Night scene from *Faust* was its greatest achievement, together with a pleasing survival, *Coppélia*, with a female Franz. I begged Lifar to retain this, and he did, as long as the brilliant Pauline Dynalix was there to sustain the role. During Diaghilev's lifetime no one in the artistic or fashionable world would dream of attending the Opéra Ballet. The snobs sent their servants to the Sunday matinées.

Lifar came into his prime as a dancer in 1931, having inherited Diaghilev's brilliant circle – Cocteau, Kochno, and others. He was full of enthusiasm at discovering his gifts as a choreographer after his brief trial in *Le Renard* under the tutelage of Larionov, during Diaghilev's final season. He had come to Paris from Kiev, sent there by his teacher, Nijinska. He was a last-minute replacement and technically below standard. Hard work with Cecchetti had turned him into a dancer; the artistry he already possessed, and his *Le Fils Prodigue* established him as the most exciting discovery since

Nijinsky. He was vastly ambitious. His prestige was sufficient to allow him to ride roughshod over the civil service hierarchy existing in the French national theatres and enabled him to give the younger dancers an opportunity to shine. He had an understanding director in Jacques Rouché, a millionaire who spent his own money to supplement the rather meagre government subsidy. He gave inspiring classes, sufficiently unorthodox to provide a relief from the normal academic routine, adding excitement but leaving the school untouched. In a very short time the ballet had recovered its dignity as a profession. Once again a ballet première was a great occasion. Such distinguished critics as Levinson, Svetlov, Chaikeivitch, and Wolkonsky, who had sometimes been grudging toward Diaghilev in his later years, sang Lifar's praises without reserve. Cocteau, Vaudoyer, Picasso, Derain, Milhaud, Poulenc, and others treated him as a distinguished colleague.* Since Vestris, whose biography he wrote, no other dancer had so completely dominated the Parisian scene. No one savoured his success, fame, and, at times, notoriety more than Lifar. He was completely uninterested in financial rewards and was generous to a fault, aiding the many impoverished Russian refugees without ostentation. He turned author, publishing biographies and manifestos on his theories of the dance that were a confusing mixture of classicism and revolt, but full of interesting material.

Lifar regarded Diaghilev with filial piety and was at all times a fierce defender of his reputation. All this acclaim certainly went to his head, though he retained a sense of humour and could always tell a story against himself. On one occasion I saw him leaf through the index of a foreign book on ballet (in spite of his position he was and still is largely unrecognized outside France). 'What, only two or three mentions of my name! It is like writing history without including Napoleon,' and he threw the wretched book in the wastepaper basket. On another occasion he told me of his exciting visit to Rio. 'I was standing on the deck as we came into port when I suddenly noticed that everyone was kneeling as if in prayer – good, I thought, here is a public that really appreciates an artist. Then I turned round and saw behind me Cardinal Verdier giving his blessing! Still, they were a wonderful audience and I had a triumphant tour.' The cardinal was so enchanted by this story that he gave Lifar

*Today he is a member of the French Institute, an exceptional honour for a dancer-choreographer.

a photo signed 'To a prince of the dance from a prince of the Church'.

Lifar was obviously frequently embroiled in headline-making quarrels of a highly theatrical nature. In New York he challenged Massine to a duel. It was an anticlimax. Massine's only reaction was to say, 'Go take an aspirin.' Later he fought a duel with the equally histrionic Marquis de Cuevas. Naturally the press was informed and photographers were present. One of them received a scratch and they resumed their friendship. Lifar took friendly criticism remarkably well and never bore a grudge; there were far better things to do, and hatred was not in his character. The war proved his undoing. It came at the very moment when he had formed his ideal company and was at his peak as dancer, choreographer, and personality. He cannot be blamed for keeping the Opéra alive during the occupation; to have done otherwise would have thrown hundreds out of work. What let him down was his monstrous ego, his indiscretion and particularly that of a devoted brother who boasted of his enormous influence with the occupying power. He could not see himself purely as an artist. He had to be in the very centre of things, playing a mysterious role in the political scene. It had to be 'Moi et Hitler, moi et Pétain, moi comme gardien de la culture française.' His autobiography, a fantasy, shows him involved in everything, a man with a mission that must be kept secret, a man of the Resistance, the superdiplomat. Certainly he met many highly placed Germans who flattered him, as they had Jean Cocteau, Sacha Guitry, and many others, including Maillol, Derain, and Despiau. Like them, he had seized the opportunity of helping friends in danger whenever possible. When I assisted in trying to rehabilitate Lifar after the war, following a B.B.C. announcement about his probable execution, I found him guilty only of vanity and an over fertile imagination, expressed by such remarks as 'I am a conqueror in art as Hitler in war' or his brother's reported boast, 'Such is Serge's influence with the German High Command, he can do anything.' I never heard reports of his being mean or underhanded, even from those who disliked him. When the occupation began he summoned the corps de ballet and told them, 'German officers will certainly ask you out to parties. You are under no obligation to go. If you refuse, do so tactfully.' The fact that he escaped with a year's suspension from the Opéra and that, on retirement, he received a letter of commendation from de Gaulle would have scotched all rumours had he not published such a highly coloured account of his war activities. His love of scandal certainly cost him the decoration he so richly deserved. The government might have proved magnanimous in the case of an artist who did so much for his adopted country.

Today Lifar has turned painter with some success; his name is still prominent in Paris, and every dancer speaks of him with gratitude and affection. For me he will always remain an artist whom I respect and a friend to whom I am devoted. I remember with nostalgia holidays in Venice and the south of France. Three scenes in particular come to mind: a visit to the Teatro Olimpico in Vicenza, where a crowd of tourists look up from their guidebooks in amazement as Lifar bounds onto the stage and, in spite of a surfeit of his favourite pasta, shows flashes of his former self; Lifar with Tcherina on the bare stage of the Fenice in Venice walking through *Giselle*, still, in that rehearsal sketch, the most romantic Albrecht of them all; finally, Lifar, plump and with retirement overdue, dancing *Icare* at Covent Garden. Some of the audience titter, the next day the critics are brutal, but how appropriate and tragic that the last time I see him dance is in the part of the man who attempted to fly and failed.

His story does not end with his decline and retirement. He had appeared at the Cambridge Theatre, London, during his exile from the Opéra, with a dazzling company that included Renée (Zizi) Jeanmaire, Olga Adabache, Ludmilla Tcherina, Alexander Kalioujny, and, one of the rare truly elect, Yvette Chauviré, of whom much more later. Jeanmaire had appeared during de Basil's ill-fated post-war season at Covent Garden, the one strong personality in a depleted company. De Basil swore that he had never met with a more strong-willed dancer: she smiled and had her own way. It was obvious that here was something totally new in French ballet and that the Opéra was too rigid for one of her temperament. We saw another defector from the Opéra, Colette Marchand, dancing with the Metropolitan Ballet, an admirable small company that first revealed the talents of Svetlana Beriosova but which was sadly under-financed. The value of a great institution lies in the rebels it produces when its own creative impulse is dormant.

II. Chauviré. One night in Paris I met one of the dressers in a café near the Opéra. We sat down for a drink, and she enthralled me with some hair-raising backstage gossip in the great tradition of Halévy's *La Famille Cardinal*.* She ended up by saying, 'Mademoiselle Chauviré is quite different. *There* is one who will succeed by her talent alone, no short cuts for her.' It was the first time I had heard the name of Chauviré, who very shortly was not only to become the most outstanding French dancer since the heyday of the romantic movement, 'La Chauviré nationale', but also to be loved by the Russian public as one of their own.

I first saw her in the only accurate film of ballet life, *La Mort du Cygne*, afterwards bought up by Hollywood and reissued in a caricature of the original version. Mia Slavenska was the heroine, and it also introduced a child, Janine Charrat, who later became famous as a dancer and choreographer; Yvette Chauviré played the girl who finally abandoned dancing. A film reveals little of a dancer's personality. It remains a substitute as far removed as convenience food is from a chef's creation, or as instant coffee is from the real thing. My true introduction to Chauviré was, as it should be, in her greatest role, Giselle. I had gone with Vera Volkova to a matinée of Lifar's company at the Cambridge Theatre in London. We both found ourselves crying. Here was a French Giselle in a French ballet, with all the fine detail, all the understanding of romantic tradition, but combined with a depth and sincerity that were exceptional. How admirably she understood the village girl and the meaning of the grape harvest! It was within her own experience. This was the true French countryside – and I am well aware that the scene is set in Germany. Her involvement in the village scene was total, and she brought the dances of the corps de ballet, which often break the continuity of the drama and seem irrelevant, right into the picture in a way that I have not seen equalled. There are so many facets to this veteran ballet that we tend to take for granted. Like Ulanova, whom I was to see much later, Chauviré carried the character of Giselle over into the second act, making the ballet a whole rather than two parts. We were unmistakably in France, the real France of the countryside, miles from the bustle of the boulevards.

For a time Chauviré took lessons from Boris Kniasev, a Russian, who found himself so carried away by a performance that he seized

---

* A minor French classic by Halévy: a most amusing series of short stories that deal with the intrigues of the family of a young girl in the Opéra corps de ballet.

a bouquet from another dancer and laid it at her feet with a shout of 'Ma Chauviré!'

III. Roland Petit. Lifar had awakened the Académie de la Danse from its long sleep and had created a new generation of dancers. When he returned after his brief exile, the drive was no longer there. He had been in absolute control too long, as had Petipa at the Maryinsky, and the positive reaction, which was to prove fruitful for such a short time only, was due to the dancers he himself had formed. A national ballet is indispensable, but so are the breakaway groups. Unfortunately economic conditions now make the appearance of such comets no longer possible. A millionaire or a foundation may come to the rescue, but in the long run such groups rapidly become part of the establishment.

In Paris the sympathetic and highly intelligent Irène Lidova, wife of the photographer Lido, had gathered round her a small concert group inspired by a young dancer of Franco-Italian parentage, Roland Petit, one of those who found the Opéra too restricting. The group soon grew into a brilliant ensemble that included Renée Jeanmaire, Colette Marchand, Irène Skorik, Nina Vyroubova, Violette Verdy, Claire Sombert, Hélène Constantine, Jean Babilée, and Oleg Briansky. Boris Kochno emerged from retirement to become artistic adviser. For five years Les Ballets des Champs Élysées and its successor, Les Ballets de Paris de Roland Petit, dominated the creative ballet world, the true successors to Diaghilev in his *école de Paris* period. The thrill and shock of the ballet first night had returned, with new painters and musicians to be launched.

Given Petit's extraordinary flair, his restless nature, and his ability to mould his ballets round individual dancers, this new company was born to be ephemeral. Petit was torn between ballet and American-style music-hall dance, between the classics and jazz. He left behind him some masterpieces that will defy revival. He was producer, choreographer, and, when Kochno left, artistic director, the only dancer to succeed in this last role. Like Graham Greene he created a number of lightweight entertainments that were truly entertaining.

His masterpieces were *Les Forains, Le Jeune Homme et la Mort, Les Demoiselles de la Nuit, Les Amours de Jupiter, Carmen* (with certain reservations), and *Le Loup*.

Les Forains, with a brilliant décor by Bérard and bittersweet music by Sauguet, dealt with a group of itinerant circus artists, a common enough theme but full of brilliant inventive touches such as the dance of the Siamese twins, which was pathetic but never sentimental. These circus folk were true professionals, proud of their work, whatever the audience reaction. It was only when the show was over and the caravan packed that we became aware of their poverty and eternal disillusionment.

In *Le Loup*, which introduced a new and exciting painter, Carzou, and a new composer, Dutilleux, Petit treated a major subject, the intolerance of the mob for a stranger who seemed to threaten its way of life. This was his finest piece of choreography, one that did not rely simply on brilliant touches of stagecraft for its effect. Jean Babilée as the Wolf and Claire Sombert as the village girl he loves gave two of the finest performances I have ever seen. His ferocity tamed by love and her tenderness and desire to protect him, expressed by their whole bodies in pure choreographic terms, made this a deeply moving experience. I have seen *Le Loup* with other casts, including Petit himself. It remained a superb ballet but lost some of its emotional impact. Everything that Sombert does has a rare quality.

Le Jeune Homme et la Mort, conceived by Jean Cocteau, resorted to shock tactics. It was something that cannot and should not be repeated; the shock was a double one, to the artists while it was being rehearsed, and to the audience. It was rehearsed to jazz and danced to Bach's Passacaglia in C minor without the fugue. The contrast between the nobility of the music and the sordid drama of a death by hanging resulted in more than just a paragraph in the tabloids. The ballet was made by Jean Babilée's completely danced interpretation, Natalie Philippart's entrance as Death, both strong and gentle, and Georges Wakhevitch's attic setting. The apotheosis, nearly always an anticlimax or a cliché in ballet, reconciled music and story. Once again Cocteau, who had so repeatedly amazed Diaghilev, brought off a major *coup de théâtre*. He was concerned with death in many of his films, notably *Orphée*, but here the theme became condensed without the kind of involved mythology that, when it flags, can verge on the ridiculous. A study of Cocteau and the ballet is long overdue; an admirable subject for the pen of Richard Buckle.

Les Amours de Jupiter, with costumes and scenery by Jean Hugo, never made a strong impact on the audience and has been long forgotten, undeservedly so. It revealed an important aspect of Petit's work, his ability to deal with a sensual subject, the *Metamorphoses* of Ovid, without a single lapse of taste. Its positive virtue was the complete translation of a classical myth into the ballet medium, but without the too-obvious elegant stylization that fails to convince and carries one straight into the twentieth century. This was a minor masterpiece of French decadent art, the most erotic ballet I have seen on the stage yet without a single ugly or vulgar movement.

Babilée must rank amongst the most exciting male dancers I have seen, including the Russians, but he was great only for a very short period. He was a freak who broke all the rules. At times he rode his motorcycle to the theatre and stepped straight onto the stage to dance a dazzling Bluebird. He was a natural athlete and a star personality. This star quality is a mystery. It often – though not in Babilée's case – has nothing to do with artistry or technique. It certainly is something far removed from the manufactured commercial article, packaged at great expense by an enterprising management. The public recognizes it immediately; the critics may find numerous faults, but they applaud nonetheless. Such a dancer may often distort the choreographer's work, and equally often he may lend colour to the colourless, so that without him a particular ballet cannot be revived. Babilée and Renée Jeanmaire were both stars and artists. Jeanmaire made *Carmen* her own. It had many changes of cast but was never the same without her. This was Mérimée's *Carmen*, and only in the Habañera, danced by Petit himself, was there a betrayal of both Merimée and Bizet. As in *Les Amours de Jupiter* Petit proved that the sensual and erotic are far removed from the pornography that has disfigured so many more recent works.

Such 'personal' choreography was the strength and also the failing of Petit. He took an acrobatic cabaret dancer, Danielle Darmance, was inspired by her particular gifts, and built round her a light work, *Le Bal des Blanchisseuses*, which, without her, failed to hold up. In a company that is not his, Petit seems lost, using an idiom that owes more to the fashion show than to ballet. His *La Péri* for Fonteyn and *Sick Rose* for Plisetskaya had nothing to tell us either about those remarkable dancers or himself. *Ballabile* for the Royal Ballet is more successful, but it belongs amongst his lesser entertainments. Recently Petit has come into his own again with his company at Marseilles where he has a completely free hand.

The excitement of his premières has returned and as an art director he stands supreme. He is a narrative choreographer in a class of his own and a dancer who combines character and panache.

His version of *Coppélia* aroused considerable controversy with the usual cries of 'hands off a masterpiece'. Is the allegedly original *Coppélia* a masterpiece? Was it ever one? Is it even a museum exhibit since the role of Franz is no longer danced by a woman? I must confess to acute boredom at the cliché of the doddering senile Dr Coppelius. Petit gives it logic, drama, pathos and wit, situating it firmly in France where musically it belongs. And what a joy to be aware of the music once again.

Three of the dancers in the first companies were outstanding on all counts: Irène Skorik, Violette Verdy, and Nina Vyroubova. Skorik, half Russian and half French, was never really at home in Petit's repertoire. She had a magnificent line, made for the full-length classics; at the same time she was a dancer in search of a choreographer. She was intensely musical, in love with Wagner; she also wished to act. She was highly critical, too critical for a dancer, continually questioning what she was doing, and was never able to fulfil her quite exceptional promise, though for a long time she danced with a Munich company that never travelled abroad. Today she has turned actress. She missed greatness by a hair's breadth.

Violette Verdy started with Petit as a child and went on to gain international fame with Balanchine. From the first she showed enormous will power in her dealings with two strong-minded choreographers. When Petit went through a phase of wishing to have his dancers' noses reshaped by a plastic surgeon, she refused point blank. Later, though she became a faithful interpreter of Balanchine, she never let herself become a passive instrument, a musical phrase, as did so many of his company.

The third of his dancers, Nina Vyroubova, the only pupil of the great Trefilova to assimilate her teaching – and Trefilova was a difficult teacher who taught seated and whispered her corrections – was one of the rare outsiders to become a *première danseuse étoile* at the Opéra, and to partner Lifar. She had so many of her teacher's gifts, plus the temperament to shine in a romantic ballet such as *Les Sylphides*, the spirit of which she caught to a perfection that I have only seen equalled by the Swedish ballerina Elsa Marianne van Rosen.

The weakness of French ballet is the closed door, which so few have penetrated. You are either in the Opéra since childhood, frustrated from inside by a director who may have little interest in the art or a minister whose policy calls for great spectacles, or frustrated from outside by total lack of opportunity to do more than give a few concerts with a scratch group, or to appear for a brief period as a guest artist in a foreign company.

Claire Sombert, a subtle and highly intelligent artist, one of my 'greats', and her occasional partner Michel Bruel are in this kind of a predicament. Apart from *Le Loup*, I had to wait for the Cuban Dance Festival to see the real Sombert in a deeply moving performance of *Giselle*, where the French couple stole the thunder from Maximova and Vasiliev, with whom they alternated. This was French dancing at its finest. Fernando Alonso nudged me and said, 'Even her faults become virtues,' and I agreed. France and the world missed seeing a rare artist of the dance and a male dancer who enchanted Russian audiences and critics when he appeared as a guest artist, a rare happening. Sombert's dancing to music by Albinoni remains one of my treasured experiences; that rare thing, good music made visible.

20. The Soviet Ballet

THE year was 1956. The first season of the Bolshoi Ballet had long been announced at Covent Garden. Would it come off, or would there be a sudden cancellation? A Soviet athlete had taken refuge in her Embassy after having been charged with stealing a hat at C & A, a London department store, and this trivial incident, blown up by the press, might disrupt everything. The sense of anticipation was tremendous. I was called almost daily by people whom I scarcely knew to ask me if I could get them tickets. 'We met at so and so's party,' they said. I was very rude; it was not to the box office that I referred them. The publicity was enormous, and people who had never previously shown any interest in ballet wanted to be in on the event. It had been the same with Maria Callas at Covent Garden, where I heard a smartly dressed group of people asking for information about the plot of *Tosca*.

The first night nearly did not come off as planned. The whole episode revealed an interesting attitude of professionalism in the theatre. The Russians told David Webster, the General Administrator of the Royal Opera House, that their rehearsals were not sufficiently advanced for them to give of their best, especially in view of the fact that the Covent Garden stage was so much smaller than their own Bolshoi. Webster pointed to the queues that had been waiting in the street for seventy-two hours and said that it was essential to keep faith with the public. The Russians replied that it was not keeping faith with the public to give anything less than their best. London deserved the best, and it would take them another few days. It was all very calm, polite, and sincere, a seeming deadlock. Then Webster, always a master diplomat, replied that he fully understood their point of view. He explained that the most distinguished and influential audience had booked their seats months in advance, and that, if dates were changed, they had so many other engagements it would mean their missing the season altogether, with serious repercussions. He believed that this world-renowned company would surely be able to respond to such a challenge and that he and his staff would do everything to help. He made his point and everyone collaborated magnificently in spite of language difficulties.

It had been quite different in France during the rehearsals at the Opéra for the season that was killed by the fall of Dien Bien Phu. I had gone over for the occasion. The French stage crew was almost solidly communist and at the same time hostile to foreign companies, as we found to our cost when Sadler's Wells visited Paris. The Russians, eager for perfection in this first visit to the West, piled on rehearsals. As lunchtime approached the stagehands began to grumble; comrades or not, at *midi* every sensible Frenchman tucks his feet under a table, and that was that.

I have already written of my first exposure to Soviet dancers and my complete disillusionment. I had slightly modified my opinion since seeing Raïssa Struchkova at a concert performance and watching snippets of rehearsals in Paris. I had been asked to return as a guest critic for the *Daily Mail*, a paper not then giving much dance coverage, and also to broadcast first-night impressions for the B.B.C.'s transmission to Russia.

That first night was one of the most memorable in my whole career. It was dominated, as was the whole season, by the incomparable artistry of Galina Ulanova. She was an artist in the old Maryinsky tradition, lyrical with gently flowing movements, and at the same time with something new, a subtle combination of Anna Pavlova and Isadora Duncan; she was supported by a superb company of what I can only describe as total dancers. Her Juliet transcended the choreography to become Shakespeare's heroine. There was a wonderful passage at the very beginning when the child Juliet is romping with her nurse and catches sight of herself in the mirror. She sees she is no longer a child and that the security of the nursery has gone for ever. She is pleased but at the same time frightened of what the future holds in store. The whole episode passes in a flash. Scene by scene the character is developed. The Juliet of the balcony is a passionate Italian woman. Finally there are the curtain calls, a trifle clumsy at first. Juliet is dead and Ulanova seems bewildered by the noise, an intrusion on her other personality. I remembered what the Indian philosopher Ananda Coomaraswamy had written about art : that the first step is perfect craftsmanship and then, rarely, by an act of grace, the artist so identifies herself with the character that she becomes that character.

Later in *Giselle*, a ballet that I knew by heart, I recognized once again that complete identification between artist and subject. I saw a number of new facets in the role. In simple terms Giselle is a *prima ballerina assoluta*. At her very first entrance she must conceal this essentially dominant fact from herself and her public, and be a simple village maiden. She will come to an untimely end, but she must be unaware of this and live for the moment only. I recall how superbly Ulanova achieved this, with her downcast eyes and her slightly awkward hands. Then follows the tragedy of what Gautier called 'la douce folie'. I have written elsewhere of the violent contrast between the two acts; Act I, the body, Act II, the spirit. I feel now that I was wrong; this was altogether too superficial a description. The Giselle of Act II is still earthbound and loving, forgiving and resisting the forces of evil. Passion still exists, but it is tempered by pity and understanding. For me Ulanova gave this veteran ballet a new dimension. It was an ageless poem about perfect love. I knew that all my life I had been waiting to see such a dancer, and that all my previous experience had gone toward a complete understanding of her art. Here was a marvellous balance of emotion and intellect.

She was delicate and no longer young. She was already thinking of retirement. 'The dancer's tragedy is that when she really understands what it is all about the body rebels,' she said. Lavrovsky told me he had never seen her dance more movingly than during that London season. Her few appearances at Covent Garden had made her as great a legend in England as in Russia.

What was impressive in the Bolshoi company as a whole was the great importance given to character roles such as the Nurse (Iraida Olenina) and Lady Capulet (Yelena Ilyuschenko) in *Romeo and Juliet*, the mother in *Giselle*. This was something entirely new to Western ballet, where such roles are usually given to the older classical or *demi-caractère* dancers, who rarely have the figures, the temperament, or the presence to fit into the narrative and to provide the necessary *realism*, a word of great importance to the Russians. Not one of these classics involving a dramatic narrative has ever seemed to me convincing outside Russia and Cuba, and it has certainly inhibited the impact of the ballerina.

The male dancing was a revelation as we had expected, but more on the character than the classical side. The role of *danseur noble* had been neglected in favour of an over-emphasis on athleticism; it should of course exist, but here it was too prominent. It was welcome at the time when male dancing was still suspect in this country.

The scenery, very much pre-Diaghilev, was disappointing but more than compensated for by the music. Under the leadership of the partially blind conductor Yuri Fayer one felt one was hearing these familiar scores for the first time; although ballet music, however well known, is taken seriously by Soviet musicians, Fayer has never been surpassed in Russia. Apart from Ulanova there were some admirable soloists. Raïssa Struchkova, who had the misfortune to be dancing at the same time as Ulanova, became a firm favourite in England. Her blind dive into the arms of her partner and husband, Lapauri, was a moment to be waited for in the atrocious *Walpurgis Night*, one that almost justified this hackneyed work. In the dramatic roles she was capable of great subtleties of interpretation. The young Nina Timofeyeva, today an outstanding dancer, made her debut in *Swan Lake*, anxiously watched by Ulanova, whose protégée she was. Already Ulanova was revealing her gifts as a coach, gifts that eventually led to a second career.

She is a magnificent judge of a dancer, even when that dancer is performing one of her own great roles with a completely different interpretation. She does not seek to turn out a lifeless copy. 'How do you see the role?' she asks. She makes the dancer think and feel. I once saw Galina and Yuri Fayer helping a young dancer from Tadjekistan rehearse the double role of Odette-Odile. Galina put her completely at her ease, treating her as an equal who needed some advice about the stage, and Fayer let her tap out her rhythms on his knee. I wish a camera could have recorded this scene, which not only showed two great artists at their best, but underlined the strength of the tradition that exists in Russia.

I had been trying to meet Ulanova before the season started. Her translator, Nina Latta, a talented actress, was a great friend of mine and had attempted to arrange a rendezvous. Ulanova was busy, tired, and feeling her way cautiously, and I had no luck. After my first-night notice, which is now displayed in a cabinet in the foyer of the Bolshoi, and my broadcast, which had been reproduced in the Soviet press, she suddenly asked Nina to arrange a meeting. It took place in her sitting room in a hotel in Norfolk Street off the Strand. She had ordered lobster and Beaujolais, a novelty for her and, as a combination, a novelty for me. She looked totally different off the stage; more like a sympathetic university don than a ballerina. I held her in awe. I was glad that I had seen her great performances before meeting her; for her I was a totally unknown quantity, totally outside her experience. She plied me with questions about Pavlova and Karsavina, while I tried to draw her out about her own interpretations. It marked the beginning of a friendship that has lasted for twenty years, with constant meetings in London, Moscow, Varna, and Havana.

She is unlike any other theatrical personality I have ever met. Reserved to the point of shyness, she said one day that being a living legend was to live in isolation. People were frightened to drop in, and it made for loneliness. Genuinely modest, with a quiet sense of humour that enables her to laugh at herself, she has tremendous understanding and sympathy with the young. I have never heard her raise her voice. As chairman of a jury of some eighteen opinionated people from a number of countries, she can always see two points of view and arbitrate through reason, never using her fame as a lever. Her tolerance tended to lead to long meetings, but everyone left well satisfied. The night I met her for the first time she was genuinely puzzled, used as she was to success in her own country, that I, a Westerner who had seen so many of the great ones, her childhood heroines, had put her in a class of her own. 'I am going to dance The Dying Swan. You saw Pavlova so many times. Promise me that you will come to all the performances. You may like one of them. My interpretation is totally different. Mine is a struggle against death.' I told her of a conversation with Fokine in which he had said that this role was one that could be left to the dancer to interpret in her own fashion. What mattered was that it was not just a solo dance but something that needed interpretation. It has been much abused, but when created it was revolutionary. The divertissement till then had been an occasion for a display of fireworks; this was not in fact a divertissement at all, but a one-person ballet.

During that 1956 season I saw much less of Ulanova after our first intimate meeting. The atmosphere had become strained after the invasion of Hungary, but the British did not allow politics to interfere with their enthusiasm or with their personal relations with the company. The stagehands tried hard to fraternise with their opposite numbers; the respective managements met in the canteen. The Russians, however, were nervous, withdrawn, and constantly summoned to their Embassy for briefings on some situation or other that might have led to the abrupt termination of the season. Ulanova in particular shunned all personal publicity; the gossip-column intrusion into private lives is unknown in the Soviet Union. One day she fled almost in panic before a battery of cameramen assembled outside a cinema when it was heard that she was attending a performance. This led to a separation between her interpreter, Nina, and herself. Lord Waverley, the chairman of Covent Garden, and Lord Drogheda, his colleague, handled the situation magnificently, determined that politics must not be allowed to interfere with art, which in itself was a complete means of communication. This had been an understood thing in Napoleonic days, when even scientific expeditions were allowed to continue unhindered by wars or politics. Waverley and Drogheda always maintained a friendly contact with the company, realizing the many difficulties of this totally strange environment. Ava Waverley provided a quiet second home for Galina, taking her on shopping expeditions and introducing her to a few selected friends, amongst them Lord Alexander of Tunis. Ulanova met the Queen Mother and afterwards told me of the tremendous sympathy she felt for her.

A great contrast to that hotel supper in Norfolk Street was in her flat in Moscow many years later. It was an impromptu affair; the guests were the Alonsos and myself. Galina only spoke Russian, the Alonsos a number of languages, but no Russian, and my Russian was of the kitchen variety. The atmosphere was completely relaxed as she cooked us a delicious meal, but we had a great deal to say to one another, and mime could not carry us very far. Suddenly she had a bright idea, a friend who spoke English. She rang him up and we crowded round the phone for translations. The unfortunate linguist must have been disturbed a dozen times during that very happy Moscow night.

The last time I saw her that first season was when Lord Waverley, whom I had always thought of as a monolithic and unbending figure, presented her with a set of suitcases. Spontaneously she kissed him on both cheeks and he blushed. After that incident I saw a new Waverley. Whenever we met he asked after her with warmth and affection. To David Webster she was always 'the miracle woman'. These were the friends she made in London and always remembered with pleasure.

My greatest reward came in 1973, on the occasion of my seventieth birthday party, when Ulanova paid her first solo visit to London and made a speech in my honour. Like Lord Waverley, I blush when I remember the generosity of her action in undertaking the long journey and the tribute she paid to her old friend.

Shortly after the Bolshoi's first London season, my opposite number, Ella Bocharnikova, then director of the Bolshoi School, paid a visit to London, visited the Royal Ballet School, and stayed with us in the country. She became a close friend and my cicerone in Moscow on many occasions. She prepared me for all that I was to see in her country and showed me photographs of her three prize pupils, Maximova, Vasiliev, and Ryabinkina, who were then in the top class.

After that first taste of the Bolshoi, I visited the Soviet Union on half a dozen occasions to watch the ballet, visit the schools, and twice as a member of the international jury for the Moscow ballet contests, the last time as Vice-President. I owe a debt of gratitude to Ekaterina Furtseva, the Minister of Culture at that time, who died while this chapter was being written. She opened every door for me, and we had many interesting discussions. She may have been a re-doubtable figure, but she had a sense of humour and was a strong supporter of ballet.

Before going into detail I want to give some reasons, that soon become obvious, for the supremacy of the Russians as dancers, and I am not now writing of ballet as a whole. This is a dancing nation, as one could see on any collective farm where a man with a squeeze box could electrify the workers into a superb ensemble. I once saw Vasiliev join in such an impromptu dance; the distance between farm worker and professional was one of training, experience, and exceptional talent, but not of the will and ability to express emotion in movement.

In its origins the dance had come from the people; the finest teachers in the world had then brought a classical discipline to them. What is particularly interesting is that those very teachers had themselves fallen under the Russian influence. It had always been written, and I firmly believed it until I soaked myself in the atmosphere and looked up the records, that the Russian school as we know it had been created by three foreigners, Petipa, Johannsen, and Cecchetti. It had also been said that the Russian school was the French school the French themselves had forgotten. This needs con-siderable modification. Petipa and Johannsen were rapidly assimi-lated into the Russian scene, Cecchetti far less. Already in the early nineteenth century the Great Patriotic War had made the Russians turn to national themes and develop a Russian choreographic tradition dealing with contemporary life. It is true that the French had forgotten their school in the sense that romanticism had become a formula, that the male dancer had lost his role and degenerated into a *porteur*, and that ballet was looked on as an entertainment and not an art. There is a lithograph by Doré showing the Opéra corps de ballet in a ragged formation making eyes at a wealthy man seated in the stage box. Gautier himself recognized that the Russian attitude toward ballet was far more serious – and that arch-romantic, father of *Giselle*, did not take ballet so very seriously himself. In Russia the serf dancers and actors kept a firm hold on realism as opposed to naturalism and formalism, prolonging the active life of the romantic ballet.

The vast extent of the country could and does nourish the repertoire as it had in Europe when there was still a peasant class. Dancing in Russia, in field and factory, army and navy, is a natural means of expression. One could see this precious heritage when Diaghilev first conquered the West with the dance of the Polovtsian warriors from *Prince Igor*, and we see it still when the classically trained dancers of the Kirov perform *Taras Bulba*.

This gift has been fostered by nobles, the court, and the Soviets, so that there were, and are, none of the difficult economic problems that exist in the West. A more recent factor is the vast new audience so different from the *abonné* or subscription public – balletomanes who counted the fouettés aloud, keeping their opera glasses focused on an individual dancer. The new public wants to see a spectacle and to participate in action clearly told in movement. The stories themselves, which were a pretext for dancing, and so often still are in the West, became important in their own right. The new ballets might be called propagandist in the sense that so much theatrical art is – the works of Beaumarchais, Ibsen, and Galsworthy for instance – but the people could identify themselves with characters in *The Red Poppy*, *The Flames of Paris*, and *Spartacus*; even *Giselle* becomes the story of the peasant and the aristocrat.

Another important factor is the role of the intelligentsia. Ballet has always occupied the attention of scholars, as it once did in France when it earned the critical praise of Voltaire. Stanislavsky's scattered writings on the subject, assembled by Natalia Roslavleva, have had a serious influence on the art. Even toward the decline of the Petipa era such writers as Volynsky, Svetlov, and Levinson analysed it in depth. Volynsky even placed himself at the barre at the age of seventy in order to gain a further insight.

This then is the solid background. It has paved the way for a teacher of genius, Agrippina Vaganova. She herself was an indifferent ballerina but, as a pupil of Nicolas Legat and an admirer of Fokine, who had entrusted her with the mazurka in *Chopiniana* (*Les Sylphides*), she had assimilated all that had gone before and was very much aware of the present and the future. Vaganova wrote that 'those who assert that the old ballet has spent itself and should be forgotten are deeply wrong ... If art, indeed, should reflect contemporary life, it does not mean that classical examples of its past should disappear ... Our dancers, educated according to the principles of contemporary classical training, are able to cope with *any* difficulties ... As to eccentric-acrobatic elements, they should occupy the modest one per cent that is their only worth.'

This outlook on classicism, which was backed by Lunacharsky, the able minister of culture, with Lenin's approval, together with her development of classical teaching, not only served ballet during the revolutionary period but laid the foundations of the Soviet school.

The Russians have two other trump cards : the difference in outlook and temperament between Moscow and Leningrad, and the dancers' total commitment.

Although, technically speaking, all the schools are the same and Leningrad dancers are often taken over by the capital, there is a marked difference in the atmosphere of the two cities which must have an effect on the dancers. Before the revolution, Saint Petersburg carried the great tradition of classical ballet with its strong French influences; Moscow was more Slavonic, more interested in experiment. Vaganova taught the dancers in Leningrad, but though her teaching became universal it could, like a language, be used with a number of different accents. It is this kind of rivalry that so greatly enriches the dance. Our own ballet is closer to that of Leningrad, and the Kirov-ex-Maryinsky approach finds more favour in England. For my part, leaving aside the genius of Ulanova, a Leningrad product, I find the Muscovites more exhilarating. Carried to extremes their exuberance may overflow into vulgarity, though the word is harsh. They believe in what they are doing; the temperament is not assumed and often carries such conviction that one is only critical after the event. In Russia alone have I truly enjoyed a *divertissement* in spite of its lack of content. Some of the pas de deux, in particular Messerer's *Spring Waters*, exploit the new technique to the full, and are both exciting and lyrical. The Russians are not frightened of vulgarity; the only thing they fear is anaemia. There is no sexual suggestiveness, a statement that cannot be made about Western vulgarity. When they are vulgar, it is the vulgarity of exuberance, the brashness of youth, that carries an audience with it, so that even the blasé balletomane is forced to applaud. There are today eight schools and thirty-two companies, those in such remote places as Perm and Novosibirsk being outstanding, as well as many folk-dance groups, all of which continue to nourish the art of the dance.

The words *total commitment* should be used for all dancers. In the Soviet Union they have a very special meaning. From the moment a pupil has passed through the school the dancer is secure for life. The knowledge gained on the stage is ploughed back into the tradition. Not only are there dancing dynasties, there is still a Petipa and a Gerdt descendant; Ulanova's mother was a dancer. The retired dancer is carefully studied as a potential teacher and placed in the right position, as a coach, a company teacher, a teacher of folk dance or a teacher of amateurs in a Pioneer group, a school of general education, or as an athletic trainer. Hence the wonderful record held by Soviet Russia in skating, the circus, and gymnastics. The ballet becomes a powerhouse for movement. On any night the stage boxes hold as many as forty dancers watching the performance and discussing it critically and constructively.

This is not the place to write of politics, but the question of defection, a word that really means breach of contract, cannot be ignored. The dancer is more secure than the general, the scientist, the writer, or the politician. He has a lifetime of security and privilege. His education has cost the state a vast sum of money. To defect seems to the Russians to be unpatriotic, an act that leaves his comrades in the lurch, especially during an important foreign tour. It is often done on impulse and afterwards regretted. The only way of stopping it would be to allow the dancers to appear as guest artists abroad for a limited period. I believe that, given this freedom and trust, the majority would return to the greater security and opportunity provided in their own country. Their experience would also enrich the dance, especially the opportunity of working with a number of choreographers. Nureyev has never ceased to sing the praises of the Russian school and has, apart from the manner in which he left Russia, been a valuable propagandist for that school; a true patriot *malgré lui*! Makarova, too, upholds the Russian school. Once she reproached Nureyev with 'dancing like them'. His reply, worthy of an earlier dancer, Louis XIV, was 'Je danse comme moi!'

The Russian male dancer is virile, a superb partner and an athlete. The *danseur noble* is comparatively rare today, as in the past. Pierre Vladimirov, whose memory is still honoured in Russia, was outstanding in Imperial Ballet days. In the West until recently the *danseur noble* was considered to be slightly effeminate. When I became a member of the jury at the first Moscow dance contest at the Bolshoi I was immediately struck by Baryshnikov, who later became one of the defectors. His technique was that of a great virtuoso, not surprisingly, but his dancing was infinitely subtle. His solo, *Vestris*, was commonplace enough choreographically; performed by a lesser artist it would have been a typical charity *divertissement* number. Baryshnikov danced it with wit and deep insight into the character of the man who, when asked if he was suffering from an injured ankle, replied, 'When this is known the whole of Paris will be in mourning.'

It goes without saying he won the gold medal.

Now that he is in touch with new choreographic developments it seems likely that Baryshnikov will have a range no other male dancer has known since Nijinsky. The cardboard princes will come to life, Petrouchka will suffer and finally triumph, and the Cocteau-Petit *Le Jeune Homme et la Mort*, possibly dated, will once again produce the shock impact given it by the remarkable Babilée, a left-over from the *épatisme* of the later Diaghilev years.

The Panovs were altogether a different case, one that was brutally handled. They did not defect, but gave due warning and asked for permission to leave. For the reasons I have stated, that permission may justifiably have been refused, but to prevent them from dancing at all was both inhumane and stupid, an act so negative as to be incomprehensible to the normal person. Much the same was done in the star era in Hollywood, where a company would punish an actor by leaving him under contract but workless. In America, however, there were some means of redress available, and the actor was not turned into an outlaw. This attitude has badly damaged the great good will built up since 1956, and saddened all sincere admirers of the Soviet ballet. It is a painful subject that cannot be avoided. Let us hope that it will never be repeated. There is little anti-Semitism, at any rate, in the ballet world; many of the leading dancers are Jewish. It is Zionism that the Russians cannot understand, the attitude of a foreign allegiance. The right to move freely, even within Russia, has never been admitted – even in tsarist days there were limitations – and the outcry in the case of the Jews could have a serious backlash, especially when it is backed up by hooliganism in theatres abroad. The high esteem in which Laurence Olivier was held, and the tactful intervention of Harold Wilson, helped secure the Panovs' release. It might have taken place sooner had there been fewer demonstrations and disruptions. Whatever Nureyev may have done in the eyes of the Soviet, surely it is time that they allowed his mother to visit him in the name of humanity and at the very least for better public relations. I write as an admirer of Russian Ballet and of its large-hearted people, the vast majority.

The Soviet critic's view of ballet is an interesting one that in part is valid throughout the world. Ballet must be positive and life-enhancing; its subject matter must always contain an element of the heroic. This is limiting, and the immature boy-scout conception of heroism can reach ridiculous lengths. I have even heard of an unideological *Swan Lake*! In the original story Odette and her prince commit suicide by throwing themselves into the lake; through their sacrifice the evil genius is defeated. The apotheosis shows very clearly that they are triumphant and live happily ever after in some spirit world. This is perhaps lending too much meaning to a fairy tale designed for dancing. In the Soviet version the prince fights with and overcomes the demon, and he and Odette live happily ever after in this life. If nothing else, the fight between the prince and the magician is exciting and prevents von Rothbart from being a cardboard figure. I can see little difference and no consistency in this happy ending, since Giselle is allowed to have dealings with the supernatural – and I doubt whether it has ever led an audience to believe in Wilis!

On the other hand, this insistence on some standard of heroism or idealism avoids many of the morbid and often indecent passages that disfigure so many modern works and should have no place in ballet. There is everything to be said for idealism in art so long as it is not carried to ridiculous extremes. There must be a distinction between the subject matter and the manner in which it is treated.

Ballet is a branch of the theatre and, if it is to be taken seriously, it should be capable of dealing with a wide range of emotions. If we ruled out from the stage all unpleasant subjects, then the whole Elizabethan theatre, Shakespeare included, would be taboo as well as Ibsen and Brecht. If we look on ballet as poetry we have the precedent of Verlaine and Baudelaire; if we look at it as painting we have an outstanding example in Goya, whose subject matter is often undeniably horrific.

What matters is that the translation into choreography must be complete. There is no place for natural movements that do not leave room for the imagination, or for crudities that shock. Ballet must be realistic. This applies to all art at all times and everywhere, if it is correctly applied. It must in fact be true to its particular medium; it must carry conviction and communicate, not necessarily a story, but an emotion. Realism and naturalism must never be confused. Every art has its conventions; there is nothing natural about singing or dancing a drama. What is natural must be translated into the language of the particular medium in order to become real. A bronze bust is real, but a waxwork figure can never be real and very rarely seems natural.

This is obvious, but the Russian insistence on the principle means in practice that every participant on the stage is acting as well as dancing. The ballet librettist has an important role to play. It is this lack of realism that has killed *Petrouchka* and *Carnaval* today.

Finally *formalism* – a bad word. In Russia it means the frills without the substance, *parler pour ne rien dire*. This does not rule out the storyless ballet. The English ballet critic has long been aware of this fact, but the word has not become part of his jargon.

Within this framework criticism in Russia is serious and on a high level. It tends to be heavy, lacking in light and shade, and much of it suffers from the fact that it believes itself to be objective. The dance is frequently written about by the older dancers. Negative criticism is discouraged. There are some outstanding critics and historians, amongst them Yuri Slonimsky, Natalia Roslavleva, and Vera Krassovskaya.

Let us return to the dancers. Ulanova was succeeded as *ballerina assoluta* by Maya Plisetskaya, her complete opposite. Plisetskaya has beauty, with the most perfect neck and shoulders and the glamour of a star, both on and off stage, a true star without the chi-chi mannerisms inculcated by a publicity agent. She is highly intelligent with a strong will of her own, something not often seen in the Soviet Union, and she usually has her own way. Her influence has been a valuable one for the future. She is definitely not *goût anglais* and her opinion of English critics, frequently expressed in strong language, is good for us and must be a considerable relief to her. It is only fair to say that in England we have only seen one side of her, the flamboyant. She is technically, if one uses the word in a quantitative sense, the most astonishing dancer I have ever seen. She has speed, amazing extension, and accuracy. In classics such as *Swan Lake* Odette seems lost; it is always Odile we see. *The Dying Swan* becomes a bravura piece with snaky arms that might have come from some Oriental dance. It is in *Don Quixote* that Plisetskaya almost comes into her own. No one could dance more excitingly. One must applaud, not at the end but throughout the dance, as the impossible is made easy. The wit, however, is missing; there are no contrasts. In Alberto Alonso's *Carmen*, created for her, and her favourite role, there is none of the subtlety of Alicia Alonso, who also danced it. It is as little Spanish as the Petipa ballet *Don Quixote*, as far removed from *Mérimée* as Cervantes, or from Bizet as Schedrin's appalling orchestration.

Plisetskaya has a dual personality: her other aspect is sensitive, restrained, and truly romantic, musical as well as purely rhythmic, and this side of her art has never been seen in England. I shall never forget her role in *Spartacus* before it was danced on pointes – the night before the battle and then the scene of mourning when she becomes every woman, shocked and solitary. Her restraint is magnificent, it has true dignity, the very embodiment of Roman heroism. Later, in a ballet she choreographed herself, she portrayed Anna Karenina with complete identification and a subtlety I had never suspected she possessed. She has also proved herself a remarkable screen actress. All this suggests that she needs the discipline of a strong narrative and that her extraordinary facility for difficult technical feats is her greatest enemy.

It would serve no purpose to go through a list of dancers, there are so many and they are so varied, but it would be ungrateful not to name four who have given me particular pleasure. Ekaterina Maximova became a ballerina straight from school and was formed as an artist by Ulanova. Her dancing is full of light and shade, she can perform fireworks with the best of them but also be a true romantic in *Giselle*. She has, however, been over-exposed; this has become more obvious with each successive year. She is a romantic by nature but has been forced in too many directions. Vasiliev, who partners her, and who also became a *premier danseur* straight from school, is the most athletic and virile dancer I have ever seen, a view confirmed by Fyodor Lopokhov. He accomplishes the seemingly impossible with such consummate ease, with so perfect a line, and with such a feeling of strength held in reserve that he is able to avoid appearing acrobatic, as so many Soviet male dancers do. He does not exhibit the extra effort needed to achieve the little bit more that upsets the balance of the whole. He is a *danseur noble*, but he lacks any subtle dramatic ability. One is almost tempted to say that in his case he does not need it, there is so much drama in every leap as he dominates the vast stage of the Bolshoi and even succeeds in cutting the football-field stage of the Kremlin Theatre down to size.

Maris Liepa forms a strong contrast. He is the complete dancer-actor. His arrogant Roman in *Spartacus* is one of the truly great dramatic performances, one that would have delighted Fokine, who was so insistent on period style, something so often lacking in Soviet ballet, especially amongst the men. His portrayal of the complex Karenin is in violent contrast, showing a thorough understanding of Tolstoi's character.

My fourth dancer, Natalia Bessmertnova, I first noticed in the classroom. She bears an extraordinary physical resemblance to Pavlova. She has less brilliance than the other ballerinas, she is capable of technical errors, and her performances vary from day to day. Yet everything she does seems to come from within; there is something gentle and serene about each movement that is all the more evident when compared with the bold attack of her rivals. They all have the superb Vaganova back, still to be mastered in the West, and the thrilling leaps once the province of the men alone. This is often at the expense of the superb line that used to be a major feature of the old Russian school, a line stretching to infinity. There are too many dropped wrists and finicky *ports de bras*. Bessmertnova has none of these impurities. She moves one deeply in such a showy role as the ballerina in *Casse-Noisette*, which in Russia is doubled with that of Clara. She lives in the child's dream world and gives the ballet the true atmosphere of a fairy tale in a way that I have never seen before, though Tchaikovsky's music demands such an interpretation. Grigorovitch's choreography has given a new life to this ballet. It is one of those rare cases where a classic is improved in a modern version. In so many of the Bolshoi classics second thoughts and technical over-elaboration have brought about a departure from the noble simplicity of the original. In becoming showpieces, they have lost charm and credibility. The Kirov company has been the greater guardian of tradition because the teaching of Dudinskaya has kept close to that of Vaganova. Kolpakova and Komleva are splendid examples of the Kirov at its best.

The Soviet ballet scene represents a struggle between athletic prowess and poetry, between tradition and innovation. It turns out more exciting dancers than any other country in the history of the art. Which direction it will take depends on the choreographers and the public. To understand the Soviet ballet completely it is essential to see the dancers on their own stages, where their effectiveness is doubled. Tatty touring productions and weary dancers do them less than justice. It is also necessary to travel within Russia itself or to see the visits of the other companies to Moscow. Perm has produced two dancers in Nadejda Pavlova, gold medal winner in Moscow in 1973, who seems to have everything, strength combined with exceptional lightness, and Irina Tchenchikova. They will certainly prove of world class, if they are carefully nursed. Alas, the little Pavlova, scarcely emerged from school, has already undertaken an American tour.

An evening of ballet in Russia always provides the contrast and surprise that turned me into a confirmed balletomane and has kept me one.

The words 'Russian ballet' mean so many things to so many people that I shall quote, slightly amended, a definition I wrote in a monograph *The Russian Genius in Ballet*. It is a purple patch, but I must indulge myself:

The Russian school combines the grace of the French and the strength of the Italian as developed through the Russian physique and temperament. It has always been firmly rooted in the people and their folk dance. Russian dancing is an arrow shot into the air, the parabola shown by the fountains of Peterhof. It is total dancing, the complete expressiveness of the body. It is the break through the technical barrier. It is simplicity in the grand manner. It is thought and emotion, will and instinct. It is Pavlova's final flutter as the Dying Swan, her flirtatious gaiety with a fan. It is Karsavina, the girl, awakening a woman after her rose-drenched dream. It is the Polovtsian warrior Bolm, the tragic

and finally triumphant Petrouchka, Nijinsky. It is the spirit and fine
carriage of Semenova. It is Ulanova – Giselle transforming a sentimental
anecdote into a deathless story of love; Ulanova – Juliet rising to the
challenge of a masterpiece. It is Plisetskaya as Anna Karenina living
in movement the greatest character in her literature.

It is a dialogue between Petipa and Vaganova, whose busts face each
other across the rehearsal room in Rossi Street. They speak to one another from Saint Petersburg to Leningrad.

21. Competitions

IN 1967, my last year as director of the Royal Ballet School, I came upon a rich and new experience as welcome as it was unexpected, the membership of juries at international dance contests, first at Varna and then at Moscow. It is of course impossible to grade artists but, if eighteen very experienced members of a jury from a number of countries voting in secret ballot find themselves in agreement about the top three contestants out of a hundred, those top three must have considerable talent.

These contests have been won by some dancers already well known, such as Vasiliev and Maximova; they have also discovered and launched dancers who were unknown. It was not the medals that counted but the chance of meeting leading personalities from all over the world in committee, in discussion groups, in a relaxed atmosphere in excursions or round a bar. Galina Ulanova, Fyodor Lopokhov, Moiseyev, Grigorovitch, Anissimova, and others from Russia; Chauviré, Daydé, Bessy, Lifar from France; Alicia and Fernando Alonso from Cuba, Agnes de Mille and Jerome Robbins from the United States, Sonia Gaskell from Holland, Erik Bruhn from Denmark, and the leading teachers and choreographers from Japan, Rumania, Czechoslovakia, Poland, Bulgaria, Hungary, Finland, Sweden, Denmark, Greece, East and West Germany, and Belgium. We saw dancers from all these countries, as well as from Mongolia, Ulan Bator, Uzbekistan, and other Soviet republics. The arrangements for translations and interpreters worked to perfection. Two years of travel could not have given one such an experience. One was continually reminded that this art was truly international and that the language of ballet could have many accents and intonations. That was the important thing. Constant exposure to one's own national idiom tended to result in the belief that it was the only correct one, and justifiable national pride turned into thoughtless chauvinism. It was a question of 'tom-ah-tos and toe-may-toes'. In many cases the teaching in some particular country had been faulty; this soon became obvious through the marking.

I was in a strong position. For some reason Great Britain would have nothing to do with these contests and, as an independent, I had no personal interest. As Vice-President of the jury I could scrutinize the votes and I was delighted to see how impartial they were; the Russians, in particular, who had the majority of candidates, were very critical of their own dancers.

I presided over the conferences, during which the topic was invariably either 'In which direction will ballet go in the future?' or 'What is the meaning of modern?' Everyone agreed that classical training must remain the basis of all ballet and there agreement ended. Paradoxically the Russians were the diehard conservatives, the Americans the left-wing revolutionaries. The split had nothing to do with politics. Many of the Marxist countries, Cuba in particular, sided with the American point of view.

The public, both in Bulgaria and Russia, was keen on novelty, often to the embarrassment of the authorities, who frowned on anything that hinted of sex. Béjart's choreography was applauded to the echo by the public but viewed with suspicion by the authorities. During all these many discussions only one man introduced politics. I promptly shut him up and was thanked for it. I afterwards learnt that he had been expelled from the party and was trying to work his passage back.

As had been the case in Australia, I found myself more and more interested in the Bulgarians and their country. I prolonged my stay, paid further visits, and wrote a book of impressions, *Heroes and Roses*. These are the contacts that ballet brings all over the world, ignoring race and politics. Would that sport could fulfil a similar function.

It was in Bulgaria that I renewed my friendship with Alicia and Fernando Alonso, which led to two long visits to Cuba. The Cuban candidates in the dance competitions had astonished everyone, proving the only serious rivals to the Russians, and I was eager to study the school that had produced them.

22. The Cuban Ballet

I WAS first invited to Cuba in 1967, to be present at an international dance festival held at the picturesque García Lorca Theatre, the Opera House from which Caruso had once fled in costume and make-up during one of the many revolutions. Dancers had assembled from all over the world to appear as guest artists in the classics, and Ulanova was a guest of honour.

I had seen most of the dancers on their own stages, and I had also seen the Cuban ballerinas for a brief period at Varna. It was their company, and especially their school, that aroused my interest.

Alicia and Fernando Alonso had graduated in American Ballet Theatre, where the young Cuban ballerina had greatly profited by the example of her namesake Alicia Markova. Alberto Alonso had been a member of the de Basil company, where he was always known as 'Kooba'. A remarkable family these Alonsos. Their mother, whom I met, had founded a society, Pro Arte Musicale, that included ballet in its activities. Fernando married the young Alicia when she was sixteen, and they left to gain experience and, if possible, fame in America. It was not long in coming. When I first saw her she was a strong ballerina, but I did not realize her full potential. She was found to be suffering from a double detached retina and became almost completely blind. She could only view the stage from a great distance, relying on her partner and Fernando to act as her eyes. This handicap undoubtedly developed her will to succeed and sharpened her already keen intelligence. By using binoculars she managed to take in more than the average sighted person. I marvelled at her attention to detail as a producer.

The Alonsos were staunch patriots. Throughout the American triumphs they never lost sight of the ideal of a Cuban National Ballet based on Madame Alonso's firm foundation. They would visit Cuba from New York at every free moment, spending their own money, to dance and produce at home. They sent for such fine teachers as George Gontcharov and Mary Skeaping to train their dancers. The will and knowledge existed, but the situation was even more precarious than that of our early Sadler's Wells, especially during the inefficient and corrupt regime of Battista.

When Castro came to power, even before his rule had been firmly established, he visited them very early one morning, waking them from a sound sleep. He knew the struggles they had had and the great contribution that they could make to Cuban artistic life and prestige. He offered them *carte blanche* to establish a school and a company. He had taken over the expansive grounds of the Country Club as a centre for artistic education. There he had built schools for music, drama, painting, modern dance, and ballet, with the old club house as a centre. The portrait of a former chairman painted by Oswald Birley, staunch supporter of Diaghilev and de Basil, still occupied a place of honour. The old headquarters of Pro Arte Musicale remained the focal point for the company. The landscaped architecture of the schools was a work of art, completely functional and cool, without the need of air conditioning under the scorching summer sun.

There the Alonsos set to work, unknown to the rest of the world. Fernando proved himself a great teacher, one of the most outstanding I have ever seen, able to give the impetuous Cubans a strong classical discipline and to harness and make use of their natural exuberance. The Cubans, like all Latins, are an excitable race, but voices were never raised in the classroom. Alicia took her place at the barre and was carefully corrected by her husband. The placing was meticulous. Fernando gave reasons for every correction, and a class for fifteen dancers turned into fifteen private lessons, yet there was no unnecessary talk. Every one of those dancers had to become a potential teacher. He formed four remarkable dancers of world class, whom I named 'Cuba's jewels': Aurora Bosch, Loipa Araujo, Mirta Pla, and Josefina Mendes. They were the medal winners who had so impressed the judges at Varna and later in Moscow, the only rivals to the strong Russian contingent. The boys were still a problem as everywhere else outside Russia, and they were greatly helped by Azari Plisetsky, Maya's brother, who became Alicia's partner for many years.

From my first visit I could see the emergence of a new school with a method and personality of its own, the youngest school in the history of our art. In its classicism it was closer to Leningrad and especially to England than to Moscow. The tempi in the classics were slower, sometimes excessively so, but the balance was extraordinary, never the slightest disturbing wobble, almost slow motion, followed by exciting bravura passages so that the dance never became monotonous.

The most unusual feature was the blending of two civilizations, the European and the Latin-African. The school was completely integrated and, after the first surprise, one no longer noticed a black prince or Giselle's African mother. At times the inborn African rhythm intruded on the peasant scenes in *Giselle*, until firmly disciplined by Fernando.

It was the dual personality of the company that enabled the third member of the family, Alberto, to come into his own as choreographer, 'marrying' Cuban folkloric subjects to the classical foundation. There was no narrow ideological canon as in Russia, and the repertoire included ballets by Balanchine, Maurice Béjart, and others.

What astonished me was the reaction of the public. No pop group or football team could have had more faithful or good-natured fans. They cheered everything, before, during, and after a step; they tore up their programmes and showered the stage with confetti. Finally Fernando asked me to make an appeal for restraint, which I did every day for a week in newspapers and on radio and television. I tactfully made the appeal on behalf of the dancers, saying that they could not hear the music, which was true. After that the enthusiasm remained but was shown in the right places. Each one of the 'jewels' had her faithful band of admirers, who would chant her name at curtain fall. One night a fan of Loipa's distributed a poem he had written in her honour. I remember he compared her to a palm tree, which I suppose was a compliment; they are very beautiful trees. The stage door was besieged, and anywhere in the street one might be accosted in the usual manner, 'Pst, Galina [to Ulanova], Pst, Arnold, which of the ballerinas do you prefer?' When Alicia Alonso or Galina Ulanova entered the auditorium, the audience rose as for royalty in England, and I shared some of the reflected glory as a TV commentator. The full programme was covered by television, and I did interviews from a box in each interval. There was also an hour-long ballet discussion every week on the radio and many columns in the newspapers. The whole country was seized by a balletomania such as I had never experienced before. They were proud, and rightly so, of their great achievement, and they felt that it belonged to them. Alicia was the First Lady of Cuba.

The work they did was tremendous, apart from the customary grind all dancers know. Each one of the ballerinas taught in the main school, and the Alonsos were establishing schools and companies in the other provinces. There were extra performances for schools and groups of workers in big halls, each one a grand gala. There were also civic duties, such as planting coffee in the new agricultural belt around Havana, in which everyone took part. The ballet company, with its perfect coordination, beat all the other groups in their assignment. (They were spared the heavier task of cutting the sugar cane.) I myself was exhausted after an hour in the blazing sun and covered from head to foot in red soil. One night I came across Loipa Araujo as a home guard, in smart uniform with a rifle, on duty outside the ballet headquarters. This balletomania had infected the diplomatic corps, who often attended rehearsals and gave parties for the company. Composers, painters, and poets looked on the ballet as a branch of their own art.

Foremost amongst the balletomanes were the members of the British Embassy, headed by the Ambassador and his wife, Richard and Barbara Slater. The ballet was a strong bond between the nations. The company was shown films of the Royal and the Bolshoi Ballets, and the Cuban ballets were filmed by their own company members.

It was suggested at an impromptu party at the British Embassy that I return the following year for a long stay to lecture to the public, in the schools, and to arrange seminars for the budding critics. Britain was playing an active role in transport and agricultural development, why not add ballet appreciation?

I could not resist becoming a part of this society of balletomanes. It had all the well-remembered excitement of the early days of the Camargo Society, the Ballet Club, and Sadler's Wells, where one could watch daily progress in the most congenial surroundings – and in this case be fortified by my growing friendship with the Slaters and the Alonsos, soothing Daiquiris, rum-soaked snow with limes, and Havana cigars.

I enjoyed the lectures immensely. There were thirty of them, given in a delightfully relaxed atmosphere, starting in a small hall and ending up in a theatre. I never knew who my translator might be. It was often a distractingly attractive ballerina, sometimes the Alonsos themselves, but always someone who knew the subject. The questions were searching, particularly at the school, and there were long discussions. I could see more future critics than there were newspapers. The mass enthusiasm of the first year was still there, but now it was tempered by knowledge. The copies of the English dance magazines passed from hand to hand, 'What did Mr Buckle mean by this, Mr Bland by that, Mr Kennedy by t'other?' The company was sad that politics debarred it from going to America where the Alonsos had learnt their *métier*, though they visited Canada and France and toured the whole of the communist world, including Outer Mongolia where the warm-blooded Cubans suffered from the intense cold. Faithful American friends made the long journey via Madrid to see them, another proof, if proof were needed, of the power of the dance to promote understanding.

In my visit to the school I saw that the discovery of the 'four jewels' was not just a lucky chance. The auditions were as stiff as anywhere, the standards high, and boys were increasing in number. Many of those I saw have since become prize winners in Varna and Moscow. I also took the opportunity to see other types of dancing and to observe their influence on the Cuban ballet. Nowhere was the evolution of ballet from folk dance to stage more apparent. Alberto Alonso had married a great rumba dancer, Sonia Callero, who also joined in the daily ballet classes and joined the company in appropriate works. In class or in private life one would not have picked her out from the mass. She was handsome, as are most of the Cubans; Graham Greene wrote that the Cubans turned out attractive women as if by conveyor belt. Even the women traffic police, with their berets set at a saucy angle, were graceful and attractive. Owing to the American blockade clothes were in short supply, but the Cubans were superbly dressed and their stage costumes were impeccable. It was on the stage that the pretty, quiet Sonia became a beauty with an electrifying personality, an extraordinary transformation. The rumba, which when not dull was often vulgar, became a dance of allurement with subtly changing moods ranging from flirtation to passion but without a single suggestive movement. The dance was beautifully choreographed with a discipline rarely seen in Spanish dancing – the classical principle at work once again.

I also saw various folk dances, mainly African in origin, but some of them with strong Western influences going back to the days of slavery and based on the popular ballroom dances of the time. Many of the dancers were in their late eighties, somnolent and seemingly crippled until the drums roused them. A French ethnologist, himself a Negro, was able to tell them which tribe they came from through the style of the dance. Unfortunately the young people watched with only mild interest and no longer joined in. In a very few years this rich inheritance will have been dissipated.

One night a banquet was held in the vast square in front of the cathedral. All around us there was dancing. A spotlight would focus on a particular house or rooftop; minuets and waltzes could be seen through the elegant windows, wild voodoo dances high on the roofs; an unforgettable spectacle, surely the greatest dance gala ever to be staged. There were a number of cabarets and nightclubs in Cuba where the dancing reached a very high standard, particularly the vast open-air Tropicana with its many stages, the highest reaching right up into the treetops. The Cuban sense of colour, and the quality of the lighting and production, made these spectaculars into something very special. When I left, such luxury was being abandoned, doubtless with every justification, though there was plenty of money to spend and no consumer goods to buy.

On leaving Cuba I gave the company a book I had written on the work I had seen, incorporating much of the material of my lectures. It was published there as part of the celebrations in honour of the company's first quarter century, a beautiful example of Cuban book production. I also wrote a preface to Tana da Gamez's book on Alicia Alonso, published in the United States – where Alicia is only now being allowed to dance once more!

When the Alonsos made the long journey to be present at my seventieth birthday dinner I had a welcome surprise. After all those years Alicia could see again; a new operation had proved successful. Her long reign as a ballerina was coming to an end, and now a new career as producer and choreographer lay ahead. She had already proved herself in that most difficult of all houses, the Paris Opéra, with her fine productions of *Giselle* and *Le Pas de Quatre*, unhampered by the heavy binoculars; truly a heroine of the dance.

23. Renvoi

I STILL maintain a close link with ballet, as a governor of the Royal and London Festival Ballets and of the Royal Ballet School, and as a member of various advisory bodies concerned with dancing in education.

The young author of *Balletomania* would have found this last activity unthinkably solemn and remote in 1934, but since then he has come to see the value of a dance discipline all over the world, both as physical and mental training. At first a few of us had to fight the physical educationalists, who were strongly opposed to any disciplined movement in dance, though we always had a number of headmistresses and, much later, headmasters on our side. The physical educationalists held that dance was to be free, that any repression was wholly bad, and that movement acted as a release. I could never discover the logic of this, especially after having watched the results in many schools. Games are no fun without rules, and children recognize this. There are many instincts civilized man must learn to repress, and one should begin at an early age. The dancing of primitive people is guided by a strict set of rules. It must be if the magic is to work. I am not opposed to freedom of expression and improvisation, which is important, but only after a certain discipline has been taught. Rules first, then freedom. That also is the essence of good manners.

The opposing parties have now become staunch allies as gymnastics have become closer to dancing. I discovered this recently at a top-level conference at the Gulbenkian Foundation, presided over by Peter Brinson and with Lord Annan present. It was expected to be controversial, even heated. It proved highly constructive.

Today ballet is considered an O-level subject in the General Certificate of Education, another breathtaking advance from 1934. It is still in an experimental stage and is not intended to produce dancers or teachers of dancing, though it may nourish them. It will certainly train the audience of the future. These products of balletomania have proved most rewarding.

Since this new section was written, I have enjoyed the dancing of Antoinette Sibley, Monica Mason, Antony Dowell, and David Wall, and of Maina Gielgud, who has inherited the real Terry touch, Eva Evdokimova, the gold medallist at Varna, Karen Kain, the Canadian, an admirable classicist as well as a splendid interpreter of Petit's choreography, his first real Carmen after Jeanmaire, who created the role, and especially Lynn Seymour, in a class of her own as a great dramatic dancer with a range that encompasses pure ballet to Duncan. Few dancers have contributed more to choreography than Seymour. Her influence on Macmillan from the time of *The Burrow* is obvious, she has truly been his muse. Ashton has compared her to Karsavina and Duncan. She showed her versatility as Natalia Petrovna in his superb *Month in the Country* and in his dances in the Duncan manner. Where so many admirable dancers in Britain and America today are physically immature, Lynn is a woman who can convey woman's emotions. She belongs among the very great in my experience and it will be interesting to see if she succeeds in her new choreographic career. Her *Leda*, inspired by Yeats, created for television, was superbly sensual and showed a rare understanding of the medium and the poet. The standard is high, particularly amongst the men, and the tradition remains unbroken.

Ballet has given me a rich life, something far greater than the experiences in the theatre itself and the memories that are mine. It has given me extensive travel, good companionship, a deeper understanding of painting and the sculpture that I love so dearly, and a special insight into the character of alien civilizations. 'Show me how people dance and I will tell you what they are.' This ancient saying is true even in such a sophisticated and highly regulated art as ballet, a language with so many varied dialects, many of which are new since *Balletomania* was written over forty years ago. My views may have been narrow then, when the one criterion we had was the Diaghilev Ballet and its immediate followers. Today ballet's possibilities are unbounded. Many primitive forms of movement will disappear, to be absorbed in the rich and wonderful world of the dance, which constitutes a social history of mankind.

APPENDIX

Guest List at the Seventieth Birthday Dinner, The Ritz, 23 September 1973

Dr and Mrs Alberts
Mr Donald Albery
Mr and Mrs Fernando Alonso
Mr Richard Arnell
Mr and Mrs Michael Ayrton
Sir Sydney and Lady Barratt
Miss Doris Barry
Miss Phyllis Bedells
Mr Richard Behrens
Mr James Cleveland Belle
Mr and Mrs Bryce Blair
Mr and Mrs David Blair
Miss Caryl Brahms
Mr Peter Brinson
Mr Justice Browne
Miss Louise Browne
Mr Richard Buckle
Mr William Cavendish
Mme Yvette Chauviré
Miss Mary Clarke
Mr and Mrs John Coast
Dr Arthur Connell
Mr George Milford Cottam
Sir Trenchard Cox
Mr Anthony Crickmay
Mr Clement Crisp
Mme Liane Daydé
The Cuban Ambassador and
    Señora de Sota
Dame Ninette de Valois
Mr Anton Dolin
Viscount and Viscountess Eccles

Mr and Mrs Edward
    Kelland Espinosa
Mr and Mrs Dwye Evans
Mr and Mrs Alan Fairley
Mme Tamara Tchinarova Finch
Sir Michael and Lady Fraser
Miss Sonia Gaskell
Sir John Gielgud
M. Claude Giraud
Lord Goodman
Mr Ram Gopal
Mr Charles Gordon
Miss Kathleen Gordon
Mr and Mrs Sandor Gorlinsky
Mr and Mrs Nigel Gosling
Miss Beryl Grey
Mr and Mrs Ivor Guest
Mr and Mrs Alan Hall
Mrs Arnold Haskell
Professor and Mrs Francis Haskell
Mr and Mrs Stephen Haskell
Lord and Lady Hastings
Mr Nicholas Hinton
Mr and Mrs Victor Hochhauser
Mr and Mrs Ian Hunter
Mr Stanislas Idzikovski
Mr Hugh Jenkins, M.P., and
    Mrs Jenkins
Mr Eric Johns
Mr Kurt Jooss
Mr and Mrs Victor Kempner
Miss Muriel Kerr

Mr Svend Kragh-Jacobsen
Mr and Mrs Gordon Latta
Baroness Lee of Asheridge
Mr John Lehmann
Mr Michael Le Marchant
Mr Serge Lifar
Mr and Mrs Frederick Lloyd
Sir Joseph Lockwood
Dr Brigitte Lohmeyer
The Marquis and
   Marchioness of Londonderry
The Soviet Ambassador and
   Mme Lunkova
Mr and Mrs Ian MacPhail
Dame Alicia Markova
Mme Donka Minkova
Mrs Doris Langley Moore
Professor Sir Claus and Lady Moser
Mr and Mrs J. D. Newth
Mr Milen Paunov
Miss Ailne Phillips
Mr and Mrs Enzo Piazotta

Mr Alexis Rassine
Mr and Mrs L. Rotherham
Miss Lynn Seymour
Lord Shackleton
Mr and Mrs Donald Sinden
Mr and Mrs Richard Slater
Mlle Claire Sombert
Mr Norman St John Stevas, M.P.
Mr Sven Svenson
Mr and Mrs John Tooley
Mme Galina Ulanova
Dame Peggy van Praagh
Mrs Douglas Vivian
Mme Vera Volkova
Mrs Nobuko Vuenishi
Viscountess Waverley
Sir George and Lady Weidenfeld
Mr and Mrs Alan Wilkinson
Mr Peter Williams
Mr G. B. L. Wilson
Mr and Mrs Michael Wood
Mr and Mrs Paul Wyeth

MESSAGES WERE RECEIVED FROM:

Ballet Nacional de Cuba
Mme Irina Baronova
Mr Cyril Beaumont
Miss Minsa Craig
Mme Violetta Elvin
Dame Margot Fonteyn
Miss Celia Franca
Sir Robert Helpmann
June
Nora Kaye and Herbert Ross
Mme Tamara Karsavina

Mrs Yehudi Menuhin
Mr and Mrs Alan Paton
Dame Marie Rambert
Mme Natalia Roslavleva
Mrs Mrinalini Sarabhai
Scottish Theatre Ballet
Constantin Sergeyev and
   Natalia Dudinskaya
Mr G. Sevastianov
Mme Tamara Toumanova

Index of Ballets et Cetera*

*Including ballet and opera companies, ballet theatres and schools, dance festivals, plays, movies, revues, magazines, books, operas, and movements in art.

Index of Persons

MORE ABOUT PENGUINS
AND PELICANS

Penguinews, which appears every month, contains details of all the new books issued by Penguins as they are published. From time to time it is supplemented by our stocklist, which includes around 5,000 titles.

A specimen copy of *Penguinews* will be sent to you free on request. Please write to Dept EP, Penguin Books Ltd, Harmondsworth, Middlesex, for your copy.

In the U.S.A.: For a complete list of books available from Penguins in the United States write to Dept CS, Penguin Books, 625 Madison Avenue, New York, New York 10022.

In Canada: For a complete list of books available from Penguins in Canada write to Penguin Books Canada Ltd, 2801 John Street, Markham, Ontario L3R 1B4.

In Australia: For a complete list of books available from Penguins in Australia write to the Marketing Department, Penguin Books Australia Ltd, P.O. Box 257, Ringwood, Victoria 3134